A WORLD HISTORY

A WORLD HISTORY

WILLIAM H. McNEILL

NEW YORK

OXFORD UNIVERSITY PRESS · 1967   LONDON

TORONTO

HUMAN SOCIETIES, distinguished from one another by differing styles of life, are very numerous, and have existed from pre- and proto-human times throughout mankind's history. Civilizations are unusually massive societies, weaving the lives of millions of persons into a loose yet coherent life style across hundreds or even thousands of miles and for periods of time that are very long when measured by the span of an individual human life. Being both massive and long-lived, civilizations must perforce also be few. Indeed, from the time when human societies first attained civilized complexity and size, no more than four different major civilized traditions ever co-existed in the Old World; and in the New, where Amerindian development remained always weak and retarded, no more than three distinct civilizations ever emerged.

These facts allow an overview of the history of mankind as a whole. To be sure, the effort to hold simultaneously in mind what was happening in widely separated parts of the earth requires us to focus attention on certain aspects of reality and to pass others by. The same is true of the study of more detailed segments of the human past—think, for instance, of the idiosyncratic experiences of each town and village that are so ruthlessly neglected in our standard national histories! As in cartography, each scale has advantages and shortcomings, and an appropriate amount of detail. Too much information will obscure the whole; too litttle will deprive history of its verisimilitude and disguise the open-ended surprisingness of human experience. Historians of the nineteenth century erected a frame for national histories that continues to command general assent; and in the twentieth century, American textbook writers arrived at a rough concensus concerning the history of something called Western Civilization. But for world history, an agreed criterion has not yet appeared. What to omit and what to pay attention to remain very much matter for debate and disagreement.

Because of these disagreements, it seemed worthwhile to write this brief account of mankind's past. The success of my book *The Rise of the West* (Chicago, 1963) made it plausible to believe that a shorter work, suited for use as a college text, would make my personal vision of the whole history of mankind more accessible to students—a vision which, however imperfect, still has the virtue of being cohesive and intelligible, something that can be grasped and remembered and reflected upon afterwards.

The organizing idea is simple: in any given age the world balance among cultures was liable to disturbance emanating from one or more centers where men succeeded in creating an unusually attractive or powerful civilization. Neighbors and neighbors' neighbors were then tempted or compelled to change their own traditional ways of life, sometimes by outright borrowing of techniques or ideas, but more often by adjusting and changing things to suit the local scene more smoothly.

In successive ages the major loci of such disturbance to the world altered. It therefore becomes possible to survey the epochs of world history by studying first the center or centers of primary disturbance, and then considering how the other peoples of the earth reacted to or against what they knew or experienced (often at second or third hand) of the innovations that had occurred in the prime centers of cultural creativity.

In such a perspective, geographical settings and lines of communication between different civilizations became centrally important. Archaeology, technology, and art history provide important clues to ancient relationships which the surviving literary record sometimes disguises.

This book was written during the summer of 1964 and revised in the summer of 1965. The Carnegie Corporation helped to finance its preparation and the reproduction of a set of readings for an experimental course in world history. Students who took that course, both in the College and in the Extension Division of the University of Chicago, during the academic year 1964–65 earned my gratitude by cheerfully serving as guinea pigs. I owe special thanks also to Professor John A. Wilson of the University of Chicago, who read Part I, and to Professor Immanuel Hsu of the University of California at Santa Barbara, who checked the passages dealing with the Far East. Both detected errors and infelicities which have, hopefully, been removed.

W. H. M.

Chicago, Illinois
December 1966

Contents

PART III

World Maps in Color

*Prepared by the Cartographic Department of the Clarendon Press, Oxford,
and printed in Great Britain by Cook, Hammond & Kell, Ltd., London*

Text Maps

Chronological Charts

List of Plates

xi

A WORLD HISTORY

Part I

EMERGENCE AND DEFINITION OF THE MAJOR

EURASIAN CIVILIZATIONS TO 500 B.C.

The first great landmark of human history was the development of food production, which permitted an enormous multiplication of human numbers, and laid the basis for the emergence of civilizations. How, when, and where hunting and gathering gave way to farming and pastoralism is uncertain. One of the earliest and most important instances of this transition took place in the Middle East, perhaps between 8500 and 7000 B.C. Thence, through migrations and borrowings, few of which can be reconstructed by modern scholars, grain cultivation spread into Europe and India, China, and parts of Africa. The Americas, monsoon Asia, and west Africa may have seen independent inauguration of agriculture, though this is not certain, nor are the dates known at which the cultivation of plants became central to human life in these parts of the globe.

The second great landmark in mankind's history was the emergence of skilled and complex societies we call civilized. Here the primacy of the Middle East is undisputed. Man's earliest civilized communities developed in the valleys of the Tigris-Euphrates and the Nile between about 3500 and 3000 B.C. The Indus valley followed suit soon afterwards. At first civilized complexity required very special geographical conditions. Only on irrigated land could rich crops be harvested year after year from the same fields; and only where irrigation was needed did large numbers of men find it necessary to co-operate in digging and diking. An agricultural surplus that could support specialists, together with habits of social organization embracing large numbers of men, thus could and did emerge in the flood plains of the principal Middle Eastern rivers, and, until much later, not elsewhere.

About a thousand years thereafter, men began to extend civilized complexity to rain-watered land. The invention of the plow was here fundamental. It permitted ancient farmers to harness the strength of animals to the tasks of cultivation, and thereby allowed the individual farmer to increase his food production very substantially. This made available an agricultural surplus such as had previously been reserved for irrigated land. In addition, civilization demanded a distinctive social order. It required a sharp polarization between rulers and the peasant majority to compel the latter to part with their surplus crops in order to support the courts and palace cities that rulers and aristocrats gradually built up. A significant variation depended on sea trade, which allowed rulers of such an island as Crete to gather the fruits of the entire Mediterranean coastline and sustain a palace city at Knossos on the strength of mercantile enterprise.

A fourth great change in human relationships brought steppe pastoralists and warriors to the fore for the first time. This happened soon after 1700 B.C., when techniques of chariot warfare were perfected somewhere along the northern fringes of Mesopotamia. Chariots gave dominion to warriors who knew how to tame horses, and since the great center of horse raising was on the steppes, it was warrior tribes of central Asia and the Ukraine, speakers of Indo-European tongues, who reaped the principal advantage. These warriors overran all of Europe, western Asia, and India. Others, who had somehow acquired the techniques of chariot warfare, also conquered the peasants of the Yellow river valley in China.

In Europe, India, and China, interaction between pre-existing agricultural peoples and the new masters of the land laid the groundwork for the emergence of three new and enormously successful styles of civilization. The pace of their development was roughly comparable, so that by 500 B.C. a distinctive European

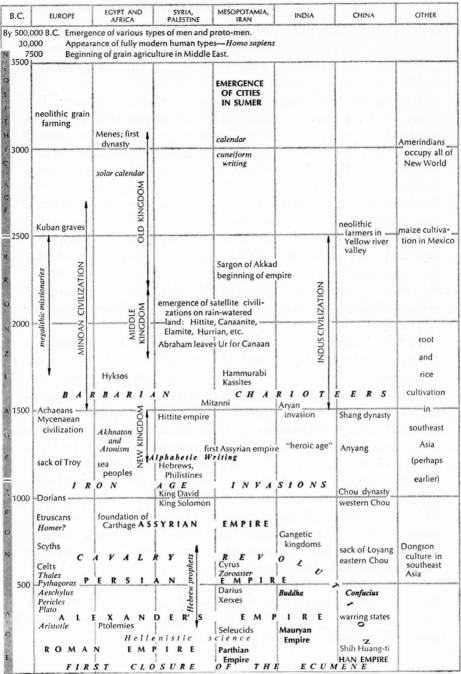

B.C.	EUROPE	EGYPT AND AFRICA	SYRIA, PALESTINE	MESOPOTAMIA, IRAN	INDIA	CHINA	OTHER

By 500,000 B.C. Emergence of various types of men and proto-men.
  30,000   Appearance of fully modern human types—*Homo sapiens*
  7500   Beginning of grain agriculture in Middle East.

N E O L I T H I C   A G E
B R O N Z E   A G E
I R O N   A G E

3500

3000

2500

2000

1500

1000

500

EUROPE:
neolithic grain farming
Kuban graves
megalithic missionaries
MINOAN CIVILIZATION
B A R B A R I A N
Achaeans
Mycenaean civilization
sack of Troy
I R O N
Dorians
Etruscans
Homer?
Scyths
C A V A L R Y
Celts
Thales
Pythagoras   P E R S I A N
Aeschylus
Pericles
Plato
A L E X A N D E R' S
Aristotle
R O M A N   E M P I R E
F I R S T   C L O S U R E

EGYPT AND AFRICA:
Menes; first dynasty
solar calendar
OLD KINGDOM
MIDDLE KINGDOM
Hyksos
Akhnaton and Atonism
NEW KINGDOM
sea peoples
foundation of Carthage
Ptolemies
Hellenistic science

SYRIA, PALESTINE:
emergence of satellite civilizations on rain-watered land: Hittite, Canaanite, Elamite, Hurrian, etc.
Abraham leaves Ur for Canaan
Mitanni
Hittite empire
Alphabetic Writing
Hebrews, Philistines
King David
King Solomon
A S S Y R I A N   E M P I R E
Hebrew prophets
Seleucids
Parthian Empire
O F   T H E   E C U M E N E

MESOPOTAMIA, IRAN:
EMERGENCE OF CITIES IN SUMER
calendar
cuneiform writing
Sargon of Akkad beginning of empire
Hammurabi
Kassites
C H A R I O T E E R S
Aryan invasion
first Assyrian empire
I N V A S I O N S
R E V O L U T
Cyrus
Zoroaster
E M P I R E
Darius
Xerxes

INDIA:
INDUS CIVILIZATION
"heroic age"
Gangetic kingdoms
Buddha
Mauryan Empire

CHINA:
neolithic farmers in Yellow river valley
Shang dynasty
Anyang
Chou dynasty
western Chou
sack of Loyang
eastern Chou
Confucius
warring states
Shih Huang-ti
HAN EMPIRE

OTHER:
Amerindians occupy all of New World
maize cultivation in Mexico
root and rice cultivation in southeast Asia (perhaps earlier)
Dongson culture in southeast Asia

3

type of civilization had emerged in Greece; an equally distinctive Indian style of civilization had become manifest in northern India; and in the middle reaches of the Yellow river, Chinese civilization had likewise asserted itself.

The Middle Eastern center had a more complicated history. The effect of the chariot conquest on Mesopotamia and Egypt was comparatively superficial, since before long, local peoples learned how to use chariots to oust their conquerors. Three civilized empires, based in Egypt, Asia Minor, and northern Mesopotamia, then competed for supremacy in the Middle East until a new wave of barbarian invasion struck. The newcomers were equipped with iron (actually soft steel) weapons, and the great empires of the Bronze Age broke under the attack of tribesmen armed with the new and more abundant metal. But once again the effect of barbarian conquest was transitory. New empires arose, climaxing in the unstable political unification of the entire civilized area of the ancient Middle East, first under the Assyrians and then under the Persians.

As a result of this tangled development, what had once been separate civilizations in Egypt and Mesopotamia, not to mention the constellation of satellite civilizations that had arisen on rain-watered land around and between the two great river valleys, all began to merge into a new cosmopolitan Middle Eastern style of life. A decisive formulation of a Middle Eastern world-view appropriate to this cosmopolitan civilization took place among the Jews, whose religion, as shaped by the prophets of the eighth to sixth centuries B.C., was as vital and persuasive as the Buddhism of India, the Confucianism of China, or the philosophy of Greece, all of which also found their initial expression before the end of the sixth century B.C. With the clear and emphatic fourfold patterning of Eurasian civilization that thus came into focus by 500 B.C., an initial, constitutive phase of world history came to a close.

To explore this initial period of civilized history, when the main lines and distinctive emphases within which most men subsequently were to live first printed themselves upon human minds and feelings, will be the aim of Part I of this book.

I

In the Beginning

HUMAN history begins with the emergence of *Homo sapiens* from proto-human populations. The process was undoubtedly very slow, but by about 100,000 years ago scattered hunting packs of biologically modern kinds of man roamed the savanna lands of Africa and perhaps also inhabited regions with suitably mild climates in Asia as well. These earliest human communities depended in part on skills inherited from their proto-human ancestors. The use of wood and stone tools, for example, seems to have started long before fully human populations had come into existence. Elementary language, and habits of co-operation in the hunt, were also proto-human in their origin. So, perhaps, was the domestication of fire.

What mainly distinguished fully human populations from the man-like creatures who flourished before them was a prolongation of infancy and childhood. This meant a longer time when the young depended on parents, and a correspondingly longer time when the elders could teach their offspring the arts of life. From the child's side, slower maturation meant prolonged plasticity and a much-increased capacity to learn. Enlarged learning capacities, in turn, increased the frequency of selective preservation of inventions and discoveries made, presumably, more or less at random. When this occurred cultural evolution began to outstrip the comparatively slow pace of biological evolution. Human behavior came to be governed far more by what men learned in society than by anything individuals inherited biologically through the marvelous mechanisms of the DNA molecules. When cultural evolution took over primacy from biological evolution, history in its strict and proper sense began.

The earliest men. Nothing is known for sure about the spread of the earliest human populations from their cradleland, if indeed there was a single geographical center where modern man first evolved. Minor biological variations certainly arose — witness the racial differences among existing mankind. But when and where modern races defined themselves is unclear. Fortunately the historian can afford to neglect such questions because the variables affecting human conduct through time are not, so far as anyone can tell, defined by biological variations among different human populations.

Even cultural differentiation may not at first have been very conspicuous. At any rate, hand axes and other stone tools show remarkable uniformity over wide areas of the Old World and across comparatively vast periods of time. Indeed, about nine-tenths of *Homo sapiens'* time on earth saw men confined to a life of hunters and gatherers, using simple tools of wood and stone, familiar with fire, and living so far as we can tell in an almost unchanging way from generation to generation.

Surviving stones, shaped to human purposes by skilled chipping and flaking, cannot reveal much about the life of their makers. Presumably, as long as men lived mainly by hunting, and supplemented animal flesh with whatever they could pick up — grubs and insects, edible roots, stalks, and seeds — they lived a roving life, like the few surviving primitive hunters of modern times. Very likely bands were small, numbering from twenty to sixty persons under normal circumstances. Occasional contact with neighbors was certainly a feature of primitive life. Probably such contacts were usually reduced to regular ceremonies, when neighboring bands came together to celebrate the fact of survival and to transact unusual business. On such occasions, marriages might be arranged between members of different groups, and rare objects like cowry shells were certainly exchanged. Hostilities between neighboring bands probably also occurred, at least occasionally, but evidence is really lacking since surviving stone blades and axe heads could be used equally well for hunting animals or for killing other men.

Ecological influences. The comparative stability of the earliest hunting style of life suggests that adjustment to the environment became very exact. Each band inherited adequate customary responses to every situation that might arise. In the absence of important changes in the ecological balance of plants and animals within which early human hunters found their niche, perhaps human life would still adhere to the patterns of behavior appropriate to small, roving bands of hunters and gatherers. If so, human cultural evolution would have assumed a vastly slower pace, more akin to the rhythms of biological development from which it emerged than to the headlong rush of history.

In some important parts of the earth, however, the natural environment did not remain stable. Instead, climatic changes along the northern limits of human (and proto-human) habitation time and again transformed the ecological background, and in doing so presented men with a series of critical challenges to their powers of adaptation and invention. This in all probability was what unleashed the potentialities of cultural evolution from the tight mesh of use and wont that defined but also restricted the lives of ancient hunters.

The ecological changes that triggered human history are all related to the latest retreat of continental ice from the northern hemisphere. Glacial ice began to melt back from Europe and northern Asia and America about 30,000 years ago. On the bared ground, tundra and thin forest first developed. Along the Atlantic face of the Old World the drift of cyclonic storms across the warm waters of the Gulf Stream established a comparatively moist and equable climate in western Europe. As a result, vegetation grew lushly and sustained a large population of sub-arctic herbivores: mammoth, reindeer, bison, and many more. This in turn constituted a rich food resource for primitive men and other large-bodied predators to feed upon.

But before men could take advantage of these possibilities some basic inventions were needed. In particular, men had to learn how to sew skins together to make an artificial pelt that might keep even hairless humans warm in a very chilly landscape. This in turn required awls and something to serve as "thread" — perhaps sinews or thongs of raw hide. The necessary inventions were made, allowing bands of hunters who were skeletally all but indistinguishable from modern men to invade the tundra and forest of western Europe some 25–30,000 years ago. Earlier human or para-human populations, the so-called Neanderthal men, whose skeletal structure differed substantially from that of any surviving population, disappeared as the newcomers advanced.

Tools and weapons of stone are not the sole evidences of their life which these invading hunters left behind. For it was they who made the famous cave paintings of southern France, and who left a few other enigmatic traces of their magico-religious ceremonies in the earth's dark recesses. What may have been the ideas that led hunters of perhaps 18,000 years ago to make images of their prey on the walls of deep dark caves cannot be known today. Very likely elaborate myths explained the relationships of men to the animals they killed. Perhaps the rites of caves were intended to propitiate the animal spirits and encourage fecundity: but we can only guess.

The arctic big-game hunters of western Europe depended on the herds, and the herds depended on grass, mosses, and other vegetation. When the further retreat of the ice and the warming of the climate allowed thick forests to form, these food resources were cut off. The great herds disappeared and a new style of human life had to be worked out. The caves were abandoned and the men who had used them perhaps followed the dwindling sub-arctic herds northward and eastward as the ice retreated. In western Europe, forest browsers, like deer and cattle, arrived with the trees, and human hunters (perhaps new arrivals) quickly learned to prey upon them. But the hunting bands that spent their life pursuing deer and cattle left comparatively few traces in the archaeological record. Other populations, however, learned to exploit aquatic food resources by inventing simple boats, nets, and fish hooks. Relatively sessile communities thus developed, since boats had to come back to harbor and there were only certain spots where suitable shelter from storms could be had. Great rubbish piles, composed mainly of the remains of shellfish, accumulated on such sites. They allow modern archaeologists to study the sequence of occupation and to trace changes in tool assemblages through time.

Other parts of the world are far less well explored than western Europe, and it is not yet possible to reconstruct in any detail what may have transpired elsewhere while these changes were taking place along the Old World's northwestern fringe. It seems probable that changes were not so drastic. Western Europe's juxtaposition of glacial ice and the Gulf Stream induced far more radical alteration of climate and biosphere than occurred elsewhere; and so far as the still rather limited exploration allows us to guess, it appears that changes in human occupancy and modes of life in other parts of the world were correspondingly less drastic. An exception, perhaps, should be made for the Americas, for it was the melting back of the glacial ice that permitted bands of hunters to move up the Pacific coast of Asia and cross to Alaska. Thence they drifted southward until they penetrated all parts of the American continents and adjacent islands. Dates for the first human occupation of the New World are in dispute, but it is likely that the earliest hunting bands began to spread through North America between 10,000 and 15,000 years ago. Human occupation of the world's other habitable continent, Australia, appears to be much older, and probably goes back to a time when a land bridge united that continent with southeast Asia.

Changes brought by agriculture. Primitive hunting bands had probably not reached Tierra del Fuego at the southernmost tip of South America by the time a new style of human life achieved clear definition in the general region of the Middle East. For it was probably between 7000 and 6500 B.C. that a few human communities located in the hilly region to the north and east of Mesopotamia began to reshape their natural environment by cultivating plants and domesticating animals. Wheat and barley were their most important crops; sheep and goats, their most numerous domesticated animals. The first food-producing communities preferred wooded ground. It was easy to kill a few dozen trees by slashing off the bark all round their trunks. This exposed the forest floor to sunlight, so that seeds planted in the loose leaf mold around the standing trunks of the dead trees could grow and flourish. Then after two or three crops had depleted the soil, fertility could be renewed by burning the dried-out trees and scattering the ashes over the ground. Then, five to ten years after the plot had first been carved out of the forest, primitive farmers moved on. Having exhausted the soil of their small plots, they simply repeated the whole cycle elsewhere, letting their abandoned fields grow back to woods and slowly return to something like their original state. This sort of cultivation still survives in a few remote parts of the world. Geographers call it slash and burn agriculture.

The first farmers needed three implements which had been unimportant for hunters: an axe to cut and girdle the trees, a hoe to stir the leaf mold for the reception of seed, and a sickle to harvest the ripened grain. Sickle and hoe could be made entirely of wood, but the axe had to be of stone, tough enough to withstand the shock of heavy blows without shattering. Flint, which hunters had long been accustomed to chip into arrow heads and knife blades, was useless for such purposes for it was too brittle. Other kinds of rock, mainly granites and basalts, had to be shaped into axe heads by prolonged grinding and polishing, producing a distinctive "neolithic" or New Stone Age style of tool.

In addition, neolithic farmers developed a number of other important additions to the hunter's tool kit. Baskets and clay pots for storing grain and other possessions became important and, for people who were no longer constantly on the move, possible. Mudbrick houses, looms for making cloth, oven-fired pottery suitable for boiling cereals and other foods, and the arts of baking and brewing all came rapidly into use. The village community replaced the roving band as the fundamental unit of human society. The discipline of regular and laborious work in the fields, together with the need for measurement of time to identify the right season for planting, distinguished the farmer's from the hunter's style of life. Foresight and restraint were also needed, for even in a time of hunger it was necessary to save a proper amount of seed grain to

assure future harvests. Courage and habits of violence, so necessary
for hunters, had little importance for farmers.

Finally, human numbers vastly increased when men ceased to be
mere predators upon the natural environment. Instead of remaining
a rather rare species, men began to form dense settlements and by
their activities altered the natural balance of plant and animal life
radically, partly by intention and partly in ways quite unforeseen
and unintended.

Somewhere in monsoon Asia a type of agriculture centered upon
root crops may have arisen independently of the Middle Eastern
style of grain-centered cultivation. Many experts also suppose that
food production originated independently in the Americas and in
west Africa. Archaeological investigation has not yet elucidated
the question, and since the earliest farmers usually left very slight
traces behind them, it may never be possible to reconstruct the
geographical and chronological facts precisely.

The earliest civilization. Nevertheless, Middle Eastern grain agriculture and domesticated animals deserve to be accorded a special
place in human history, for it was from this style of life that the
earliest civilization emerged. This occurred in the land of Sumer
which lay along the lower reaches of the Tigris and Euphrates
rivers on the flat alluvial plain bordering the Persian Gulf. Primitive farming techniques had to be radically altered before the
annually renewed river silt from which the land of Sumer was built
could be made to produce rich crops. In the forested hills of the
Middle East enough rain fell in early summer to sustain the growing grain until the harvest. This was not the case further south,
where summer rains almost never fell. Hence, only by bringing
river water to the fields to irrigate the crops could a harvest be
assured. But the construction and maintenance of the necessary
canals and dikes called for the massed labor of hundreds or thousands of men and for a much tighter social discipline than had prevailed in the earliest farming communities. In neolithic villages it is
likely that the small biological family constituted the ordinary
working unit. Each family normally consumed the produce of its
own plot or plots of cropland, and there was no need of organized
co-operation among larger numbers, save perhaps on ceremonial,

religious occasions. Everyone was equally enslaved to the vagaries of the weather, and all were equally free, since the principal differentiation was between age groups and the two sexes. This simple social structure altered radically in the river bank environment. For the scale of operation necessary for controlling the river's waters required that the labor of the majority of the people be directed by some sort of managerial elite.

How a managerial class first arose is not certain. Conquest of one people by another may have divided society between masters and servants, managers and managed. On the other hand, experts in the supernatural, whose special status was certainly age-old in human society, may have served as the catalysts for a far-ranging process of functional specialization. In subsequent times Mesopotamian myths explained that gods had created men to be their slaves, so that food and clothing and the other necessities of a well-appointed

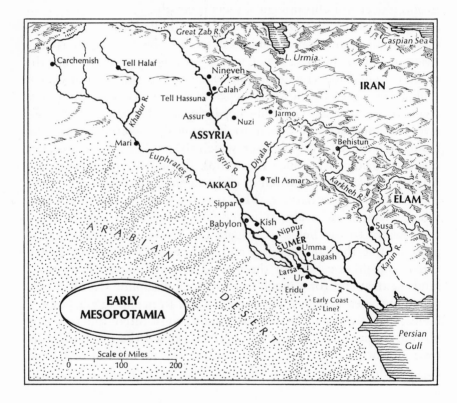

divine household — i.e. a temple — would be provided for the god's enjoyment without he himself having to take the trouble of producing them.

We also know a little about how these ideas were applied in practice. Thus, at Lagash an inscription divides the land of the city into three categories, depending on what sort of dues its possessors owed the god. Very likely the heaviest dues did not leave the farmers enough to eat. This then made it necessary for them to work for the god during part of the year, i.e. to labor on irrigation works or at some other project planned by the priests. In this way some of the grain and other agricultural products paid into the temple by farmers were paid out again as wages for work that was done at the direction of the god's special servitors, the priests.

Such a system obviously permitted the labor power of thousands of men to be concentrated for carrying through big projects. It also permitted specialization, for many full-time artisans had to employ their best skill in order to feed, dress, amuse, and worship the god with the sort of pomp and luxury needed to assure the divine good pleasure. By virtue of their emancipation from the ordinary routine of farming life, these specialists were able to develop skills and knowledge far greater than men had ever before attained. Civilization thereby came into existence in a short thousand years, between about 4000 B.C., when the first settlements appeared in the lower Tigris-Euphrates valley, and 3000 B.C., when written records that can be read by modern scholars start to cast a fitful light upon the social and intellectual dimensions of Sumerian culture.

Sumerian inventions. Technical developments were at first very rapid. Metallurgy, wheel-spun pottery, wheeled vehicles, sailing vessels, sculpture, monumental buildings, and — perhaps most important of all — the plow, appear almost simultaneously in the archaeological record. A distinctive art style, exemplified primarily in the miniature form of seal-engraving, also defined itself rather quickly. Other skills that left no traces for modern archaeologists certainly accompanied these developments. Weaving and dying of woolen textiles, for example, which later provided Mesopotamian cities with a major export commodity, and the elaborate pageantry of temple services must date back to the very beginning of Sumerian civilization. In addition, the arts of measurement assumed unparalleled importance and precision. Construction of canals and dikes and of monumental temple structures, raised high above the plain like artificial mountains, called for precise measurement and careful planning.

Far more critical, however, was the measurement of time, for the fundamental rhythm of the farming year depended on the correct anticipation of the seasons. The moon's waxing and waning was the most conspicuous marker of elapsed time; but the cycles of the moon did not fit evenly into the solar year, and the priests had therefore to observe, measure, and correlate the celestial movements of both the sun and the moon before a reliable calendar could be created. The maintenance of such a calendar may, indeed, have been the most important service priests offered early cultivators. Knowledge necessary to maintain a calendar also constituted an important basis for priestly pre-eminence in society. Ordinary farmers perhaps felt that men who could foreknow the seasons thereby demonstrated their special relation with the gods and deserved deference. It is possible that the organization of irrigation works, with all the technical and social consequences that flowed from that departure, was begun under the direction of priests whose social leadership rested, in large part, on their ability to predict the seasons.

Writing. From the point of view of subsequent history, the most remarkable priestly invention traceable to Sumer was the discovery of means whereby spoken words could be recorded. This was done by making marks on soft clay with a sharp reed end. If a permanent record was wanted, an all but indestructible document could easily be produced by baking the clay, either in the sun or in an oven. It is to such baked clay tablets that we owe all our detailed knowledge of ancient Mesopotamia. The script that slowly emerged from this practice is called cuneiform, i.e. wedge-shaped.

At first, Sumerian priests used writing mainly to record deposits in and withdrawals from temple storehouses. A persistent problem here was how to find ways to record the names of the men who engaged in these transactions. Eventually the effort to record individual men's names in recognizable form induced the priests to resort to equivalences between syllables in men's names and the sound of some easily pictured word. Then, by developing enough standard syllable pictures the scribes could easily learn to record all the sounds of ordinary speech. Writing of complete sentences, and of sacred stories, religious invocations, laws, contracts, and many other sorts of documents thus became possible soon after 3000 B.C.

Conventionally, and not without reason, historians use the invention of writing to mark the divide between prehistory and history. Since writing that can be read by modern scholars allows so much deeper insight into the activities of men long since vanished from the earth, this distinction still makes sense, despite all the advances of archaeology which have recently blurred the sharp demarcation that once existed between these epochs.

It seems probable that all known forms of writing derive directly or indirectly from the Sumerian invention. Other early peoples, who invented other scripts, seem to have done so only after hearing of the possibility of writing from travelers who had knowledge of the wonderful skill Sumerian priests had unlocked by striving to record unambiguously just who had and who had not paid his debts to the god.

Irrigation. By about 3000 B.C., when written records begin to allow a more detailed knowledge of ancient Sumer, water engineering had attained very considerable elaboration. All the readily irrigable land had already been brought under cultivation. A dozen or more cities, each with several thousand inhabitants, dotted the irrigated landscape, and within each city the god's house or temple constituted by far the largest and grandest structure. Nippur appears to have enjoyed a certain primacy among Sumerian cities. Priests from all parts of Sumer probably gathered there from time to time at the temple of Enlil, god of the storm. Exchange of news and views, and the transaction of all sorts of business between the separate Sumerian cities, presumably took place on such occasions. The cohesion and uniformity of Sumerian civilization could scarcely have been maintained in any other fashion.

When quarrels broke out between adjacent cities, no doubt the conferences of priests attempted to adjudicate the points of dispute. But as Sumerian water engineering approached its geographical and technical limits, quarrels were likely to become really serious, because as irrigation canals became larger and longer every new withdrawal from the rivers began to affect the water supply available downstream. Peaceable adjudication of disputes over water rights, which in a dry season might quickly become a life-and-death affair, was therefore not always possible. As a result, war between neighboring cities, and presently among rival coalitions of cities, became an important and recurring feature of Sumerian life. In addition, defense against outer barbarians was always difficult. The river valleys lay wide open on all sides to hostile assault, and the wealth so spectacularly accumulated through irrigation and specialization of artisan skills made the Sumerian cities worthwhile objects of attack.

Military force and monarchy. As a result, by 3000 B.C. Sumerian cities had developed a military organization that rivaled the importance of priestly leadership. Kingship may initially have been based upon a theory that the gods delegated someone as their representative among men. In times of peace such a dignitary would be chief priest; but in time of war he had either to lead the army in person or else find some younger and more vigorous man to do so on his (and the gods') behalf. When warlike relations between adjacent cities became normal, the importance of military leadership increased at the expense of ritual and other peacetime functions. Sometimes frictions arose between priestly and military leaders, for the needs of defense were imperious when rivals still threatened and decisive victory had not been won. But clearly, there was no possibility of decisive victory as long as the separate cities of the Sumerian plain maintained their independence. Only a single administration empowered to distribute water and settle other quarrels among the various cities could end civil strife. Such an imperial state might also reasonably be expected to hold the barbarians of the borderlands in awe through the overwhelming force it could assemble in case of provocation.

The great difficulty lay in devising means whereby an imperial monarch could effectively control distant parts of his domain. The earliest great conquerors appear to have kept a large military household around their persons at all times. In order to maintain a body of several thousand armed men, rulers like Sargon of Akkad (*c.* 2250 B.C.) found it necessary to travel incessantly from place to place. An annual income of plunder from hostile communities was probably also essential. Such a predatory regime was inherently precarious. Any military reverse sufficed to induce local communities to refuse to admit the monarch's armed men when next they knocked at the city gates. But the only alternative was to scatter garrisons out among the subject communities to assure their obedience; and this meant the dispersal of the monarch's striking force, and endangered his superiority in the field over local rivals. Moreover, garrisons stationed for long periods of time away from the king's person might cease to obey their distant monarch's commands, even when such commands could be reliably transmitted to them.

In the face of such difficulties ancient Sumer never attained peace for very long. Deep-set local loyalties to the separate cities within which Sumerian civilization had originally developed undermined all efforts at imperial unification, and shifting coalitions and alliances among rival cities failed to balance each other off so exactly as to prevent frequent resort to war. Thus the problem of maintaining peace at home and an effective guard against outsiders was never solved. Nevertheless, just because the problem remained critically important, it provided the principal growing point for Sumerian as well as for later Mesopotamian civilization. Improved weapons and more massive, better organized military forces were one result. Administrative and political devices for controlling men at a distance were another. Some of these Sumerian inventions have remained fundamental to civilized governments ever since, for such basic elements as published law codes, bureaucratic appointment to office, and official postal services all date back to ancient Mesopotamia. There are even traces of official propaganda designed to convince people that the land of Sumer had "always" been united under the supreme jurisdiction of one god and one king.

Long before the inadequacy of these devices for maintaining peace and order had been definitively demonstrated, important aspects of Sumer's civilization attracted the attention of neighbors far and near and stimulated them to alter their own ways in the light of Sumerian achievements. A survey of the first phase of the diffusion of Sumerian civilization will therefore engage our attention in the next chapter.

II

Diffusion of Civilization

First Phase to 1700 B.C.

BETWEEN about 4000 and 1700 B. C. human societies were affected by the spread of two concentric disturbances. It was as though someone at about a three-thousand-year interval had dropped stones into the middle of a pond. Geographical and social irregularities meant that the propagation of the two successive waves did not follow an exact geometric pattern, but instead darted ahead here, lapped round an island of conservatism there, or somewhere else stopped short in face of an impenetrable climatic barrier. Yet despite such complexities, the simile is useful. Within all the variety of landscape the Middle Eastern sort of neolithic farming continually spread to new ground, wherever temperature, rainfall, and natural forest cover permitted. Then, some distance behind, more complex societies which we can properly call civilized also propagated themselves successfully on new, especially hospitable ground.

Pastoralism. As slash and burn grain-cultivation spread, and the number of men dependent on this mode of life increased, two important modifications of the earliest farming pattern assumed major importance. First, in the great steppe region of Eurasia, lying north of the hill and mountain zone where agriculture had arisen initially, there were few trees and correspondingly few locations naturally suited to slash and burn cultivation. On the other hand, the wide grasslands that gave the steppe its special character were particularly well suited for the maintenance of herds of domesticated animals. Hence, hunters of the steppe, when confronted with the array of skills the earliest farmers had developed, were making an effective adjustment to their geographical environment when they accepted animal domestication and rejected the laborious digging which grain cultivation required.

A distinctive pastoral style of life thus emerged, acquainted with agriculture but disdainful of it. A similar, though hotter and dryer, environment existed south of the mountains, where the grasslands shade off into desert throughout a great arc north of the Arabian peninsula. In this zone too, pastoralism developed as a variant of neolithic farming techniques. The assortment of domesticated animals in the southern region tended to differ from the larger-bodied beasts favored in the north. Sheep, goats, and donkeys could better withstand the shortages of summer fodder inherent in a semi-desert climate than could more voracious cattle and horses, whose greater size helped them to survive the winter cold of the northern steppe.

The emergence of pastoralism as a distinct mode of life on the northern and southern flanks of the agricultural world cannot be dated precisely. Probably no large number of people lived as pastoralists before 3000 B.C. Long after that time, adaptation to nomadic life on the steppe was not complete. Such an apparently simple technique as riding on horseback, for example, did not become common until after 900 B.C., perhaps because a life in the saddle demanded not only a saddle and bridle but also adjustments of clothing (trousers) and housing (tents or wagons) and a general lightening of household impedimenta.

Pastoralists were, like hunters, parasites upon herbivores. They were like hunters, too, in pursuing a wandering life, moving comparatively large distances in search of grass for their animals. Pastoralists often followed a more or less regular migration pattern designed to discover the richest feeding grounds for their herds at each season of the year. Above all else, shepherds and herdsmen had to protect their herds from rival carnivores, whether those rivals were animals or other men. Such a life required a chief, who could decide the route of march and take command of the entire community in time of emergency whenever rivals attempted to intrude upon the community's traditional pasture lands or steal their flocks and herds.

Warlike organization and habits of violence characteristic of successful big-game hunters remained near the surface of such a life, whereas the earliest farming communities were remarkably peaceable and egalitarian. This contrast gave pastoralists a distinct advantage in any military collision with mere farmers. Indeed, pastoralists enjoyed so great an advantage that they were always tempted to try to domesticate their fellow men by conquering and exploiting them as ruthlessly as they did their animals.

The subsequent history of mankind in the Old World turned upon an interplay between the superior numbers made possible by farming existence and the superior politico-military organization required by pastoralism. This balance tipped sometimes in favor of one, sometimes in favor of the other protagonist, depending on fluctuations in social organization and cohesion, and on developments in technology. Accidents like the appearance of a great conqueror and empire builder or the outbreak of devastating plague also played their part in disturbing the balance from time to time. Everywhere and always its fluctuations harrowed and disturbed human society, but bloody collisions between farmers and herdsmen also pricked men on to make experiments in living they might otherwise have never ventured. After about 3000 B.C. the pace of social evolution all across Eurasia was, therefore, vastly accelerated by the enlarged variety of human society resulting from the divergence between farming and pastoral styles of life.

The plow. The invention of the plow also altered and diversified the texture of human life in a very significant way. Somewhere, sometime before 3000 B.C., but perhaps not long before, men learned how to harness the strength of their animals to the tasks of tillage. This had several important consequences. It united grain growing and animal husbandry as never before, making each dependent on the other. It also imparted to the Middle Eastern style of mixed farming — which thus achieved a mature definition — some important advantages over other types of cultivation.

First of all, the plow made grain-growers fully sedentary. Obviously as the number of farming communities multiplied, forest land suitable for slash and burn cultivation became more and more difficult to find. The response was to migrate from the original centers in the hilly country of the Middle East, thus spreading agriculture in all directions. But some farming communities remained behind and had to return at more and more frequent intervals to fields that had already been tilled. Under such circumstances the luxuriant fertility of virgin soil could no longer be expected. Plowing, however, allowed men to cultivate far more land than they could hope to do with hoes and digging sticks, so that by gathering a less abundant crop from more land the farmer could maintain or even increase his food supply.

Moreover, it was soon discovered that a fallow field, i.e. a field kept in tilth but not planted with grain, would recuperate far more rapidly than if the land were simply allowed to go back to weeds. By alternating cropland and fallow, therefore, a plowman could maintain himself indefinitely in one spot. The lessened fertility of plowed acres as compared with the virgin soil used by slash and burn cultivators was compensated for by a more systematic and convenient layout of fields. Stumps, after all, seriously obstruct uniform, careful cultivation, even with a hoe. Indeed, what we conceive a field to be — a comparatively smooth, uniformly culti-vated piece of land in which seeds of only one botanical species are usually planted — is the creation of the plow, whose size and awk-wardness in turning, together with its inability to adjust to the small hummocks and hollows characteristic of a forest floor, re-quired men to remake the landscape far more drastically than the forest farmers had done.

Small, rectangular fields began to appear all over the Middle East as a result of plowing the same soil time after time. As this oc-curred, Middle Eastern farmers often found themselves able to raise a considerable surplus of food even on land not refreshed by river silt or watered by irrigation channels. In such societies animal power had so effectually begun to supplement merely human mus-cles that a few men could be spared from the immediate tasks of feeding themselves. This made civilization possible, even beyond the limits of irrigation. And it was not long, as we shall see pres-ently, before the new possibility of creating and sustaining civilized social complexity and specialization of function on rain-watered land was acted upon in regions suitably close to the original seat of civilized life.

Thus between 3500 and 2500 B.C. the rise of pastoral communi-ties on the one hand and of plowing villages on the other greatly enriched the variety of human styles of life and prepared the ground for a geographically massive spread of civilized complexities to all regions of the Eurasian continent where temperatures and rainfall permitted the growing of grain on a large scale.

Egyptian civilization. Prior to about 2500 B.C., however, the spread of civilized forms of society required very special geographical circumstances. Only in irrigable river valleys could the techniques then known support the corps of specialists needed if civilized levels of skill and knowledge were to be attained. Several smallish rivers within fairly short range of Sumer met these requirements. The Jordan, for example, and the Karun river, which today flows into the Tigris near its mouth but in ancient times made its independent way to the Persian Gulf, both saw very ancient cities rise along their banks; and it is probable that archaeologists will uncover several others like them elsewhere. But these river valleys were too small to become seats of a society massive enough to stand comparison with Sumer, or with the other antique civilizations that were arising simultaneously in the Nile and Indus valleys.

Until the 1930's, the civilization of Egypt was believed to be the most ancient of the earth. But Egyptologists now agree that their predecessors' chronological estimates were seriously in error. The traditional beginning of Egyptian history was the unification of Upper and Lower Egypt under King Menes. This probably occurred about 3100 B.C., at a time when Sumerian cities already had several centuries of development behind them.

Small but unmistakable traces of Sumerian influence upon the earliest phases of Egyptian civilized development have been discovered. It seems probable, therefore, that seafarers from the head of the Persian Gulf made their way around Arabia to the Red Sea and there came sporadically into contact with the peoples inhabiting the narrow Nile valley. Techniques and ideas already familiar to the Sumerians were of particular value to the natives of an environment that was in so many ways similar to that of the lower Tigris-Euphrates. Irrigation, metallurgy, writing, the plow, wheeled vehicles, and monumental buildings had all appeared in Mesopotamia by about the time of Menes. All, in short order, were fitted to Egyptian use by a process of imitation and adaptation.

Mediterranean Sea

PALESTINE

Dead Sea

Pelusium

DELTA

Sais
Busiris

Avaris

HYKSOS, 1680 B.C.

LIBYA

Heliopolis

Memphis

LOWER **EGYPT**

Fayum

Heracleopolis

Nile R.

MT. SINAI

Hermopolis

Akhetaton (El-Amarna)

Lyconpolis

UPPER **EGYPT**

Red Sea

Abydos

Thebes • Karnak
Luxor

ANCIENT EGYPT

Ombi

Syene
CATARACT

Scale of Miles
0   50   100

Nile R.

Abu Simbel
CATARACT
NUBIA

Egypt's political unification created conditions whereby a very rapid assimilation of those elements in the Sumerian tool kit that appealed to the Egyptians could and did take place, while elements incompatible with local tradition or geographical conditions were repudiated. In other words, Egyptian civilization came rapidly into existence, with a stylistic coherence and institutional framework of its own. What had taken a thousand years or longer in Mesopotamia required less than half as much time in Egypt, thanks to the advantage the Egyptians had of being able to profit from Sumerian experience.

Important differences between Egyptian and Sumerian social structures made Egyptian civilization both more perfect and more fragile. Everything in Egypt focused upon the court of the god-king or Pharaoh. In Sumer, the gods were believed to be invisible, though man-like in their needs and traits of character and behavior. The Egyptians, on the other hand, declared their king to be a god. Immortal himself, he could also confer immortality upon other men. Here was a powerful motive for obeying the Pharaoh, since a grateful god-king might be expected to reward those who had served him well in this life by graciously allowing them to share his divine immortality as ever faithful servants. Defiance of the Pharaoh, on the other hand, forfeited all hope of life after death.

The Old Kingdom. The peculiar geographical conditions of the Nile valley also helped political centralization. Formidable deserts on both flanks of the Nile made the valley almost immune from any really dangerous foreign attack. Occasional raids by the Nubians from the south or by Libyans from the west lacked the weight of numbers that made barbarian attack such a serious problem in Mesopotamia. Moreover, within the valley itself, the slow, stately Nile current could carry boats northward without difficulty, while the return trip could be made almost as simply by raising sails to catch the north-to-northeast wind that blows across Egypt nearly all the time. Shipping up and down the Nile was so easy that it eclipsed all other forms of transport. No part of the fertile soil was far from the river's edge, and from almost any place along the bank a ship could carry goods or men upstream or downstream all the way from the marshy delta at the river's mouth to the first cataract. Under these circumstances, to control the shipping on the river was to control the entire country. And it is in the nature of things that vessels moving upstream and downstream are easier to observe and control than is any form of overland transport that does not have to follow definitely prescribed routes. Hence, the devices for upholding a central, imperial administration which were painfully and imperfectly developed in Mesopotamia were not needed in Egypt. The divine ruler, with a few obedient and eager servants stationed at intervals along the river, could command the entire country without difficulty.

What happened was that the god-king's household extended itself over the navigable length of the Nile valley, bringing the whole flood plain within a single administrative unit. At one stroke, therefore, Egypt solved the problem of internal peace and order which was proving stubbornly insoluble in Sumer at the time when Menes united Upper and Lower Egypt so effectually.

The Pharaoh's household also constituted the principal framework within which Egyptian civilization took form. Artisans and administrators attached to the god-king's household summoned the pyramids into being and originated the scarcely less wonderful conventions of Egyptian art within three to four hundred years of Menes' conquest. Hieroglyphic writing, glazed tiles and pots, exquisite carpentry, together with music and dancing and other skills less well known from archaeological remains, all grew up within the same royal household. If such skills existed elsewhere at all, they did so only in pale and imperfect provincial forms.

Such concentration upon a single center had the advantages that large-scale enterprise is always able to attain. The great pyramids, for example, could be built only by mustering the rural manpower of all Egypt during the season of the year when no work needed to be done in the fields; and only a single commanding center such as the Pharaoh's court could do so. On the other hand, the rigorously centralized regime of ancient Egypt was inevitably fragile too. Everything depended on the willingness of men far removed from the Pharaoh's presence to obey him or his agents. Throughout nearly nine hundred years, during the period of the Old Kingdom (c. 3100–2200 B.C.), this appears nonetheless to have been effectively the case, save for brief periods of transition from one dynasty to another.

Even at the height of the Old Kingdom, sharp local diversity lay just beneath the surface of Pharaonic uniformity. This is particularly evident in the confusion that continued to reign among Egyptian deities. Local gods, often conceived in animal or semi-human forms, commanded local loyalties, and nothing like the coherence of the Sumerian pantheon ever emerged. Local sanctuaries and priesthoods presumably preserved these incompatible pieties. In course of time some of them began to develop elaborate ceremonies and started to construct buildings comparable in scale to those of the ancient temples of Mesopotamia.

Nevertheless, it was not disobedient priesthoods but rebellious local officials who ultimately disrupted the centralization of the Egyptian government. The educated class of scribes, who recorded their dismay at the disintegration of Pharaonic order, felt this fragmentation of Egypt to be profoundly wrong. Nevertheless, for more than a century after 2200 B.C. the country remained divided, as Mesopotamia almost always had been.

A sharp decay of most aspects of the Egyptian civilization resulted. Local rulers did their best to maintain high art and other attributes of the Pharaonic dignity, but more straitened resources meant the decay of luxury and often of expertise as well. Yet even in time of outward disorder and political division, the ideals of Pharaonic civilization survived. Nearly a thousand years of the Old Kingdom had rooted the ideals firmly in the soil of the Nile valley.

The Middle Kingdom. Hence it is not surprising that after nearly two centuries of political division, Egypt was again united by a new conqueror from the south who made his capital not at Memphis, near the apex of the Nile delta, but far upstream, at Thebes. The so-called Middle Kingdom, thus established, lasted until about 1800 B.C. when the land of Egypt once again broke up into local and competing sovereignties, each ruler claiming to be the legitimate Pharaoh of all the land.

Art styles and other evidences of cultural continuity suggest that the rulers of the Middle Kingdom set out deliberately to model themselves on their predecessors' achievements. Yet there were important differences. Temple architecture became more and more elaborate. Local landlords and magnates, whether priests or laymen, continued to enjoy far greater importance than had been the case in the days of the Old Kingdom. Egyptian society and civilization therefore became less dependent upon a single center, and correspondingly more resilient in face of political disaster. Yet these advantages were purchased at the cost of the loss of the supreme artistic refinement and stylistic coherence which had characterized the culture of the Old Kingdom at its height (i.e. *c.* 2600–2400 B.C.).

In view of the fact that the next major landmark of Egyptian history was conquest in force by barbarian strangers from Asia known as Hyksos, this dispersion of cultural leadership during the Middle Kingdom was probably critically important for the survival of the Egyptian style of civilization. Had a single Pharaonic household still, as in the days of the Old Kingdom, comprised the entire circle of Egyptian expertise, its destruction would also have destroyed Egyptian civilization: but before the Hyksos appeared, this risk had been removed through multiplication of lesser centers of specialized skill and knowledge within the structure of Egyptian society itself.

The Indus civilization. Far less is known of the other great civilization that emerged in the third millennium B.C. in the Indus valley. The script used by the Indus peoples cannot be read by modern scholars, so that an all-important avenue for scholarly understanding of the Indus culture is still closed. Archaeological investigation of Indus sites is also incomplete, and some of the digging that was done was done poorly. Nevertheless, certain deductions seem legitimate from what has already been discovered. The Indus civilization had two great urban capitals, one located at Harappa and the other several hundred miles downstream at Mohenjo-daro. Precocious political unification, analogous to that of Egypt in the days of the Old Kingdom, offers the best explanation for the great difference between these two cities and the far smaller country towns and villages which seem to constitute the only other kinds of Indus sites.

ANCIENT INDUS
SITES

■ City or town
• Village
Modern names shown in brackets

Scale of Miles

0   300

[Kabul]

(Kyber Pass)

Indus R.

[Rawalpindi]

(AFGHANISTAN)

Jhelum R.

Chenab R.

Ravi R.

[Kandahar]

Sutlej R.

Rupar

Harappa

Kalibangan

[Delhi]

Jumna R.

B A L U C H I S T A N

Judierjo-
daro

Mohenjo-daro

Chanhu-
daro

THAR OR INDIAN DESERT

[Jodhpur]

[Karachi]

Indus R.

Early Coast Line?

Lothal

Arabian Sea

KATHIAWAR

Narbada R.

(I N D I A)

[Bombay]

HIMALAYA

Contact with Sumer is certain, since seals and other small objects of Indus manufacture have been discovered in Mesopotamia in strata dating from about 2500 B.C. In all probability sea-borne contact with Sumer therefore played the same role in accelerating the growth of Indus civilization as it did in the earliest stage of Egyptian development. Just as in Egypt, the art style and mode of writing developed by the Indus peoples apparently bore no relation to Sumerian prototypes. Stimulus to develop their own distinctive styles of life was what Egyptian and Indus peoples took from the Sumerians. Only at the very start, before local styles had been defined, can traces of direct imitation or awkward mimicry of Sumerian techniques be expected. Examples of such imitation have been found in Egypt, but ground water has so far prevented archaeologists from penetrating to the lowest levels at the twin capitals of Indus civilization, Harappa and Mohenjo-daro, where similar evidences of direct imitation might perhaps be found.

Both Mohenjo-daro and Harappa are divided between an elevated citadel or sanctuary and lower-lying city blocks. Some areas contained long rows of identical rooms — sleeping quarters for some sort of conscript or slave labor perhaps. More than this can scarcely be deduced about the social structure of ancient Indus society. The analogy of both Egypt and Sumer suggests that a society organized by priestly colleges for the more sumptuous service of the gods was probably at the heart of Indus civilization; but we cannot be sure.

The chronological span represented by the mounds of rubble constituting the two capital sites can be stated with fair assurance, since cross dating with Sumer through seals and other imports at either end is possible. On this basis it seems probable that Indus civilization flourished from about 2500 to 1500 B.C. The two great cities were destroyed by attackers who, having slaughtered the inhabitants and burned the towns, did not care to take up residence themselves. Almost certainly, Aryan-speaking tribesmen from the north were the barbarians who thus destroyed the Indus cities and disrupted Indus civilization. The destruction was nearly complete. Only the elements of Indus civilization which were accessible to village piety and comprehensible by untutored understandings survived into later times. The special knowledge and high skills once possessed by the (presumably priestly) leaders vanished when the barbarians killed or dispersed them, between 1500 and, at the latest, 1200 B.C. A similar fate might have overtaken Pharaonic Egypt had not the political development of the Middle Kingdom allowed a dispersal of the skills and knowledge required to maintain Egyptian civilization, long before the Hyksos attacked and overran the land.

Mesopotamian civilization, 2500–1700 B.C. While these great changes transformed the life of Egypt and the Indus valley, civilized life did not remain stable and constant in Mesopotamia. Yet nothing so fundamental as had taken place between 3500 and 2500 B.C. in the land of Sumer could recur in the centuries that followed. The problem of frontier guard against barbarians eager to plunder the riches of the irrigated plain was never solved for long. The no less intractable problem of keeping peace among the cities themselves was solved only by a common subjection to the alien, and often hated, rule of some barbarian or half-barbarian conqueror.

Amid unending political and military turmoil, two important changes should be noted. First, soon after 2000 B.C., the Sumerian language ceased to be spoken on ordinary occasions. It was supplanted by various Semitic languages, of which Akkadian was the first to achieve literary definition. The displacement of Sumerian from everyday usage seems to have taken place gradually. Semitic speakers from the desert fringes must have moved in in such numbers as gradually to reduce the Sumerian language to the status of a sacred tongue, to be learned in schools and intoned at religious festivals. The obvious necessity of addressing the gods in their familiar language, however, preserved Sumerian for many centuries. The fact that the priests had to learn Sumerian, as we might learn Latin today, required them to create bilingual word lists and other school helps. This, in turn, is what first permitted modern scholars to decipher and read Sumerian once they had mastered Akkadian with the help of bilingual inscriptions using old Persian.

Secondly, little by little and despite frequent setbacks, territorially extensive political empires gained in coherence and stability. Bureaucracy, law, and trade helped to cement large kingdoms, and the device of using written letters and instructions to communicate with distant officials made it possible for a monarch to make his will reliably known to men he had never seen and in places where he might never appear in person.

Centers of political power tended to migrate upstream. This was so partly because salting of the soil as a result of evaporation damaged and eventually destroyed the fertility of the oldest fields in the extreme south of Mesopotamia. In addition, in any military collision the city upstream always had the advantage, since it could cut off the canals and interrupt the water supply of those downstream. As a result Akkad began to dominate Sumer by the time of Sargon (c. 2250 B.C.); and Babylon, still further north, became the capital of Mesopotamia by the time of Hammurabi (c. 1700 B.C.), one of the few kings who succeeded briefly in uniting all of the Tigris-Euphrates flood plain under his sway.

In Hammurabi's time, too, Babylonian priests boldly reworked the corpus of Sumerian and Akkadian learning to exalt the name and powers of Marduk, Babylon's divine proprietor and protector. Thus, for example, the so-called "Creation Epic," which recounts how the world was made in terms echoed later by the Book of Genesis claims Marduk as the chief of the gods. This was done by substituting his name for that of Enlil, the storm god of Nippur, who certainly enjoyed primacy among the gods of the Sumerian original. In other respects also, scribes and mathematicians in Hammurabi's age proved themselves unusually venturesome. For example, complex arithmetic calculations appear for the first time in tablets from this age; and then for more than a thousand years nothing new of any significance in mathematics is to be found.

The geographical shift from Sumer to Akkad and from Akkad to Babylonia, and the linguistic transformation that accompanied this northward migration of the center of wealth and power, did not much modify the fundamental continuity of Mesopotamian civilization. The ideas first worked out by Sumerian priests to explain the world and man's relation to the gods stood the test of time. So did the early technological adjustments to life in the river flood plains. Remarkably small change came to either of these aspects of Mesopotamian civilization. Invention and slow improvement tended to concentrate instead on political and military matters where, as we have seen, the arts of imperial administration were gradually elaborated.

Transition to rain-watered lands. Geographical enlargement of the civilized area of the Mesopotamian valley itself, together with the rise of Egyptian and Indus styles of civilization in the distant river valleys of the Nile and Indus, obviously constituted an important reinforcement to the ranks of human civilization. Yet as long as such complicated societies required irrigated river valleys for their development, they had, perforce, to remain rare and exotic forms of human life, islanded in a sea of barbarism. Only when rain-watered land could also be made to sustain specialists in sufficient numbers to make civilized societies possible could civilizations dominate the globe. This was a process that took nearly four thousand years to come to its completion, starting not long before 2000 B.C. and finally accomplished only in the nineteenth century of the Christian era.

Details of how the transition to rain-watered land first actually occurred are unknown, although the fact is indisputable. By about 2000 B.C., for example, Mesopotamia had come to be ringed around by a series of satellite civilizations, or proto-civilizations, of which the Hittite society in Asia Minor and the Canaanite in Syria and Palestine are by far the best known. Egypt's deserts forbade any comparable development on the flanks of the Nile valley, but it is possible, perhaps probable, though not yet attested to archaeologically, that elements of Indus civilization filtered southward and eastward to affect the lives of non-irrigating peoples in southern and central India.

It is not difficult to state what was needed for civilization to be able to flourish on rain-watered land. First, farmers had to be able to produce a surplus of food. Second, some social mechanism had to transfer food surpluses from the hands of the farmers who produced them to an array of specialists, who could then freely elaborate high skills and arcane knowledge without having to spend most of their time working in the fields, like the peasant majority.

We have already seen how the spread of plowing enabled ordinary farmers on many soils and in most seasons to produce an agricultural surplus. This was an indispensable preliminary to the establishment of civilization beyond the limits of irrigation. Yet the exact origin and early diffusion of plow agriculture is quite unclear. Equally the origin and nature of the social mechanisms that transferred food from its producers to specialized consumers really escape modern knowledge. Conquest and trade were probably the two principal factors. But conquerors and merchants impinged variously upon pre-existing forms of social leadership to produce rather considerable structural variations among the civilized and proto-civilized societies that began to grow up beyond the limits of river valley irrigation.

In northeastern Asia Minor, for example, the discovery of a number of clay tablets written by Assyrian merchants about 1900 B.C. allows a glimpse of emergent Hittite civilization. At that time local rulers had already begun to gather an entourage of soldiers, priests, merchants, and artisans — thus anticipating on a small scale the courtly life that developed a century or so thereafter at the Hittite capital of Hattusas. Many aspects of Hittite life were direct importations from Mesopotamia. Cuneiform writing, for example, and some of the myths of Mesopotamian religion were borrowed outright. At the same time, important elements from local tradition survived. The result was an amalgam of Mesopotamian provincialism and local uniqueness. Hittite art sensitively reveals the resulting cultural duality, for despite a close relation with Mesopotamian prototypes the sculpture of Hattusas has an unmistakable style of its own.

Hittite society comprised several different ethnic groups, and it seems likely that conquest of one group by the other lay at the bottom of the social differentiation upon which Hittite civilization arose. Only after local chiefs and rulers had a certain amount of wealth or labor power at their disposal could civilized merchants really begin to do business. The goods produced in distant civilized areas were likely to be too expensive to interest ordinary farmers, and the things civilized merchants sought in exchange — e.g. metals, timber, or other raw materials — often required rather elaborate operations for their transport or other preparation. It seems altogether likely that the men who organized local manpower for such enterprises and who bought cloth, metal goods, and other wares from civilized traders were able to do so by virtue of wealth and power they had initially acquired as leaders of one ethnic group in the conquest of another. The prominence of armed men, and the squat heaviness characteristic of Hittite sculpture, certainly suggest the heavy tread of conquerors, who found themselves in a position to require rents and services from their victims on a scale sufficient to maintain small cities in which artisans and other specialists could cater to the conquerors' tastes.

Substantially the same pattern of social evolution appears to have occurred in other parts of Mesopotamia's borderland. Canaanites on the west may have been more mercantile, less military; but in the hill country north and east of the Tigris valley, Hurrians and Elamites developed their own variations on the civilized Mesopotamian style of life by following a predominantly military route — or so our very imperfect information suggests.

At a still further remove, in the steppe country beyond the mountains, pastoralists were particularly interested in metal that might improve their weaponry or enhance the splendor of their dress. By about 2500 B.C., for example, chieftains of the Kuban valley, north of the Caucasus mountains, began to furnish their graves with handsome bronze weapons and jewelry. Bronze made the already warlike barbarians of the steppe even more formidable. They proved able, in fact, to conquer their neighbors far and wide. Thus, for example, during the following six to seven hundred years, bronze-wielding barbarians swarmed from the steppe and overran all of western Europe, conquering and in time absorbing pre-existing populations. Habits of violence and admiration of the military virtues were implanted deeply into the European consciousness by these Bronze Age barbarian invasions. Europe also became Europeanized in speech, since, except for Finns, Estonians, Magyars, and Basques, all the modern inhabitants of Europe speak languages derived from an ancient tongue (or closely related tongues) brought from the western steppelands of Eurasia by the Bronze Age conquerors.

This family of languages is called Indo-European because its various branches are spoken not only in Europe but in Persia and northern India as well. This modern distribution attests to the fact that when their rude prowess had been reinforced by the possession of up-to-date bronze weapons, the steppe barbarians also found it possible to conquer eastward and southward. In the Middle East, for example, small bands appear to have established themselves as rulers among the hill people called Hurrians; the same was true of the Kassites further east. Even the Hyksos, whose main ethnic component was Semitic in speech, also may have incorporated a few Indo-European speakers into their ranks. The Aryan conquest of the Indus valley and the destruction of the ancient Indus civilization which ensued constituted one extreme wing of this barbarian migration. Other less well-known tribes (Tocharians) moved even further eastward, perhaps at a later date, as far as the borders of China.

Further consideration of the character and consequences of this vast movement of peoples will be reserved for the next chapter.

Sea-borne civilization. While interaction between civilized techniques and barbarian societies was producing these striking changes in the ethnic map of Eurasia, another, less massive but not unimportant, sea-borne contagion also transformed human lives and cultures in the Mediterranean and along the Atlantic coast.

Minoan Crete offers the principal example of an early sea-borne civilization. The island itself was not settled much before 4000 B.C., when Mediterranean seafaring presumably began. Cretan rubbish piles betray clear signs of commerce with Egypt by about 3000 B.C. Full-scale civilization emerged on the island nearly a thousand years later, for the famous palace of Minos was first built about 2100 B.C. By about the same time an as yet undeciphered form of writing, together with metallurgy, magnificent pottery, a charmingly naturalistic art style, and all the other appurtenances of archaic civilization had put in their appearance.

The wealth required to maintain the artisans and other specialists who created the splendors of Minoan civilization came mainly from sea commerce — or so it seems. Minoan ships traveled widely in the Mediterranean. Search for the copper and tin needed to make bronze may have been the main lure to distant voyaging. At any rate, traces of Minoan settlements have been discovered in Sardinia, near old copper mines. Crete itself exported timber and olive oil to the Levant and to Egypt. In addition Minoan merchants probably served as middlemen between civilized artisans of the eastern Mediterranean and raw-material producers of the north and west.

Exactly how Minoan society was organized remains beyond the

scope of modern knowledge. Minos was probably a title like Pharaoh, and the ruler's powers were probably based more on his religious than on his military or administrative role. Warfare was clearly far less important than it was on the mainland. So far as can be discovered, Knossos, the capital, was not defended by any wall; and arms and armor are not in the least prominent among Cretan remains.

The religion upon which Minos' power rested was related to cults that survived into historic times in Asia Minor. The central deity appears to have been a "Great Mother" goddess, whose special symbol was the double axe. In addition, bulls and snakes were objects of special reverence. Bull-dancing, i.e. acrobatic religious performances in which youths seized the charging animal's horns and leaped high over his back, was an important rite. Spanish bull-fighting may descend from this ancient religious sport.

As compared with the severe, stolid character of Hittite sculpture, Minoan art strikes a modern observer as light, graceful, spontaneous. Naturalistic drawing of fish and other aquatic forms of life, and a conventionalized but vivacious portrayal of human beings, bespeak a gayer and less violent outlook than that revealed by Hittite and other continental societies, where military struggles and the oppression of conquered peoples were the central realities of civilized and proto-civilized existence.

Further west in the Mediterranean, when Cretan civilization was at its height, another center of high culture existed on the island of Malta. This island appears to have been the site of the "mother church" of a "megalithic" religion. All that is known for sure is that a large number of tombs and other structures made of very large rocks came to dot the coastlands of western Europe and north Africa all the way from Morocco to southern Sweden. Why men took the trouble to make such structures cannot now be determined. Presumably missionary-priests persuaded the local inhabitants that such efforts were worthwhile, and both organized the necessary manpower and taught local peoples the skills needed to construct these massive monuments. In all probability the teachers of this religion held out hope of an immortal existence in islands of the blessed lying far to the west beyond the sunset. The tombs and

other megalithic structures presumably helped to assure such
happy immortality. It seems probable that the ideas of megalithic
religion were related in some way to Egyptian cults of the dead;
but exactly how this linkage may have been forged is not clear. Indeed, since written records do not exist, the doctrines of the
megalithic religion may only be surmised on the basis of Irish and
other Celtic folklore of much later times.

The geographical distribution of megalithic remains in Europe
and Africa makes it clear that the bearers of this culture traveled
by water, and must, indeed, have been rather expert seamen. In all
probability their vessels were simple coracles, i.e. wickerwork
covered by hides to keep out the sea. With such light, simple boats
it was possible to sail long distances by hugging the shores and
landing whenever a storm threatened. Accidental voyages across
the open sea obviously could occur whenever a boat got caught in
an unexpected storm. It is possible, for example, that the Canary Islands were populated as a result of just such an accidental voyage.
At any rate, a Stone Age people who may have been descendants
of megalith builders inhabited those remote islands when Europeans first discovered them in the fourteenth century of the Christian era. As a matter of fact, voyages all the way across the Atlantic, sailing as Columbus was later to do before the northeast trades,
were technically possible even with such simple vessels as those the
ancient megalith-makers possessed.

The expansion of megalithic proto-civilization to the Far West
occurred between about 2500 and 1700 B.C. By the latter date, barbarian conquerors descended from pastoralists of the Eurasian
steppe reached the Atlantic shores of Europe, and there subdued
the peaceable megalith builders. Occasionally, the new masters of
the land used the old megalithic skills to erect structures like
Stonehenge in England. These standing stone circles, of which several besides Stonehenge exist, probably represent a monumental
version in stone of a style of religious architecture that had originated as a circle of tree trunks.

Southeast Asia and the Americas. Elsewhere in the world, so far
as we can tell, no such striking changes took place in the centuries
between 3000 and 1700 B.C. The spread of agriculture continued,

and in the monsoon regions of Asia a type of garden cultivation that concentrated mainly on root crops acquired greater and greater importance. At some early period the monsoon cultivators added rice to their crops. In suitable regions rice soon became the staple of this style of cultivation.

The garden culture of monsoon Asia differed from the field culture familiar in the Middle East in two respects: (a) rice plants were transplanted from special seed flats (i.e. treated like roots or other plants that can be propagated by transplantation of offshoots) and (b) animal power was not vitally necessary to supplement human muscles in the work of cultivation. These differences meant that the southeast Asian garden style of cultivation was more intensive and much more labor-consuming than field agriculture of the Middle Eastern type. Very dense peasant populations could and did soon develop in the monsoon region of Asia on the basis of this sort of cultivation.

As a result, between 2000 and 1000 B.C. (and perhaps beginning earlier), a series of populous human communities arose along the river banks and coastal plains of southeast Asia, spreading all the way from Bengal to southern China. These societies depended on rice and root crops for their food and developed considerable skill as seafarers. Yet nothing comparable in complexity to the civilizations of the Middle East arose. Specialization of skills, and the organization of comparatively large numbers of men into a single political and economic unit, did not occur on the scale familiar in the Middle East, perhaps because the climatic conditions of the monsoon region made the common effort required for large-scale irrigation unnecessary, and indeed, in wetter regions, absurd.

How far early Asian seafarers may have penetrated among the islands of the Pacific cannot be said, since archaeological study of these parts is very spotty. Expansion, perhaps geographically more extensive than anything the megalithic folk of Europe accomplished, probably occurred, for seafaring in regions ruled by the predictable monsoons and trade winds is relatively easy, even for primitive craft; whereas the storm-beset north Atlantic is one of the most unruly oceans of the entire world.

In the New World, the roving bands of hunters who had percolated across Bering Strait with the retreat of the last ice cap occupied all of North and South America by about 3000 B.C., when archaeological traces of human occupation begin in Tierra del Fuego at the tip of South America. Before that time cultivation of maize and other crops had begun in central Mexico, southwestern United States, and (though dates are here more problematic) perhaps also in Peru and adjacent regions of South America. This agriculture did not at once provoke the rise of cities and civilization, however. Simple village life continued to prevail in the most advanced parts of the New World until a few centuries before the Christian era.

Despite many uncertainties and glaring gaps in our information, it is clear that mankind's cultural achievements by 1700 B.C. were impressive. By comparison with the rates of cultural advance which had prevailed in earlier ages, the pace of social change had assumed a dizzying rapidity. Within less than two thousand years, three irrigation civilizations had arisen in the central region of the Old World; a large number of lesser satellite civilizations had grown up on rain-watered land, and attenuated echoes of civilized achievements had reached both the barbarian warriors of the northern steppelands and shore dwellers of the Mediterranean, the Atlantic, and, perhaps, also the Indian Ocean. A less variegated, less supremely skilled, and far less well-known cultural advance had also taken place in monsoon Asia.

In short, civilized history, in all its complexity, was well launched. Peoples as yet untouched by the skills and greed engendered within civilized societies were everywhere in retreat before the restless probing of civilized and semi-civilized adventurers, pioneers, warriors, traders, missionaries, mining prospectors, and land grabbers.

III

Cosmopolitanism in the Middle East

1700–500 B.C.

DURING a period of about three hundred years, beginning soon after 1700 B.C., the civilized world was overrun by barbarian conquerors. Hill peoples living north and east of Mesopotamia, tribesmen from the desert fringes of Syria, Palestine, and northern Arabia, together with wide ranging war bands originating from the northern steppe combined in varying proportions to attack all existing centers of civilized life. The range of these barbarian conquests was never again equaled. In outlying civilized areas where the social structure sustaining specialized skills was not very tough, the barbarian conquests destroyed most of what had been achieved. At the two extreme edges of the civilized world, in Crete and in India, little but smoking ruins survived the Achaean and Aryan assaults, both of which probably reached their climax between 1500 and 1400 B.C.

Nearer the center, where civilized styles of life were more deeply rooted, the consequences of barbarian conquest were less drastic. Mesopotamian and Egyptian civilizations survived with only local and temporary setbacks. The barbarians who took power in each land (Hyksos in Egypt about 1680 B.C., Kassites in Mesopotamia at about the same time) were interested in enjoying what they had conquered. They therefore needed help from priests, scribes, and other experts to keep both gods and men in

order so that rents, taxes, and luxury goods produced by specially
skilled workmen might continue to flow in. As a result, the structure of society upon which civilization depended did not break
down. Indeed, traditional forms of Mesopotamian and Egyptian
cultural expression underwent surprisingly little change.

Technique of chariot warfare. The range and force of these barbarian conquests was closely linked with an important advance in
the technique of warfare. The barbarian conquerors possessed light
war chariots and fleet horses to pull them. From the security of a
galloping chariot they were able to launch a shower of arrows
against any opposing military array with almost complete im-
punity. Battle tactics were to feint a charge a few times, showering
the enemy with arrows on each approach, and then mount a final
attack in which all the chariots charged home at once and overran
the opposing forces.

The advantages enjoyed by chariotry in the seventeenth century
B.C. may be compared to the advantage of a tank force when
pitted against unsupported infantry in the second quarter of the
twentieth century A.D. Mobility, firepower, and armor, three prime
determinants of battle, all favored the charioteers. Their greatest
weakness lay in the fact that chariots, and the equipment needed
by a chariot warrior, were very expensive. Bronze weapons and
armor, horses, and the skilled carpentry, leather-work, and other
artisan crafts required to construct a serviceable chariot added up
to an enormous cost. Chariots had consequently to remain comparatively few. The chariot age was therefore an age of aristocracy,
when military supremacy, and with it economic and political preponderance, rested in the hands of a very small elite.

When and where the full elaboration of chariot warfare originated is not certain. Iran or Azerbaijan, where civilized artisan
skills, above all the art of the wheel-wright, were easily accessible
to tribes of horse-raising pastoralists, would appear to be the most
likely places for the initial development of chariot warfare. The
most likely date is shortly after 1700 B.C., for it was then that the
rapid expansion of barbarian conquest got under way.

As the chariot's advantages became fully apparent, it acquired an
enormous prestige. Even in regions where wooded landscapes made

45

bow fighting largely ineffective, e.g. in northern and western Europe, barbarian tribes hastened to acquire the master weapon of the age. This appears to have been the case in Greece, for example. Certainly the tactics of the Achaean warriors before the walls of Troy as reported by Homer make no sense. Homer's heroes do not use bows, but instead dismount before fighting and use their chariots merely as conveniences in getting to and from the field of battle. This deprived the chariot of any but ceremonial significance. Further east, however, more open landscapes made the bow a practicable weapon. The Aryans who invaded India as well as those other charioteers who established their rule in China's Yellow river valley before 1400 B.C. used the chariot rationally, as a moving platform from which to launch a shower of arrows.

With the perfection of techniques of chariot warfare, barbarian horse raisers began to enjoy enormous military advantages. Conquest became easy, even with only a handful of chariots. Landed aristocracies of the sort which had begun to build provincial civilizations all around the flanks of Mesopotamia shortly before 2000 B.C. became much easier to establish, for the difference in military power between a few men with chariots and everybody else had become enormous. As a result, after an initial period of mere destructiveness, which brought both the Indus and the Cretan civilizations low, the barbarian conquerors began to construct their own rougher, militarily more formidable, style of civilization in both Greece and India. Classical Greek and Indian civilizations took their origin in this way. The same appears to be true of distant China, where the arrival of chariot warriors probably inaugurated the Shang dynasty. (Traditional Shang dates according to the shorter chronology are 1525–1028 B.C.) The Shang, to be sure, were the second dynasty recorded in Chinese tradition, but archaeological investigation suggests that the first rulers of China — the Hsia — presided over no more than unusually large neolithic village communities, whose inhabitants made fine pottery but had acquired few of the other material attributes of high civilization.

It therefore appears that the invention of the chariot, and the great differentiation this introduced on the battlefield between mounted and unmounted men, set the stage for the beginnings of each of the three great outlying civilizations of the Old World. The military and aristocratic governance of Mycenaean Greece, Aryan India, and Shang China, and the simultaneity with which these regimes arose, created a loose kinship that extended across the entire breadth of Eurasia. The indirect influence from Mesopotamia, along whose flanks the war chariot was first perfected, also established a real if remote interrelationship among all the great civilizations of the Old World.

Three Middle Eastern empires. The significance of the chariot conquerors for the old and firmly rooted civilizations of the Middle East itself was not so great. The invaders promptly created a number of extensive and loosely administered feudal empires. The members of each victorious war band scattered out across the countryside and set themselves up as landlords and masters of the pre-existing populations. Rather rapidly the conquerors adopted at least some of the ways of civilization. The Hyksos, for example, whom the Egyptians hated as foreigners, went very far toward accepting the manners and rituals of ancient Egyptian religion and civilization. In Mesopotamia the assimilation of the Kassite barbarians was even more complete.

Despite this acculturation, the ancient peoples of the Middle East did not willingly accept subjugation to barbarian masters. It was not long before local leaders, beginning sometimes on a very small scale, borrowed the techniques of chariot warfare in order to throw off what was still felt to be an alien yoke. In Egypt, for example, a local princeling of Thebes in the south led a rebellion against the Hyksos, and drove them entirely from the Nile valley by about 1570 B.C. In Mesopotamia it was the king of Assyria, far to the north, who led the "native reaction" by throwing off barbarian overlordship (about 1380 B.C.). The Hittites too recovered from the initial shock of exposure to the new type of warfare by acquiring chariots for themselves, and soon became a third great power, disputing distant Syrian borderlands with Egypt, the strongest single state of the age, and with Assyria.

The discovery of an Egyptian file of diplomatic records from the fourteenth century B.C. allows modern scholars a vivid glimpse of the international aristocratic life of these three great empires. Akkadian cuneiform was the language of diplomacy. Kings' daughters were given and accepted in marriage to seal alliances, thus incidentally diffusing styles of courtly life and civilization. Professional charioteers, gathered into garrisons, constituted the core of the fighting forces. They were paid both with booty and with gold or other valuables that accrued to the ruler by taxation. Egypt, whose coffers were replenished by gold mines in Nubia beyond the first Nile cataracts, had the largest supply of gold and therefore could afford to maintain the best army. Pharaoh recruited mercenaries from every borderland of the Nile.

Noble warriors, tamers of horses and masters of the battlefield, were unruly subjects. A warrior king might indeed persuade them to follow his banners toward almost any sort of reckless adventure; but no well-ordered bureaucracy could flourish in states built around the rude consensus of aristocrats of the chariot. Hence, the Egyptian, Hittite, and first Assyrian empires were loosely consolidated states, chronically liable to local rebellion. Whenever a local princeling or landed magnate took offense at an act of the central authority he could defy the distant king and his agents with ease, and could only be brought to book if a majority of his fellow aristocrats sided against him and with the king. The chariot nobility did this in the most practical of all possible ways, either by obeying the royal summons to come into the field against the rebel or by refusing to do so. The king's power was thus very effectively restricted by the consensus of his mighty men. The same rude consensus restrained individual nobles from random and irresponsible revolt or disobedience.

Chivalric courtesies among fighting men, and a ruthless oppression of mere peasants and servitors, characterized the cosmopolitanism of these Bronze Age empires. In the long run the extreme social distance between the ruling warriors and the rest of society constituted a profound weakness. But as long as ordinary men could not bring any armaments into the field of battle that could stand against the tactics of chariot warfare, aristocratic cosmopolitan chivalry prevailed.

The Iron Age. Soon after 1200 B.C., however, the widespread use of a new and much cheaper metal than the bronze upon which aristocratic charioteers had depended changed the military balance drastically. Once again numbers began to tell on the battlefield. The new metal was iron, worked into what metallurgists call "semi-steel," and produced from ores that were far more common and therefore cheaper than the copper and tin needed to make bronze.

Iron smelting required an entirely new set of skills. To make bronze, ingots of copper and tin had to be heated until the metals became liquid, whereupon the hot fluid was poured into moulds and allowed to cool. To produce tough, durable weapons and tools of iron however, the smiths of antiquity had to learn how to hammer impurities from a hot but far from molten mass (the bloom). After repeated heatings and hammerings, the finished article had to be plunged suddenly in cool water or oil. Slower cooling gave time for crystals to form in the iron, producing a rigid, brittle material that was of no use for making weapons or tools.

There is some reason to believe that the secrets of iron manufacture were first discovered in northeastern Asia Minor, well before 1400 B.C. But it was only after the disruption of the Hittite empire by invaders from the north that ironsmiths began to spread knowledge of the new technique widely through the Middle East and into barbarian Europe as well.

The first major consequence of this technical advance was another general wave of barbarian invasion which lapped round the great empires of the ancient Middle East and toppled them one after another between 1200 and 1000 B.C. The military success of the Iron Age barbarians rested upon the psychological cohesion of rudely egalitarian communities in which every man could be an effective soldier because there was no deep division between masters and their subjects like that which had long prevailed in the civilized regions of the world. Aristocratic charioteers, necessarily few in number, surrounded by sullen subjects and riven by traditional rivalries, were no match for such a massed assault.

The new invaders of the Middle East came from the same border regions whence their predecessors of the Bronze Age had come: the steppe and mountain regions to the north and east, and the desert fringes on the south. Many peoples later to become famous were among these migrant bands: Medes and Persians in Iran; Philistines, Hebrews, and Aramaeans in Syria and Palestine; Phrygians and Dorians in the Aegean area. Most of the invaders were organized tribally, and each conquering host established its own local political institutions, sometimes (as among the Hebrews) linked informally into a broader confederation that came into operation in time of unusual emergency.

Effects of iron. The use of iron had important economic as well as political and military effects. The new metal was sufficiently abundant to make it possible for farmers to make sickle blades, plow shares, and other agricultural tools of iron. This gave an increased efficiency to farming, especially in regions where clayey soils made breaking the earth comparatively difficult.

In some parts of the Middle East the free peasantries that sprang up in the lee of the Iron Age invasions were in a position to trade some of their crops for artisan products — including, first and foremost, iron tools and weapons, but also such things as wheel-spun, kiln-baked pottery and spoked cart wheels, whose manufacture required special skills beyond the reach of any ordinary farmer. Even when landlords and tax gatherers reasserted themselves in Middle Eastern society — a phenomenon not long delayed — this sort of local circulation of goods between town and country continued to exist. A corps of humble town artisans, possessing skills and producing goods needed by the peasantry, came permanently into existence. No matter what military or political disasters and disruptions subsequently visited the region, this local specialization survived or quickly re-established itself.

As the advantages of economic specialization thus penetrated down to the very bottom of the social scale in the Middle East, civilization became fully and firmly indelible for the first time. No important segment of the population any longer remained entirely outside the network of exchange and interdependence. This was, perhaps, the greatest achievement of the Iron Age. Social differen-

ANCIENT
MIDDLE EAST
c. 1200 B.C.

Scale of Miles

0   500

Mycenaean		Hittite
Egyptian		Mesopotamian
Invasions of iron-age era		
Steppe		Desert

Caspian Sea

Black Sea

Mediterranean Sea

Red Sea

Persian Gulf

IRAN

PERSIANS

Persepolis

MEDES

Susa

ASSYRIA

Nineveh

Assur

MESOPOTAMIA

Babylon

BABYLONIA

Mari

Euphrates R.

Tigris R.

ARAMAEANS

ARABIA

SYRIA

MITANNI

CHALYBES

Caucasus

Kuban R.

Aras R.

HITTITES

Hattusas

Halys R.

PHRYGIANS

LYDIANS

Troy

Aegean Sea

GREECE

Mycenae

DORIANS

ILLYRIANS

THRACE

Danube R.

CRETE

CYPRUS

Beirut

Jerusalem

HEBREWS

PHILISTINES

Gaza

EGYPT

Memphis

Thebes

Nile R.

LIBYA

51

tiation and specialization which had originally been the product of most unusual geographical and social circumstances became permanently part of the agricultural society of the Middle East. Civilized social complexity and specialization had finally, after some two thousand years, become normal.

By contrast, the political arrangements resulting from the Iron Age invasions were very unstable. Struggles among local tribes and tribal confederations soon led to the reappearance of substantial territorial states. The Assyrians were the most successful empire builders. They were able to draw fighting men from among a hardy and numerous local peasantry. Other assets were the imperial tradition and governmental techniques of ancient Mesopotamia whose cultural heirs and defenders the Assyrian kings consciously felt themselves to be. Egypt, on the other hand, having barely been able to repel three successive hosts of would-be invaders (1220 to 1165 B.C.), remained thenceforward immured within the boundaries of the Nile valley, intent only upon keeping intruders at arm's length and preserving the cultural inheritance of the most ancient Pharaohs.

Despite ruthless and almost incessant warfare, the Assyrian empire never became really secure. Subject peoples like the Israelites and Babylonians rebelled repeatedly. Drastic retaliation, such as the removal of all leading families from the kingdom of Israel to Babylonia (721 B.C.), did not prevent the renewal of disorder as soon as a plausible opportunity presented itself. Yet not rebellion from within but another major revolution in the technique of warfare was what finally overthrew the Assyrians. This military revolution occurred between 850 and 700 B.C., and its major locus was upon the steppes. In essence it was absurdly simple: during these centuries steppe nomads began habitually to ride on horseback. They thereby became cavalrymen, with all the advantages of mobility conferred by this simple method of exploiting the strength and speed of horseflesh.

The cavalry revolution. We are so accustomed to the idea of riding on horseback that it is likely to seem the most natural way to use a horse. Why then did it take men so long to become habitual riders? As a matter of fact, men had occasionally mounted on horses' backs long before 2000 B.C. But until saddle and stirrups had been invented there were serious difficulties. In the crisis of military action, a mounted bowman had to have both hands free for shooting. Any unexpected change in his horse's motion put the rider in danger of falling ignominiously from his mount in the very face of his foe. Charioteers solved this problem by entrusting driving to one man, shooting to another. Cavalrymen had to do both at once. This required a division of labor not between two men but between the lower torso, which controlled the horse, and the upper, which controlled the bow. Under these circumstances only long habituation on the part of both horse and rider could secure the sort of reliable co-ordination needed to make riding safe. The centaur of Greek legend and the cavalryman of history thus in fact each constituted a remarkable symbiosis between very different biological species, and we should not be surprised that it took a long time for riding to become important in war.

But when riding did become common, its military importance was similar to the earlier invention of chariotry. By mounting their horses' backs, bow in hand, whole tribes of nomads acquired a mobility and striking power superior to what any infantry army, however well organized and disciplined, could attain. Hit-and-run raids from the steppes, harassing caravans, and burning villages became safe and easy. Only an equally mobile, better disciplined, or more numerous cavalry force could hope to stop such raids. This the Assyrians could not supply. Their homeland was not good horse-raising country, lacking enough grass. Horses therefore remained comparatively rare, the pride of rulers and nobles but far beyond the reach of the Assyrian rank and file.

Soon after 700 B.C. peoples known to the Greeks as Cimmerians and Scythians exploited the new cavalry power of the steppe by launching extensive raids against the Middle East. Successful cavalry raids encouraged revolt in the rear. Rebellious Babylonians from the south, Medes from the Iranian highlands to the east, and Scyths from the northern steppe combined their forces for the final overthrow of the Assyrian state in 612 B.C. The victors divided the spoils: the Scythians returning homeward to the northern steppe, their horses laden with plunder, while the Medes and Babylonians

THE CAVALRY REVOLUTION
800 B.C.—500 B.C.

Steppe

Desert

Persian Empire about 500 B.C.

divided up the Assyrian empire with a newly ambitious Egypt.

The victors soon fell to quarreling among themselves. In particular Babylonia and Egypt started a struggle for control of Palestine and Syria, in the course of which the small kingdom of Judah, having opted for an alliance with Egypt, met the vengeance of King Nebuchadnezzar of Babylon (ruled 604-581 B.C.). Babylonian armies captured Jerusalem in 586 B.C., destroyed the city, and deported its inhabitants to Babylon. This episode in the political turbulence of the age, in itself not specially remarkable, turned out to be critically important for the evolution of Judaism.

The Persian empire, 558-330 B.C. Within less than half a century, a new conqueror, Cyrus the Persian (ruled 558-529 B.C.), emerged from the eastern highlands and united nearly all of the Middle East under his sovereignty. His successors, Cambyses (ruled 529-521 B.C.) and Darius the Great (ruled 521-484 B.C.), added Egypt and northwest India to the Persian empire. The Persians protected the critical steppe frontier by hiring border tribes of horse nomads to check raids from the more distant grasslands. When this arrangement threatened to break down, both Cyrus and Darius led the full muster of the Persian field army out into the steppe, in hope of over-awing if not of defeating the nomad cavalrymen. Cyrus lost his life in such frontier warfare, and the great Darius met with only indifferent success when in 513 B.C. he invaded Europe and penetrated the Scythian homeland by invading what is today part of southern Russia.

In the civilized heartland of the Middle East itself the Persians at first undertook to restore local freedoms and traditional religious and legal systems to all the peoples they annexed to their empire. Cyrus accordingly allowed the Jews to return to Jerusalem, and a few did so. He simultaneously restored or recognized the authority of the ancient priesthoods of Egypt and Babylon on condition that they support his regime. But Cambyses, the son of Cyrus, and Darius found it necessary to withdraw such special privileges when local pieties and priestly aspirations proved fertile seedbeds for revolt. As a result, Cyrus' successors abandoned his policy of liberation, and the old techniques of Assyrian administration were quickly revived and even improved on. Disheartened by repeated

failures to secure effective local independence, the resistance of
the Middle Eastern peoples to the political supremacy of an alien
but distant overlord tended to weaken. Nevertheless, the Persian
empire survived only a little more than two hundred years, and
was destroyed in the end (330 B.C.) not by native revolt but by
attack from a still semi-barbarous Macedonia, lying on the distant
western fringe of the empire.

Before we leave the Middle East and turn our attention to India, Greece, and China, we should consider, if only briefly, three
key developments of Middle Eastern civilization which these long
and tumultuous centuries brought into much sharper focus than
before. The first of these was the evolution of techniques of empire; the second was the invention of alphabetic writing; the third,
the rise of ethical monotheism.

The techniques of empire. Generally speaking, the institutional
basis for a cosmopolitan society had first been worked out in ancient Mesopotamia before the Bronze Age invasions of the eighteenth century B.C. A political order dominated by bureaucrats, i.e.
by administrators whose powers inhered in their offices rather than
in their persons, had been well developed under Hammurabi. The
same principle was revived by the Assyrians and adopted by the
Persians with no important changes. The network of appointive
officials remained quite thin on the ground. A royal governor responsible for a comparatively large territory could not oversee or
control what happened in all parts of the province entrusted to him.
In practice he had to deal with a wide variety of local administrative authorities — temple priesthoods, city magistrates, territorial
princelings, or some other type of local power-wielding elite.

Use and wont defined most such relationships quite closely: the
amount and nature of any tax payments or military service local
authorities rendered to the governor; legal jurisdictions of king,
governor, and local authority; religious and other ceremonial observances required to keep good relations with the gods; in short,
any matter that brought officialdom into contact with local life
tended to become encrusted by custom. Thereafter, either partner
found it difficult to alter the relationship. This meant both a limit

upon the ability of the king and his governors to mobilize the resources of the entire society for war or any other purpose, and a
modicum of stability for the imperial government itself, since traditional tributes and services could more or less be counted upon
without having to be renegotiated or forcibly collected each year.

Such principles of government were not new in the first millennium B.C., but the Assyrians, Babylonians, Medes, and Persians
applied them to larger territories and for longer periods of time
than had ever been done before. The main reasons for their success
lay in the persistent military superiority enjoyed by the rulers of
large territories against lesser rivals. Important improvements in
military administration lay behind this imperial preponderance.
The Assyrians, for example, developed something approximating a
professional officer corps, and formed regular units, arranged into
tens and hundreds. A successful officer might expect promotion
from lesser to greater commands at the will and discretion of his
superiors. Radical rationality — promotion according to merit and
demonstrated success in action — had far greater scope in such a
system than in the civil administration proper. Moreover, annual or
almost annual campaigns kept the imperial army in good fighting
trim, easily capable of overcoming any improvised local resistance
and of over-awing most threats from across distant borders.

In Sargon of Akkad's day (c. 2250 B.C.) the maintenance of a
standing army had presented enormous difficulties since goods
could not be concentrated at any one place on a sufficient scale to
maintain a sizable force. But distributing armed men across the
countryside, wherever food and other supplies for their maintenance could be found, risked dissolution of the central power.
Sargon had met this dilemma by sustaining his army on the basis of
perpetual plundering of conquered territories. Hammurabi had
stationed his soldiers on landed estates, and tried to enforce regular
service by keeping careful records of each man's military obligations. Under the Assyrians and Persians the ancient dilemma remained, but improvements in transport and communication had
blunted its horns. It was now possible for the imperial court to attract toward itself a sufficient flow of goods to allow a fairly substantial force — the royal bodyguard — to be maintained at all

times. The full imperial muster could not be kept under arms, but had to be scattered across the countryside between campaigns, and then summoned for service when needed. But as the size and professionalism of the royal bodyguard increased to the scale of the Persians' 10,000 "Immortals," the central imperial authority acquired an automatic military superiority over any ordinary rival. The mere existence of such a royal bodyguard compelled even distant provinces to obey the imperial summons to arms, since everyone knew beforehand that disobedience would bring swift and overwhelming retaliation. Only some quite unusual constellation of forces, such as that represented by the Scythian cavalry raids in the seventh century B.C. or by the well-organized Macedonian army that Alexander led into Persia in the fourth century B.C., could upset the military preponderance of such an imperial establishment.

Herein lay the secret of Assyrian and Persian political-military successes. And in the larger frame of world history the development of such a fundamental instrument of power as a standing army, supplemented by a semi-professional militia for campaigns, certainly marks a major landmark of political evolution. Both Roman and modern European armies based themselves on the administrative principles first worked out by the ancient Assyrians and Persians.

Behind the professional standing army lay economic and technological advances that allowed concentration of goods on a scale sufficient to maintain comparatively large numbers of men under arms year in and year out. Systematic road building helped. The Assyrian army regularly built highways suitable for use by wheeled vehicles. This facilitated supply service for the troops, and vastly accelerated their marches toward distant flanks of the empire. Roads also cheapened and speeded movements of men and goods in time of peace.

In addition, a series of legal and customary definitions of merchants' rights and privileges facilitated trade over comparatively long distances and between mutually alien and distrustful populations. Babylonian law in the second millennium B.C. had already taken account of the needs of merchants, and in their days of imperial greatness the Assyrians and Persians continued to accord important legal protection to traders. Merchants, for example, were exempt from military service. Important cities where merchants and artisans congregated enjoyed surprisingly extensive rights of self-government in return for payments of money tribute. Even more important, the roads were — in principle if not always in practice — policed by the imperial government. Hence any local entrepreneur who tried to live by plundering passing caravans could expect retaliation from imperial officials commanding local garrisons, or at the hands of detachments of the field army itself. Inter-regional traders and the imperial armies thus supported one another in a more or less conscious and deliberate alliance. The two constituted the principal institutional growth point of the ancient Middle East between 1700 and 500 B.C.

Alphabetic writing. The growing preponderance of imperial political and military institutions had wide and complex ramifications. For example, merchants, officials, and other participants in inter-regional affairs required a common language. They found it after about 1000 B.C. in Aramaic. They also needed a simpler mode of writing. From its inception in Sumerian temples, the art of writing had been confined to a learned few, who had to go to school for long years in order to master the numerous syllabic symbols employed to represent spoken language. But before 1300 B.C. radical simplification of the art made writing comparatively easy to learn. This in turn offered the possibility of literacy to much broader segments of society.

Experimentation with simpler modes of writing seems to have concentrated along the eastern Mediterranean coast, from Sinai to the Taurus mountains. This region lay between Egypt and Mesopotamia, where the completely different hieroglyphic and cuneiform styles of writing offered themselves as models, but where the elaborate school systems required to train boys to full mastery of those complicated scripts did not exist. Under these circumstances, half-educated scribes, with no vested interest in ancient correctness, dabbled freely with simplified scripts. Their efforts produced numerous "alphabets" based on the principle that if a single sign is used to symbolize each distinguishable consonantal sound, then about thirty signs suffice to record human speech. For the Semitic languages which were spoken in the region, vowels sounds do not really have to be written down, since it is easy to supply the correct vowels for insertion between written consonants. Even today Arabic and Hebrew continue to omit vowels.

The precise time at which alphabetic writing originated cannot be established with certainty. By about 1300 B.C. it had become common in Syria and Palestine. The discovery of numerous potsherds used to record very ordinary transactions suggests that alphabetic literacy soon percolated fairly widely through the urban society of the region. Scribes of Mesopotamia and Egypt of course repudiated the new styles of writing, and for sacred uses the older cuneiform and hieroglyphic scripts continued in use until near the Christian era. But for ordinary affairs, alphabets, slightly adjusted to fit different languages, spread in every direction from their Syrian place of origin and offered a new medium through which more popular literatures could attain a degree of permanence.

The importance of the invention of alphabetic writing may be compared to the importance of the introduction of iron which occurred at roughly the same time. Iron tools and weapons democratized warfare and society by making the distinction between rich and poor less sharp. It also, as explained above, made civilization really endemic for the first time by bringing rural peasants and urban artisans into a mutually beneficial exchange relationship. Similarly, alphabetic writing democratized learning by allowing ordinary men to master the rudiments of literacy. Through the alphabet the higher intellectual traditions of civilized society, which had formerly been the preserve of special colleges of priests, became accessible to laymen and commoners as never before. Even more important, alphabetic writing made it far easier for laymen and commoners to contribute to the literary heritage of civilized communities, thus widening and increasing the variety of that heritage very considerably. Without the existence of alphabetic writing, for example, it seems unlikely that the utterances of a simple shepherd like Amos or of any of the other Hebrew prophets would have been preserved to influence men's thoughts and conduct from that day to this.

The effect of iron and of alphabets, therefore, was to establish civilized styles of life far more securely than ever before, by making a fuller participation in the economic and intellectual pursuits of civilized life accessible to a larger proportion of the total population than before. Yet one must not exaggerate. The gap between town and country remained very great, and with only rare and evanescent exceptions, the peasantries of the Middle East entered only passively and as victims into political affairs. Equally, they shared very little in the high culture of the cities, clinging stubbornly to local folkways, pieties, and resentments against harsh tax collectors, dishonest merchants, and greedy landowners whose ways were not their ways and whose very existence seemed, to peasant eyes, an evidence of profound injustice and unrighteousness.

The rise of monotheism. Alienation of the peasantry was only part of the problem confronting the cultural leaders of the Middle East between 1700 and 500 B.C. Old styles of thought and feeling, frozen into fixed forms by the priestly piety and learning of ancient Mesopotamia and Egypt, were not adequate to account for facts newly apparent in a growingly cosmopolitan age. Thus, for example, when Egyptian armies and diplomats crisscrossed Asia, Syria, and Palestine, sometimes successfully and sometimes not, it became impossible to believe that the divine Pharaoh's will was everywhere and always supreme among men, as a god's will ought to be. And when political power and economic wealth moved up the Tigris-Euphrates valley, first to Babylon and then to Nineveh, leaving the once flourishing cities of Sumer to decay or utter desolation, religious hymns and rituals which treated Sumer as the center of the world and the gods' principal concern no longer commanded easy and automatic assent. Such discrepancies between present facts and the inherited pieties were even more acute for lesser peoples inhabiting the regions between Egypt and Mesopotamia, for they found themselves more and more at the mercy of foreign armies and alien masters, who knew little and cared less for the myths, rituals, and deities that local priesthoods honored.

Generally speaking these discrepancies provoked one of two opposing responses. Some men explained the gap between pious expectation and reality by saying that the gods were displeased by failure to perform traditional rites precisely and properly. What was needed therefore was a more faithful adherence to ancient precedents, whereupon the gods might be expected to set things right once more. Rigid conservatism and conscious archaism, seeking to discover and revive old forms that had been lost and forgotten, was the appropriate behavior for those who accepted this explanation.

Others argued that earlier ideas about the governance of the universe and man's place therein needed to be amended or even replaced by new revelation. Yet even radical religious reformers often claimed to be merely restoring forgotten truths that had been obscured with the passage of time. And, on the other side, conservative archaists could become effective revolutionaries, if their version of the truth and correct service of the gods conflicted in some important respect with current religious practice. As a matter of fact, the really important movements that made lasting changes in men's world outlook combined the appeal of a return to a better (sometimes fictitious) past with an appeal to the authority of new revelation.

The intellectual and religious evolution of ancient Oriental society tended toward ethical and transcendental monotheism. But only the Jews were able consistently to carry the trend to a logical, unambiguous conclusion. Other peoples, even when they exalted one deity above others and magnified the power of some particular god until it extended over the entire universe, nevertheless could not jettison traditional polytheisms altogether.

In Babylonia, for example, the priests claimed universal dominion for Marduk. Old hymns and rituals were "corrected" to eliminate everything which had become repugnant to the priests' sensibilities. Thus, for example, passages in Sumerian hymns referring to the divinity of kings were simply expunged. But after this sort of purification of ancient texts, further alteration stopped, and a fixed body of canonical literature, derived for the most part ultimately from ancient Sumer itself, endured throughout Assyrian times with almost no change at all. The antiquity and authority of such a religion was no doubt impressive, yet it offered little to comfort individual persons afloat in the great cosmopolitan empires of the age.

Egypt's religious evolution was more stormy. When the Egyptians, having driven the Hyksos invaders from their land, embarked on their imperial venture into Asia, they seem at first to have been exhilarated by the wonders and excitements of the great world they encountered outside the Nile valley. In the fourteenth century B.C. a clique of reformers and religious radicals arose, who argued that the innumerable gods of Egypt and other lands were all false. Only Aton, the glorious sun, everywhere the same and everywhere beneficent to men, together with Pharaoh who, like the sun, was also beneficent and — at least in principle — also universal, seemed to the reformers to bear the true marks of divinity. When the Pharaoh Amenhotep IV (1380–62 B.C.) came to the throne he espoused these ideas. Renaming himself Akhnaton, he set out to use all the traditional powers of his office to overthrow the old rites and pieties of Egypt. This roused a counter-fanaticism among priests and conservatives, so that after Akhnaton's death the Atonist faith was persecuted as energetically as it had briefly persecuted the older forms of Egyptian religion. Thereafter the Egyptians gave up all effort to reorganize their religious tradition to take account of the new realities that easier intercourse with distant peoples brought to the fore. Rigid conservatism in all things, treasuring each jot and tittle of ancient learning because of its immemorial antiquity, became the prevailing attitude of mind. The older the better, so that in art, for example, sculptors copied Old Kingdom works, and did so with such skill that modern scholars cannot always be sure which are from the third millennium B.C. and which were made two thousand years later!

The political history of the ancient Middle East accorded with this psychological turn. After 1100 B.C. Egyptian power shrank back to the narrow valley of the Nile, whose natural defenses gave pause even to the Assyrians and made the Persian empire over Egypt persistently insecure. Egypt, in short, both in thought and deed, turned her back upon the rest of the world, and by so doing was able to preserve her age-old political and cultural identity until Roman times.

Early Judaism. The really fruitful thinking of the first millennium B.C. occurred not in either of these ancient centers of Middle Eastern civilization, but in two marginal areas: Palestine and Iran.

Palestine lay between Egypt and Mesopotamia, aware of the cultural traditions of both but sharing fully in neither. In similar fashion, eastern Iran lay on the cultural watershed between Mesopotamia and the rising civilization of India. Hence, in both Palestine and eastern Iran when local conditions stimulated men to explain afresh the working of the universe, they found not one but two competing systems of thought at hand. Under these circumstances simple assimilation or modest adjustment of civilized myths to suit local needs and traditions was not really satisfactory. Instead, a freer and more radical religious revelation became possible. Serious and sensitive men in both places set out to wrestle with the perennial problems of human life without being able to rely upon ready-made, self-authenticated, and immemorially ancient bodies of doctrine.

In this struggle to define anew men's relations to the supernatural, the Judaic tradition, centered in Palestine and recorded in the Hebrew scriptures, proved critically important, for it became the seedbed not only of modern Judaism, but of Christianity and of Islam as well.

Biblical tradition traced the Hebrews back to Abraham, who left the Sumerian city of Ur (perhaps about 1900 B.C.) to take up a nomadic life along the desert fringes of Mesopotamia and Syria. Abraham reputedly migrated the length of the fertile crescent that caps the Arabian desert until he and his followers arrived in the land of Canaan, later called Palestine. There is nothing intrinsically improbable about this traditional account.

The next major episode in Hebrew history, the Egyptian bondage, is more puzzling, for Egyptian records and chronology are difficult to reconcile with the Biblical story. Perhaps some Hebrews migrated into Egypt with the Hyksos, and were later subjugated by native Pharaohs; but this is purely speculation. Moses, the leader of the Exodus, may have been in touch with Atonist religion; but of this there is no evidence, other than his Egyptian name. The Biblical account of how the oppressed Hebrews left Egypt and resumed a nomadic life in the Sinai peninsula may be based on historical happenings. The covenant with Yahweh and Moses' lawgiving at the foot of Mt. Sinai seem, indeed, exactly what a people

HEBREW PALESTINE

Boundary of the Kingdom of David about 1000 B.C.

Israel (to 722 B.C.)   Judah (to 586 B.C.)

Mediterranean Sea

Sidon
Damascus
Tyre
Dan
BASHAN
Acco (Acre)
Sea of Galilee
MT. CARMEL
Nazareth
Samaria
Joppa
Jericho
Rabbah
Jerusalem
Ascalon
Gaza
Hebron
Dead Sea
Beer-sheba
MOAB
Raamses
Pelusium
THE NEGEB
Route of the Exodus
WILDERNESS OF ZIN
EDOM
E G Y P T
ARABIAN DESERT
Route of the Exodus
SINAI
Ezion-geber
PENINSULA
Gulf of Suez
Gulf of Aqaba
MT. SINAI
Red Sea

Scale of Miles
0   25   50

who had forgotten customary ways of living in the desert would require.

Most modern scholars are of the opinion that the Hebrews who invaded Canaan and occupied the hill country of Palestine soon after 1200 B.C. came freshly from the desert, and that only a few of them (perhaps one or two of the twelve tribes) had been in Egypt or acknowledged the religion of Moses. Nevertheless, a codified law and a god of battles who had proved his power by protecting his people from the wrath of Egypt were clearly assets to tribesmen who lacked political or cultural cohesion. Hence, it is not surprising that the religion of Yahweh became the rallying point for military operations against the Canaanites. On the other hand, as soon as the Hebrews began to settle down to agriculture, they naturally resorted to the gods of the land, the baals, whose power to guard the crop and fertilize the fields had been attested by long experience.

The worship of Yahweh could not merge into the fertility cults of Canaan. Memories of the desert and of the good old days when Yahweh's followers smote the Canaanites and destroyed their idols kept old antagonisms alive. Hence, when the need for defense against Philistines and other neighbors compelled the Hebrews to unite under the leadership of a king, the mighty men who fought first for Saul and then for David naturally rallied under Yahweh's warlike banner. The rapid expansion of David's kingdom (c. 1000 B.C.), however, opened the way for courtly luxury and closer relations with neighboring states. This in turn provoked bands of prophets to denounce, in Yahweh's name, all the new-fangled corruptions resulting from the inroads of civilization and to renew attack on the baals. Elijah was the most famous of these early prophets.

Prophecy took a new turn when individuals, inspired by a burning sense of God's power and will, denounced social injustices in passionate poetry, which was then recorded and preserved. The earliest literary prophet was Amos (c. 750 B.C.). He was followed by a long line of others until the time of Daniel (c. 150 B.C.). During this period, the Hebrew prophets remoulded the religion of Yahweh. Instead of a tribal war god, as he had become during the time of the invasion of Canaan, the prophets universalized

Yahweh's power. At the same time, they declared that God was both just and merciful, punishing wrongdoers yet ready also to forgive those sinners who repented in time.

Yahweh had always been a jealous god, requiring the undivided loyalty of his people and repudiating all rivals. It was therefore comparatively easy for the Hebrew prophets to develop the worship of Yahweh into an uncompromising monotheism. No other people of the Middle East could become monotheists and also remain true to their traditional faith, for they had all inherited polytheistic pantheons. Yet monotheism seemed the only really satisfactory explanation of a world in which distant monarchs and unforeseeable events originating hundreds of miles away profoundly affected local affairs. In such an age, religious localism no longer accorded with common sense and everyday experience. Traditional rites rang hollow, but only the Hebrews were able to give full expression to the widely felt need for religious universalism. Their definition of ethical monotheism constituted therefore one of the greatest and most enduring achievements of ancient Oriental civilization.

The institutional form that the worship of Yahweh assumed was also of great importance for subsequent religious evolution. As long as the Hebrews enjoyed political independence, the cult of Yahweh centered upon temple rituals conducted in the capital. Hebrew political strength weakened after King Solomon's death (c. 932 B.C.) when the kingdom split into two parts: Israel in the north with its capital at Samaria, and the smaller kingdom of Judah in the south with Jerusalem for its capital. Then, as we have seen, when Israel was conquered by the Assyrians in 722 B.C., its leading families were deported, and a similar fate befell Judah at the hands of the Babylonian conqueror, Nebuchadnezzar, in 586 B.C.

The exiles from Israel lost their identity (the ten "Lost Tribes") and merged into the general population of the Middle East. In the northern kingdom, therefore, the religion of Yahweh survived only on a simple peasant level. Adherents of this faith were later known as Samaritans. Jews, who inherited the far richer tradition of Judah, despised the Samaritans as men who had allowed true religion to become contaminated with superstition.

A far different fate befell the exiles from Judah. Not long before the conquest of Jerusalem a strenuous effort had been made to purify the worship of Yahweh. In the course of this reform the sacred scriptures were organized into the books of the Old Testament, almost as known today. Hence, when the leading families of the land found themselves exiled in Babylon, far from Yahweh's temple, they at least possessed the sacred texts and could read and study them. Weekly meetings of the faithful at which the teacher (rabbi) explained the scriptures thus replaced temple services, and became the central cult act of what we may henceforth properly call the Jewish religion. Even when Cyrus the Persian permitted the exiles to return to Jerusalem (only a few actually did so), services in the restored temple did not displace local weekly meetings for reading the scriptures. Most Jews could not attend the temple, for many remained scattered in distant lands among alien peoples. They nevertheless retained the full conviction of their religion, reinforcing their hopes by pondering the promises of the holy texts.

Religion was thus separated from locality. Jews could in most outward things behave like the people around them, speak diverse languages, and dress and act in different ways while yet remaining faithful to Yahweh. Religion, in short, became disentangled from other aspects of human culture. Instead of remaining dependent upon sumptuous conduct of services in the temple at Jerusalem, or requiring its adherents to live in a single area and follow more or less uniform customs, the Jewish faith became capable of flourishing wherever a few of the faithful might gather to study and meditate upon the scriptures.

The exile also worked an important change in the emotional tone of the Jewish faith. Emphatic predictions of a future righting of wrongs had always been a prominent feature of prophecy. But the experience of the exile in Babylon gave the future an even greater importance. Jews were compelled to ask themselves: Why does God allow the wicked to prevail? Why does He punish his faithful servants so harshly? Two theories emerged from this questioning. Some, like Ezra and Nehemiah, emphasized the need for an even more scrupulous adherence to God's will as revealed in the scripture, since present sufferings were obviously due to God's displeasure with shortcomings of the past. But others, in particular the great poet Isaiah, developed the idea that God was purging his people, trying their patience and testing their fortitude, in order to reward the remnant on a great "Day of Judgment" when the world would come to an end and all its injustices be finally swept away. To men buoyed by such a vision, the greater the sufferings of the present, the nearer seemed the Day of Judgment, and the more important it was to adhere carefully to God's prescriptions as recorded in scripture.

Since different passages of the holy books seemed to contradict one another on many points, and since there were many personal problems which no scriptural instruction seemed to meet, the rabbis had to exert much ingenuity in applying scriptural laws to daily life. Doing so they gradually evolved a code of conduct that answered almost every problem a man could raise, and gave everyday life meaning and value. Such a belief and such a moral code was like a beacon amid the flaccid cultural landscape of the ancient Middle East, whose great cities were populated in large measure by men who had lost their ancestral religious roots without acquiring any real convictions or new moral codes that were adequate to urban conditions. In the major cities, therefore, where other faiths broke down, Judaism flourished, and amid all uncertainties and hardships of the age, strengthened its hold on its adherents' minds.

The canon of scripture was not closed until long after 500 B.C. and the rabbinical commentaries upon them did not attain definitive form until several centuries after the Christian era. Nevertheless, by 500 B.C. the peculiar emphasis and unique vitality of Judaism had become clearly apparent.

Zoroastrianism. Meanwhile, far to the east, on the other flank of the Mesopotamian world another religious movement attained major importance in the sixth century B.C. The reform of Persian religion associated with the name of Zoroaster differed from the development of Judaism in being the work of a single great prophet, who repudiated and denounced the traditions of his people and sought to make all things new. The Parsis of modern India trace their religion back to Zoroaster, but the connecting links are obscure. It is not certain, for example, what if any of the sacred writings preserved by the Parsis should be attributed to Zoroaster himself. The most ancient part of those writings, the *Gathas,* are written in a crabbed form of the Persian language, many passages of which remain almost unintelligible to modern scholars.

It is difficult therefore to know details of what Zoroaster taught. Dispute also rages as to where and when he preached. The only indisputable landmark is the fact that King Darius of Persia (d. 484 B.C.) used Zoroastrian phrases in some of his inscriptions. This suggests that he was himself an adherent of the faith. It seems likely that in Darius' time the Zoroastrian doctrine was still fresh-minted, the work of a man seeking to explain and order the changing world in which the Persians found themselves as they launched their imperial career.

Zoroaster's message was lofty and abstract. He preached the glory of a supreme, incorporeal, and universal deity, Ahura Mazda. Mazda was locked in cosmic strife with Ahriman, the principle of evil. Every good man's duty, clearly, was to enlist on the side of Light and obey Ahura Mazda's injunctions, as mediated through the prophet Zoroaster. These involved modest cultic observances (blood sacrifice was expressly forbidden) and moral conduct toward other men. As reward, Zoroaster promised prosperity in this world and immortality hereafter. He also seems to have believed that the end of the world would come in due season, at which time Ahura Mazda would signify his triumph by sending a purifying freshet of molten metal to engulf the wicked. The forces of Light, divine and angelic as well as human, would then rejoice together and forever in their victory.

Zoroastrianism never became the faith of any people who were not Persian; and even among the Persians probably only a limited circle of aristocrats and courtiers espoused the prophet's doctrine in its entirety. After the time of Xerxes (d. 465 B.C.), for example, inscriptions left by Persian monarchs referred to deities and concepts that were incompatible with Zoroaster's teachings (as reconstructed by modern scholars anyhow). Hence it does not appear that strict Zoroastrianism long prevailed even in the Persian court. Yet the political power the Persians won under Cyrus and stabilized under Darius meant that the religion of Zoroaster became at least vaguely known to all the various peoples whom the Persians ruled over. Thus certain features of later Judaism — for example, such concepts as angels and a fiery damnation of the wicked — may have been borrowed from or influenced by Zoroastrian doctrine.

Zoroastrianism had no such world-transforming career as Judaism and its two daughter religions, Christianity and Islam, were to have. Yet Zoroaster's teaching deserves to rank with the utterances of the great Hebrew prophets as a serious and fervent effort to give religious direction and order to the flux and uncertainty of the cosmopolitan world of the ancient Orient. Zoroastrian dualism explained evil more plausibly than any strictly monotheistic faith could do. Dualisms which traced their origins indirectly to Zoroaster have therefore cropped up repeatedly in the Judeo-Christian-Moslem traditions; but Zoroastrianism itself barely survives, and not without extensive later emendation, among the Parsi community of India.

The Definition of Indian Civilization

to 500 B.C.

THE warlike invaders who destroyed the Indus cities about 1500 B.C. inaugurated a dark and barbarous age in India. It is likely that several waves of Aryan invaders drifted southward across the mountains, requiring as much as three hundred years to complete the migration. During all this time, rival bands of warriors wandered with their cattle from place to place, stopping to reap a crop from time to time, before again moving on. The wanderers fought one another and subjugated the native populations they found on the ground. Bands gradually penetrated to new parts of India, spreading Aryan speech and breaking down the earlier isolation of forest peoples in the interior, whom the newcomers easily overpowered because of their warrior habits and better armament.

By slow degrees, however, the wanderers began to settle down to a more stable agricultural life. Herding ceased to have the pre-eminence it had enjoyed in the heroic days of roving and conquest. The more laborious tasks of working in the fields supplanted the leisured routine of warrior herdsmen. But even after the invaders had become fully agricultural, Aryan expansion into the further reaches of southern and eastern India continued. Their style of slash and burn cultivation required sporadic migration to new ground when old fields had become exhausted.

Remains from the "heroic age" of Indian history are few. Lacking well-built cities or permanent places of residence, the early Aryans left little for archaeologists to discover. To be sure, there are literary texts descended from this age. But these owe their preservation to the fact that priests later adapted them for use in religious rituals. In the process, the original texts underwent protean changes as they were passed orally from one generation to the next. As a result, it is often impossible to know what is genuinely ancient and what may have been added later. Nevertheless, both the *Rig Veda*, the holiest and probably the oldest collection of Sanskrit poems that has been preserved, and the *Mahabharata*, a vast epic poem, include passages that describe how noble archers engaged in duels with rival heroes by exchanging volleys of arrows while careening across the field of battle in horse-drawn chariots. Such passages attest that India, like Greece and the Middle East, experienced an aristocratic chariot age.

Then, about 900 B.C. chariot tactics ceased to prevail in India. Iron spread to the subcontinent, and just as it did in the Middle East, allowed poor men who could not afford to keep horses and chariots to protect themselves with armor. The coming of iron therefore overthrew aristocratic predominance. As iron altered the balance of forces on the battlefield, small states arose in which each fighting man had his share in making political decisions. Evidence for the existence of such armed, rudely egalitarian communities comes mainly from the north, especially amid the foothills of the Himalayas; but it is possible that similar political arrangements had once had a much wider distribution before the great centralized monarchies of the Ganges valley began to overpower merely local polities. It is indeed only when these old-fashioned clan republics succumbed to the forces of some Ganges king — a process in full career about 600 B.C. — that we hear of their existence.

Shift to the Ganges. Iron had another important effect on Indian life. Tools made of the new metal facilitated clearing the jungle, especially in the Ganges valley, where the heavy rains of the monsoon sustained lush vegetation and made the soil, once cleared of its trees, into unusually fertile farm land. Rice, which, as we saw, was probably first domesticated by garden cultivators of southeast

Asia, added greatly to the productivity of the Ganges valley. Wheat and barley, the two staples of Middle Eastern agriculture, yielded far less food per acre of cropland than did rice. Denser populations could therefore be sustained in lands suited to rice culture. Permanent occupation of particular fields went along with rice cultivation, for the diking, digging, and terracing needed to bring irrigation water to the paddy fields was too laborious to make moving to a new location seem in the least attractive. Thus fully sedentary agriculture, with permanent village and town centers and a population that could be taxed easily because it could not afford to flee into jungle fastnesses, all arose in the Ganges region as a result of the establishment of rice cultivation.

By about 800 B.C., therefore, the Ganges valley had achieved the prerequisites for a fresh growth toward civilized complexity. This time the Indus valley was left far behind. Old-fashioned shifting cultivation still prevailed in the Indus region. No firm, large-scale political structure could be raised upon the backs of a population that could melt off into the forest whenever a royal agent came to demand taxes or some other sort of onerous service. To the east, on the contrary, the rice paddies both tied their cultivators down and gave them such a productive type of agriculture that they could afford to part with considerable quantities of their crop and still survive.

Several great monarchies served by professional administrators and by professional soldiers therefore began to develop in the Ganges valley at a time when the Indus (and presumably also south India about which we know nothing) were still divided among innumerable small kindreds, united, if at all, only by the unstable suzerainty of some high king, who lacked real administrative authority beyond his own immediate circle of personal followers. In the Ganges region, however, the development of effectively centralized monarchies implied the rise of courtly centers, where high artisan skills could and did develop rapidly. Inter-regional trade also became important, and even lapped over from its center in the Ganges region to add a new and potentially very significant element to Indus valley life. Archaeological evidence shows that seaborne trade with Mesopotamia was resumed by about 800 B.C.

In all these respects, the development of India differed from that of the Middle East only in being somewhat retarded and somewhat less well recorded. Yet the new style of life which began to emerge in India after 800 B.C. was quite different from that prevailing in the cosmopolitan world of the Assyrian and Persian empires north and west of the Hindu Kush. The unique character of the emergent Indian civilization centered on the institution of caste and the ascetic transcendental emphases of Indian religion. Each of these requires a little explanation.

Caste. A modern caste is a group of persons who will eat with one another and intermarry, while excluding others from these two intimacies. In addition, members of any particular caste must bear some distinguishing mark, so that everyone will know who belongs and who does not belong to it. Definite rules for how to behave in the presence of members of other castes also become necessary in any plural society where such contacts are frequent. When an entire society comes to be organized on these principles, any group of strangers or intruders automatically becomes another caste, for the exclusive habits of the rest of the population inevitably thrust the newcomers in upon themselves when it comes to eating and marrying. A large caste may easily break into smaller groupings as a result of some dispute, or through mere geographical separation over a period of time. New castes can form around new occupations. Wanderers and displaced individuals who find a niche in society are automatically compelled to eat together and marry one another by the caste-bound habits of their neighbors.

How or when Indian society came to be organized along these lines remains unclear. Perhaps the Indus civilization itself was built upon something like the caste principle. Or perhaps the antipathy between Aryan invaders and the dark-skinned people whom they attacked lay at the root of the caste system of later India. But whatever the origins of caste, three features of Indian thought and feeling were mobilized to sustain the caste principle in later times. One of these was the idea of ceremonial purity. Fear of contaminating oneself by contact with a member of a lower, "unclean" caste gave Brahmans and others near the top of the pyramid strong reasons for limiting their association with low-caste persons. From the other end of the scale, too, the poor and humble had strong reasons for clinging to caste. All but the most miserable and marginal could look down upon somebody, a not unimportant psychological feature of the system. In addition, the humbler castes were often groups that had only recently emerged from primitive forest life. They naturally sought to maintain their peculiar customs and habits, even in the context of urban or mixed village life, where men of different backgrounds and different castes lived side by side.

Other civilized societies usually persuaded or compelled newcomers to surrender their peculiar ways, and assimilated them in the course of a few generations to the civilized population as a whole. In India, on the contrary, such groups were able to retain their identity and autonomy indefinitely by preserving their own peculiar customs within the caste framework, generation after generation.

The third factor sustaining the caste principle was the doctrine of reincarnation and "varna." The doctrine of varna declared that all men were divinely divided into four castes; the Brahmans who prayed, the Kshatriyas who fought, the Vaisyas who worked, and the Sudras who performed unclean tasks. Official doctrine classified the first three castes as Aryan, the last as non-Aryan, and insisted upon hierarchical rank from Brahmans at the top to Sudras at the bottom. Reality never corresponded even remotely to this theory. There were hundreds if not thousands of castes in India, rather than the four recognized in Brahmanical teaching. But apparent injustices and anomalies disappeared when the doctrine of reincarnation was combined with the doctrine of varna. The idea of reincarnation, indeed, gave logical explanation and justification to the system by explaining caste as a divinely established institution, hereditary from father to son, and designed to reward and punish souls for their actions in former lives. This undoubtedly helped to stabilize the confused reality. A man of unblemished life, born into the lowest caste, could hope for rebirth higher up the ladder. Conversely, a man of high caste who failed to conform to proper standards could expect rebirth in a lower caste. He even risked reincarnation as a worm or beetle, if his misbehavior deserved such a punishment.

Clearly, the caste system as observed today did not exist in ancient India. Yet modern castes are the outgrowth of patterns of social organization that are as old as the oldest records. Early Buddhist stories, for instance, reveal many episodes turning upon caste distinctions, and passages in the *Rig Veda* and other ancient writings imply caste-like practices and attitudes. By 500 B.C. we can at least be sure that the seeds from which the modern caste organization of society grew had already sprouted luxuriantly on Indian soil.

Caste lessened the significance of political, territorial administration. Everyone identified himself first and foremost with his caste. But a caste ordinarily lacked both definite internal administration and discrete territorial boundaries. Instead, members of a particular caste mingled with men of other castes, observing the necessary precautions to prevent contamination of one by the other. No king or ruler could command the undivided loyalty of people who felt themselves to belong to a caste rather than to a state. Indeed, to all ordinary caste members, rulers, officials, soldiers, and tax collectors were likely to seem mere troublesome outsiders, to be neglected whenever possible and obeyed only as far as necessary. The fragile character of most Indian empires resulted in large part from this fact. A striking absence of information about war and government is characteristic of all early Indian history; and this, too, presumably reflects Indian peoples' pervasive emotional disengagement from the state and from politics.

Caste also made it easy for Indian civilization to bring new groups within the pale. No very radical adjustment of previous customs and habits was required of the newcomers, who simply became one more among the already innumerable castes of the land. Correspondingly, very primitive and ancient patterns of thought and behavior remained latent within the fabric of Indian society, perpetuated by peoples who in adjusting themselves to the necessity of living amid strangers had nevertheless, through the vehicle of caste, retained their primitive ancestors' magical rites, charms, and habits of thought.

Transcendental religion. Disregard for war and politics and tolerant hospitality for widely divergent customs were also emphasized by India's unique religious evolution. Until quite recently in India, religious doctrine was transmitted exclusively by word of mouth from teacher to pupil. Any earnest inquirer after truth might sit at the feet of more than one teacher. Hence, all sorts of blending and interlacing of different doctrines easily occurred. Moreover, there are no dates to help sort out the development of religious thought. The bulky religious literature that has survived is couched in time-lessness, and contains remarkably few references to events or per-sonages that can be identified with a particular time and place. Any effort to disentangle strands of thought must therefore be logical rather than historical. Nevertheless, the logical sequence may match the historical stages of development. We simply cannot be sure.

Surviving records are, of course, all written in Sanskrit, the lan-guage of the Aryan invaders. They brought with them a pantheon of deities, among whom the principal war leader and strongest per-sonality was Indra, destroyer of cities and god of thunder and storm. Other gods embodied other natural elements and forces — sky, air, earth, water, and the like. A priesthood accompanied the invaders also. Its function was to invoke the gods, offer sacrifice, and by other appropriate rituals to ward off divine displeasure. Prosperity in peace and in war, long life, and good health were the goals of these pious observances.

Nothing in this religion seems notably different from the aims and attitudes of other barbarian tribes of Indo-European speech: Greeks, Latins, Celts, Germans, Iranians, Slavs, and the rest. All of them revered aspects of the world of nature which had been en-dowed with more or less definite personalities. Details of the pantheon varied from case to case, but it seems clear that the fun-damental world-view expressed by these early Indo-European reli-gions had been built up by priestly specialists who were at least vaguely aware of how the Mesopotamians conceived the divine rulers of the universe as a quarrelsome company of capricious per-sonalities. The pervasive though inexact resemblances between the Sumerian pantheon and those of the different Indo-European peo-ples cannot be accounted for in any other way.

The Vedas and Brahmanas. Our knowledge of Aryan religion derives from the Vedas. The Vedas, used as handbooks of religious ritual, comprise songs that were recited aloud during sacrifices, to-gether with other passages instructing the priests what to do during the ceremony. In course of time, the language of the Vedas became more or less unintelligible, even to priests. A great effort was there-upon made to preserve details of accent and pronunciation, by in-sisting on exact memorization of texts from master to pupil across the generations. Every jot and tittle of the inherited verses was felt to matter, since a misplaced line or mispronounced word could nullify a whole sacrifice and might even provoke divine displeas-ure.

Preoccupation with correctness of detail speedily shifted empha-sis from the gods of the Aryan pantheon to the act of worship and invocation itself. Aryan priests may also have learned about magi-cal powers claimed by priests of the Indus civilization. At any rate, some Brahmans began to argue that by performing rituals cor-rectly they could actually compel the gods to grant what was asked of them. Indeed, proper sacrifice and invocation created the world of gods and men anew, and stabilized afresh the critical rela-tion between natural and supernatural reality. In such a view, the importance and personalities of the separate gods shrank to trivial-ity, while the power and skill of the priesthood was greatly magni-fied. These extravagant priestly claims were freely put forward in texts called Brahmanas. These were cast in the form of commentar-ies on the Vedas, purportedly explaining what the older texts really meant, but often changing meanings in the process.

The Upanishads and mysticism. Priestly claims to sovereign authority over gods and men were never widely accepted in an-cient India. Chiefs and warriors might be a bit wary of the power of priestly magic, but they were not eager to cede to the priests the primacy claimed by the Brahmanas. Humbler ranks of society also bridled at priestly presumption. This is proved by the fact that a rival type of piety took hold in India and soon came to constitute the most distinctive element in the whole religious tradition of the land. Another body of oral literature, the Upanishads, constitutes our evidence of this religious development. The Upanishads are not systematic treatises nor do they agree in all details. Yet they do express a general consensus on important points.

First of all, the Upanishads conceive the end of religious life in a radically new way. Instead of seeking riches, health, and long life, a wise and holy man strives merely to escape the endless round of rebirth. Success allows his soul to dissolve into the All from whence it had come, triumphantly transcending the suffering, pain, and imperfection of existence.

In the second place, holiness and release from the cycle of rebirths were attained not by obedience to priests nor by observance of ceremonies. The truly holy man had no need of intermediaries and, for that matter, no need of gods. Instead, by a process of self-discipline, meditation, asceticism, and withdrawal from the ordinary concerns of daily life, the successful religious athlete might attain a mystic vision of Truth — a vision which left the seer purged and happy. The nature and content of the mystic vision could never be expressed in words. It revealed Truth by achieving an identity between the individual soul and the Soul of the universe. Such an experience, surpassing human understanding and ordinary discourse, constituted a foretaste of the ultimate bliss of self-annihilation in the All, which was the final goal of wise and holy life.

The themes and attitudes expressed in the Upanishads are so different from the worldly and practical tone of the Vedas and Brahmanas that anyone who is not himself a mystic is likely to ask how the change can be accounted for. Perhaps ascetic practices had been known to the priests and holy men of India before the Aryan invasion. If so, the Upanishads' recipe for the religious life may represent an intrusion into Sanskrit literature of attitudes and ascetic disciplines which were of pre-Aryan origin.

Moreover, it seems likely that the ascetic, other-worldly emphasis of the Upanishads began to attract attention among the speakers of Aryan tongues only when the small, more or less egalitarian communities of free men, which had arisen in northern India during the Iron Age, began to crumble before the greater power of centralized bureaucratic kingdoms of the Ganges valley. Perhaps, therefore, men who found their familiar way of life no longer possible were attracted to asceticism precisely because strangers and agents of distant rulers had destroyed the social and political order their fathers had known. On such a hypothesis, men who were de-

scended from warriors and rulers found a substitute for their own
lost liberties in the private and personal pursuit of holiness, conducted, for the most part, in the freedom of forest retreats, far
from the ordinary haunts of men. It was in such places that the
Upanishads were created, when a master of ascetic discipline attempted to pass on to others the secret of his experience.

Still a third explanation is physiological. Skeptics of course have
no difficulty in recognizing that prolonged fasting, sleeplessness,
and deliberate repression of breathing can produce unusual bodily
sensations. When men are prepared by an eager expectation to in-
terpret visions seen under such circumstances as a confrontation
with some divine, ultimate reality, the experience acquires overwhelming emotional and personal importance.

Yet to anyone who has experienced a mystic vision such explana-
tions are simply irrelevant. Initiates who share a memory and who
live in hope of the renewal of their spiritual transport know the self-
validating force of the experience. Justification is unnecessary, explanation impossible, doubt inconceivable — or so the words and
behavior of thousands upon thousands of mystics strongly suggest.

The godless asceticism recommended by the Upanishads and the
meticulous performance of rituals demanded by the Brahmanas
certainly seem opposed. Yet the Brahman priests of ancient India
found an easy way to reconcile these contradictory ideals. They
argued that the way of the Upanishads was appropriate toward the
end of a man's life, after he had spent his youth honoring priests,
observing ceremonial prescriptions, and raising a family. In this
fashion the doctrines of the Upanishads were accepted into Brahmanical religion, and the priests, whose pretensions to authority
were directly assailed by Upanishadic doctrine, serenely survived
as purveyors of religious ritual for ordinary men.

Jainism and Buddhism. About 500 B.C., however, the emergence
of Buddhism and of Jainism presented the Brahmans with a more
serious challenge. These two religions had historical founders, both
of whom were probably alive in the year 500 B.C. although exact
dates are not known in either case. Jainism was established, or re-
formulated, by Mahavira; Buddhism arose around the charismatic
figure of Prince Gautama. The two religions had much in com-

mon. Both in a sense popularized the ideas that had been abstractly expressed in the Upanishads, for both Mahavira and Gautama, the Buddha, made personal annihilation and escape from the cycle of rebirth the supreme goal of religious striving. The two religions differed in some important details of doctrine, and Jainism never attained Buddhism's popularity. It remained a faith for an elite, demanding strenuous asceticism, even to the point of starvation unto death, of its initiates.

Buddhism, on the contrary, was built around a moderate regimen. In his youth, Gautama tried asceticism, but he then decided that severe maltreatment of the body was not the way to escape from the suffering of existence. Instead he recommended a quiet middle way between ordinary self-indulgence and the severities of the practicing ascetic. He himself, and his numerous followers, divided their time between contemplation, religious discussion, and begging. During the rainy season, Gautama was fond of remaining in the same spot with a group of like-minded men around him. In the dry season he wandered from place to place, living on alms. Throughout he sought to cultivate an inner holiness by pursuing the "noble eightfold path," that is, the cultivation of right views, right aspirations, right speech, right conduct, right livelihood, right effort, right mindedness, and most important of all, right rapture. Gautama, the Buddha, never made explicit what the word translated as "right" in these phrases meant. He taught by example not abstractly. His followers attempted to model their own lives on his, and observed the rules he laid down when some particular problem was brought to him for advice.

During Gautama's lifetime, therefore, a body of followers arose who found the way of life he prescribed to be so satisfying that even after his death (c. 486 B.C.) they continued to live in communities that followed his rules, and honored the holy Buddha that Prince Gautama had embodied so perfectly. Writers of English ordinarily call such communities "monasteries." The later Christian monasteries did in fact resemble them quite closely, since many of the Buddhist communities came in time to possess buildings and income-producing property donated by pious laymen who felt the need for holy men's aid along the path of salvation.

In this fashion, what had begun as a temporary association between master and followers attained a corporate durability which has lasted uninterruptedly until our own time. Buddha's teachings, to be sure, underwent great elaboration and radical change in the course of time, but the institutional continuity of communities of monks remains unbroken. The lives, feelings, and acts of hundreds of millions of men have been affected by these communities and by the religious ideals they preached and embodied. Despite the fact that the land of its birth later repudiated Buddhist forms of piety, India's main impact upon peoples outside her borders came in the guise of missionaries who spread the doctrine and the practices of the Buddhist religion into China, Japan, Korea, and almost all the lands of southeast Asia.

In India itself, during the first centuries of its existence, Buddhism popularized, moderated, and defined the Upanishadic style of religiosity. Thereby, Buddhism helped to imprint a distinctive other-worldly, mystical, and ascetic tradition upon Indian civilization as a whole, and defined directions of growth from which later Indian thinkers and holy men never departed. Yet despite its early successes, Buddhism did not in the end prevail. Instead, a revived and transformed Brahmanical religion — Hinduism — proved capable of winning and holding the allegiance of most Indians. How this happened must be reserved for later consideration, but it is worth pointing out the practical weakness in Buddhism that made this great reversal possible. In its early forms, Buddhism had no rituals for the ordinary emergencies of human life — birth, death, marriage, coming of age, and the like. The texture of ordinary life therefore continued to call for the services of the Brahmans, and the need for Brahmans kept alive Vedic learning and priestly pretensions in all their complexities. The Buddhist way of life offered a complete guide only to the unusual individual who renounced normal family life and devoted himself entirely to the pursuit of holiness. Others could not afford to do without traditional rites and priestly assistance. For the ordinary crises of life early Buddhism had nothing to offer. India therefore never became a thoroughly Buddhist land, and Indian civilization never entirely fitted itself to a Buddhist mould.

Nevertheless, it seems fair to say that by about 500 B.C., when caste and the characteristic emphases of Indian religion had both come into focus, Indian civilization as a whole had defined its enduring character and special bent. Great elaboration and cumulatively great transformations of course lay ahead, yet a cultural identity recognizably the same links contemporary India with the ancient India of Buddha's time.

Simultaneously, among the Greeks another definite and new style of civilization had emerged. We must next consider how this happened.

V

The Definition of Greek Civilization

to 500 B.C.

HILE India worked its way toward the definition of a new and distinctive civilization on one flank of the ancient Middle East, on its other flank another new civilization was also emerging: the Greek. The principal stages of early Greek history closely resemble what we know or can surmise about Indian development. But the end product differed fundamentally. The Greeks put political organization into territorial states above all other bases of human association, and attempted to explain the world and man not in terms of mystic illumination but through laws of nature. Thus despite a similar start, when fierce "tamers of horses" — like those of whom Homer later sang — overran priest-led agricultural societies, the Indian and Greek styles of civilization diverged strikingly by 500 B.C.

Mycenaean Vikings. One great difference existed from the start. The Aryans of India remained landsmen, whereas the earliest Greek invaders of the Aegean region took readily to the sea, infiltrating Knossos in Minoan Crete and establishing themselves among the Aegean islands as well as on the Greek mainland. The first Greek-speaking rulers of Knossos made very little change in the archaeological remains of Minoan civilization, although they did develop a new script (Linear B), which recorded an archaic form of the Greek language. About 1400 B.C., however, Knossos was destroyed, perhaps by some piratical raid launched from the new-sprung capital at Mycenae on the Greek mainland. For the next two hundred years a series of sea raids — interspersed perhaps with more peaceable trade — carried Mycenaean ships to almost all the coasts of the Mediterranean. Three separate attacks were launched against Egypt by a coalition of "sea peoples" in which Greeks probably took a minor part. In the year 1190 B.C., however, the Egyptians successfully repelled the last of these ventures, and a remnant of the invading host settled in Palestine to become the Philistines of Biblical history. A similar raid (traditionally dated 1184 B.C.) against Troy at the mouth of the Dardanelles became the focus around which Homer's tales of heroism clustered.

The city-state. Soon after 1200 B.C. these far-flung enterprises came to an end. A new wave of invaders, the Dorians, came down from the north and overran the centers of Mycenaean power. With the Dorians or very soon after came iron, with all the usual political consequences. Aristocratic charioteers, who had controlled war and politics in the days of Mycenae's greatness, were overthrown by local tribes of iron-wielding warriors. Such groups were always ready to migrate to any new spot where better crop land or pasture could be found. The Dorian invasions therefore proceeded piecemeal, and involved many secondary displacements of peoples. In particular, refugees from the Greek mainland took ship and established a series of new settlements across the Aegean on the coast of Asia Minor. These regions were subsequently known as Ionia and, further north, Aeolia. For protection against the older inhabitants the Greek settlements clustered on defensible peninsulas and other suitable places on the coast. Since the refugees (like the Hebrews of the Exodus) had no pre-existing pattern of leadership or code of custom to which all unthinkingly subscribed, they had to invent a visible set of laws and system of government to assure effective co-operation in the new settlements. In so doing, they created the earliest Greek city-states.

Moses had faced a similar problem a century or two before when he led the children of Israel from Egypt into the desert. The legislation with which he organized the community in its new environment became the kernel of later Judaism. The self-governing city-states created by Greeks on the coast of Asia Minor had almost as great an importance in world history. For by inventing the city-state or *polis* (hence our word "politics"), the Greeks of Ionia established the prototype from which the whole Western world derived its penchant for political organization into territorially defined sovereign units, i.e. into states. The supremacy of territoriality over all other forms of human association is neither natural nor inevitable, as the Indian caste principle may remind us. Hence, if Westerners owe their religions to Hebrew refugees from Pharaoh, we also owe our politics to Greek refugees from the Dorians, who had to reorganize and rationalize their traditional society in order to survive in a new and hostile environment just about two centuries after Moses had led his people into the desert and out of Egypt.

Development on the mainland toward supremacy of the polis was slower. Semi-migratory kindreds had first to settle permanently on some particular piece of land, and then had to combine with neighboring kindreds into a single territorial unit to constitute a polis. The line of evolution is fairly clear. Violence diminished, population grew, land became scant and fixed farming became the rule. As the population settled down, local chieftains found it convenient to settle disputes by sitting in council at some fixed center under the presidency of a high king. When the full council could not be in session it often seemed desirable to appoint individuals to look after matters of common concern, and to check the king in any attempt he might make to extend his authority. In this fashion magistrates arose, who were appointed for a limited term and entrusted with a delegated and, in course of time, legally defined authority. In some of the emergent city-states the kingship itself became a magistracy; in other cases kingship remained hereditary in a particular family.

Colonization and trade. As population continued to grow, emigration overseas offered a solution for some of those who lacked enough land to live on at home. In ancient times, emigration was not usually an individual or family affair, but was organized by groups of several hundred persons at a time. Numbers were needed for protection. Numbers also permitted new settlements to retain a fully Greek character amid barbarian populations even as far away as Sicily and southern Italy, or the northern Aegean and Black Sea coasts. Greek colonies were fully self-governing from the start, although religious ties with the mother city were always maintained.

Colonization helped trade, for the new cities often acted as middlemen between up-country barbarians and the older Greek cities. This sort of trade got an enormous fillip when a few Greek cities began to specialize in producing wine and olive oil. These were comparatively precious products and required special climate and skills. Oil and wine could, however, be quite easily stored and shipped in jars. Barbarians within reach of Greek navigation quickly learned to value these products, and could offer grain, timber, or other raw materials in exchange. It soon became obvious that vintners and olive-growers had a great advantage in such trade. Their products were comparatively rare and precious. Barbarian nobles would pay a lot to get what they could not produce at home. They were therefore ready to supply far greater quantities of grains and other raw materials to the Greek cities where this sort of commercial agriculture took root than these same cities could possibly produce on the land that lay within their own boundaries.

This pattern of economic exchange had fundamental importance for all of classical history. First of all, it made possible the creation of comparatively large cities in olive- and vine-growing coastlands, for such cities could feed themselves on imported grain. Secondly, it brought farmers into the commercial life of the towns as active and absolutely vital participants. In the older Middle Eastern societies, agricultural surpluses came onto the urban markets largely in the form of economically unrequited rents and taxes. A passive and withdrawn peasantry, regarding rulers and townspeople as their oppressors and natural enemies, was an inescapable concomitant of such a relationship. Not so in Greece. The farmer with his wine and oil regarded himself and was regarded by others as the ideal type of citizen, entering the market freely as a buyer and seller, and expecting also to play his part in public affairs when the dry season

ANCIENT GREEK WORLD

• Greek

○ Phoenician

Atlantic
Ocean

GAUL

E U R O P E

SPAIN
Tagus R.
Homeroscopium
Maenaca
Gades
Ebro R.

Rhine R.
Rhône R.
Massilia
Emporium
Po R.
Alalia
CORSICA
SARDINIA
Rome
Cumae
ITALY
MAGNA
GRAECIA
Tarentum
Croton
SICILY
Syracuse
Carthage
Leptis

Mediterranean Sea

Danube R.

Tyras
Olbia
Chersonesus
Byzantium
Apollonia

Black Sea
Sinope
Phasis
Trapezus

PHRYGIA
LYDIA
GREECE
Athens
Knossos
CRETE
Cretan Sea
Cyrene
Ionian Sea
Aegean Sea

LIBYA

AFRICA

CILICIA
PHOENICIA
CYPRUS
Tyre
Al Mina

ASSYRIA
Tigris R.
Euphrates R.
Babylon

ARABIA

Red Sea
EGYPT
Naucratis
Memphis
Nile R.

Scale of Miles
0   500

MACEDONIA
THRACE
Byzantium
AEOLIA
Phocaea
IONIA
Ephesus
Miletus
RHODES
Aegean Sea
Chalcis
Eretria
Athens
Delphi
Corinth
Mycenae
Sparta

Miles
0   100

89

interrupted the tasks of cultivation and permitted him the needful leisure.

Effects of the phalanx. About 650 B.C. a momentous change in military tactics gave a secure basis to the common farmer's participation in political life. This was the invention of the phalanx — a densely massed infantry formation eight ranks deep whose members were trained to run and charge in unison. A skillful charge delivered by several thousand armored men moving as a single mass proved capable of sweeping cavalry or any other kind of opposing force off the field. As this became obvious, every city had to organize and train as big a phalanx as possible from among the citizenry. Anything that interfered with strengthening the phalanx endangered the city. If danger was acute, as happened for example in Sparta in the seventh century B.C., when a revolt of enslaved subjects threatened the Dorian rulers with disaster, the response could be drastic. The Spartans actually made themselves into a perpetual garrison in their own land, requiring that each citizen between the ages of twenty and thirty live in a barracks and eat in a military mess. No other city reacted so extremely as Sparta did, but no other Greek city was able to develop so professional a fighting force either. Others contented themselves with remodeling older aristocratic institutions in such a way as to give decisive weight to an assembly of all who were able to equip themselves for the phalanx with shield, helmet, sword, and spear.

The introduction of the phalanx had still another pervasive and profound influence. Every young man who could possibly afford to buy the necessary armor and weapons spent long hours with his fellow youths practicing the rhythms and skills needed to fight effectively in the phalanx. Speed, strength, and courage were only part of what was required. In addition every man had to learn to keep time to the beat set up by the war chant, so that the wall of shields would not break when the phalanx charged across the field of battle. Every man's safety depended upon his neighbor keeping his place in the ranks, for each man's shield helped to cover the right side of the man next to him. Conspicuous personal feats of arms were as much out of place in such a situation as cowardice or inability to keep pace with the rhythm of the charge, for anything that broke the line threatened immediate disaster.

Long hours spent in rhythmic exercises with a group of other men has an exhilarating, almost hypnotic, effect. In all probability such exertions rouse instinctive resonances inherited by all men from extremely remote ancestors, who by dancing around their camp fires presumably expressed and at the same time created the socio-psychological solidarity required for effective co-operation in the hunt. The aim and climax of the phalanx drill was battle; and this, too, roused fiercely primitive impulses deriving directly from the ethos of the human and proto-human hunting pack.

Perhaps because of these resonances with the most elemental level of human sociality, every Greek citizen and soldier who endured the long hours of training needed for skillful service in the phalanx and had then undergone the fatigues and dangers of a campaign and known the fierce joys and sudden exertions of battle emerged from such adventures marked for life by a deep sense of solidarity with all those who had shared these experiences with him. This intense sentiment became the basis for a fiercely collective pride in the greatness and glory of the city to whom all equally belonged, and in whose service all might find personal fulfillment and an unusually vivid sense of personal freedom by submitting to a common rhythm and demanding regimen.

It is not therefore surprising that with the introduction of the phalanx the Greeks altered their ideal of personal behavior. In the earlier aristocratic age, individual self-assertion and conspicuous consumption had been generally admired. Feats of individual prowess, such as those celebrated by Homer, and personal display of luxury went hand in hand. The phalanx, however, made close conformity to a norm absolutely mandatory in military matters. This principle was soon carried over into civil life as well, so that it became ill-mannered, un-Greek, improper to live luxuriously or, indeed, to differ in any conspicuous way from one's fellows. Competitive self-assertion was instead transferred to the collective concerns of the polis. Not the individual but the city became the hero.

Dominance of the polis in Greek culture. So powerful and compelling was the psychological pull of the polis that almost every aspect of Greek cultural activity was speedily caught up in and — as it were — digested by the new master institution of Greek civilization. Religion, art, literature, philosophy, took shape or acquired a new accent through their relationship with the all-engulfing object of the citizens' affection. A few remarks about each of these facets of Greek life will make their relationship to the polis clearer.

First, religion. In the dark age following the Dorian invasion, each local king and clan chieftain conducted religious observances on behalf of his household and followers. Later, these traditional religious duties were often treated as magistracies, to be occupied temporarily by one or another high-born aristocrat. Such religious functionaries were usually quite indifferent to the vast discrepancies of doctrine they had inherited, for Greek religion had been compounded of two distinct elements. Stories associated with the Olympian gods, whom the Greeks had brought with them from the north (a pantheon resembling the pantheon the Aryans brought to India), confronted other myths associated with the ancient goddesses of fertility who had been worshipped in the land before the Greeks arrived.

Priests of the oracle at Delphi together with poets who regarded themselves and were regarded by others as divinely inspired did something to bring order into this confusion. Hesiod (8th century B.C.) in particular attempted to organize the various discrepant myths into a coherent whole. But Hesiod and his greatest predecessor, the mighty but theologically unsystematic Homer, could not really reconcile the innumerable contradictions that resulted from the superimposition of two incompatible religious systems. This logical disarray opened wide the gate for private speculation about the nature of the world and man's place in it. In this way philosophy was born.

Religious development moved in another direction. Ordinary men and politicians were not seriously troubled by the obvious conflicts among traditional myths. As long as traditional modes of invocation and worship of each deity were reasonably clear it was enough to know that one god was appropriate for one occasion and another for a different occasion. But as the wealth of Greek cities increased, and especially when it became common for rich men to vie with one another in financing public worship, a great deal of inventiveness was devoted to the elaboration of traditional rites into sumptuous spectacles. In the course of this ritual elaboration, elements of the Olympian worship and elements derived from the older cults of the land were intermingled. This was conspicuously the case in Athens, for example, where during the Panathenea — one of the religious high points of the year — a great procession symbolically linked the ancient mystery cult center at Eleusis to the Acropolis by going from one to the other. Similarly, the worship of Dionysus — a johnny-come-lately among the gods who had no place among the Olympians — became the occasion for dramatic presentations of myths drawn indiscriminately from the Olympian and from the pre-Olympian religious traditions. In this practical fashion the rising polis, through public cult ceremonies, mingled and, by mingling, effectively reconciled the discordancies of the Greek religious heritage.

Art, too, or at least those monuments that survive, came largely within the polis frame during the sixth century B.C. Construction of public temples gave employment to masons and architects. The creation of cult statues for such temples, not to mention the embellishment of temple walls and pediments, offered scope for sculptors. Classical Greek art was fundamentally shaped by the requirements of this sort of public use. Individual portraits were quite inappropriate to an art aiming at the portrayal of gods and heroes. Instead, an ideal type of human beauty was called for, and Greek artists succeeded in achieving it with a surety of touch that has stirred admiration ever since.

It was not until after 500 B.C. that the rise of the drama set the polis mark upon Greek literature. Prior to that time, poetry had been shaped to aristocratic tastes, and tended to glorify individual self-assertion and aggrandizement. This was pre-eminently true of the greatest and most influential of all Greek poets: Homer. Homer probably lived sometime between 850 and 700 B.C. in Asia Minor; but his poems deal with Mycenaean heroes, and clearly reflect information about that age which must have been transmitted orally, perhaps by a bardic tradition. Modern archaeological discovery has tended to increase the plausibility of Homer's account of the wrath of Achilles and of Odysseus' travels; but the *Iliad* and *Odyssey* contain some clear anachronisms to prove that the poet lived much later, as the Greeks of the classical age themselves always believed. Homer's compelling statement of the heroic ideal, combining fierceness and joy in action with a haunting sense of the inevitability of eventual defeat and death, entered fundamentally into the Greek view of life. For just as a well-trained phalanx rushed into battle like a single being, animated by a single will and inspired by a common ferocity, so each individual Greek of the classical age tended to regard his particular polis as though it were one of Homer's heroes, and was easily persuaded to strive for the collective gain and glory of his city regardless of personal costs or consequences. In this simple fashion the Greeks were able to reconcile the egalitarianism and self-effacement required by the phalanx with the older, aristocratic, and self-assertive ideal enshrined in Homer's poetry. To harness heroic violence and unbridled self-assertiveness effectually to the service of the polis as the Greeks were thus able to do was really quite as remarkable as the simultaneous transvaluation taking place in India with the rise of the ascetic, mystical idea at the expense of earlier Aryan this-worldliness.

Despite the general success of the polis ordering of things, a few individuals fretted over the logical inconsistencies of Greek religion and traditional world-view. As trade developed, opportunities to learn about the wisdom of the East multiplied. Inquiring Greeks soon discovered that among the priestly experts of the Middle East there was no agreement about such fundamental questions as how the world was created or why the planets periodically checked their forward movement through the heavens and went backward for a while before resuming their former motion. It was in Ionia that men first confronted this sort of question systematically enough to bother recording their views. These, the first philosophers, sought to explain the phenomena of the world by imaginative exercise of their power of reason. Finding conflicting and unsupported stories about the gods to be unsatisfactory, they took the drastic step of omitting the gods entirely, and boldly substituted natural law instead as the ruling force of the universe. To be sure, the Ionian philosophers did not agree among themselves when they sought to describe how the laws of nature worked, and their naïve efforts to explain an ever wider range of phenomena did not meet with much success.

Nevertheless, their attempts at using speculative reason to explain the nature of things marked a major turning point in human intellectual development. The Ionian concept of a universe ruled not by the whim of some divine personality but by an impersonal and unchangeable law has never since been forgotten. Throughout the subsequent history of European and Middle Eastern thought, this distinctively Greek view of the nature of things stood in persistent and fruitful tension with the older, Middle Eastern theistic explanation of the universe. Particular thinkers, reluctant to abandon either position entirely, have sought to reconcile the omnipotence of the divine will with the unchangeability of natural law by means of the most various arguments. Since, however, the two views are as logically incompatible with one another as were the myths from which the Ionian philosophers started, no formulation or reconciliation ever attained lasting and universal consent. Men always had to start over again to reshape for themselves a more satisfactory metaphysic and theology. Here, therefore, lay a growing point for all subsequent European thought which has not yet been exhausted.

Indeed, the recent successes of natural science seem to have vindicated the Ionian concept of natural law in ways and with a complexity that would have utterly amazed Thales (d. c. 546 B.C.) or any of his successors, who merely voiced what turned out to be amazingly lucky guesses. How did they do it? It seems plausible to suggest that the Ionians hit upon the notion of natural law by simply projecting the tight little world of the polis upon the universe. For it was a fact that the polis was regulated by law, not by the personal will or whim of a ruler. If such invisible abstractions could govern human behavior and confine it to certain roughly predictable paths of action, why could not similar laws control the natural world? To such a question, it appears, the Ionians gave an affirmative answer, and in doing so gave a distinctive cast to all subsequent Greek and European thought.

Limitations of the polis. It would be a mistake to leave the impression that all facets of Greek life fitted smoothly and easily into the polis frame. The busy public world left scant room for the inwardness of personal experience. Striving for purgation, for salvation, for holiness, which found such ample expression in the Indian cultural setting, was almost excluded. Yet the Greeks were not immune from such impulses, and through the ancient mystery religions, as well as through such an association as the "Order" founded by Pythagoras (d. *c.* 507 B.C.) they sought to meet these needs. But when such efforts took organized form, a fundamental incompatibility between the claims of the polis to the unqualified loyalty of every citizen and the pursuit of personal holiness quickly became apparent. This was illustrated by the stormy history of the Pythagorean Order. Either the organized seekers after holiness captured the polis, as happened for a while in the city of Croton in southern Italy, or the magistrates of the polis persecuted the Order, as happened in Pythagoras' old age. There seemed no workable ground of compromise in this, the earliest recorded instance of conflict between church and state in Western history.

The fundamental difference between Greek and Indian institutions as shaped by about 500 B.C. was made apparent by this episode. The loose federation of cultures allowed by the caste principle in India experienced no difficulty at all in accommodating corporations of seekers after holiness such as the communities of Buddhist monks. By contrast, the exclusive claim upon the citizens' time, effort, and affection which had been staked out by the Greek polis allowed no sort of corporate rival.

Enormous energies were tapped by the polis. A wider segment of the total population was engaged in cultural and political action than had been possible in any earlier civilized society, and the brilliant flowering of classical Greek civilization was the consequence. Yet the very intensity of the political tie excluded ranges of activity and sensitivity that were not compatible with a territorial organization of human groupings, and sowed seeds of civil strife between the Greek cities which soon proved disastrous. But every achievement involves a surrender of alternatives: it is merely that the Greek achievement, by its very magnitude, casts an unusually clear light upon what it also excluded.

VI

The Definition of Chinese Civilization

to 500 B.C.

IN the Yellow river's middle reaches the great stream leaves the barrenness of the Inner Mongolian steppe and cuts through soft loess soil on its way toward the flood plain below. Rain falls sporadically in this region of fertile, easily worked soil, sometimes in cloudbursts that bring flash floods; but there are many seasons of scant rainfall when the crops suffer from drought, and occasional years when the rains, which depend upon the furthest northward reach of the monsoon, simply fail to arrive.

In this precarious environment neolithic farmers began raising crops of barley and wheat about 2500 B.C. In addition, the early farmers of the Yellow river valley raised some rice, the staple of monsoon Asia. But in a region where water was likely to be critically short, rice could never displace the less productive but more drought-resistant Middle Eastern grains.

Three distinct types of neolithic settlements have been discovered in this mid-region of the Yellow river valley. One of them, the so-called "Black pottery" culture, developed rather large villages, sometimes protected by stout earthen walls. Such details as the shapes of their large ceremonial pots closely resemble elaborate bronze vessels dating from the early period of Chinese civilization. Hence it seems likely that the Black pottery people were ancestral to the historical Chinese, although it would be unwarranted to assume that the peoples who produced the other, different pottery styles did not also contribute to the emergent Chinese civilization.

Nevertheless, Chinese civilization did not develop spontaneously from the Black pottery villages. The earliest known archaeological site which is unmistakably Chinese is the capital city of Anyang, dating from about 1400–1100 B.C. It revealed some important differences from the material remains left behind by the farming folk of the Black pottery villages. In particular, royal graves contained horse skeletons, bronze weapons and accoutrements, and chariots. Such features are, of course, strongly reminiscent of the nearly contemporary chariot conquerors of the Middle East, Greece, and India. Two other telltale traces are the compound bow (specially strengthened to make it short yet powerful and thus useful in the confined space of a chariot) and the rectangular layout of the city itself, with two main streets crossing at right angles in the center of the walled area.

Some scholars are so impressed by the uniqueness of Chinese civilization and by the distances separating the Yellow river valley from western Asia as to repudiate the idea that there could be any important connection between Chinese and Middle Eastern affairs in such early times. The peculiarities of Chinese writing and the high technical virtuosity of Chinese bronze casting also impress those who deny that Chinese civilization might have arisen through stimuli offered by events occurring far to the westward. But once chariots had been perfected, men who knew how to use this new and overwhelming weapon must have found it as easy to subdue peaceable cultivators of oases in central Asia as others did to conquer Mesopotamia, Egypt, India, and the Aegean lands. Moreover, oases of varying size were more or less continuously strung out all across central Asia, being located wherever a stream came plunging down from the high snow-capped mountains into the deserts that lay at the feet of the Himalayan, Altai, and Tien Shan ranges. Indeed, the Yellow river valley was in a sense no more than the largest and most easterly of these oases, being located on a stream that was powerful enough to break through the desert barrier, regain rain-watered land, and penetrate at last to the ocean itself.

Chronological relationships are compatible with the idea of diffusion of chariot technology eastward as well as west and south, for there is about a two-hundred-year gap between the time when conquering charioteers first appeared in the Middle East and the time when similar military equipment is known to have reached China. But archaeological digging has not been undertaken at any of the intermediary oasis sites where traces of the passage of chariot conquerors might be expected. Obviously until such confirmation has been found, any westward connections attributed to the rulers of the earliest distinctively Chinese society must remain hypothetical.

The Shang dynasty. Later tradition gave the name Hsia to the first human rulers of China. No archaeological finds can be definitely attached to the Hsia, unless, indeed, the Black pottery villages represent the material remains of that age. Anyang, on the other hand, definitely belongs to the second dynasty recorded in Chinese history, the Shang. The shorter of the two traditional chronologies assigns the dates 1523–1028 B.C. to the Shang dynasty, and modern scholarship can find no reason to question the correctness of this record. Anyang was, according to the traditional story, the third and last capital of the Shang, but precise identification of the earlier seats of government has not yet been made.

Clearly, caution is called for in interpreting such an incomplete archaeological record. Conquerors, if indeed they came by the oasis route through central Asia, probably intermarried with local women, sent their sons' sons onward to the next oasis, and the next, during a period of some two centuries. Hence one need not assume any massive influx of Indo-European barbarians, such as flooded into India at about the time the Shang dynasty established itself in China. Moreover, it seems clear that the conquerors soon adopted much of the culture of their new subjects; or to express the matter more precisely, it seems probable that when the Shang aristocracy established itself over the farming populations of the Yellow river valley, the rulers began to collect rents and used part of their income to support a body of artisans, whose skills rapidly improved as they became professional. Some of the skills seem to have been new to China, e.g. bronze-founding and wheelmaking — both of them vital to the charioteers' armament. But new skills could be harnessed to old uses, as the elaborate bronze ceremonial vessels which have been dug in thousands from Shang graves prove. For these pots conform in many cases to shapes already familiar among the Black pottery folk. The incised patterns, geometrical, yet sometimes zoömorphic, which decorate these pots, may also have derived from an older wood-carving art style familiar to the Black pottery people.

An important feature of the discoveries at Anyang was a great collection of "oracle bones." These are bones or sometimes tortoise shells that were consulted by priestly diviners of that ancient society in the hope of finding the answers to various urgent questions about the future. "Will it rain?" and "Will the barbarians attack?" are the sort of questions asked. The diviners, being conscientious professionals, anxious to improve their skills in interpreting the signs vouchsafed by the gods, sometimes recorded both the question and the answer. They did so in a style of writing directly ancestral to modern Chinese ideographic script — so much so that modern scholars found no great difficulty in reading the oracle bones from the time when they were first discovered.

Not much can be deduced about Shang society and government from the brief records inscribed on the oracle bones. Nor do other archaeological materials allow us to say much more than that Shang society was warlike and aristocratic, and supported a small group of highly skilled artisans who produced objects of great refinement for their noble masters. The great bulk of the population labored at the tasks of cultivation without taking any active part in the life of the court and noble households. It seems probable that the Shang "empire" was parceled out among warrior chieftains who were only remotely subject to any superior central authority. But evidence is really too scant to permit definite conclusions.

The inscriptions on the oracle bones do provide somewhat fuller information about Shang religious ideas. The names of several gods and goddesses appear, though their function is seldom made explicit. Some seem to be embodiments of a mountain, river, lake, or of a similar natural feature. In other cases, symbols whose exact meaning cannot really be recovered probably refer to ancestral spirits. Human sacrifice was practiced by the Shang, and a dead king was followed to his grave by a whole retinue of followers and courtiers. Such traits as these, repugnant to later Chinese sensibilities, remind us of how close to barbarism Shang society remained.

The Chou dynasty. In 1051 B.C. or thereabouts the Shang dynasty was overthrown by the Chou, who were conquerors come from the western borderlands of China in the Wei valley of modern Kansu. There is no reason to doubt the essential accuracy of Chinese traditional history, which divided the Chou period into two halves: the early or western Chou (1051–771 B.C.) when the capital remained in the Wei valley, and the later or eastern Chou (771–256 B.C.) when the capital was located near the center of the Chinese world at Loyang.

During the first of these periods, the central administration may have been able to exert more or less effective control over a considerable area of northern China. But in 771 B.C. a sudden barbarian attack overwhelmed the capital, destroyed the direct imperial line, and paralyzed the central authority. Even when a scion of the ruling house assumed the imperial office at Loyang, thus inaugurating the eastern Chou dynasty, an effective central authority was not restored. Instead a series of rival local princes disputed power and precedence with one another, engaging in an unending series of diplomatic and warlike encounters. Their struggles gradually became more ruthless as rival princes extended and strengthened their power through improvements in the arts of administration and war.

This period, traditionally called the age of the "warring states," saw a rather rapid geographic expansion of Chinese civilization. Refugees from the increasing violence at the center helped to spread Chinese culture and skills to surrounding peoples, and in doing so sucked them into the political vortex. Princely efforts to find new allies among the barbarians had the same effect. These processes brought the coastal regions of north China into the circle of Chinese culture for the first time, and extended the frontier of the Chinese style of life as far south as the Yangtse valley. China, in short, was rapidly becoming geographically recognizable as the China of later ages.

from aristocratic families with traditional claims to political eminence. This was true even of democrats like Pericles, who dominated the political scene in Athens between 460 and 429 B.C. and
gave his name to Athens' greatest age. After his death, during the
long and bitter Peloponnesian war against Sparta and her allies
(431–404 B.C.), the division of interest between farmer-soldiers
and the landless rowers of the fleet became so serious that old-
fashioned aristocratic and ultimately land-based leadership found-
ered. Thus Pericles was succeeded by Cleon, a capable and un-
scrupulous commoner. After Cleon's death in battle (422 B.C.) the
former aristocratic monopoly of political leadership was never
entirely restored.

A more portentous change was the decay of polis loyalty. This
change was felt throughout the Greek world, wherever the old
simplicities, which required and permitted nearly every adult male
to farm and fight in the phalanx beside his fellows, gave way to
more complex social differentiations among such groups as merchants, artisans, farmers, soldiers, sailors, slaves, foreigners, landowners, and sharecroppers. The long struggle of the Peloponnesian
war drastically accelerated this process. Everywhere (even within
Athens itself) oligarchs and conservatives tended to support
Sparta, while democrats sympathized with Athens. Since outside
intervention on behalf of one or the other party was always a
possibility, both the temptation and the opportunities for treason
multiplied. The old idea according to which private interest and
ambition should be subordinated to the welfare of the polis as a
whole could not withstand such pressures. One after another the
separate cities of Greece lost their internal cohesion as party rivalry
degenerated into wholesale resort to threat, assassination, and exile.

The classical age. But before the polis world dissolved into
squalid civil strife, for a period of almost fifty years, from the time
of Xerxes' great disaster in 480–79 B.C. until the outbreak of the
Peloponnesian war in 431 B.C., Athens in particular and the Greek
world at large experienced a golden age which was more concentrated in time and space and more perfect in its expression than any
comparable period of human history.

In another and even more important sense China was also becoming her historic self in the age of the Chou. For it was under this dynasty that the ideas that became basic to all later Chinese civilization found their first clear expression. In addition, in the later Chou period, arts of bureaucratic government and a system of society hospitable to bureaucratic centralization emerged in each of the rival states into which China divided. To be sure, idea and practice did not come into reasonable harmony until after the establishment of the Han dynasty (202 B.C.), yet the main elements and emphasis of the Chinese style of civilization had become manifest some three centuries earlier, i.e. by about 500 B.C.

From the very beginning, the Chou conquerors appear to have eliminated some of the more barbarous aspects of Shang religion. Human sacrifice and ritual slaughter ceased. Very likely the conquerors explained their usurpation of supreme power by claiming a mandate from Heaven. This idea certainly became a cornerstone of later Chinese political thought, and may, as Confucius believed, date back to the propaganda of the first Chou conquerors. As later developed, the theory held that Heaven, which was conceived as a vaguely anthropomorphic supreme deity, granted rule over earth to a specially selected agent, the "Son of Heaven" or emperor. As long as he behaved piously and correctly, the Son of Heaven could expect to continue to remain in office. Impiety or rude, improper behavior, on the other hand, invited the withdrawal of Heaven's mandate, whereupon some other man might be chosen for the role of ruler on earth.

Connected with this political theory was an elaborate cosmology, which traced parallels between heaven and earth in great detail. As the heavens turned on the pole star, for example, earthly affairs were supposed to turn upon the emperor, who was responsible not only for matters of war and politics but for the weather and all other terrestrial phenomena that might affect human activity. A good emperor brought peace and good harvests, a bad one brought the reverse. Behavior in accordance with carefully prescribed rites constituted the essence of the emperor's duty. Only so could earth and Heaven attain the harmony and smooth interaction of one upon the other which was necessary for human welfare.

Such ideas as these both exalted and severely limited the emperor's power. One clear implication was that there could be only one Son of Heaven. All other rulers must derive authority from him through some sort of delegation, real or fictitious. In the early Chou period, the emperor's power was real enough to create no serious problem for theorists. Local noble families held land on a sort of feudal tenure, which quickly became hereditary. The centrifugal tendency inherent in such a system was counteracted by palace schools in which the sons of nobles were trained not solely in military skills like archery but also to a knowledge of the rites they would have to perform when they became heads of families and responsible for the welfare of all under their command. Knowledge of these rites implied also familiarity with the ideas behind them, i.e. with the theory of political legitimacy and human social order that made the Son of Heaven supremely responsible for all that happened on earth. Proper performance of the necessary rites also required literacy, so that the young nobles of Chou China had to learn at least the rudiments of the difficult Chinese script. They thus combined the skills and duties of ruler, warrior, priest, and scribe, and in their own persons performed functions which in Middle Eastern society had long since been distributed among separate professions.

After 771 B.C., however, reality and theory began to diverge from one another in distressing degree. The later Chou rulers no longer enjoyed the practical authority their predecessors had in fact exercised. The titular Son of Heaven became one of the weaker rulers of a small state near the center of the Chinese world, while upstart princes near the frontier built far more powerful kingdoms for themselves, and professed only the merest lip service — if that — to the old pieties of Chou religion and cosmology. Effective efforts to collect larger amounts of taxes and to mobilize more dependable armies became the price of survival in the age of the warring states. This required princes to find men to serve them who were willing to go beyond precedent and treat others as mere instruments for the realization of the purposes of state. It required, in short, the elaboration of civil and military bureaucracy.

Confucianism and Taoism. Recurrent and increasingly violent war, with all the pressures toward maximization of state power which such contests created, accorded ill with the older belief that correct observance of traditional rites was the key to all good order among men and to earthly prosperity as well. Outright repudiation of the pieties of the past was one possible response. This point of view was advanced ruthlessly and rationally enough by a number of practical statesmen and men of affairs, known collectively as "Legalists." But their radical repudiation of traditional piety did not prevail in the end. Instead, it was the stoutly conservative yet

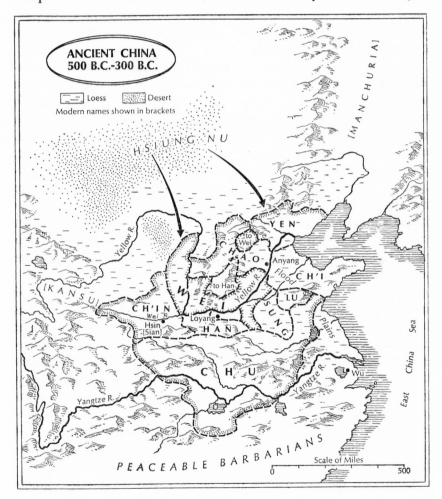

ANCIENT CHINA
500 B.C.-300 B.C.

Loess   Desert
Modern names shown in brackets

modulated piety of Confucianism that put a stamp on Chinese society which lasted until our own time.

Such an outcome was far from clear in Confucius' own lifetime (551–479 B.C.). The Sage, indeed, regarded himself as a failure, for he was never called upon to govern; and he believed that an educated man's virtue could only find its full expression through the exercise of power and responsibility. It is ironical to reflect that through his disciples he governed China for a vastly longer period and in a more profound and important sense than could possibly have been the case had Confucius been entrusted, as he always desired, with the conduct of affairs in one of the competing states that existed during his own lifetime.

Even his eventual success would have seemed absurd to Confucius, for he believed that he added nothing to the wisdom of the ancients. In a sense he was perfectly correct in denying that his ideas were new. For Confucius looked back with deepest nostalgia to the days of the early Chou, and beyond that to the Shang, Hsia, and to the legendary age of the divine emperors. Then, he felt, times had been good because Heaven and earth had stood in correct relationship to each other. This vision of the past set the stage for Confucius to wrestle with the central problem of his day: How could a good man live well in a bad world? For if the harmonious relationships which ought to prevail between Heaven and earth were lacking, as was all too evidently the case, what should a wise and good man do?

Confucius' answer was cool, unsystematic, moderate. A good man, he said, should pursue virtue in all the ordinary circumstances and confrontations of life. He should know and observe ancient rites whenever possible. He should be good, wise, and brave, whenever possible. He should respect superiors, and expect deference from his inferiors in rank. He should be prepared to govern wisely and well when entrusted with office, but should not demean himself by departing from the gentlemanly code exemplified and described by Confucius in order to attain power improperly. Such power was incompatible with virtue, and virtue, according to Confucius, was always the supreme end of human life.

Confucius did not believe that nobility was necessarily hereditary. On the contrary, he seems to have thought that a proper education could make the right sort of young man into a gentleman even if his father had come from some humble walk of life. Education, building upon a natural aptitude, might thus open a path whereby ambitious and capable men could hope to rise toward the top of the social scale. This was to become a very prominent and important aspect of traditional Confucian China, and constituted a break with naïvely aristocratic ideas of earlier Chou times.

Confucius flatly declined to speculate about the realm of the spirits. He never doubted their reality or power, but when the world of men was in such confusion and disorder, he preferred to direct attention to the human aspect of things, dismissing the mysteries of Heaven and of ancestral spirits as improper objects of scrutiny. Better to learn traditional rites by which good men of the past had dealt with Heaven and the ancestors than to speculate vainly upon divine nature or powers!

Confucius' disciples recorded his sayings and passed them on to later ages, perhaps in edited form, as the wisdom of their revered master. Tradition credits Confucius with arranging the "Five Classics" of later Chinese learning, but this is probably fictitious. Nevertheless, the codification of a body of traditional Chinese writings into a recognized canon was completed by about Confucius' time. This had great importance later, since study of the classics became the mark of the well-educated man, and ability to quote aptly from one or another of these books and to use the written language in a pure, classical style became the hall marks of Chinese gentlemen. By sharing intense study of a limited number of texts (including of course such works as the *Analects* in which Confucius' sayings were collected) the Chinese of later generations shaped a common core of shared experience from which fundamental attitudes and values, the cement of Chinese civilization, naturally emerged.

Confucian emphasis upon decorum and self-control could not satisfy everyone. Too much was left out: the depths of human passion and the mysteries of nature had no place in a well-regulated Confucian world. Other schools of thought that took these aspects of reality seriously commanded considerable attention in China.

The most important of these was Taoism. This was an ill-defined tradition built around a body of more or less secret knowledge. Taoists emphasized magical charms and rituals that were supposed to impart health and long life, and might confer other and more unusual powers over human and natural forces, e.g. the ability to fly through the air. In a later age, and partly under the stimulus of Buddhism, Taoism attained something approaching a doctrinal definition. But in Confucius' time Taoists appear to have been more like Siberian shamans or the medicine men of the Amerindian tribes than like the philosophers of Greece or the holy men of India.

Nevertheless, the existence of Taoist adepts gave a balance to the ancient Chinese world-view that Confucianism alone could not supply. Moderation and self-discipline needed its complement of mystery and magic to satisfy the ordinary range of human needs and to express the fluctuating feelings of men who lived in hard and uncertain times. By complementing each other, the one supplying precisely what the other lacked, Confucianism and Taoism constituted an unusually stable pattern of thought, which lasted, with many changes and later enrichment yet without fundamental interruption, from Confucius' time until the twentieth century of the Christian era. No other cultural tradition has lasted so long and governed the lives of so many millions of men. China's comparative isolation from other high cultures helped to assure such stability; but the intrinsic attractiveness of the Chinese way, combining common sense with endless subtlety, contributed to its long and brilliant success.

VII

Changes in the Barbarian World

1700 to 500 B.C.

HE cosmopolitan massiveness of Middle Eastern civilization and the rise of three new high cultures in India, Greece, and China obviously increased the variety of civilized influences playing upon the barbarian world. In the remoter habitable regions of the earth, so far as anyone knows, no very important changes occurred. In Australia, for example, an age-old style of hunting life maintained the even tenor of its way, unaffected by anything occurring elsewhere. In the Americas, also, no very dramatic developments can be discerned from the archaeological record. Cultivation of maize and other crops became more and more important, and centers of comparatively dense population began to arise on the central plateau of Mexico and further south in what is today Guatemala. Events along the west coast of South America are more obscure, owing to unsettled questions of chronology, but it seems probable that Peru lagged somewhat behind Mexico in development toward a populous agricultural community.

Sub-Saharan Africa also remained apart from the rest of the world. In all probability, cultivation of edible roots and other crops made considerable progress in west Africa, while the east coast of the continent was visited at least occasionally by seafarers from civilized ports. The Egyptian style of civilization penetrated some distance up the Nile into Nubia, but what if any contact there may have been between Nubia and the deeper interior of the continent, is simply not known. Extensive archaeological investigation will be necessary before anything approaching a reliable picture of the ancient history of sub-Saharan Africa will become possible.

The Mediterranean. In the part of Eurasia closer to the main centers of civilized developments, we are better able to discover major landmarks of change. The western Mediterranean, for example, was the scene of successful colonization not merely by the Greeks, but by representatives of Middle Eastern civilization, the Phoenicians and Etruscans, as well. The most successful Phoenician colony was Carthage, in north Africa, established not long before 800 B.C. Other Phoenician colonies dotted the north African coast and occupied the southern and western portions of Sicily. A second civilized people from the east, the Etruscans, whose exact origin is one of the standing puzzles of ancient history, also appeared in the western Mediterranean about 800 B.C., and established a series of towns in central and northern Italy. These outposts of Middle Eastern styles of civilization, together with the numerous Greek colonies in eastern Sicily and southern Italy, spread familiarity with the advantages of civilized life to all the coasts of the Mediterranean. From these centers, knowledge of and admiration for at least some aspects of the life of the coastal cities tended to seep inland along trade routes.

Westward from the steppes. This geographically modest extension of the civilized sphere of influence was dwarfed by the continuing expansion of the formidable steppe warrior peoples. We have already encountered steppe warriors as conquerors of civilized populations: Kassites, Hyksos, Mycenaeans, Aryans, and the rest. Other steppe warriors exercised their prowess in the conquest of less-developed lands, above all in Europe where a long series of westward displacements from the steppe into forested land gathered momentum a little before 2000 B.C. The final result, as we saw above, was to impose upon the whole continent a barbarian level of culture.

The spread of cavalry tactics after about 900 B.C. brought the steppe peoples into much closer relation to the Middle Eastern centers of civilization than before. Successful raids such as those made by the Scythians in the seventh century B.C. introduced rude warriors and pastoralists to the luxuries and delights of civilization. The long series of border wars and hit-and-run raids which became normal thereafter, meant that the steppe tribesmen were under constant temptation to organize themselves into stronger and more cohesive units in order to make their raiding more formidable. The Scythians, for example, after migrating from central Asia to southern Russia (probably just before 700 B.C.), erected a tribal empire in the Ukraine, and soon entered into extensive trade relations with the rising Greek world to the south. The basic exchange was Scythian grain for the oil and wine produced in the city-states of the Aegean coastlands. As a result of such trade, by 500 B.C. the Scythian aristocracy of southern Russia was beginning to acquire a taste for Greek luxuries.

Further to the west, Celtic-speaking tribes exploited the mobility that came from riding horseback to expand their dominion widely through western Europe. The center of Celtic dispersion was what is now southern Germany. This was a region where tribes that had been squeezed from the westernmost bay of the Eurasian steppe — i.e. the central plain of Hungary — had to adjust their habits to a new, forested environment. The main problem was that the bow, the standard weapon of steppe nomads, could not be used very successfully in a forested landscape, since arrows too often would be deflected from their target by twigs and branches. The ancient Celtic warriors solved this problem by inventing a great two-handed sword, designed to be used from horseback. Armed with these great blades, the Celts overrode earlier occupants of France, Spain, Britain, Ireland, and nothern Italy. They also raided sporadically even further afield into such regions as Greece, Asia Minor, and central Italy.

Like the Scythians, the new masters of western Europe were often interested in the luxuries of Mediterranean civilization, so far as they could get hold of them. In Spain, for example, Carthaginian traders and colonists allied themselves with the Celts at the expense of the earlier, subjugated inhabitants of the land. In what later became France, Greek trade had begun to reach northward from the port of Massilia (modern Marseilles, founded about 600 B.C.). The pattern of exchange was similar to that in southern Russia.

The militarization of society that these conquests by peoples deriving ultimately from the steppe brought to Europe created one of the basic conditions of later European development. Yet it also cost the destruction of some of the megalithic achievement of an earlier age. Long voyages in small craft could not be undertaken safely when the masters of the shoreline were inclined to treat a stranger as an enemy to be robbed and killed if he did not seem too strong. On the other hand, much of the megalithic priestcraft probably survived, perhaps in edited form, among the Celtic Druids.

What happened on the eastward flank of the steppe world is not nearly so well known as are events in Europe. This is because archaeological study of central Asia is still in a most imperfect state, and rash guesswork remains the only alternative to complete ignorance. It seems likely that the arts of horsemanship and the skills of nomadry spread eastward through the grasslands rather slowly. One people after another, living in or near the steppe, picked up the necessary skills from neighbors further west. Any tribe already equipped to live the life of a full-fledged nomad would migrate eastward only as a last resort, since this meant moving from better pasture land to worse. The reason is that rainfall and temperature both decline as one moves eastward along the Eurasian steppe toward Mongolia.

As a result of this geographic fact, by the time all the steppe had been filled by nomad groups — not until about 400 B.C. — a regular and very powerful east-west gradient came into operation. The high plateau of Mongolia constituted a very harsh environment and required great hardihood of both man and beast. Westward the steppe extended all the way to the Hungarian plain, becoming warmer and better watered as the altitude decreased and the rain-bearing Atlantic winds came nearer. Any political disturbance of life on the steppe therefore was likely to impel fugitives and/or conquerors westward, where better grass and a better climate beckoned. Hence, across the centuries a steady drift westward manifested itself. Scythians, starting in the Altai, moved to the

Ukrainian steppe. Turkish tribes replaced them in central Asia, only to follow the Scyths westward in time, making room for the Mongol-speaking peoples who came pressing in the Turks' rear.

Steppe warriors, owners of herds of horses, and accustomed from childhood to life in the saddle, were very formidable fighting men. Raiding the richer, civilized regions lying to the south of the steppe zone was a constant temptation. Any weakening in the guard which civilized rulers maintained against such raids was quickly discovered by casual parties of nomad horsemen, probing southward on the lookout for whatever they could pick up. A few striking successes in small-scale raids quickly induced thousands of nomads to join a successful captain. Nomad harassment could therefore quickly snowball into a massive assault, unless civilized resistance could somehow be organized in time. In western Asia, the principal early example of this phenomenon was the Scythian participation in the siege and sack of Nineveh, the Assyrian capital, in 612 B.C. But, as we have already seen, soon thereafter the Medes and the Persians found a way of coping with the nomad danger, by hiring tribes of nomads to stand guard against their fellows along the frontier of the Middle East.

Eastward from the steppes. In the Far East it is possible that the sack of the Chou capital in 771 B.C. was also the work of nomad raiders, operating from a base somewhere in central Asia. Unfortunately, information about this episode in Chinese history is too scant to tell whether steppe nomads, mounted and equipped for cavalry warfare, were the destroyers of the western Chou dynasty or not.

Some modern scholars think that raiders from the steppe penetrated all the way to the Pacific, reaching the coast near the southern border of modern China. By about 700 B.C. a proto-civilization had arisen in this region, based in large part on seafaring. The archaeological remains left by these "Dongson" peoples show surprising similarities to archaeological materials from the western steppe region of Eurasia. Perhaps therefore when the arts of cavalry warfare were still new a few venturesome horsemen did move southward from the Altai region through Szechuan and overran the coastal "Dongson" peoples, whose seamanship had permitted the accumulation of enough wealth to make them tempting objects of attack.

Exactly how far Dongson seamen may have penetrated is an unsolved problem. The winds and waters of the south Pacific are comparatively quiet and dependable during the greater part of the year. Even with small craft and inexact navigation, it is possible to travel long distances across such an ocean. The Malay peoples of Borneo and the southern Philippines probably descend from these early seafarers. Not long before the Christian era they sent a stream of colonists to the island of Madagascar at the other side of the Indian Ocean — a fact attested by the survival today of a Malay tongue as the main speech of that distant island. It is also possible that other seamen may have penetrated into the depths of the Pacific. A few vessels may even have reached the American coast and taught Amerindians how to smelt tin and copper to make bronze.

Such a transoceanic contact would account for the otherwise very puzzling resemblances between Amerindian art from early Mexico and Peru and the art of the southeast coastland of the Asian mainland. Other ideas, for example, the association of the four points of the compass with colors, also crop up on both sides of the Pacific and may attest some early transoceanic contact. On the other hand, the crops upon which Amerindian civilizations were based were not derived from the Old World, and some scholars think that even if a few boatloads of castaways crossed the ocean successfully at an early date they contributed nothing of importance to the emergence of Amerindian civilizations. Such a view assumes that the art of bronze casting and the other resemblances that seem to link the Old World with the New are either accidental or arise from independent inventions or convergent evolution.

Whatever the truth may be in this matter, the fact remains that the level of culture and technical skill possessed by the Amerindians never caught up with the achievements of the Old World. The major centers of innovation and the most important seats of civilization continued to be in Eurasia, where no fewer than four major civilizations had defined themselves by 500 B.C.

Summary. Between 1700 and 500 B.C. the geographic area within which the influences of high cultures began to make a difference in how men lived became much larger. The rise of new centers of civilization was accompanied by the development of a high barbarism in the steppes and in such favored regions as western Europe, southern China, and (although we know almost nothing about it) in southern India too. Civilization had indeed become endemic, capable of establishing itself wherever reasonably fertile agricultural land was to be found.

The story of the next two thousand years, from 500 B.C. to A.D. 1500 is the story of, among other things, an ever renewed though not always successful expansion of civilized styles of life at the expense of the neighboring barbarisms. It is also a story of rough equilibrium between the four major centers of civilization in the Middle East, India, Europe, and China. The second part of this book will undertake to sketch the main turning points and leading characteristics of this era of cultural balance.

An historical atlas and a dictionary of dates are valuable reference works for anyone interested in history. The best atlas for world history is *Westermanns Atlas zur Weltgeschichte* (Braunschweig, 1956), which has unfortunately never been issued in an English edition. William Robert Shepherd, *Historical Atlas*, 9th ed. (New York, 1964), is the standby for the English-speaking world. William L. Langer, ed., *An Encyclopedia of World History*, rev. ed. (Boston, 1952), is standard and very useful for checking dates and refreshing one's memory about the sequence of events.

Numerous books purport to deal with world history. Some are collective works, like the Cambridge histories: *The Cambridge Ancient History*, 12 vols. (Cambridge, 1923–39), *The Cambridge Medieval History*, 8 vols. (Cambridge, 1913–36), and *The Cambridge Modern History*, 13 vols. (Cambridge, 1902–12); new editions of both the modern and ancient histories are in progress. Others bear the stamp of an individual mind and therefore, though more coherent, are also controversial, since no one man can master the learning of every field of history. Four such books have some claim to a general reader's interest: H. G. Wells, *The Outline of History* (London, 1920); Oswald Spengler, *The Decline of the West*, 2 vols., 2nd ed. rev. (New York, 1931); Arnold J. Toynbee, *A Study of History*, 10 vols. (London, 1934–54); and my own, William H. McNeill, *The Rise of the West* (Chicago, 1963). Toynbee's work has also appeared in abridged form, D. C. Somervell, ed., *A Study of History*, 2 vols. (London, 1946, 1957).

Two sorts of additional reading obviously clamor for a student's attention: translations of ancient texts and modern studies of the past. Translations of the Bible and of the classics, like Homer, are very numerous and with generations of scholarship have attained a high precision. It therefore seems captious to try to recommend one translation as against another for works of this sort. Other civilized traditions are not nearly so richly represented in English translation. For the ancient Middle East, James B. Pritchard, ed., *Ancient Near Eastern Texts Relating to the Old Testament*, rev. ed. (Princeton, 1955), offers an excellent and arresting selection of documents; and N. K. Sandars, tr., *The Epic of Gilgamesh* (Penguin, 1960), makes easily available a cheap edition of Mesopotamia's chief literary monument. For Indian culture, W. T. DeBary, Jr., et al., eds., *Sources of Indian Tradition* (New York, 1958), gives a fine selection of passages from the Vedas, Upanishads, and other early texts. A companion volume, W. T. DeBary, Jr., et al., eds.,

116

Sources of Chinese Tradition (New York, 1960), does equally well in assembling and excerpting from early Chinese texts. In addition, Arthur Waley, tr., *The Analects of Confucius* (New York, 1939), and Arthur Waley, tr., *Shih Ching, Book of Songs* (Boston, 1937), are worth attention from students of history.

Many works dealing with ancient times lard their pages liberally with translated extracts from ancient texts. Interplay between translation and commentary often gives a better introduction to the subject than unsupported translations, particularly when the culture under consideration is deeply unfamiliar. Good examples of this literary genre for the ancient Middle East are: Samuel Noah Kramer, *Sumerian Mythology* (Philadelphia, 1944); Henri Frankfort, et al., *Before Philosophy* (Penguin, 1941); J. A. Moulton, *Early Zoroastrianism* (London, 1913). For Indian culture, Edward Conze, *Buddhism: Its Essence and Development* (New York, 1959), Sir Charles Eliot, *Hinduism and Buddhism: An Historical Sketch*, 3 vols. (London, 1921), and Heinrich Zimmer, *Philosophies of India* (New York, 1951), are all helpful. The same may be said of Fung Yu-lan, *Short History of Chinese Philosophy* (New York, 1948). Two works on early Greek thought belong here: John Burnet, *Early Greek Philosophy*, 4th ed. (London, 1930), is a sober, standard, and painstaking account, whereas F. M. Cornford, *From Religion to Philosophy: A Study in the Origins of Western Speculation* (London, 1912), stands at the opposite pole, being brilliant, speculative, and provocative.

Perusal of photographs of ancient works of art and other material remains constitutes a second and very valuable avenue along which a student of the ancient past may travel. It has the great advantage that no translator stands between you and the original work; in addition, relatively large numbers of works may be passed before one's eyes easily in a short period of time simply by turning the pages of a well-illustrated book. This allows comparisons, and comparisons may generate insights into changing modes of sensibility, across both space and time — if the student takes the pains to keep in mind a loose space-time grid within which to fit each particular work of art. As a supplement and corrective to the often excessive verbalism of historians — whose sources, after all, are usually written — serious attention to art and art history is to be recommended highly. For prehistoric art, H. G. Bandi, H. Breuil, et al., *Art of the Stone Age* (New York, 1961), is good. For the art of the ancient Middle East, the following: André Parrot, *Sumer: The Dawn of Art* (New York, 1961); André Parrot, *Arts of Assyria* (New York, 1962); Henri Frankfort, *The Art and Architecture of the Ancient Orient* (Penguin, 1959); W. Stevenson Smith, *Art and Architecture of Ancient Egypt* (Penguin, 1958).

The magnificent volume, Heinrich Zimmer and Joseph Campbell, *The Art of Indian Asia*, 2nd ed., 2 vols. (New York, 1955), serves better than any text could do to demonstrate the radiation of Indian culture into southeast Asia. Ludwig Bachhofer, *A Short History of Chinese Art* (London, 1947), offers a technical yet convincing stylistic analysis of the early Chinese bronzes. An even more striking work of stylistic analysis is Henri Frankfort, *Cylinder Seals* (London, 1939), which by means of the one object which has survived abundantly from ancient Mesopotamia relates changing artistic motifs to alterations in the social and political order of that ancient society. A more telling illustration of the inter-relationship between art history and social development as a whole could scarcely be imagined.

Unfortunately, heavily illustrated art books are bound to be expensive, and this limits their utilization. An easy, though not entirely satisfactory, alternative is offered by University Prints, an agency which sells individual photographs of a wide variety of art objects, loose leaf and for very modest sums. If a teacher wishes to equip all members of a class with the same photographs in order to be able to study and discuss them easily, University Prints offers a flexible and readily accessible resource. Their address is 15 Brattle Street, Cambridge 38, Mass.

Books of modern scholarship may be grouped by subject, as follows: HUMAN EVOLUTION AND PREHISTORY. W. E. LeGros Clark, *The Antecedents of Man* (Chicago, 1960); Kenneth P. Oakley, *Man the Tool-Maker*, 4th ed. (London, 1958); Robert Ardrey, *African Genesis* (London, 1961); Sol Tax, ed., *Evolution after Darwin*, 3 vols. (Chicago, 1960); Carleton S. Coon, *The Origin of Races* (New York, 1962); M. F. Ashley Montague, ed., *Culture and the Evolution of Man* (New York, 1962); and J. G. D. Clark, *World Prehistory, An Outline* (Cambridge, 1961). Theoretical rather than historical, but a very thoughtful little book, is Robert Redfield, *The Primitive World and Its Transformations* (Ithaca, N.Y., 1953).

ANCIENT MIDDLE EAST. Henri Frankfort, *The Birth of Civilization in the Near East* (Bloomington, Ind., 1951); V. Gordon Childe, *What Happened in History* (Penguin, 1943); Samuel Noah Kramer, *The Sumerians: Their History, Culture, and Character* (Chicago, 1963); John A. Wilson, *The Burden of Egypt: An Interpretation of Ancient Egyptian Culture* (Chicago, 1951); W. Stevenson Smith, *Interconnections in the Ancient Near East: A Study of the Relationships Between the Arts of Egypt, the Aegean, and Western Asia* (New Haven, Conn., 1965); O. R. Gurney, *The Hittites*, rev. ed. (Penguin, 1961); George Steindorff and Keith C. Seele, *When Egypt Ruled the East*, rev. ed. (Chicago, 1957); A. T. Olmstead, *A History of Assyria* (Chicago, 1923); Donald Harden, *The Phoenicians* (New York, 1962); William F. Albright, *The Archaeology of Palestine*, rev. ed. (Penguin, 1960); T. H. Robinson and W. O. E. Oesterley, *History of Israel*, 2 vols. (Oxford, 1932); H. H. Rowley, ed., *The Old Testament and Modern Study* (Oxford, 1951); A. T. Olmstead, *A History of the Persian Empire* (Chicago, 1948); R. C. Zaehner, *The Dawn and Twilight of Zoroastrianism* (New York, 1961); Jack Finegan, *Light from the Ancient Past: The Archaeological Background of Judaism and Christianity*, 2nd ed. (Princeton, 1959); David

Diringer, *The Alphabet: A Key to the History of Mankind*, 2nd ed. rev. (London, 1953); Ignace J. Gelb, *A Study of Writing*, rev. ed. (Chicago, 1964); Otto Neugebauer, *The Exact Sciences in Antiquity*, 2nd ed. (Providence, R.I., 1957); R. J. Forbes, *Metallurgy in Antiquity* (Leiden, 1950); and Charles Singer, et al., eds., *A History of Technology*, I: *From Early Times to Fall of Ancient Empires* (Oxford, 1954).

EUROPE. J. G. D. Clark, *Prehistoric Europe: The Economic Basis* (New York and London, 1952); C. F. C. Hawkes, *The Prehistoric Foundations of Europe to the Mycenean Age* (London, 1940); V. Gordon Childe, *The Dawn of European Civilization*, 6th ed. (New York, 1958); J. D. Evans, *Malta* (New York, 1959); J. D. S. Pendlebury, *The Archaeology of Ancient Crete* (London, 1939); R. W. Hutchinson, *Prehistoric Crete* (Penguin, 1962); A. R. Burn, *Minoans, Philistines and Greeks, B.C. 1400–900* (London, 1930); Chester G. Starr, *Origins of Greek Civilization, 1100–650 B.C.* (New York, 1961); M. I. Finley, *The World of Odysseus* (New York, 1954); Eric R. Dodds, *The Greeks and the Irrational* (Boston, 1957); Alfred E. Zimmern, *The Greek Commonwealth*, 5th ed. rev. (Oxford, 1931); M. Pallottino, *Art of the Etruscans* (London and New York, 1955); Raymond Block, *Origins of Rome* (New York, 1960); T. G. E. Powell, *The Celts* (New York, 1958); and B. H. Warmington, *Carthage* (London, 1960).

THE EURASIAN STEPPE. V. Gordon Childe, *The Aryans: A Study of Indo-European Origins* (New York, 1926); Tamara Talbot Rice, *The Scythians* (London, 1957); M. Rostovtzeff, *Iranians and Greeks in South Russia* (Oxford, 1922); George Vernadsky, *Ancient Russia* (New Haven, 1943); and William M. McGovern, *The Early Empires of Central Asia* (Chapel Hill, N.C., 1939).

INDIA. Stuart W. Piggott, *Prehistoric India to 1000 B.C.* (Penguin, 1950); R. E. M. Wheeler, *Early India and Pakistan, to Ashoka* (London, 1959); R. E. M. Wheeler, *The Indus Civilization*, The Cambridge History of India, supplementary volume (Cambridge, 1953); R. C. Majumdar and A. D. Pusalker, eds., *History and Culture of the Indian People*, I: *The Vedic Age* (London, 1951); and J. H. Hutton, *Caste in India: Its Nature, Functions and Origins* (Cambridge, 1946).

CHINA. Herrlee G. Creel, *The Birth of China* (London, 1936; reissue, 1951); Li Chi, *The Beginnings of Chinese Civilization* (Seattle, 1957); Cheng Te-k'un, *Archaeology in China*, I: *Prehistoric China* (Cambridge, 1959); Cheng Te-k'un, *Archaeology in China*, II: *Shang China* (Cambridge, 1960); Chang Kwang-chih, *Archaeology of Ancient China* (New Haven, Conn., 1963); William Watson, *China: Before the Han Dynasty* (New York, 1961); L. C. Goodrich, *A Short History of the Chinese People*, 3rd ed. (New York, 1959); and three controversial but fascinating works, Herrlee G. Creel, *Confucius, the Man and the Myth* (New York, 1949; new title, *Confucius and the Chi-*

nese Way, New York, 1960); Joseph Needham, *Science and Civilization in China,* multivolumed (Cambridge, 1954–   ); and G. F. Hudson, *Europe and China* (London, 1931).

OTHER PARTS OF THE WORLD. Most of the rest of the world barely enters the historic record before 500 B.C. Three works on African prehistory, however, deserve mention here: Sonia Cole, *The Prehistory of East Africa* (New York, 1954); J. Desmond Clark, *The Prehistory of Southern Africa* (Penguin, 1959); and George Peter Murdock, *Africa: Its Peoples, and Their Culture History* (New York, 1959). As for the New World and southeast Asia, it seems best to suggest relevant works as part of the bibliographical essay appended to Part II of this book.

Part II

Equilibrium Among the Civilizations

500 B.C.–A.D. 1500

For about 2000 years, between 500 B.C. and A.D. 1500, no single center of civilized life enjoyed definite preponderance in the world. Before that time, the Middle East had taken first place, influencing neighbors and neighbors' neighbors, even across long distances, because aspects of the way of living familiar to men in the Middle East struck others as definitely superior to what they themselves had previously known. But as the civilizations of India, Greece, and China assumed distinctive shapes, the bearers of these civilizations ceased to feel any inferiority vis-à-vis the Middle East and became correspondingly impervious to influences issuing from such an alien source. On the margins, barbarians now had several variant models of civilized life from which to choose, and often sought to mix elements of one civilization with aspects of another in order to retain a fuller autonomy for themselves.

The four distinctive civilized styles of life which had arisen in the Old World by 500 B.C. were roughly equivalent to each other. Throughout the ensuing centuries, growth and modification within each of these civilizations never ceased. The area of the earth occupied by each civilization tended to expand. This, of course, increased the bulk and variety within each civilized heartland and reduced the insulating barbarian zones between. Contact from one end of Eurasia to the other tended, despite some setbacks, to in-

Timeline chart (read left column as dates, B.C. above 1 AD, A.D. below):

B.C. / A.D.	WESTERN EUROPE	EASTERN EUROPE	MIDDLE EAST AND NORTH AFRICA	EURASIAN STEPPE	CHINA	INDIA AND SOUTHEAST ASIA	OTHER
	Celtic expansion	Persian wars — Xerxes; PERSIAN EMPIRE; Athenian empire; Peloponnesian war; Hippocrates	PERSIAN EMPIRE		*Confucius*	*Buddha*	
400	Gauls sack Rome				warring states		
300	Rome unites Italy	Plato; Aristotle; Euclid; MACEDONIAN EMPIRE				Alexander's conquest; MAURYAN EMPIRE	
200	Hannibal's war	Praxiteles; Aristarchus of Samos	SELEUCIDS; PTOLEMIES		Shih Huang-ti unites China	Asoka	
	RISE OF ROME — FIRST CLOSURE OF THE ECUMENE	Hipparchus					
100	Lucretius; Cicero; Vergil; JULIUS CAESAR			HSIUNG-NU	HAN DYNASTY; Ssu-ma Ch'ien	spread of Indian culture to southeast Asia	
1 AD	AUGUSTUS	CRUCIFIXION; St. Paul; Jewish revolt: destruction of the temple; Gospels written	PARTHIANS	KUSHANS			
	Claudius; Domitian; Tacitus			TURKISH DOMINANCE			
100	Trajan	Jewish revolt					
	Marcus Aurelius	codification of Greek science: Galen, Ptolemy				reinvigoration of Hinduism	
200	civil war and invasion; Plotinus; Mani			EPHTHALITES; Attila; JUAN-JUAN	barbarian invasions	decimal numbers	"classic" period in Amerindian civilizations begins
300	restoration of Roman empire; Huns; CHRISTIANITY BECOMES OFFICIAL RELIGION			SANIAN DYNASTY	SPREAD OF BUDDHISM	classical Sanskrit; Kalidasa; GUPTAS	
400	GERMANIC INVASIONS; sack of Rome; St. Augustine; St. Patrick; Clovis						Ghana in West Africa

Banner across center: THE ECUMENE

500
- St. Benedict
- JUSTINIAN partial restoration of Roman or Byzantine empire
- Buddhism established in Japan
- Polynesian dispersal begins

600
- Slav infiltration into Balkans — AVARS
- Mohammed — ISLAMIC CONQUESTS
- SUI DYNASTY / CHINA REUNITED
- Nara period in Japan

700
- Austrasian invasion
- Moslems in Spain, battle of Tours
- Leo III, the Isaurian, Moslem repulse
- iconoclastic controversy
- OMMAYADS
- Chinese control of oases of central Asia
- Li Po
- printing invented
- Moslems in Sind

800
- Charlemagne, Roman emperor
- battle of Talas
- Uighur empire
- Tibet
- overthrow of Buddhism
- Shankara
- end of classic period of Amerindian culture

900
- Viking, Magyar, Arab invasions
- BULGARS
- ABBASID CALIPHATE
- T'ANG DYNASTY
- TURKISH DOMINANCE

1000
- Cluniac reform
- conversion of Magyars and of Norway
- conversion of Rus, Basil II, Byzantine recovery, final East-West schism
- Papal reform, battle of Manzikert
- ibn-Sina
- Islamic conversion of steppe tribes
- compass, gunpowder invented
- Mohammed of Ghazni; conquest of northern India
- Lady Murasaki

1100
- St. Anselm, Abelard
- Hellenic Renaissance
- FIRST CRUSADE
- al-Ghazali, Omar Khayyam
- ibn-Rushd
- SUNG DYNASTY
- Chu Hsi
- slave sultanate of Delhi

1200
- St. Francis
- fourth crusade
- Alexander Nevsky — TURKISH
- MONGOL DOMINANCE
- Rumi
- Genghis Khan
- EMPIRE
- TURKISH DOMINANCE

1300
- collapse of the Hohenstaufen empire
- St. Thomas Aquinas
- Papacy at Avignon
- Dante
- battle of Kossovo
- BLACK DEATH EPIDEMIC
- Hafiz, ibn-Khaldun
- Persian art at its peak
- Tamerlane
- Cheng-ho voyages to India
- MING DYNASTY
- Chichen Itza in Yucatan

1400
- Great Schism
- Hundred Year's war, Italian Renaissance
- capture of Constantinople by Turks
- capture of Granada
- Kabir
- TURKISH DOMINANCE
- Aztecs in Mexico
- Incas in Peru

123

crease in frequency as the centuries passed. This permitted leaders of one culture to borrow or adapt items from other civilizations which happened to interest them. Such cross-cultural borrowing was, indeed, one of the principal stimuli to innovation within each separate civilization. Yet such borrowings were always voluntary, spontaneous, never forced.

In other words, each of the major civilizations of the Old World retained its autonomy for a two-thousand-year period. The relationship between the four may be thought of as an equilibrium. Any important disturbance tended to affect other parts of the system, but no one civilization ever attained such scale or power as fundamentally to alter the fourfold balance of the whole.

The equilibrium among the world's civilizations did, nonetheless, suffer a series of shocks which constitute the major bench marks of world history during this period. First Greek and then Indian civilization spread widely beyond their original borders. Yet the Hellenization of the Middle East, like the Indianization of China and Japan, proved in the end to be only a superficial, temporary phenomenon. In both cases strong native reactions eventually repudiated most of the alien elements accepted eagerly in earlier generations. Then for a third time the world's balance seemed threatened by the sudden rise of Islam and its successive stages of expansion, first throughout the ancient Middle East, north Africa, and Spain (632–1000), and then into India, eastern Europe, and central Asia (1000–1453). India, indeed, lost political independence entirely and Hindu culture ceased to be fully autonomous. Moslem overlords and rulers joined forces with converts to Islam (who were drawn mainly from the lower castes) to put Hinduism under restrictions and pressures that profoundly affected its subsequent development.

Still a fourth disturbance, emanating this time from western Europe, finally upset the cultural balance of the earth. The process began after A.D. 1500 when European enterprise first opened the Americas and explored the rest of the earth's habitable coastlines. Yet in a real sense, it was not until 1850 that the Western world attained such crushing superiority over the other major civilizations of the earth as to compel the leaders of all non-Western societies to abandon their ancestors' ancient ways and surrender their age-old cultural autonomies in order to enter upon a desperate effort to "modernize" by borrowing skills from the West.

Consideration of this, the modern period of world history, will be reserved for the third part of this book. In Part II we will deal with the intervening period, when more definitely than at earlier or in later times, each separate part of the civilized world went its own way, paying only marginal attention to what was happening elsewhere.

VIII

The Flowering of Greek Civilization

500–336 B.C.

N 499 B.C. the Greek cities of Ionia rebelled against the Persian rule they had acknowledged since 546 B.C. when Cyrus the Great had conquered Asia Minor from King Croesus of Lydia. Five years later the revolt was suppressed. Miletus, the leading city of the Ionian coast, was sacked. Victory in this first round of war between Greeks and Persians rested clearly with the latter. Nevertheless, King Darius was not satisfied, for Athens and Eretria, two obscure Greek cities, had dared to send a few ships from across the Aegean to aid the rebels. A punitive expedition, sent in 490 B.C., plundered Eretria but failed to capture Athens. To be sure the Persians did land at Marathon, twenty-six miles from Athens, expecting treason from within to open the city's gates. But the scheme failed. The Athenians won a brisk skirmish at Marathon by attacking the Persians as they re-embarked on their ships, and a runner brought the news to Athens before the Persian fleet could arrive (hence our modern "marathon" races). As a result, when the Persian ships did show up the traitors in Athens made no move, and the discomfited invaders then withdrew across the Aegean.

These clashes were the prelude to a serious attempt on the part of the Persians to conquer European Greece. In 480 B.C., Xerxes, King Darius' son and successor, mustered his imperial field army, some 60,000 strong, for the attempt. The Persians made very elaborate preparations indeed. A floating bridge was constructed across the Hellespont, supplies were stored at depots all along the Thracian coast, and diplomatic missions were sent to persuade the Greeks to submit. Many cities and the influential Greek oracle at Delphi decided to accept Persian terms before it was too late. But some twenty cities, loosely confederated under Spartan leadership, refused to yield. A Spartan detachment vainly attempted to stop the Persian host at Thermopylae in the north. The Athenians then were compelled to evacuate their city, which was plundered and burned by the advancing Persians.

Yet until the Greeks submitted, such victories remained indecisive, for the Persians had great difficulty in supplying their army in an unfriendly and ravaged land. Xerxes therefore tried to bring matters to a head by attacking the Greek fleet, which had taken refuge in the Bay of Salamis just east of Athens. In the narrow strait between the island of Salamis and the mainland the superior numbers of the Persian fleet could not be brought to bear, so that the Greeks, by skillful and resolute maneuvering, were able to win a decisive victory (480 B.C.). After this failure, Xerxes decided that he and the larger part of his army would have to return to Persia, since supplies sufficient to feed the entire force over the winter were simply not available in Greece.

Next spring, accordingly, a sharply reduced Persian force confronted the combined armies of the Greek cities at Plataea, where, once again, victory rested with the Greeks (479 B.C.). Simultaneously, the Athenians carried the war across the Aegean, where the mere appearance of their warships encouraged a number of Ionian cities to revolt.

The Persians never again undertook full-scale operations against Greece. Hostilities dragged on until 446 B.C. Almost annually the leagued Greek cities dispatched a fleet early in the summer to attack Persian strongholds along the Aegean coast; and each fall the fleet came back, almost always with some new success to its credit. Athens took the lead in these operations since Sparta, the greatest land power of the Greek world, refused to continue active operations after the immediate threat of Persian invasion faded.

ATHENIAN EMPIRE
c. 432 B.C.

⬚ Athenian Empire ⬚ Spartan Allies

Effects of Athenian naval warfare. The indefinite prolongation of naval warfare brought great changes to the internal balance of the Athenian polis. Citizens who owned little or nothing could always serve as rowers in the warships. They thus rendered a military service to their polis that became just as important as service in the phalanx. The fleet, in other words, gave a major military role even to the poorest citizens, who had formerly been unable to afford the equipment needed to fight with the phalanx. Moreover, the pay for rowing service together with the chance of picking up some rich booty from the sack of a new-won town became, for a large number of Athenian citizens, a very welcome addition to their annual income.

Even before the great Persian invasion, Athens had become a democratic city. But at first the voting rights of the poorer citizens were insecure, being more the result of efforts by aristocratic politicians to find new support among the lower classes than of any effective strength or organization among the poor themselves. But when rowing in the fleet became a normal summer's occupation, the poor took on a military role that entitled them to be heard in affairs of state. The democratic constitution thus became secure for the first time. Old-fashioned farmer-infantrymen were pushed to the margins of Athenian political life. They lived too far from the city to attend the meetings of the assembly regularly, whereas when the fleet was at home, the urban poor often had little else with which to occupy their time.

Very soon Athens' eager pursuit of aggressive naval war alarmed some of the more conservative Greek cities. In 467 B.C., for example, the island of Naxos declined to send the usual contingent of ships and men to war against the Persians. The Athenians interpreted this as treason. They turned their armament against Naxos, defeated the islanders, and assessed a money tribute. Subsequently other allies were treated in the same way. As a result, what had begun as a free league of cities against Persia by degrees became an Athenian empire, which at its height exercised dominion over some fifty cities, great and small, scattered all around the Aegean.

Despite the democratic form of Athenian public life, for a long time the city's leaders and military commanders continued to come

After their surprising success against the imperial majesty of Persia, the Greeks came to feel extraordinary confidence in themselves and in their way of life. Awed no longer by the pomp and secret wisdom of the East, sublimely sure of themselves and eager to explore the world within and about them, Athenians in particular and other Greeks in somewhat lesser degree, found themselves able to combine thought and action in such a way that each supported and urged the other onward. Who, after all, could doubt the essential goodness and excellence of Athenian institutions when the city had won and continued to win such successes overseas? And yet who could doubt that there was much to learn from the new experiences, strange new products, and novel ideas that converged upon a city that had so suddenly become the mistress of the eastern Mediterranean? The Athenians were proud of their past, committed to their present, and eager to explore anything new in their future. Imbued with supremely venturesome confidence, they proceeded to give classical expression to almost every aspect of Greek culture: drama, philosophy, history, rhetoric, architecture, and sculpture.

Drama. "Goat songs" honoring the god of wine, Dionysus, were sung by masked choruses in several Greek cities, but only in Athens did these crude beginnings develop into tragedy. In the course of the fifth century B.C. music, staging, costumes, and dancing all became much more elaborate. Choruses began to undergo prolonged training when it became customary to conduct competitions for the best performance at the great festivals of Dionysus. Antiphonal singing between leader and chorus developed into dramatic dialogue. Presently, two actors were presented on the stage simultaneously, later as many as three. With this development, the chorus retreated from the center of attention and assumed a secondary role, commenting, warning, or setting the mood for the action of the play whose main thread was now carried by the actors.

The tragic performances of ancient Athens presented a magnificent spectacle. All male citizens could attend freely, for the festivals were still regarded as public acts of worship. The cost of putting on each performance was met by rich men who found satisfaction in competing for the prize. Even the most stupid citizen could respond to the rhythms of dance, song, and language — for the words were sung by the chorus and the actors' lines also conformed to poetic meters. These aspects of Greek drama are almost entirely lost to moderns. All that survives is the texts of a few of the plays, together with a number of fragments of others. Yet these mutilated remains continue to arouse admiration, partly because of their poetic greatness, partly because of the ideas they express. This admiration is and remains genuine because the tragic poets of ancient Athens took advantage of the traditional celebrations handed down to them to construct stories that confronted fundamental problems of human life. In doing so they touched upon themes that command perennial interest, being in some sense universal to all men.

Three great poets worked this remarkable transformation of the ancient goat songs: Aeschylus (525–456 B.C.), Sophocles (496–406 B.C.), and Euripides (484 or 480–406 B.C.). For their subject matter they drew on the common stock of stories about gods and men which had been handed down from immemorial antiquity — what we call myth, but what the Greeks themselves thought of as ancient history. But the tragic poets seem to have felt free to alter details of the traditional stories if it suited their purposes to do so. They exercised their own personal insight and imagination even more freely in trying to explain the relations of gods to men, of fate to free will, and of private to public duty — to mention only a few of the themes they dealt with.

Yet although all three of the great tragedians remained faithful to conventional forms and limits, it does not take much penetration to recognize that with Euripides tragedy was beginning to lose its usefulness for the exploration of serious moral and theological questions. The older poets, Aeschylus and Sophocles, shared traditional pieties with the majority of their audience. The changes, adjustments, subtleties, and queries they brought to bear upon traditional moral and religious ideas did not disrupt but rather enlarged and reconfirmed the general structure and validity of old viewpoints by giving them poignant and sophisticated expression. Not so Euripides. He had grown up in a later generation, when traditional convictions had already eroded among intellectually inclined young Athenians. Yet in public Euripides had to conform — or pretend to conform. Anything else would have been felt as a desecration of what was, after all, a religious ceremony. He solved his problem by almost scornfully bringing forth some formula of conventional piety. This served to unravel the plot or save a situation which, on the human dramatic level, Euripides presented in an iconoclastic way that implicitly contradicted the glib and easy answers his divine messengers and oracles provided for the difficulties of life.

Clearly, what had happened was that the intellectual elite of Athens no longer shared the presuppositions of the mass of the citizenry. A man like Euripides no longer believed in the reality or powers of a god like Dionysus, whose festival he, as a tragic poet, was required to celebrate! Small wonder, therefore, that after his time no other great poet rose in Athens to carry on the tragic tradition. Instead, it soon became customary to revive the classic tragedies. Fresh dramatic creation was confined to comedy, where wit, suspense, and the foibles of human character could be explored without raising any of the deeper issues of the human condition as the tragedians had, throughout the fifth century, been able and eager to do.

Philosophy. Philosophers took over where the tragedians left off. This is attested by the dialogue form assumed by most of Plato's writings. The great advantage of philosophic dialogue was that it need not conform to outworn conventions, nor did it have to appeal to the entire citizen body of the Athenian polis. Any reflective, leisured man familiar with Attic Greek and curious about the nature of things could read what Plato wrote: he could agree or disagree, read and reread the dialogues, or discard them as futile. But neither author nor reader depended on the assent of the crowd and the approval of public officials who were responsible for arranging traditional religious celebrations. Dramatic poets were bound by all these ties. Hence when a pervasive and basic rapport between the mass public and the most advanced thinkers of Athens ceased to prevail — a circumstance already hampering Euripides — further investigation into the nature of man and his place in the world could only occur through the more private, personal medium of philosophic dialogue.

Athens had not been an important early center of Greek thought. But when she became mistress of the Aegean, philosophers as well as other strangers converged upon the city. The temper of the Athenian populace was distrustful. Thus, for example, a famous philosopher and personal friend of Pericles, named Anaxagoras, was exiled for impiety, having argued that the sun was not a god but merely a red-hot stone.

Another group of wise men, the sophists, met a much warmer reception in Athens. Their profession was to train young men in the art of rhetoric. Speaking well was, of course, very necessary for a political career in a democratic city such as Athens, for nothing important could be done without persuading the Assembly of the citizens. But when teachers and pupils began to think and talk about words and speeches, they soon became aware of the fact that language and argument had rules and were themselves subject to analysis. This was a very exciting discovery. Some of the sophists appear to have believed that a thorough mastery of the rules of logical argument would unlock all the mysteries of the universe if men had but the wit and daring to do so.

The sophists distrusted mere custom and habit. Such an attitude could be very disruptive, for in the cold light of logic what binding force was there in the polis law itself, which varied from city to city and from nation to nation in an utterly illogical way? Why should not a bold and courageous man penetrate the veil of convention and base his action upon the nature of things, to be discovered through precise manipulation of the logical tools of language? Indeed why not? Especially if the bold young man in question happened to belong to a political faction or social class that had little chance of winning control of the government through constitutional procedures. Hence it was mainly young men of wealth who felt the fascination of the radical sophist challenge to the legal frame within which public life proceeded. Sophistry justified them in their withdrawal of loyalty from the polis, for they were the men who found the demands placed upon them by the democratic polis of Athens to be a more and more unwelcome burden — especially during the disastrous years of the long war with Sparta (431–404 B.C.).

During these same years another enigmatic figure wrestled with the moral and political questions that had been raised by the sophists. His name was Socrates (d. 399 B.C.), a native Athenian, who served as soldier and magistrate when called upon to do so, and who yet could not persuade himself that the laws and government of Athens were really just, wise, or good. Socrates spent his time arguing in public places with anyone who cared to risk the shock of discovering, under Socrates' insistent and incisive questioning, how inadequate his opinions and convictions really were.

Socrates wrote nothing. He is known to us mainly through Plato's dialogues, in which he almost invariably plays the role of interlocutor. Plato's portrait may be retouched to make Socrates conform to Plato's own views and preferences. The comic poet Aristophanes (d. 380 B.C.) and the historian Xenophon (d. 354 B.C.) also left literary portraits of Socrates that bear small resemblance to Plato's protagonist. Yet despite obscurities, it is clear that Socrates, like his disciple Plato, was a radical conservative. In effect, he attempted to use the sophists' tools of linguistic and logical analysis to support traditional values, hierarchies, and standards by finding a universal truth or reality behind mere conventions of the here and now. It is far from clear whether or not Socrates ever satisfied himself that he had found such universal truths. Yet when a cabal of democratic politicians brought him to trial in 399 B.C. on the charge of having corrupted the youth and of disbelieving in the gods of Athens, he preferred to die rather than repudiate his mode of life. He asserted that he must obey the dictates of justice first and always, even at the risk of colliding with man-made laws such as those according to which the Athenians condemned and executed him.

Plato (427–347 B.C.) was a young man when Socrates took poison and died according to Athenian law. Like many of the other Athenian young men who had gathered around Socrates to hear him deflate the pretensions of upstarts, Plato was of noble birth, and even claimed descent from Athens' early kings. Perhaps for this reason, the great issue for Plato was always political: how to put things right so that good men would rule and justice prevail. But true reform required true knowledge, without which one man's opinion was no better then another's, and there could be no escape from the harsh party strife which was tearing Athens apart. To the pursuit of this sort of knowledge he therefore dedicated his life. In doing so, he brought together almost all the strands of earlier Greek thought and gave to subsequent Western philosophy much of its vocabulary and many of its most central problems: for example, the relation of soul and body, knowledge and opinion, idea and reality, and naïve but necessary questions as to the nature of the Good, the True, and the Beautiful.

Plato wrote two dialogues in which he sketched an ideal state founded upon truth and justice; but when he tried to translate his ideas into practice he met with utter failure. This happened at Syracuse in Sicily, for the statesman who had invited Plato to come proved unable to persuade the youthful tyrant of that city to submit to the regimen of studies Plato prescribed. Toward the end of his life Plato appears to have found in intellectual activity and writing a partial substitute for political leadership, which he felt belonged to him by right, but which his rigid and unpopular views made impossible in a democratic city like Athens. The Academy which he established became a center for philosophic, mathematical, and scientific work. It maintained itself as a going concern for more than 900 years — longer than any modern university has yet done — and for most of that time made Athens the major center of higher education in the classical world.

Aristotle (384–322 B.C.) was a member of the Academy for many years before he set up his own school, the Lyceum. He took naturally to the life of a professional thinker. No question under the sun — or above it for that matter — lay outside the scope of Aristotle's interest. He worked out a comprehensive, closely reasoned philosophy that provided moderate, common-sense answers to everything of importance, and left remarkably few loose ends for his followers to cope with.

After Aristotle's time, the Greek cities lost real independence, and the political spark went out of Greek life. Philosophy more and more became a guide to life, attuned to the needs of the rich and well-educated men of the Greek world. Really disturbing new thoughts and new information became taboo when the central thrust of philosophy became the task of defining a reasonable code of conduct for the well-born. With this change, the first greedy reach after truth — the eager ambition of the sophists, the tenacious search for certainty to which Socrates and Plato devoted their lives, and the voracious appetite for new knowledge which had inspired Aristotle's intellect — all faded away. The great age of Greek philosophy thus came to a close. Yet the body of ideas the philosophers had expressed, and the variety of questions about the nature of the world and of human thought, belief, and knowledge they had raised, remained to haunt later generations and inspired them with a degree of sophistication about the complexities of truth which earlier thinkers, and men unacquainted with the Greek tradition of philosophy, could never equal. The bold effort to apprehend the world by use of human reason, which the Ionian philosophers had launched in the sixth century B.C., and which was broadened and deepened so energetically in Athens during the fifth and fourth centuries B.C., was therefore not in vain, despite the eventual fraying out of faith in the powers of human reason which became apparent after Aristotle's death.

Science, rhetoric, history. The main development of Greek science came after the Macedonian conquest (338 B.C.) had brought Athens' great age to a close. Nevertheless, geometry and geometric astronomy attracted serious attention on the part of Plato and other philosophers, and Aristotle very persuasively systematized physics. Simultaneously, Hippocrates of Cos (*c.* 460–370 B.C.) founded an influential school of medicine which emphasized careful observation and diagnosis, and interpreted disease not as a result of seizure by evil spirits — the usual Middle Eastern view — but as the consequence of an imbalance of fluids (known as "humors") within the body.

Rhetoric enjoyed a very high place in Greek education. Skilled public speaking was a political necessity in democratic states and was much admired even after it lost its practical political function. Study and practice of the art of speaking generated rules of correctness, and in the end elegant and graceful elocution became an object of admiration for itself, whether or not the speaker had anything important to say. Degeneration of rhetoric into a polite accomplishment only occurred after polis sovereignty had ended. Until that time (and sporadically afterward) citizen assemblies had to deal with pressing matters which provided rhetoricians with an urgent and inescapable subject matter.

History as a distinct discipline was created by the researches of Herodotus of Halicarnassus (d. c.425 B.C.). Herodotus composed a charming and discursive account of the Persian wars, in order, as he himself says, to give "due meed of glory" to both Greeks and barbarians. He portrayed the war as a struggle between freedom and slavery and clearly believed that the surprising Greek victory proved the superiority of free, self-governing communities over even the greatest of monarchies, where all men had to bow before the will of the king. Athens was the hero of Herodotus' story, but he was always aware that men remained under the gods, and were subject to a fate which they could not control. Boasting and vainglory invited divine retribution — a theme that recurs over and over again in Herodotus' pages and which he used to explain the failure of Xerxes' invasion.

Thucydides (d. c. 400 B.C.), the second master historian among the Greeks, grew up in Athens when sophistry and rationalism were in full career. He could not believe with Herodotus that the gods intervened directly in human affairs. Instead, Thucydides thought that the body politic was like the human body, liable to disordering disease through imbalance of its parts. His subject was the long, fratricidal struggle between Athens and Sparta that began in 431 B.C. Its tortuous course, provoking civil strife on top of inter-city war, gave him ample opportunity to observe distempers in the public life of the Greek cities.

Thucydides was not at first a passive observer of the war. In 424 B.C. the Athenians elected him general, but then exiled him when he failed to prevent a serious military setback. Thereafter Thucydides took no active part in public affairs. Instead he set out to discover precisely what had been said and done on either side, in the hope perhaps of diagnosing the evils of the body politic as a necessary preliminary to being able to cure them.

Thucydides never became a cool and dispassionate observer. Nor could he simply dismiss morals and belief in the supernatural ordering of human affairs. Toward the end, as Athens entered its death struggle, Thucydides the Athenian probably began to believe that he was witnessing the punishment meted out by inscrutable divine power to a city that had defied justice, being puffed up with an overweening pride that fed upon its own success. When Thucydides saw his theme conforming to this pattern, he began to recast his narrative, making Athens take on the role of tragic hero, betrayed by flaws inherent in her own greatness. He thus applied the tradition of the tragedians to contemporary history, using the medium of prose. Herodotus had similarly carried forward the epic tradition with his history of the latest collision between Europe and Asia, one of whose earlier incidents Homer's *Iliad* had chronicled.

By combining exactitude of detail with penetrating analysis and an intense controlled passion at the spectacle presented by Athens' downfall, Thucydides made a reality of his proud claim to have written "not a prize essay for the moment, but a possession forever."

Architecture and sculpture. Among the Greeks of the classical age monumental architecture was almost entirely limited to the construction of temples and other public buildings. Traditional forms confined the architect's task to the refinement of proportion and perfection of detail. But care expended on such matters as the slight curvature of the profile of the columns and of the floor upon which they rested, gave the finished structure an optical precision and grace that could not otherwise have been attained.

Enough original sculpture survives from the fifth and fourth centuries B.C. to allow us to perceive for ourselves the technical mastery Greek sculptors attained. Later critics hailed Phidias (d. *c.*434 B.C.) as the greatest of all sculptors, but nothing that can be certainly assigned to his hand survives, although he planned the sculptural decorations of the Parthenon and may have executed some of them. His masterworks, the cult statue of Athena in Athens and of Zeus at Olympia, were finished in ivory and gold. They both, being precious, have utterly disappeared. But literary descriptions make it clear that Phidias gave these great statues an aloof majesty and serene beauty that left a strong impression even in later ages when men had ceased to take the gods of Olympus seriously. Like Sophocles the tragedian or Herodotus the historian, Phidias lived at the point in time when old beliefs and pieties still seemed valid, needing only a more precise and adequate expression. Phidias did with gold and ivory what the others did with words: reshaping and enriching older conceptions, and attuning them to the more sophisticated age in which he lived.

Later sculptors continued to command extraordinary skill, but the serene self-confidence and inner harmony which Phidias had expressed could not be recaptured by later generations. A more self-conscious, theatrical style came in, which aimed to surprise or amaze the observer. Late portraits of the gods, such as the famous Hermes of Praxiteles (d. c.320 B.C.), entirely lack Phidias' majesty. The grace and beauty of idealized humanity were thoroughly within Praxiteles' reach. Yet his Hermes seems neither great nor powerful — more a pretty plaything of the imagination than a ruler of the world.

In every field of endeavor of which we have record, therefore, Athenian certainties and self-confidence, so buoyant during the first years after the Persian wars, developed toward a more diverse, divided, and complicated outlook. Division brought dissension and sometimes provoked disillusionment. But energies that had been raised so high took a long time to dissipate themselves, and Greek cultural forms remained capable of affecting other peoples for many centuries after the first bloom of Athens' great age had faded.

Social change after the Peloponnesian war. The political and social evolution of Greece confirmed, perhaps even provoked, this cultural transformation. After the Peloponnesian war ended (404 B.C.), muted hostility between rich and poor became chronic in most Greek cities. Distrust and fear divided one class from the other. The old psychological solidarity nurtured by common service in the phalanx disappeared as citizens ceased, save in unusual circumstances, to take direct part in military campaigns.

Athenian dominion gave way to Spartan supremacy. Despite

their claim to have fought for the "liberty of the Greeks," the Spartans proved themselves taskmasters at least as harsh as the Athenians had been. Athenian power therefore soon revived; but it was the city of Thebes that first crushed Sparta on the battlefield (371 B.C.) and thus inaugurated a short-lived Theban supremacy over Greece. Intervention of the still semi-barbarian kingdom of Macedon then brought a far stronger political unit into the very center of Greek politics. But even after Macedonian military superiority had been definitively demonstrated at the battle of Chaeronea (338 B.C.), the Greeks continued to nurse a stubborn longing for local autonomy and polis independence, so that any weakening of Macedonian power stirred hope of liberation from what was in fact an extremely light yoke.

Yet after 338 B.C. the scale of economic and military organization had changed, so that separate city-states no longer exercised genuine sovereignty. A well-trained phalanx remained indispensable, but could best be had for hire. The old-fashioned citizen army depended, after all, on the sense of mutuality among the members of the phalanx. Since citizens no longer fully trusted one another, thanks to the bitterness fostered during the party struggles that everywhere accompanied the Peloponnesian war, most citizen armies could no longer function effectively. Professional troops therefore began to supplement and then to supplant citizen armies, especially for expeditions to distant parts where the campaign might last for several years. Citizens who owned enough land or other income-producing property to support themselves preferred to stay at home and eschewed the hard, heroic role their forefathers had believed to be the only one suitable for free men and responsible citizens.

As this occurred, a private sphere of life began to widen its claims on men's attention, and politics relaxed its all-engulfing hold on the Greek imagination and emotion. Poor, disenfranchised citizens, landless men, refugees, foreigners, and slaves became more numerous in the Greek world. Even citizens who continued to have a legal voice in public affairs found the privilege increasingly hollow. Single and separate cities, where the citizens' voices could perhaps still be heard, had lost control of their own fates. Greece as a whole, for that matter, had become a mere pawn on a military and diplomatic chess board which was dominated by governments commanding professional armies and navies and financial resources vastly greater than any city could hope to match.

With the decisive loss of local polis sovereignty — an event signalized by the Macedonian conquest in 338 B.C. — Greek civilization and culture lost much of its initial *élan*. Only an elite could share the refinements of philosophy as elaborated by Plato, or understand the nuances of disbelief expressed by Praxiteles' statue. The humble, uneducated, poverty-stricken multitude went one way while the rich and well-born went another; and the polis solidarities which had briefly linked them into a single whole survived only weakly and in memory, not as living reality.

Greek civilization had still a brilliant future ahead, and its power of geographical expansion had, in fact, barely begun to manifest itself when this inner erosion set it. The greatness of the initial achievement was such that men in far parts of the earth and living long afterward continued and still continue to respond with a special vibrancy to the surviving monuments of the Athenian golden age. Fundamental and enduring lines of subsequent European thought and sensibility had found their first and clearest expression in the work of these few Greeks.

Such innovation did not go unnoticed at the time. We shall therefore turn next to the manner in which neighboring peoples reacted to the Greek achievement, and in reacting forwarded the expansion of a Hellenistic style of civilization.

IX

The Spread of Hellenistic Civilization

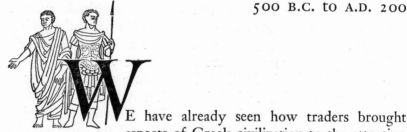

E have already seen how traders brought aspects of Greek civilization to the attention of barbarian chieftains in such backwoods regions of the Mediterranean world as Scythia, northern Italy, and Gaul. (See above pp. 87–8 and 111–12.) Closer to the Aegean center, the kingdom of Macedon acquired a somewhat deeper tincture of the Greek style of life as a prelude to conquering the heartland of Greek civilization itself. How this happened is quite instructive, for other border states have often been able to profit similarly from their position on the margins of a civilization to build a territorially larger and therefore militarily stronger power, capable, when organized with civilized efficiency, of conquering smaller rivals nearer the old center of culture.

Macedonian conquest. Macedonian kings made their courts into schools of Greek manners. The tragedian Euripides, for example, spent some time as an honored guest at the royal court of Macedon, and Aristotle tutored Alexander the Great. No doubt the Macedonian kings felt genuine admiration for Greek civilization for its own sake. But their policy of Hellenization had additional advantages. Young Macedonian noblemen on coming to court naturally acquired Greek tastes; but having done so, soon discovered that they could not lead the life of their choice anywhere but at court and in the king's service. The reason for this was that the Macedonian countryside was inhabited by a free and sturdy peasantry whose chiefs might indeed lead them into battle but could not extract heavy rents and dues from them. Hence a backwoods noble had no source of cash income such as was needed if imported Greek wares were to be paid for privately. The monarchy, deriving income from mines and from conquered cities and other dependencies, was able to import the luxuries required to live in a civilized way, and to distribute them among deserving servants of the king. In this way the Macedonian kings could maintain a corps of loyal and obedient yet proudly free and noble officers and royal agents.

When such officers of the crown undertook to teach Macedonian peasants the tactics of Greek phalanx warfare, they quickly created an overwhelming military machine. The Macedonians were numerous, hardy, and tough. They were also accustomed to obeying their superiors who now, for the first time, were willing to follow the king and give up the fierce local feuds which had previously made the Macedonian nobility utterly intractable. King Philip of Macedon (ruled 359–336 B.C.) was the first to reap the full benefit of the new configuration of forces within his country. He conquered neighboring barbarous lands — Illyria, Thrace — and then turned upon Greece. Everywhere his army met with success, presaging the even more brilliant victories that came to Macedonian arms under his son Alexander (ruled 336–323 B.C.).

Alexander's career directed Hellenism eastward. His army marched against Persia in 334 B.C. and everywhere consciously championed Greek ways. After 330 B.C., when the last Persian monarch, Darius III, was killed by his own courtiers, Alexander claimed to be the legitimate successor and avenger of the murdered monarch. Yet he did not thereby abandon his role as founder of cities — on the Greek model — and exemplar of the Greek heroic ideal. Alexander aspired to conquer the whole world, and was bitterly disappointed when his weary troops, after subduing the easternmost reaches of the Persian empire and invading northwestern India, refused to press forward into the Ganges valley. After a difficult return trip, in the course of which Alexander and his soldiers followed the Indus to its mouth and then marched overland to Babylon, the ever-victorious Macedonian died suddenly of a fever (323 B.C.).

Alexander's unexpected death, less than twelve years after he had launched his army on its great venture, became a signal for the outbreak of strife among his generals. His posthumous son and heir was among the early victims. Only after nearly half a century of warfare did three more or less stable monarchies emerge, each ruled by a Macedonian general's descendants: the Ptolemies in Egypt, the Seleucids in Asia, and the Antigonids in Macedonia. Of the three, Ptolemaic Egypt was at first the strongest. As a sea power the Ptolemies disputed control of the Aegean with the Antigonids, while on land they simultaneously quarreled with the Seleucids for primacy in Palestine and Syria.

Greek emigration. Both the Ptolemaic and Seleucid empires depended in considerable part upon Greek immigrants. Thousands of Greeks swarmed out of their homeland in the wake of Alexander's conquest in hope of finding fortunes in foreign parts. Some became government officials and administrators, others entered military service and some settled as farmers in special military colonies. But the great majority became city folk, pursuing hundreds of different occupations both in government service and in business and the free professions — working as merchants, doctors, architects, scribes, tax farmers, professional athletes, actors, and the like.

Massive emigration was both a symptom and a cause of economic setback in Greece itself. Within a century of Alexander's conquest we hear of deserted fields and empty villages. More and more the Greek countryside was abandoned by citizen farmers. Slaves and foreigners took their place. In a sense these changes simply made the society of Greece conform to a pattern already age-old in the Middle East. The close linkage between farmers and city folk, which had prevailed for a while during the first flowering of Greek culture, disappeared. A wide and all but unbridgeable social and psychological gap opened between the upper classes of the towns (many of them now landowners, drawing rents from the country) and the crude peasantry. Almost as great a gap also divided the poor of the city from the rich and educated classes who

The Development of Greek Sculpture

A POLIS WARRIOR AND CITIZEN

Aristion (the name, engraved on the base, means "good" or "noble") is wearing body armor and holds a spear, but lacks the helmet, sword, and shield that completed a hoplite's panoply.

The style of fighting and of living that made a nobleman like Aristion voluntarily dismount and join as an equal the ranks of ordinary farmer-citizens in Athens' phalanx inaugurated the classical age of Greece. The classical style of art, here seen emerging from archaic stiffness, balanced naturalism (observe the muscles of the forearm) with convention (drapery, hair, and beard) through the exercise of technical skill analogous perhaps to the political skill that kept precarious balance between heroic egoism and personal subordination to the polis during Athens' golden age.

Hirmer Fotoarchiv Munich

Stele of Aristion, 510-500 B.C., from Velanidesa in Attica. National Museum, Athens.

PLATE 1

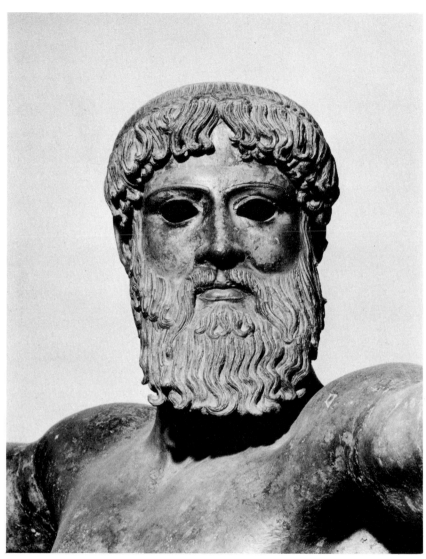

Poseidon, 470-450 B.C., found in the sea off Cape Artemision. National Museum, Athens.

CLASSIC GREEK BEAUTY

Accidents of preservation permit modern eyes to experience the aesthetic force of classical Greek sculpture at its peak only through these (and a few other) minor

PLATE 2

Head of the Athena Lemnia by Phideas, c. 440 B.C., Roman copy. Museo Civico, Bologna.

works. Both the bronze Poseidon (left) and the Lemnian Athena (right) were unknown to art connoisseurs of antiquity and cannot be assigned to any of the famous
sculptors of the fifth century B.C. In all probability we here confront two routine
products of Athenian workshops of that age.

PLATE 3

Portrait of an Unknown Roman, 1st cent. B.C. Museum of Fine Arts, Boston.

THE REPUBLIC AND EMPIRE OF ROME

These two portraits of unknown Romans show what happened when Greek sculptors put their virtuosity to work to please the Roman taste for family portraiture. Through

PLATE 4

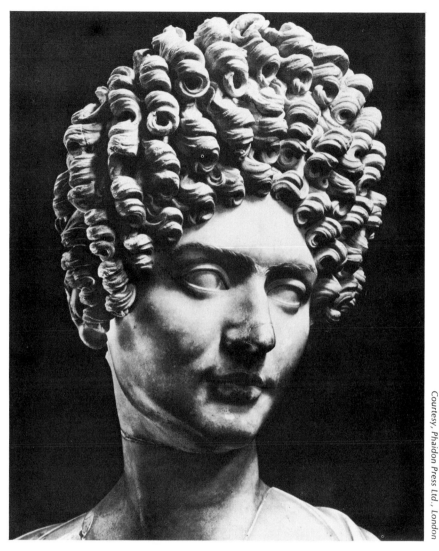

Portrait of a Roman Lady, A.D. 54-117. Palazzo Capitolino, Rome.

its simplicity and apparent realism the head on the left (first century B.C.) expresses the energy, self-discipline, and habit of command which made Rome great. The second bust dates from about a century later, when the elegant artificiality of imperial court life had superimposed itself upon the sterner virtues of the past, just as the lady's towered and patterned curls distract attention from but cannot hide the strong and haughty face beneath.

PLATE 5

Crowned Female Head, 2nd cent. A.D., from Vienne, France. Lyon Museum, France.

HOW CLASSICISM WORE ITSELF OUT

Classicism had become a genteel accomplishment for a landowning few by the second century A.D. when these two heads were made. The crowned female represents the "spirit" of a provincial town in Gaul—a conventional personification

PLATE 6

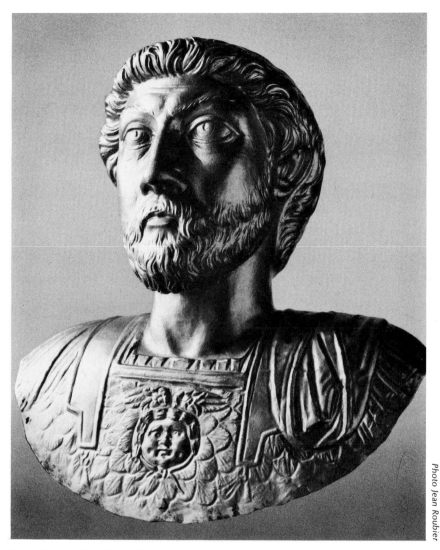

Photo Jean Roubier

Bust of Marcus Aurelius, 2nd cent. A.D. Avenches Museum, Switzerland.

invented in the Hellenistic east a full five centuries before. The skill with which the sculptor duplicated ancient motifs and style was undiminished; but his work looks backward. The bust of the Stoic philosopher and emperor, Marcus Aurelius (right), is technically less accomplished, yet manages to convey a sense of yearning for something better to believe in than worn-out gods and personified cities (like the lady opposite).

PLATE 7

Portrait of Eutropus, 3rd-5th cent. A.D. Kunsthistorisches Museum, Vienna.

THE END OF CLASSICISM

A new style, the Byzantine, begins to define itself in a bust such as this, carved sometime between the third and fifth centuries A.D. The rise of Christianity, barbarian invasions, and the breakup of the Roman Empire coincided with the shift in art illustrated here. Indeed, this bust seems to express disillusion with the world of men and a striving after transcendental truth of the sort upon which early Christianity throve.

PLATE 8

more and more dominated the political as well as the economic scene.

Such polarization of society had long been familiar in the Middle East. It was, indeed, the price of civilization, for technical limitations upon production and transportation made it necessary for some men to be deprived if others were to have the leisure to acquire and elaborate high culture. The classical age itself had not really escaped this limiting condition. Athens had been, in its days of greatness, a predator upon weaker communities all round the Aegean and Black Sea coasts. Citizens of Athens acted together to exploit their advantage, and used their wealth and leisure for public display rather than for private consumption. But collective exploitation at a distance is not necessarily milder than the pressure of a landlord upon peasants close by; and a society of cultivated landlords, with their servitors, attendants, educators, and providers of other professional services is not necessarily less humane or less civilized than an imperial community of equals whose equality is dependent in great part upon an unceasing flow of tribute, plunder, and the gains to be had from such services as the administration of justice among subject peoples.

As Greek high culture came to be the possession of an urban upper class, whose income depended primarily upon land rents or government salaries, it became far more readily exportable. Very special circumstances were required to produce a city like Athens or Sparta. But any landlord, if he commanded a sufficiently large cash income, could acquire a Greek education, learn Greek manners, and become in all respects a Greek without having to alter the social structure of his community as a whole.

As the Greeks penetrated the Middle East, therefore, the increasingly urban, upper-class character of Greek civilization facilitated its spread among the landlords and other men of means who had long dominated local society. The Greek style of life, which included such things as athletics in the nude and dancing girls as well as philosophy and poetry, appealed strongly to many of these men. Greeks, as a rule, were willing to admit such recruits to their circle as soon as the neophytes acquired a suitably Greek education and set of manners. Even humbler folk found it convenient or necessary to learn Greek, which rapidly became the dominant language of the entire eastern Mediterranean, displacing Aramaic from that position within two or three centuries of Alexander's victories.

Religious changes. At first everything seemed to go one way. Middle Eastern peoples borrowed arts and manners from the Greeks while the conquerors found little in the life of their subjects to admire or imitate. Nevertheless, before very long cultural borrowing became a two-way street. In particular, the lower classes of the towns found in Middle Eastern religions a far more adequate explanation of the world than anything available to them from the Greek tradition. No one any longer took the gods of Olympus very seriously. Their worship was inextricably tied up with public ceremonies and city-wide celebrations, whereas the poor and humble of the great cities of the Mediterranean needed a religion that could comfort them in time of personal distress, and help them to hope for a better future, if not in this life then in the next.

Educated gentlemen might still prefer the careful arguments of philosophers, who, despite important differences in detail, all agreed that wisdom required a man to refrain from extremes and not to care about anything too much, lest by caring he allow some outside attachment to disturb his philosophic calm and self-control. As long as life presented no really serious crises, such a prescription for leading a good, noble, and free private life made excellent sense in an age when public affairs were in the hands of distant monarchs and their obsequious servants. But when disaster came, which for the Hellenistic gentlemen of the eastern Mediterranean meant when crude Roman soldiers and governors trampled their gardens and demanded bigger taxes, bribes, and ransoms than they could pay, the comforts of philosophy were distant and too cold to be effective. Under these circumstances the upper classes too began to feel the need for a more personal and emotionally vibrant faith.

Several religions combining Greek with Middle Eastern elements met this need. A few Greeks were attracted to Judaism, which retained its full vigor and emotional conviction. But the repugnance pious Jews felt for some of the Greek habits and customs — in particular the nudity of the gymnasium deeply shocked Jewish sensibility — made any sort of halfway house between the two cultures difficult. Other cults, like those of Mithra, for example, and of Serapis, proved more flexible, and permitted the close marriage of Greek with Middle Eastern ideas and religious rituals. A great reflux toward a theistic interpretation of the world therefore became evident among the Greeks even before the Roman conquest drastically altered the political order of the eastern Mediterranean.

Hellenistic sciences and arts. A second fruitful interaction between Middle Eastern and Greek cultures occurred in the field of astronomy. For several centuries Babylonian observers had accumulated accurate observations of such events as eclipses, and had developed a workable way of locating events in the sky by means of a spherical grid. When the Greeks discovered these tables, they eagerly set out to explain Babylonian data by constructing geometric models of the heavens. Aristarchus of Samos (d. *c.* 230 B.C.) proposed the idea that the earth revolved around the sun, but the fact that the stellar parallax was too small to be observed with the instruments then available discredited this idea. Instead, Hipparchus of Nicaea (d. *c.* 126 B.C.) proposed the scheme which became standard in later centuries. He assumed that the stars and planets were embedded in transparent spheres which revolved around the earth at varying speeds. To account for the occasional retrograde motion of the planets he assumed that a smaller sphere revolved around a point on the surface of the earth-centered sphere and carried the fiery planet on its surface. The observed motion was therefore the sum of two independent motions which sometimes reinforced each other and sometimes worked in opposite directions. This system had the advantage that any new refinement of observation could be accounted for by inventing another sphere whose size, speed, and axis of rotation could be adjusted to produce the observed phenomena.

We are so steeped in Copernican astronomy that it is perhaps hard to understand the enthusiasm with which men accepted this geometric explanation of the heavenly motions. Such complicated machinery seems inherently implausible today; but what impressed everyone at the time and for centuries afterwards was that the mathematical precision of the scheme actually allowed prediction of planetary motions. The ability to predict where the wandering lights of the firmament would in fact find themselves at a particular time in the future seemed a certain guarantee of the correctness of the whole system.

The success of Hellenistic astronomy was further reinforced by its astrological application. The fundamental idea of astrology was that events in the heavens foreshadowed events on earth. After the linkage of Greek mathematics to Babylonian observational records it did in fact become possible to calculate the relative position of the planets at any time — past or future. With such skill, it therefore seemed possible to predict what would happen on earth. By making the assumption that the position of the planets at the time of a man's birth affected his whole life's span, a single calculation gave the key to the future for any individual. This seemed enormously impressive to the ordinary unmathematical mind. Consequently, almost from its inception — mainly at Alexandria in Egypt — the new science of astrology attained enormous and enduring popularity. Reciprocally, the demand for men who could cast horoscopes correctly kept mathematical astronomy alive through all succeeding ages. In Roman times the astronomer Ptolemy (second century A.D.) distilled Greek mathematical astronomy into a single book, which we know by its Arabic title, *Almagest*. A little later Galen (d. *c.* A.D. 200) codified Greek medicine for later ages, just as Euclid (*c.* 300 B.C.) had done earlier for geometry.

Other aspects of Hellenistic culture diversified older Greek tradition but cut no strikingly new paths. This was true of sculpture and architecture, city planning and the arts of fortification, for example. Literature tended to become academic — full of learned references — or artificial — populated by silly shepherdesses and the like. History degenerated into a branch of rhetoric, while the rhetoricians preferred a good phrase to a good idea. Such refinement and artificiality appealed of course only to the educated. The poor and vulgar also found a quasi-literary voice through the mime. This was a form of popular theater which preserved something of the bawdy tradition of Athenian comedy.

The rise of Rome. A new and politically important strand was added to the mixture of peoples and cultures in the eastern Mediterranean with the Roman conquest, first of Macedonia and Greece (146 B.C.), then of Seleucid Asia (64 B.C.), and finally of Egypt (30 B.C.). Rome began its political career as the leader of a federation of Latin cities in central Italy. A period of royal Etruscan rule ended with the establishment of an aristocratic republic (509 B.C.). The Republic was initially very strongly committed to the preservation of a simple rural Latin way of life in reaction against the corruptions of both Greek and Etruscan brands of civilization. For more than a century, Romans engaged in border wars, slowly expanding their territory, but also suffering occasional setbacks as when a raiding body of Gauls sacked the city and almost captured the capital (390 B.C.). Rapid expansion began soon thereafter so that by 265 B.C. all of Italy south of the Apennines was united under Roman leadership.

Rome's success rested partly on a numerous and hardy peasantry, disciplined and led by a hard-bitten and tenacious aristocracy that long remained profoundly distrustful of the corrupting luxury and wealth they saw among their more civilized neighbors. Additionally, the native peoples of Italy were but loosely organized into tribes and cantons, sometimes with and sometimes without a definite urban headquarters. No stubborn defense of local autonomy hindered the Romans in fastening their military and political leadership upon these peoples, especially since they were already familiar with federal arrangements within their own local political systems. Hence it proved possible to unite Italy under a single city's government without much trouble, whereas the Greeks struggled endlessly among themselves and never managed to combine local loyalties with stable attachment to any larger political whole.

Rome's rise brought on collison with the imperial city of Carthage in north Africa. Sicily, where Greeks and Carthaginians had long conducted sporadic war against each other, was the first bone of contention. Before they were able to defeat the Carthaginians, the Romans had to build a fleet, thus becoming a naval power for the first time. By 241 B.C. the Carthaginians were driven from Sicily. The island became the first Roman province, governed by a special magistrate or governor and required to pay taxes to Rome.

A second and far more severe test of Roman strength came between 218 and 201 B.C. when Hannibal, a skillful Carthaginian gen-

GROWTH OF THE ROMAN EMPIRE

265 B.C. 202 B.C.

30 B.C. 117 A.D.

Caspian Sea

PARTHIA

Tigris R. Seleucia

Euphrates R.

ARABIA

ARMENIA

MESOPOTAMIA

Red Sea

Nile R.

CAPPADOCIA

Antioch

SYRIA

CILICIA

PALESTINE Jerusalem

BITHYNIA

Black Sea

ASIA

CYPRUS

EGYPT

Alexandria

Memphis

Byzantium

Mediterranean Sea

THRACE

MACEDONIA

GREECE

Athens

CRETE

CYRENAICA

Danube R.

DACIA

Route of
Hannibal,
203 B.C.

ILLYRIA

Cannae
216 B.C.

GERMANY

ITALY

Rome

SICILY

Zama
202 B.C.

Carthage

Rhine R.

CORSICA

SARDINIA

GAUL

BRITAIN

PYRENEES

New Carthage

SPAIN

Route of Hannibal, 218 B.C.

Atlantic Ocean

A   F   R   I   C   A

Scale of Miles

0   500

152

eral, brought an army from Spain through southern Gaul and then crossed the Alps into Italy. Hannibal had expected most of the subjected cities and peoples of Italy to rise in revolt against the Romans. A few cities did indeed welcome him as liberator, but most of Rome's subjects and allies in Italy preferred a Roman to a Carthaginian master. Consequently after twelve years in Italy, during which time he was never defeated in the field, Hannibal was compelled to embark for home, because in the meanwhile a Roman expeditionary force had turned the tables on him by raising the natives of north Africa against their Carthaginian masters. At Zama in north Africa the Romans with their African allies won a final battle (202 B.C.). They forced Carthage to make a humiliating peace, transferring Spain from Carthaginian to Roman control. Thereafter the Romans remained without rival in the western Mediterranean.

Breakdown of the Republic. Involvement in the wars of the east came without delay; but for half a century the Romans held back from assuming direct political control over any part of the Hellenistic world of the eastern Mediterranean. This policy was abandoned in 146 B.C. when Macedon (already thrice defeated in battle) was made into a province and Greece was "liberated" by a foreign conqueror for the last time. Very rapidly Roman governors, soldiers, and tax farmers acquainted themselves with the refinements and luxuries of Hellenistic civilization. New tastes flowed into Rome with the new wealth derived from plunder. Simultaneously, Roman society underwent a catastrophic differentiation between rich and poor, analogous to the crisis that the Peloponnesian war had brought nearly three centuries earlier to Greece.

Civil war between rival generals, commanding increasingly professionalized troops, fastened a military dictatorship upon the Roman state. Julius Caesar (d. 44 B.C.), the conqueror of Gaul and champion of the lower classes in Rome, was the first man who seized and held extra-legal power for more than a brief period. His expressed intention of reorganizing the Roman government roused bitter opposition among his fellow Senators who thought of him as a tyrant and usurper and so slew him on the steps of the Senate house. But their act, intended to restore the Republic, merely plunged the Roman world into another round of civil war, from which Caesar's adopted son, Augustus, emerged victorious (30 B.C.).

Having won undisputed sovereignty over the Mediterranean, Augustus proceeded to borrow his defeated enemies' slogans and claimed in 27 B.C. to have "restored the Republic." He did reinstate republican forms and even entrusted the government of some of the provinces of the empire to the Senate. But Augustus was careful to keep military command in his own hands, and behind the scenes he exercised very effective control over elections and set tacit but real limits to the deliberations of the Senate. Nevertheless, the forms of republican government were not completely empty, if only because the emperor (from Latin *imperator*, i.e. commander of soldiers) was at pains to avoid hurting senatorial feelings.

The pretense of republicanism made transmission of authority from one emperor to another rather awkward, for the hereditary principle was an affront to republican theory, which held that free elections should determine political leadership. Nevertheless, the custom whereby a reigning emperor designated his successor usually worked smoothly, for all men dreaded a recurrence of civil war. As a result, for more than two hundred years after Augustus' victory the Roman world remained internally at peace, with the exception of one disastrous year (A.D. 69) when the soldiers proclaimed no fewer than three emperors in rapid succession and the imperial rivals fought out their claims in the heart of the empire. Frontier wars continued. Augustus, for example, pushed his frontiers to the Rhine and the Danube; the Emperor Claudius (reigned A.D. 41–54) began the conquest of Britain; Domitian (reigned A.D. 81–96) occupied part of Germany lying between the upper Rhine and Danube, and Trajan (reigned A.D. 98–117) conquered both Dacia (in modern Hungary and Roumania) and Mesopotamia. Two fierce Jewish revolts in Palestine also engaged Roman arms (A.D. 66–70 and A.D. 132–35) and various wars against the Parthians to the east and the Germans to the north kept Roman armies from idleness. Yet these struggles had little effect in the interior of the empire, where peace and orderliness prevailed as never before or since.

Hellenism in the Roman empire. During this long period of peace, the Roman empire witnessed a massive transplantation of Hellenistic civilization westward to Italy, Gaul, and Spain. To be sure, Latin rather than Greek became the prevailing language of these regions, so that it was Hellenistic culture in a Latin dress that rooted itself in the western provinces. Sculptors learned to carve with all the skill of their Hellenistic contemporaries, but Roman taste, emphasizing realistic portraiture, gave Roman sculpture its own distinctive character. Similarly in the field of literature, Lucretius (d. 55 B.C.), Cicero (d. 43 B.C.), and Vergil (d. 19 B.C.) — to name only the most distinguished — developed Latin into a language capable of expressing most of the Greek philosophic, rhetorical, and poetic refinements. Yet Latin could never become Greek. Latin letters and thought therefore retained always a distinctive accent, even when faithfully patterned on Greek originals or inspired by Greek example.

Within the framework of imperial administration, the provinces of the empire were organized into a series of city-states, each possessing its own local simulacrum of the public institutions, buildings, and governmental procedures which had once constituted the frame of existence for Greek and early Roman life. During the long Roman peace, provincial cities came to be dominated by local landowners. Their progress in the refinements of civilization was made at the direct cost of the peasants round about who tilled the soil and paid them rents. Gentility, but also a certain vapidity and cultural fragility, were inevitable consequences. Only a comparative handful of the population knew or cared much about the high Greco-Roman culture of the great Mediterranean world, and these favored few owed their security to the obedience of distant frontier garrisons to an emperor whom most of the soldiers had never seen. Under the circumstances it is surprising that peace lasted as long as it did, and that the privileged social position of a demilitarized landed class was not challenged until after A.D. 193, when prolonged civil war once more began to ravage the empire.

Christianity. Behind the Hellenized façade of Roman life great changes were under way during the first two centuries of the Christian era. The interaction between Middle Eastern and Greek cultures, which had begun before the Romans appeared on the scene, continued apace. The Roman state, with its rapidly proliferating bureaucracy, tax collectors, legal system, postal services, and standing army borrowed heavily from ancient Middle Eastern examples of imperial administration. More important still were changes in religion, for it was in these centuries that Christianity — a faith that combined Jewish and Greek elements with a new and most persuasive revelation — created a force that was destined to shape men's minds and feelings for millennia. Yet until after A.D. 200 Christianity, as well as other competing "mystery religions" that offered their initiates salvation from the tribulations of the world, remained relatively obscure, since it was the poor and humble of the cities who first found solace in the Christian gospel.

Despite the Greek language in which the Gospels were couched, and despite the Greek ring to some of St. Paul's (d. *c.* A.D. 64) phrases about sin and atonement, Christian theism was basically a reaffirmation of the Middle Eastern view of the nature of the world and man. The early Christians' concern for God and salvation, and their vivid expectation of a speedy end of the world stemmed from Jewish roots, and these aspects of the new faith carried greater emotional power than did the abstract complexities of trinitarian theology or other distinctively Greek aspects of the new religion.

Such analysis of the antecedents of Christianity should not disguise the fact that the events so simply narrated in the Gospels and in Acts generated something new and enormously appealing. Jesus and his disciples clearly expected God to intervene speedily and with power to set the wicked world aright. When instead the Roman authorities in Jerusalem arrested and crucified Jesus (*c.* A.D. 30), these expectations seemed at first to have been false. But soon afterwards the dispirited Apostles gathered in an "upstairs room" and suddenly felt again the heartwarming presence of their Master. This seemed absolutely convincing evidence that Jesus' death on the cross had not been the end but rather a beginning. With a great rush of renewed hope, his followers concluded that he would soon return in glory to inaugurate the long-awaited Day of Judgment. Their friend and Master, Jesus, it now seemed certain, was indeed the Messiah, prophesied from of old, who had been sent by God to save the righteous and would soon return on clouds of fire to judge the quick and the dead.

Such surprising news could not be kept quiet. On the contrary, the Apostles bubbled over with excitement and tried to explain to anyone who would listen all that had happened and was going to happen. Around this tiny kernel of excited missionaries the vast complexity of historical Christianity gradually formed — a process as surprising and world-shaking as the similar ramifications from the life of Buddha, Confucius, or any of the other great teachers of mankind.

In one important respect, however, the career of historic Christianity differed from that of any other great religion. From the beginning, learned and respectable Jews refused to accept the idea that Jesus had been the Messiah, and only a small minority of Jews ever accepted the new gospel. But St. Paul and others found willing listeners among pagans of the Hellenized cities of Syria and Asia Minor. Men who longed for a savior, but were not prepared to accept the ceremonial rules of Judaism, found the Christian message perfectly convincing. It was early decided that such converts would not have to conform to the Jewish Law. Faith in Christ (a Greek term meaning "The Anointed One" and equivalent to the Hebrew "Messiah") and a reformed life as a member of the Christian community were enough. As a result, after the Jewish Christians of Jerusalem had been dispersed in the course of the Jewish revolt of A.D. 66–70, Christian communities of the Greek-speaking cities severed their ties with Judaism entirely. No other great religion underwent such a change of environment in infancy, for Greek ideas and religious inheritance were not at all the same as Jewish, yet pagan converts inevitably brought with them many of their former habits of thought.

In particular, the combination of divine and human traits in a single person was a thoroughly familiar idea among Greeks. This aspect of Christ's existence tended therefore to attract greater emphasis. Similarly, Greek habits of logical argument demanded clearer theological definition of the relationship between God the Father, God the Son, and God the Holy Ghost or Spirit, which continued to visit and inspire Christian congregations from time to time, just as it had first visited the Apostles in Jerusalem after the crucifixion. From this emerged the subtleties of trinitarian theology. But before the abstract definition of dogma became critically important, Christians felt the need for a dependable record of Jesus' life on earth. Accordingly the four Gospels, each recording a somewhat divergent recollection of the Master's words and deeds, were written down between A.D. 70 and 100. Soon thereafter, St. Paul's letters and several other texts of exhortation or of prophecy were brought together to form the New Testament. Weekly readings from these sacred texts, together with singing and a ritual meal commemorating Jesus' last supper with his disciples, maintained the faith of the growing communities of Christians. The willingness of members of these groups to help one another, especially in time of sickness or other unusual hardship, was another very powerful support for the early church.

Despite the distrust with which Roman rulers inevitably viewed a semi-secret society which preached the early end of the world and the overthrow of Roman authority, the Christian churches continued to attract converts among the poor and disinherited of the cities. The success of Christianity, coupled with the general petering out of Greek pagan energies, was a sign that Hellenism was at long last losing its expansive power. By that time, however, peoples in Asia and Europe had transformed, borrowed, and made their own, aspects of Hellenistic civilization which seemed worth while to them. Echoes of this process extended to India and even to distant China. This we will explore in the next chapter, which will consider the development of these civilizations during the years of Hellenism's apogee, and survey the repercussions of civilized achievements upon the barbarian world as a whole.

X

Asia, 500 B.C.–A.D. 200

WHILE Hellenism was outgrowing its Aegean cradleland and becoming a diffusely genteel mode of existence, the other civilizations of the Old World did not stand still. The Macedonian and Roman conquests had consequences beyond Hellenistic and Roman frontiers, particularly in India. Simultaneously, in Mongolia the rise of the first really powerful nomad confederation triggered far-ranging migrations along the steppe. The upshot was to establish more intimate and regular communication than ever before among all civilized and many of the semi-civilized peoples of Eurasia. Despite fundamental cultural conservatism in all the main centers of civilization, the new frequency of contact across the entire Eurasian continent did stimulate peoples in critical crossroads areas to unusual creativity, especially in the field of religion.

The Mauryan empire of India. Political events are more than usually obscure because of serious chronological uncertainties, particularly with respect to events across India's northwestern frontier. When Alexander led his army into the Indus valley (327 B.C.), most of the Ganges region had already been consolidated under a single kingdom of Magadha. By disrupting local defenses and alliances the Macedonian invasion perhaps prepared the way for Chandragupta Maurya, king of Magadha (reigned *c.* 322–298 B.C.), to add the Indus region to his domain. Under his grandson,

Asoka (reigned *c.* 269–232 B.C.), central and southern India too, save for the extreme tip, was annexed to the Mauryan empire.

This vast state borrowed a good deal from Persian and Hellenistic models. Mauryan sculpture may have been produced by workmen imported from beyond the Hindu Kush. Chandragupta's palace appears to have closely resembled the Persian palace at Persepolis. Asoka's famous pillar edicts, which he set up in widely scattered parts of his empire, seem to have been inspired by the Persian royal inscriptions carved into the cliffs at Behistan. Perhaps even the Mauryan concept of universal empire owed something to the Persian and Macedonian examples.

Yet Asoka, after youthful indulgence in war and conquest, became a pious Buddhist, and devoted the rest of his life to spiritual conquests. Specifically, he sent missionaries to all parts of his realm, as well as abroad. He also erected several shrines to house portions of Buddha's ashes. For a while it seemed as though Buddhism would sweep all before it, but official patronage even when supplemented by invocations of the Buddha, perambulations of holy places, alms-giving, and other pious lay observances could not overcome the original weakness of the religion. Despite such inventiveness, it remained true that only for monks could Buddhism provide a complete way of life. Ordinary men in ordinary walks of life were still compelled to resort to Brahmans for rites appropriate to marriage, puberty, and death, not to mention all the lesser crises of human life.

Very soon after Asoka's death his empire split into warring fragments. Fresh waves of invaders came through the passes from central Asia: Greeks, Shakas, Kushans, and Parthians. These invasions were related to flights and removals on the steppe which were triggered in turn by the clash between a newly united China and the Turkish-speaking pastoralists of Inner and Outer Mongolia.

The unification of China. Amid such widespread upheaval the fundamental change, perhaps, lay in China's unification. This was the work of the ruler of the state of Ch'in. In 221 B.C. his armies, tempered in long border wars against the steppe barbarians, completed the overthrow of all rivals within China and he assumed the title of First Emperor (Shih Huang-ti) of a new dynasty, the Ch'in. The new emperor used his position to reorganize Chinese administration radically and ruthlessly. The country was divided into provinces and prefectures, on lines that lasted until modern times. He prescribed a uniform script, which also took hold and soon made older books more or less indecipherable. He completed the construction of the Great Wall of China to keep the nomads in check, and created an efficient system of posts and roads within China to allow him to rush troops to any threatened frontier or rebellious province.

This great autocrat and conqueror ruthlessly overrode local tradition, repudiating anything that set limits on his power. This meant, among other things, collision with Confucian doctrine, which sought to confine the emperor to governing according to the rites. Shih Huang-ti therefore prohibited Confucian teaching and ordered all Confucian books burned, save for a single copy of each work, which was to be preserved in the imperial archives. This decree won Shih Huang-ti the undying hatred of later generations of Confucians. More important at the time, his massive conscription of Chinese manpower for state service created general discontent, and when the great conqueror died in 210 B.C. his heir proved unable to maintain his father's power. Fresh civil war broke out, ending in 202 B.C., when the founder of the Han dynasty secured hegemony over all China. Except for one brief usurpation (A.D. 9–22) his descendants continued to occupy the imperial office until A.D. 220.

The early Han emperors came to terms with the class of landowners who, having superseded the Chou aristocracy on the land, had become the dominant element in Chinese society. Sons of these families, educated in a predominantly Confucian mould, were recruited into the imperial bureaucracy. This established a pervasive harmony of outlook between officials and landowners who effectively combined to keep peasants and other subordinate ranks of society in their proper place. One sign of the stabilization of Chinese society along these lines was a decline of intellectual controversy which had been a prominent feature of the period of the warring states. Shih Huang-ti-, for example, was identified with the Legalist school that emphasized the rights of the state over all rivals, whereas the Han emperors soon accepted Confucianism as an official ideology. Rival doctrines — Mohist, Taoist, Legalist, and others — were repressed more through official disapproval than by intellectual refutation, until, by degrees, a remarkable uniformity of outlook arose among the educated classes of imperial China.

Governments in central Asia. Long before this aspect of China's stabilization had time to work itself out, the military strength of a united China was made manifest abroad. Shih Huang-ti lost no time in taking the offensive and drove a number of tribes from Inner Mongolia across the Gobi desert to the sparse grasslands of Outer Mongolia. These refugees formed the kernel of a barbarian steppe confederation, called Hsiung-nu by the Chinese, which presently became so formidable as to constitute a worthy rival for China itself. The first Han emperor, for example, nearly lost his life on a campaign against the Hsiung-nu (200 B.C.). After this sobering experience he signed a treaty agreeing to pay tribute to the confederation and recognizing their restored dominion over Inner Mongolia.

The Hsiung-nu thereupon set out to extend their control westward across the steppe. In doing so they dislodged various Iranian-speaking peoples who fled toward the southwest, where they overthrew the Greek kingdom of Bactria, an interesting but little-known state that arose in the interstices between the decaying Seleucid and Mauryan empires, far to the east of other Greek-speaking kingdoms. Yet after a period of confusion, during which successive waves of invaders crossed the Himalayas and overran much of northwestern India, a more stable regime returned to the oases and pasture lands of central and western Asia. In 101 B.C. Chinese armies traveled westward and established the suzerainty of the Son of Heaven as far as the Jaxartes river. Some time later (exact dates are disputed), a comparatively strong monarchy ruled by Kushan kings established itself where the Greek kingdom of Bactria had formerly been, i.e. in modern Afghanistan and across the mountains into modern Pakistan. Still further west, Iranian newcomers from the steppe, the Parthians, also erected a fairly stable empire which lasted from 171 B.C. until A.D. 226.

Changes in warfare and trade. This widespread stabilization of civilized governments in central Asia became possible because of an important development in the technique of cavalry warfare. Before 100 B.C. the Parthians discovered that by feeding horses on alfalfa, specially planted and harvested, they could develop a larger, stronger, and more beautiful breed than the shaggy steppe ponies known previously. Such a horse, in turn, was able to carry a much heavier load of armor. This was important because a well-armored man and horse could render the arrows of light steppe cavalry ineffective. A company of such heavy cavalrymen could in fact return arrow for arrow, and then, when the steppe cavalrymen's quivers had been emptied, could drive them from the field and harass their retreat. Seldom, however, could armored cavalry overtake light horse. The result, therefore, was to create a stalemate between civilized heavy cavalry and the light cavalry of the steppe nomads. Neither could prevail in the other's environment. The big horses could not find sufficient nourishment in the slim pickings of the wild steppe, whereas on agricultural ground the unarmored nomads could no longer prevail against the new style of heavy armored cavalry.

Agricultural communities capable of sustaining the big horses — they could eat hay and grain when the irrigated fields needed for alfalfa were lacking — therefore had the possibility of defending themselves against nomad raiding. But the expense was great, for horse and armor, not to mention the trained professional fighting man required to use these instruments effectively, all were costly. Another difficulty was that local institutions often had to be adapted in order to concentrate enough income in the hands of individual fighting men to permit them to purchase and maintain such elaborate equipment. This usually meant subordinating a village, or several villages, to a single strong-armed warrior. But when a truly formidable class of such paladins formed in the countryside, it meant that the will of the central government could not prevail, save on sufferance and with the concurrence of this new military class. Since monarchs, peasants, and townsmen all had reason to regret such a transformation, civilized societies did not accept the new heavy-armor technology of warfare very rapidly, except in regions exposed to constant raiding from the steppes, i.e. Iran and central Asia.

Nevertheless, the shield against the steppe nomads which thus was raised in central Asia allowed civilized governments and merchants to collaborate in establishing an organized trade route, linking China with Rome by means of a well-appointed, regularly policed, and heavily taxed caravan route. Shipments of Chinese silk traveled westward to Roman Syria along this "Silk Road," while a variety of goods made the return trip — metals, glass, and considerable quantities of coin.

Almost simultaneously, Greek-speaking sea captains operating from the Red Sea discovered how to take advantage of the regular monsoon winds of the Indian Ocean to travel across the open sea from the straits of Aden all the way to southern India. Similar voyages were soon undertaken across the Bay of Bengal, linking the east coast of India to Malaya. A short portage across the isthmus of Kra then brought the voyagers into touch with Chinese vessels operating along the southeast Asian coasts. Thus a sea route, broken only by the portage across the neck of Malaya, also came to link Rome with China shortly before the Christian era.

Hundreds, perhaps thousands of persons made a living by traveling to and fro along these routes: camel drivers, sailors, guards, merchants, porters, and other common folk. They seldom left much trace in the literary record. Yet talk around campfires and in port taverns, we may well believe, spread information and misinformation about every part of the known world, throughout the bazaars of Asia all the way from Syria to China and from southern India to the Aral Sea.

Developments in the arts. No fundamental modification of any of the four major civilizations of the Old World resulted from the greater ease of communication and travel between China, India, and the Middle East. We have already seen how the Greek style of life penetrated the upper strata of Middle Eastern society, interacted with European barbarism to civilize all of Mediterranean Europe, and contributed a distinctive imprint to emerging Christianity as well. But contact with the other civilizations of the Old World did not add much more than the luxury of silk clothes to the life of Greco-Roman gentlemen.

Much the same was true elsewhere. The mainstream of Chinese culture, for example, was not affected in any important fashion by contact with the rest of the civilized world. Scholars and officials, steeped in the classics of Confucian scholarship, were as impervious to the silly notions of lowly trading folk as were their Roman equivalents, for whom a novel superstition like Christianity mattered as little as did the discredited deities of Olympus. We know far less about the lives of upper-class Brahmans in India, but they too may be presumed to have found little of interest in the gossip and tall stories of the ports and caravanserais, where the most fertile interchange between Greek, Indian, and Middle Eastern civilizations took place.

The established civilizations of Eurasia, in other words, continued on their course as before. In China the years between Confucius' death (479 B.C.) and the unification under Shih Huang-ti in 221 B.C. were particularly fertile. Various rival schools of doctrine arose to dispute pre-eminence with Confucianism and Taoism; but after the Han dynasty established peace in the land, these rivals withered or were absorbed into Confucianism. The process of absorption brought much which had originally been skipped over by Confucius into his followers' traditional learning. The usual course was to read all sorts of new notions into the Confucian classics by treating them as allegories or anagrams, which hinted at truths available only to the learned and ingenious scholar who could decipher their full meaning. In this way, as men were later to do with the Christian scriptures, a host of new ideas could be fitted within the framework of Confucianism without difficulty.

Chinese learning was further enhanced by the inauguration of history as a distinct form of literary composition. The great pioneer was Ssu-ma Ch'ien (145–86 B.C.), who compiled a multivolumed record of all the past known to him, from the beginning of things until his own lifetime. He organized China's history around the idea that each dynasty began with an especially virtuous ruler chosen by Heaven for the task, and then by degrees dissipated its initial virtue until Heaven lost patience and withdrew its mandate from the last unworthy ruler. He fitted the data of China's past into this scheme so persuasively that it became standard for all later Chinese historical writing.

We are much less well informed about the development of Indian literary and intellectual culture. The linkage of priestcraft, courtly elegance, and ascetic discipline, which achieved a classical expression in the Gupta age (A.D. 329–570), was presumably maturing; but when all dates are unsure it seems best to reserve a discussion of Indian thought and literature to a later chapter.

The Iranian regions remain tantalizingly obscure. The replacement of the Seleucid by Parthian overlordship in Iran and Mesopotamia (171 B.C.) does not appear to have had any drastic cultural consequences, at least initially. The Parthian monarchs, like the Seleucids, drew major tax revenues from the Hellenized cities of Mesopotamia and accordingly adopted a generally phil-Hellenic cultural policy. In the countryside, however, where the Zoroastrian faith survived, a more purely Iranian way of life persisted. This came clearly to political expression with the establishment of the Sassanian or New Persian empire in A.D. 226.

Art reflects exposure to new visual experiences far more sensitively than literature responds to contact with another learned tradition. This is so because it is not necessary to translate a work of art before strangers and outsiders can react to it. Literary culture, by contrast, is utterly unintelligible to the uninitiated. This is well illustrated by the manner in which contact with Greek sculpture stimulated Indian artists to perfect their own independent style of carving within a very short period. The earliest-known Indian sculpture dates from the time of Asoka. Within no more than two centuries a rich, mature style developed, well illustrated by the elaborate carving of the great Buddhist stupa at Sanchi. Art historians still debate exactly how much Indian artists were indebted to the Greeks. Yet the generally naturalistic character of Indian sculpture, its free use of Mediterranean decorative motifs, and the certainty that Indian stonecutters had ample opportunity to see numerous examples of Greek sculpture (at least as exported in cheap copies from Alexandria), all point to a real connection between the two sculptural traditions.

Astride the Hindu Kush a hybrid art style arose, using Greek forms to body forth Buddhist saviors. Buddhist missionaries spread this art across central Asia and brought it into China toward the end of the period we are now considering. As this style of art traveled eastward, Greek conventions were misunderstood. The spirit was also transmuted: what had begun as a naturalistic portrait statue of Apollo ended as a stylized evocation of other-worldly aspiration. Greco-Buddhist art really affected China only after the end of the Han dynasty (A.D. 220), when it entered deeply into and quite transformed earlier Chinese art. In this indirect fashion, we may literally watch Greek art styles spread across Asia, altering meaning and symbolic significance as they progressed.

New, cosmopolitan religions. The propagation of art styles was not, however, the most significant cultural consequence of the opening of regular communication between the separate civilizations of Eurasia. Rather, in the regions where men of different cultures met and chaffered in the bazaars there arose communities of rootless wanderers and lost souls who strove to make the harsh world in which they found themselves more tolerable by religious innovation of a sort that proved fundamental and very attractive to millions of men elsewhere throughout all later ages.

Three regions proved particularly fertile. One was in southern India, a second in northwestern India, and the third lay in the Greek-speaking regions of the Roman empire. Christianity was of course the great religious creation of the Greek-speaking populations of the eastern Mediterranean cities. Hinduism emerged almost simultaneously in southern India, while Mahayana Buddhism was doing the same in northwestern India. All three regions were active centers of long-distance trade, with big new cities where rootless men congregated. All three also were zones where several quite different older religious and cultural traditions overlapped, stimulating sensitive individuals to reorder their belief in the light of new inspiration, mystic experience, elaboration of ritual, and logic.

Something has already been said of Christian beginnings, and of the mingling of Jewish and Greek traditions that provided the new religion with its early milieu.

In southern India, Brahmanism evolved into Hinduism during the first Christian centuries in an environment where Aryan, Dravidian, and Greco-Roman influences met and overlapped. The change came gradually, for no one prophet or preacher deliberately or consciously transformed the traditional faiths of India. Rather, through a process of ritual invention, the various myths concerning the innumerable deities honored by different Indian castes began to coalesce around the figures of two rival yet complementary deities, Shiva and Vishnu. Their worshippers believed that each of these gods chose to appear to human gaze in many different forms, suited to the understanding and sensibility of particular audiences. Hence, almost any primitive cult or local peculiarity of worship could readily be attached to the cult of Vishnu or of Shiva, since every local god who in fact attracted worship was proved by that very fact to be a valid instance of divine incarnation.

Such a doctrine, nevertheless, introduced a sort of order and system into Indian religion, since, when a local cult had been identified as a form of the worship of one of the two high gods of the Hindu pantheon, worshippers could begin to share in the more sophisticated service of the god whom they had previously known only in one of his particular guises.

The really important feature of emergent Hinduism lay in this: that sophisticated worshippers of Vishnu and Shiva viewed these two deities as saviors, able and ready to rescue their devotees from the toils of their present life and raise them up the scale of being toward a blissful, perfect state. The doctrine of rebirth remained central. The simple believed that pious life and good behavior would assure rebirth in a higher caste. The educated, on the other hand, could still proclaim, with the Upanishads, that annihilation of self in the supreme reality of which even Vishnu and Shiva were but appearances, remained the goal of religious striving. Thus, by combining high metaphysics with vulgar superstition, Hinduism offered something for everyone. The combination was immensely powerful, and ended by displacing Buddhism from the land of its birth.

Before that fate overtook Buddha's followers, however, a remarkable development of the faith took place, mainly in the northwest part of India, where Indian, Greek, Persian, and steppe peoples met and mingled. This religious development probably took place at the time when the Kushan empire bestrode India's northwest frontier (1st century B.C. to 2nd century A.D.). The greatest Kushan monarch, Kanishka, was reputed in later Buddhist tradition to have been a patron of some of the most important theological pioneers of the new faith. Once again, the central innovation was belief in the existence of divine yet incarnate saviors, called bodhisattvas. A bodhisattva was a soul which, though it had attained a state of holiness deserving the release of Nirvana, nevertheless declined that privilege in order to aid others on the road to salvation. In the meanwhile, these saviors lived a spiritual existence in a super-celestial heaven where prayers and other invocations could reach them, and where they could aid struggling humanity by a sort of spiritual sympathy.

Exponents of these ideas termed their doctrine *Mahayana*, that is, the Great Way or Vehicle, thus distinguishing it from the older

Hinayana, or Lesser Way. The development certainly carried Buddhism very far from the metaphysical pessimism and ideal of personal dissolution which its founder (presumably) preached. Instead, the worshipper, by appropriate prayer and ritual invocation of a bodhisattva of his choice, could hope to become a bodhisattva himself (though perhaps only after innumerable incarnations) and thus attain a blessed life after death not fundamentally unlike that promised by Christianity.

Perhaps the resemblances between Christianity, Mahayana Buddhism, and Hinduism are to be attributed to the spirit of the times. We can readily believe that persons caught up in great trading and administrative centers of western Asia, often far from home and thrown amid strangers, welcomed the prospect of salvation. One may also argue that the kinship between Mahayana Buddhism and Christianity is due to a common Greek element. The idea of God incarnate, central to both Christianity and Mahayana Buddhism, certainly had Greek analogues — witness the all-too-human deities portrayed in Greek art. To untutored Indian eyes a statue of a god who was also a man must have required extensive explanation: and it is tempting to suggest that one of the seedbeds of the Mahayana doctrine may have been just such wonderment on the part of Indian seekers after truth and holiness.

The appearance of Christianity, Mahayana Buddhism, and Hinduism — not to mention a number of other less influential cults like Mithraism, the worship of Isis, Cybele, and others — gave men of the most various backgrounds courage to persevere even in the face of disappointment and hardship, since all these faiths held forth the hope of a future in which present injustices would be righted gloriously and forever. Moreover, these religions were independent of any particular locality or community. Like post-exilic Judaism, wherever a few of the faithful gathered together the hope of salvation burned bright. Short of that ultimate bliss, the everyday fellowship of the religious community itself provided a not ineffective solace for hardship or loneliness. All three of these religions were therefore well attuned to the requirements of urban living, as no earlier faith except Judaism had been. Since inequities and hardship were inseparable from civilized life, the appearance of such faiths very likely made the long-term survival of civilization far easier than would otherwise have been the case.

Diseases and empires. Another consequence of the intensification of contact across the Old World had a very different effect. Goods, ideas, and techniques were not the only things that traveled from one community to another. Disease germs also were transmissible, and as contacts multiplied it seems likely that various types of infection which had before been largely confined to one or the other part of Eurasia and Africa spread to new regions. Among a previously unexposed population, disease germs may cause very heavy mortality. Records from both China and Rome make clear that there were severe plagues in the first and second centuries A.D. Many parts of the Roman empire, indeed, began to suffer from depopulation, and lack of manpower became a chronic problem for the Roman authorities from A.D. 200 if not before. It is therefore not fantastic to suggest that epidemic disease, resulting from closer contact across the entire span of Eurasia and much of Africa, may have been a major factor in the collapse of the Roman and Han empires. Of course there were other factors: brute barbarian attack and internal social tensions clearly played major roles.

Yet even after the Roman peace and the Han imperial administration were both irremediably broken, the three great world religions that had come to birth in the first centuries of the Christian era — Christianity, Mahayana Buddhism, and Hinduism — continued to flourish and attracted to themselves much of the high cultural life of the troubled age that succeeded. Of all the achievements of antiquity, none remains more vigorously alive today.

XI

The Flowering and Expansion of Indian Civilization

A.D. 200–600

BY A.D. 200 Hellenism had lost its power to attract. The polite, cool, and moderate style of life recommended by Greek philosophers to Roman gentlemen no longer seemed equal to the needs of the time, especially when the long Roman peace suffered violent disruption in A.D. 193 and, after a brief rally, disintegrated squalidly between A.D. 235 and 284 into a long series of civil wars, barbarian invasions, and disputed successions to the imperial office. Simultaneously, Confucian China suffered similar disasters. The last decades of the Han dynasty were disfigured by civil wars and barbarian invasions, and the final overthrow of the dynasty in A.D. 220 simply ratified publicly the political and military confusion which had already divided China into a number of competing local states.

In the center of the civilized world, however, matters wore a very different aspect. From the Caspian to the Hindu Kush the serried array of the Iranian baronage stood guard against the raiding steppe cavalry. Their heavy horses, heavy armor, and powerful bows, together with their readiness at a moment's notice to take the field in order to protect the peasants upon whose rents they themselves depended, provided a most effective defense for the heartlands of Middle Eastern and Indian civilization. Any raiding party had to penetrate through a continuously protected countryside where the most technologically formidable warriors of the age lay in wait. Few made the attempt; fewer still repeated it.

Secure behind this barrier, both Indian and a revived Persian civilization attained new levels of elegance, sophistication, and religious virtuosity. India in particular entered upon a golden age which remained "classical" for subsequent Indian generations. Far less is known about the real cultural attainments of Sassanian Persia. Unsympathetic Moslem and Christian reports of Zoroastrian and other forms of religious heterodoxy constitute the principal basis for what little is known of Sassanian literary and religious history; and the art of the age has survived only in a very damaged state. Yet Sassanian influence upon Rome and Central Asia was almost as great as Indian influence upon southeast Asia and the Chinese Far East. It seems well, therefore, to divide the history of the centuries between A.D. 200 and A.D. 600 into two "fields of force," and consider the Indian and Sassanian achievements and influence in successive chapters, even though they coincided in time. This chapter will therefore describe the flowering and expansion of Indian civilization, and the next will deal with the achievements of Sassanian Persia.

The Gupta empire. In A.D. 320 an energetic Indian king of the lower Ganges, named Chandra-gupta,* crowned himself in a special ceremony as "universal ruler." To make good his title he then launched a series of conquests. Within less than a century, his heirs brought all of northern India from the Bay of Bengal to the Arabian Sea under their suzerainty. The Gupta empire, thus established, endured until about A.D. 570. During much of this time, warfare and major political violence seem to have been unimportant in India. We have record of only a single raid from across the mountains, which struck about A.D. 460. Within India itself chivalric conventions and religious injunctions tamed the destructiveness of warfare to an unusual degree. It was under these conditions that Indian civilization flowered in such a fashion that the Gupta age

---

* The name is identical with that of the founder of the Mauryan empire, who lived about 650 years before. To distinguish the two, it is customary to print the first Chandragupta's name as a single word and to hyphenate the second.

CENTRAL ASIAN EMPIRES
c. 400 A.D.

has ever since remained, in the estimation of both Hindus and of foreigners, the high point of the Indian past.

Despite the vastness of their realm, the Gupta rulers left scant trace behind them in the Sanskrit literary tradition. Hence what information we have is nearly all derived from reports written by Chinese, Ceylonese, and other Buddhist pilgrims. Precise political, military, geographic, and chronological facts are therefore nearly as unclear for this great age of India's history as they are for far less distinguished periods. The absence of political information is itself of course indicative of the special apolitical bent which Indian society and culture had manifested for nearly a thousand years before the rise of the Gupta empire.

The Gupta sovereigns themselves probably shared traditional Indian values so completely that they expected the realm of politics and of the state to remain relatively superficial. Thus, for example, the Gupta conquerors appear to have made it a policy to allow defeated rulers (or their close relatives) to remain in control of their accustomed lands. On a day-to-day basis, Gupta interests could be adequately cared for by a resident stationed at the vassal king's court; and on state occasions, ceremonial deference kept the Gupta emperors well content.

The Gupta kings also patronized a revivified Hinduism, and as a part of that religious policy presumably accepted the Hindu notion of law which accorded remarkably little scope to mere rulers. Instead, Hindu doctrine held that the Vedas were the highest source of authority, followed in order by commentaries on the Vedas (i.e. the Brahmanas), the example of holy men, and last of all, personal inclination, i.e. the edicts of a king or other public authority.

These views found expression in law books, called *Dharma shastras*, which were compiled during the Gupta era. They became basic for Hindu life thereafter. For example, the Dharma shastras defined the institution of caste by spelling out in detail how men of different castes should behave in a great variety of particular circumstances. The theory of castes also achieved its classical formulation in the Dharma shastras. Faithful performance of caste duties in this life, it was asserted, would prepare the soul for incarnation further up the ladder of being. Moral conduct during a series of lives would finally allow the soul to penetrate permanently into the realm of reality where all is One and one is All. But in the meantime, it was incumbent upon every man to conform to the traditions of his caste and observe the rites and practices of the group into which he had been born, no matter how crude, simple, or rationally inexplicable such customs might be.

Thus religion, law, mystical metaphysics, and crude superstition were all tied tightly together so that each reinforced the other, and — so far as we know anything at all of public and political life of the Gupta period — it appears that affairs of state also fitted neatly into the same bundle.

Sanskrit learning. Three institutions stimulated the cultural efflorescence of the age. The royal court patronized artists, writers, musicians, astrologists, astronomers, doctors, and other professional experts. Temples rivaled the courts as centers for cultural activity, for appropriately sumptuous service of the god — Shiva, Vishnu, or one of the *avatars* (incarnations) of either of them — called for the same sorts of activities as sustained the grandeur of any ordinary human monarch. Third, behind both court and temple stood an ancient school system whereby the bulky accumulation of lore bodied forth in Sanskrit oral literature was passed on from generation to generation.

In these schools, the central relationship was between a holy man and a group of disciples who came to him to learn by heart whatever traditional wisdom he had to impart. Memorization of the Vedas and other holy texts, with careful attention to correct accent and grammar, constituted the core of the educational system. Commentaries on the texts, and commentaries on commentaries, had long since proliferated beyond the limits established by even the most capacious memory, so that specialists, grouped into more or less stable "schools," divided the domain of Sanskrit learning among them.

The prestige and practical importance of the school system was tellingly demonstrated in the Gupta era by the revival of Sanskrit. In Buddha's time, Sanskrit had become a learned language intoned by Brahman priests at religious ceremonies, but otherwise forgotten. Early Buddhist writing was couched in literary versions of the popular languages of the day, all of which were derived from Sanskrit but differed from it much as French or Spanish differs from Latin. Similarly, the Mauryan empire used a number of local languages for administration. All this altered by the time of the Guptas. Sanskrit became again a living literary language, in which fresh work of utmost refinement and polish was composed.

One reason for Sanskrit's remarkable comeback may have been the growing difficulty of bridging the gap between the various local dialects. As regional differences in the everyday, uneducated forms of speech increased, the need for a *lingua franca* intelligible to all became far more acute than in the days of Asoka, when relatively small variations made differences of dialect not too difficult to overcome.

But the central fact that permitted Sanskrit's revival was the school system whereby any man aspiring to knowledge had to learn Sanskrit. A corps of men speaking the same language, and attuned to the same intellectual wave lengths, was thus maintained generation after generation. In Gupta times, this corps of educated men took over social leadership in practically every branch of cultural activity. Thereby, of course, they displaced the Buddhists, who in an earlier time had discarded Sanskrit learning as useless baggage for the soul. Some of the reasons for Buddhism's ultimate failure in India have already been suggested in Chapter IV. The readiness of Brahman Sanskritists to react energetically to the foreign stimuli that had come into India from the Greek and Iranian worlds during the preceding three or four centuries was another factor that allowed them to eclipse the increasingly well-to-do, insulated, and withdrawn Buddhists.

The enlarged horizons of Sanskrit learning were most apparent in astronomy and medicine, where the Greek imprint became clear and unmistakable. Yet the appropriation of Greek notions about the mechanics of planetary motion, together with the mathematical skills needed for casting horoscopes, did not freeze Sanskrit learning into rigid, alien moulds. On the contrary, one of the great inventions of the human mind, the decimal place system of numerical notation, emerged in India by A.D. 270. The simple numerical system of notation which we call "Arabic" and which the Arabs cor-

The Radiation and Transformation of Greek Sculpture

Photo Jean Roubier

Helvetian head from Aventicum. Avenches Museum, Switzerland.

MINGLING OF STYLES WESTWARD

This head was found in Switzerland at a Roman site. Some mingling and cross fertilization of Greco-Roman skills and style with a native art tradition (perhaps in wood?) must lie behind this strange and striking work.

PLATE 9

Athena or Roma, 2nd-3rd cent. A.D.
Lahore, Pakistan.

Buddha, 4th cent. A.D.
Lahore, Pakistan.

MINGLING OF STYLES EASTWARD

As an art style travels in time and space it alters in surprising ways. The four figures reproduced here were chosen to illustrate relationships running across all of Eurasia and some three to four centuries of time, beginning about A.D. 100 when a provincial participant in or missionary of Greco-Roman culture carved the buxom Athena (or Roma) that gazes at us from the left above. Provincial Greco-Roman art may be seen transmogrified in a second statue which comes from the same region and about the same time (above right). Here the artist used Greco-Roman motifs like the topknot and toga to portray the Buddha. In turn, Chinese sculptors seized upon the models offered by Indo-Greek Buddhist art to produce first a hybrid Chinese (opposite above) and then a fully Sinified (opposite below) version of the Buddha. Observe how the naturalistic thrust of Greek art alters and is in the end completely contradicted by the Chinese sculptor who reduced not merely the drapery but Buddha's foot itself to a flat, decorative, and delightful pattern of curves.

PLATE 10

Buddha from Shensi,
5th cent. A.D.
Gallery Sabauda, Turin.

Buddha from Honan, 5th cent. A.D.
Museum of Fine Arts, Boston.
Gift of Denman Waldo Ross
in memory of Okakura Kakuzo.

PLATE 11

Siddhārta Fasting, A.D. 300-400, from Sikri. Lahore, Pakistan.

PLATE 12

Photos, P. Chandra

Didarganj Yakshi, Mauryan dynasty, front and back views. Patna Museum, India.

THE TWO FACES OF INDIA

Asceticism and sensuality, often carried to the extreme limits set by human physiology, complemented and perhaps even sustained one another within the hospitable matrix of Indian culture. These two statues offer a dramatic, visual statement of the polarity.

PLATE 13

The Development and Radiation of Indian Architecture

Temple No. XVII, 5th cent. A.D. Sānchī.

AN ARCHITECTURAL MIRROR OF INDIAN SOCIETY

The photographs on this and succeeding pages illustrate the elaboration of Indian temple architecture between the fifth and thirteenth centuries A.D. An entrance porch, an enclosed room to house the cult image, and, excepting Plate 14, a tower rising above the spot where the image normally resided can be detected in each of these photographs, despite the great variations of ground plan and scale that characterize the temple structures.

The loose cohesion of the temples' over-all plan and their pullulating decorative and sculptural detail (compare Plates 17 and 19) hold a mirror to Indian society itself, whose central institution—caste—protected the peculiar ways and customs of an endless number of sub-groupings, and could always make room for newcomers, whether they came as humble converts from primitive hunting folk or as mighty conquerors from afar. In the same way, another gate, tower, or group of statues added to one of these temples simply enriched without upsetting the structure as a whole.

PLATE 14

Mālegitti Śivālaya Temple, c. A.D. 625. Bādāmī.

PLATE 15

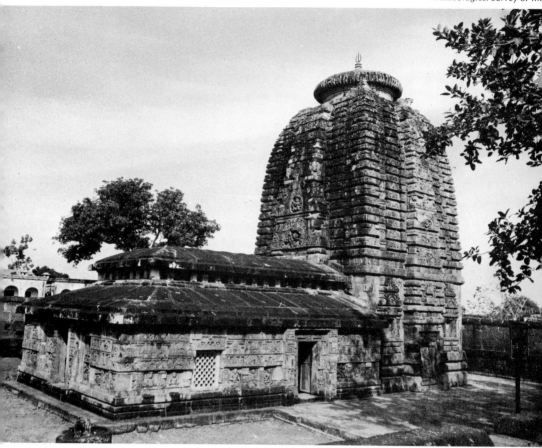

Paraśurāmeśvara Temple, c. A.D. 750. Bhuvaneśvara.

PLATE 16

Woman with a mirror, 11th cent. A.D. Bhuvaneśvara or Khajurāho.

PLATE 17

Muktésvara Temple, c. A.D. 950, general view. Bhuvanésvara.

Muktésvara Temple, sikhara, detail.

PLATE 18

PLATE 19

View of the Great Temple Compound, 8th-13th cent. A.D. Bhuvaneśvara.

TEMPLES OF SOUTHEAST ASIA

Temples built along Indian lines to house religious ceremonies deriving in large part also from India extend across a wide segment of Asia, from Tibet in the north to Java in the south, and as far east as Cambodia. In each of these regions, amalgamations took place between local religious and political traditions on the one hand and Indian cultural and religious practices on the other, so that no simple copies of Indian prototypes can be found. Yet the impact of India's religious architecture is plain to see. The acculturation of barbarian peoples to an Indian style of civilized life, here demonstrated through architecture (Plates 21-24), parallels the process we saw visually attested by the spread of Greek styles of sculpture (with appropriate modification) to Rome and western Europe (Plates 4-7).

PLATE 20

Caṇḍi Puntadewa, c. A.D. 700. Dieng Plateau, Java.

PLATE 21

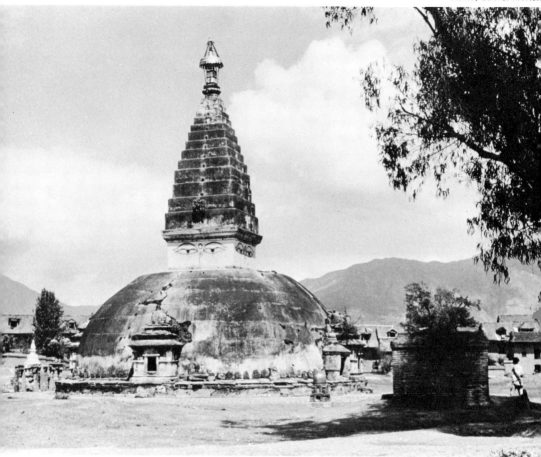

Stupā, showing the eyes of the Buddha, possibly 8th or 9th cent. A.D.
Near Kāthmandū, Nepal.

PLATE 22

The temple of Çiva, late 9th cent. A.D. Lara-Djonggrang, Prambanan, Java.

PLATE 23

Angkor Wat, early 12th cent. A.D., air view from the northeast. Cambodia.

PLATE 24

rectly attributed to India ranks with alphabetic writing as one of the master keys of human inventiveness. Once the notation had been invented, calculation became comparatively easy and rapid. As a result, both the affairs of the market place and the abstruse concerns of theoretical mathematicians were enormously facilitated. All the same, the perfected notation spread rather slowly, becoming known among the Arabs only in the tenth century A.D. and reaching Latin Christendom two centuries later still.

Sanskrit literature. The heart of Sanskrit learning lay not in natural science but in literary and linguistic labors. Preoccupation with an antique, learned, and sacred language led to the development of grammatical science. Panini wrote a grammar of Sanskrit which became classical; but when he lived is quite uncertain.

Similarly, the precise literary history of India's two great epic poems is irrecoverable, since oral transmission and elaboration across centuries left few definite traces for modern scholars to analyze. Nevertheless, it seems certain that both the *Mahabharata* and the *Ramayana* achieved their final form during the Gupta period. The *Mahabharata* is an enormously lengthy poem, roughly three and a half times as long as the entire Christian Bible. It contains a great variety of matter. At the core is an ancient story of heroic warfare between rival coalitions of noble charioteers, which must descend from very ancient bardic songs of Aryan times. Recitation of these songs somehow became part of Brahman religious ceremonies. The priests saw fit to interlard the bloody violence of the traditional tales with all sorts of homilies and stories teaching religious lessons. If the Christian fathers had reworked Homer to make the *Iliad* into a handbook of Christian doctrine, the effect would be similar. In addition, folk tales and fairy stories interrupt the narrative from time to time. Sometimes stories within stories suspend the main theme acrosss hundreds of printed pages. The *Ramayana* is shorter and more tightly organized. It is a story of the hero Rama and his wife Sita, and of the trials and tribulations that separated them through a long series of adventures until a final reunion ends the tale.

Both the *Mahabharata* and the *Ramayana* became very popular in India, and remain so to the present. Innumerable episodes provided a mine of material for subsequent literary elaboration, much as the Greek playwrights exploited Homer and Hesiod for their plots, or as Shakespeare used Italian and classical authors for many of his. The entire subsequent literary tradition of India has been shaped by this device. Between them, the two poems created a literary frame of reference and universe of discourse that still survives.

No author can be assigned to either the *Mahabharata* or the *Ramayana;* and it is clear that the texts of both poems evolved over a lengthy period of time before achieving their final shape in the Gupta period. The history of Sanskrit drama is very different, for the plays that survive usually have an author's name attached to them and bear every indication of having been composed by a single man for presentation at the royal court. The use of some Greek technical stage terms proves that Greek models had some importance for the Sanskrit theater, though exactly how much is disputed hotly, since Sanskrit drama has its own conventions and the Indian playwrights usually drew their plots from traditional materials of the epics.

Kalidasa (*c.* A.D. 400) is the acknowledged master of Sanskrit literature. His plays rank as classics, and his lyric poetry bespeaks an elegant sensibility, perhaps just a little too self-conscious and contrived to appeal strongly to our own contemporary taste. These aspects of Kalidasa's work were elaborated after his time by other courtly writers, until verbal complexity and ingenuity outbalanced and even obscured meaning.

Gupta art. Accidents of preservation make a fair judgment of the state of the plastic arts in Gupta times very difficult. Moslem conquerors later systematically destroyed the temples of northern India on the ground that they were seats of idolatry. Hence little distinctively Hindu art survives from the centers of Gupta power, which lay in the north. A few carvings from the south can be dated to Gupta times, but they are rather crude and artistically unsatisfactory. Obviously, artists faced a difficult task in giving visual form to gods whose essence was the mutability of their form, since the numerous deities of the Hindu pantheon were doctrinally linked together as successive incarnations of Vishnu or Shiva. So far as surviving monuments allow us to judge, this problem was not successfully solved during the Gupta period.

Buddhist art, on the other hand, attained a finish and perfection it never subsequently equaled. The paintings of the caves of Ajanta are deservedly famous, reflecting an elegant luxury and refinement characteristic of all aspects of Gupta culture. A few examples of Buddhist sculpture also survive, and exhibit the same artistic mastery — with just a hint of decadence — that is characteristic of the Ajanta paintings.

Religion was never separable from other aspects of India's cultural life. The law books, the two great epics, monumental temples, cult statues, and other works of visual art, not to mention the irrecoverable arts of music and dancing, were all part of Hinduism in the sense that all dealt with the relations between men and the supernatural and each in its own way helped to give definition to this critical frontier of human experience. The definitive doctrinal elaboration of Hinduism, however, came only some centuries after the end of the Gupta era, when Shankara (*c*. A.D. 870) propounded a monistic, transcendent philosophy that later defenders of Hinduism regularly resorted to when arguing against Moslem and Christian critics of India's traditional faith.

The perfection achieved in Gupta times in so many branches of cultural endeavor gave an enduring stamp to Hindu and Sanskrit culture, yet did so without injecting anything radically different or new. Maximal perfection and balance can, presumably, be attained only by refraining from major innovation. This the writers and scholars of the Gupta age faithfully did, and, by remaining gladly within the limits their predecessors had defined for them, were able to polish and improve what had been handed down in a fashion later generations never surpassed.

Eastern spread of Indian civilization. The Gupta golden age was felt far beyond India's border. The principal carriers of Indian culture were merchants and missionaries, not soldiers like those who had brought Hellenism to the Middle East, or Greco-Roman civilization to Gaul. In southeast Asia, Indian civilization abutted upon a region where no pre-existing culture offered much competition. Here, therefore, a Greater India arose. Between about A.D. 100 and

A.D. 600 a series of local states and royal courts in such areas as Burma, Sumatra, Java, Malaya, Siam, and Viet Nam eagerly strove to import as much of Indian civilization as they could.

North of the mountains, Indian merchants and missionaries confronted very different conditions. Chinese, Persian, and Greco-Roman populations were not prepared to jettison their pasts *in toto*, even when they were irresistibly attracted to some of the aspects of Indian culture — above all to the techniques of mystical asceticism which Indian holy men had long cultivated. Hence it was only selected aspects of Indian culture that took root and flourished in other parts of the civilized world, whereas Indian influence on

GREATER INDIA
400 A.D.-600 A.D.

Scale of Miles
0   500

southeast Asia was diluted only by the residual barbarisms and village simplicities of that region.

In southeast Asia legends provide some information about how Indian styles of life penetrated the peaceable village communities that existed along the shores and river banks of the Bay of Bengal and the South China Sea. Typically, a merchant from India married into a chieftain's family, and from that vantage point began to exercise cultural-political leadership over surrounding settlements until a small state emerged. Royal power in such states rested largely upon magical ideas which tied fertility of the fields to the potency of royal persons and a ceremonial stone symbol thereof (i.e. a stone phallus) — the so-called "linga." Temple and palace structures designed to house the royal person and the linga in fitting splendor soon emerged from these notions. At first the local rulers tried to reproduce Indian court life and furnishings as lavishly and correctly as possible. They even imported monumental statues and other ceremonial gear from India. Shortly before A.D. 600, however, independent stylistic development, presaging the magnificent architecture and sculpture of later centuries, demonstrated the emancipation of southeast Asian courts from their earlier tutelage.

It should perhaps be emphasized that the great bulk of the population of southeast Asia was very slightly affected by the introduction of these new styles of court life and architecture from India. Heavier labor service and taxes were perhaps the only difference villagers could notice. But the same might of course be said of the Romanization of Gaul and Britain which had been carried through some four centuries earlier. Indian expansion into southeast Asia was geographically a good deal more extensive than the westward movement of Hellenism, and also may perhaps be said to have affected more people, since the imprint of Indian models on native cultures of that part of the world has lasted until our own time.

Buddhist missions to the Far East. Buddhists played a part in the earliest phase of Indian penetration of southeast Asia, but it was Hindu religious ideas and cult practices that prevailed in most of the region, perhaps because Hinduism was more hospitable to local cults and religious practices than Buddhism could be. North of the mountains Hinduism never made any important impression. Buddhism, on the contrary, flowed like a mighty torrent into China and lapped over into Korea and Japan between A.D. 200 and 600.

The reception of Buddhism in China constituted a conscious break with Confucian traditions and values. Nothing, indeed, could be more alien to the cool, this-worldly moderation of Confucianism, with its emphasis upon family and political duties, than Indian Buddhism, which sought escape from the world and preached ascetic withdrawal from all ordinary society. Perhaps it was just this antithesis that appealed to the Chinese. For when the Han government began to lose its grip on the country as a whole, and barbarian invasion added a fresh dimension of violence to the miseries of civil war, the sage advice of Confucians, recommending moderation and decorum, must have sounded as hollow as the consolations of Greek philosophy did to Roman ears in the same age. Stronger medicine for the soul was needed in such times. The Romans found the answer in Christianity, the Chinese in Buddhism. Yet although Buddhism came to command a wide following among the Chinese, adepts in the older Confucian lore never disappeared and never surrendered their distrust of a doctrine so subversive of ordinary life and political discipline as Buddhism — at least if taken literally — appeared to be.

Efforts to get correct knowledge and true images of Buddha led several Chinese pilgrims to travel to India and visit the scenes of Buddha's life. Some of them brought back whole libraries of Buddhist texts and proceeded to organize systematic translation. But by about A.D. 600 the initial phase of eager appropriation of Buddhist learning had been pretty well completed.

Chinese Buddhists never paid much attention to the sectarian differences that divided the Indians, nor did the complex metaphysical speculations to which the Indian monks devoted their intellectual energies appeal to the Chinese. Mystical enlightenment, however, and the retreat from civil society into a community of like-minded, disciplined seekers after peace of soul did meet a need that neither the Confucian nor the Taoist traditions of China knew how to cope with. Chinese Buddhism therefore soon began to evolve in directions of its own, essentially independent of the declining curve of Buddhist fortunes in India.

Buddhism brought a distinctive style of art into China. Greek and Indian elements had already blended in central Asia to produce a stately, impressive style. In China, Buddhist art underwent rapid adjustment to the Chinese environment, so that by A.D. 600 an effective and unmistakably Chinese version had developed. Before the reception of Buddhism, Chinese art had been mainly decorative and geometrical. Buddhist art, on the contrary, centered upon a stylized yet basically naturalistic portrayal of bodhisattvas, that is, of divine helpers of mankind clothed in human form. In addition, Buddhist wall paintings and carvings often tried to tell a story which required the artist to suggest spatial and other relationships between his figures. These aspects of Buddhist art represented a notable enrichment of the Chinese artistic tradition and remained of great importance even after Buddhism itself had been sloughed off.

The impact of Buddhism on Korea and Japan was of a profounder character. Those lands boasted no very impressive pre-existing high culture. They found themselves on the extreme edge of the Chinese sphere of influence in the period when China proper was eagerly absorbing Buddhism. Hence it was Chinese civilization in Buddhist dress that attracted the kings and courtiers of Korea who, between A.D. 373 and 528, made Buddhism into a state religion in each of the kingdoms into which Korea was then divided. Japan, being more remote, was less ready to grasp the latest modes of Chinese culture. Nevertheless, a Buddhist mission that reached the land of the Rising Sun in A.D. 552 met with important success. From that time onward the Japanese islands joined the circle of the civilized (and semi-civilized) nations clustering around the imposing bulk of China.

Indian influence upon the west. Indian influence on the Iranian and Roman parts of the civilized world was far less evident than it was in the Far East and central Asia. Indeed, scholars are far from agreed that there was any important Indian impact on Europe and western Asia. The trouble is that records are lacking. If Christian and other religious ascetics of the Iranian and Roman worlds were influenced in any important ways from India, they failed to say so; and, in the nature of the case, we cannot expect records to have been made. Assuredly humble folk traveling back and forth between India and Alexandria had ample opportunity to exchange tales about the wonders of Indian ascetic practices. Indeed, we know that at least one Indian holy man reached the Mediterranean, because a "gymnosophist" burned himself publicly in Athens and by doing so excited enough wonderment that his deed was recorded. But Christian monks who saw visions and interpreted them as visions of God could not be expected to know or admit that Indian idolators had done the same centuries before. Nevertheless, the resemblances between certain details of Christian ascetic practices and the devotions of Indian sages are striking, and the style of holiness embraced so fervently by the early monks of Egypt and Syria bore a general resemblance to much more ancient Indian ascetic disciplines and withdrawal from the world. That some early Christian monks may have picked up useful hints about how to be holy from tales or personal study of Indian ascetic practices seems entirely possible, but remains quite unproven.

In the field of philosophy itself — once the pride and arcanum of Greek pagan rationalism — the new themes and mystical emphasis introduced by Plotinus (d. A.D. 270) resembled themes long familiar to students of the Upanishads. At the very least, Plotinus and his contemporaries were aware that Indian philosophy existed, and that it was as sophisticated and massive as the Greek tradition itself.

A Westerner is always likely to underestimate the magnitude of a cultural movement which affected his own past in disguised and limited ways. It is therefore well to underline the fact that the expansion of Indian civilization to southeast Asia and its impact on Chinese, Korean, and Japanese styles of life imbued the civilization of more than half the human race with a common tint. Insofar as Asia has any community of cultural tradition uniting the Indian with the Chinese, Japanese, Korean, Mongolian, Tibetan, Burmese, and Ceylonese peoples, it is due to the contagion of ancient Indian civilization, especially in its religious manifestation.

The achievement of Hellenism was no greater.

XII

Barbarian Invasions and Civilized Response

A.D. 200–600

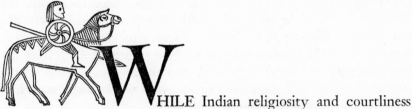

WHILE Indian religiosity and courtliness were winning converts in southern and eastern Asia, in the north the harsh shouting of warriors and the clash of arms resounded all along the length of the frontier between steppe barbarism and the civilized communities of Europe and Asia. Both in China and in Europe, civilized defenses were beaten back by advancing barbarians, but in the center of the long line the Iranians held the steppe peoples at bay. China proved capable of absorbing her invaders, and re-established imperial unity (A.D. 589) after some three and a half centuries of division and disorder. By contrast the Roman empire was never reconstituted after the great barbarian breakthroughs of the period A.D. 375–525.*

The Iranians met a more surprising fate. After their long and successful struggle against steppe barbarians and a series of hardfought but indecisive wars against the Romans of Constantinople, the Persian empire of the Sassanids collapsed before Arab invaders

---

* But the fiction carried on. In western Europe, for example, the last "Roman" emperor abdicated in 1806 and adopted the more accurate title "Emperor of Austria." In the Balkans, Greek-speaking Roman emperors reigned uninterruptedly from the "New Rome" of Constantinople until 1204. After A.D. 565 these Roman emperors are commonly termed Byzantine, but they referred to themselves as Romans, and the last claimant to the title disappeared only in 1453, when the Turks conquered Constantinople.

from the south. The conquerors were newly converted to the faith of Mohammed, which armed them with theological weapons that proved at least as effective as their (quite ordinary) horsemen, bows, and lances. Yet before the Iranians merged their cultural identity into the world of Islam, their military success against the steppe peoples and against more civilized neighbors compelled or induced Romans on the west and oasis dwellers of central Asia on the east to borrow much from them, in the process becoming what Western historians have long been accustomed to call "medieval."

During the period between A.D. 200 and 600, therefore, the northern parts of the civilized world were influenced by two distinct forces: the steppe barbarians, forever battering at the gates, countered by the Iranian example of how to organize effective defense against barbarian attack. A somewhat closer look at the course of events will show how this see-saw worked across each of the exposed frontiers of the civilized world.

The Huns and the western steppe. The nomad peoples of the Eurasian steppe may be likened to molecules of gas in a very leaky bottle. Pressure at any point spread rapidly through the entire system. Any groups of nomads displaced from traditional pasture grounds either perished or quickly seized a neighbor's pasturage by force of arms. Within a few seasons, therefore, any important disturbance of pasturage rights spread from one end of the grasslands to the other, neighbor nudging neighbor, until the weakest or least well-organized groups either died, fled into the inhospitable forest land lying north or west of the steppe, or else penetrated civilized defenses to the south, where they might become masters of agricultural populations.

We have already seen how the rise of the Hsiung-nu confederacy just before 200 B.C. started one such wave of migration (above, p. 163). Soon after A.D. 350 a similar confederation centering once more in Outer Mongolia took form. The Chinese called it Juan-juan. At its height, this war confederation exerted authority all the way from Manchuria to Lake Balkhash. As the Juan-juan power swept westward along the steppe, whole tribes and peoples fled before the assault.

One such group was known in European history as Huns. They appeared in southern Russia in A.D. 374 and immediately defeated the Ostrogoths, who had been ruling that region for a century or more. Fear of the Huns persuaded the neighboring tribe of Visigoths to seek refuge inside Roman frontiers, where that wandering horde of warriors lived off the country, alternately quarreling and making alliances with the Roman authorities. After sacking the city of Rome in A.D. 410 the Visigoths moved westward to Spain, where they set up a kingdom that lasted until A.D. 711. Several plundering German tribes soon followed the Visigoths; others submitted to the formidable Huns.

Meanwhile the Huns had set up their headquarters in the Hungarian plain, from which vantage point they raided southward into the Balkans and westward into Italy and Gaul. Yet in A.D. 453 when Attila, their last great war captain, died, the Hunnic confederacy broke up even more rapidly than it had arisen. Quarrels among rival leaders combined with rebellion on the part of some of the subjugated peoples to destroy almost overnight what had been a vast territorial hegemony.

The overthrow of the Huns' empire failed to bring any sort of order to western Europe. Some of the Germanic peoples who had been subjugated by the Huns fled south and west to Roman territory, and set up new kingdoms in north Africa (Vandals), Gaul (Burgundians), and Italy (Ostrogoths). Simultaneously, a quite different and much more lasting German advance took place in Britain and the Rhineland. Here German-speaking plowmen took over new and fertile acres which had formerly been thinly occupied by Roman (i.e. mostly Celtic) populations. This agricultural settlement proved lasting, whereas states set up by roving bands of warriors were all short-lived, like the similar barbarian regimes of north China and eastern Iran.

Steppe peoples of the east. The migrations and political changes precipitated in western Europe by the sudden appearance of the Huns were matched by similar disturbances accompanying the almost simultaneous eruption of the Ephthalites (sometimes termed Ephthalite Huns or White Huns) into eastern Iran. From this base, the Ephthalites raided northwest India, and eventually set up a predatory empire of their own, which spanned the mountains just as the Kushan empire had done before. The disorders loosed upon India by the Ephthalites brought the Gupta age and dynasty to an end. But the invaders were not more able than the Huns of Europe to establish a stable regime over the lands their bows and horses had conquered. Ephthalite power in India disintegrated into endemic civil war by A.D. 549. North of the mountains the horde was finally destroyed less than a generation later, in A.D. 567.

The fundamental weakness of these barbarian states was everywhere the same. Their rulers tried to do two incompatible things. On the one hand the victorious chieftain and his followers wanted to retain the traditional ways and manners of their predatory past. On the other, they sought to enjoy the luxuries and delights of civilized living by squeezing goods and services from their new subjects. But the more civilized the conquerors became, the less did old tribal and war band traditions hold up. Easy living and vice regularly undermined barbarian vigor and warlike effectiveness within a generation or two.

Civilized peoples as a rule disliked their barbarian masters. When opportunity offered they were predisposed to welcome a liberator who proclaimed his loyalty to old traditions and ideals. The Chinese and Persians had the greatest success in rolling back the barbarian tide in this fashion. In A.D. 552 the Juan-juan confederacy was destroyed by Chinese armies co-operating with Turks who promptly created a new steppe empire as formidable as the Juan-juan had been. Yet a dynastic quarrel within the ruling family of the new empire led in A.D. 572 to the division of the Turkish confederacy into eastern and western hordes, each jealous of the other and riven by internal quarrels.

With the threat and pressure from the steppe reduced in this way, a new Chinese dynasty, the Sui, swept away the last of the barbarian states of north China and reunited the entire country in A.D. 589. China's military and cultural dominance over the adjacent barbarian peoples was thereby unambiguously re-established.

Almost the same rhythm of events manifested itself along the eastern frontier of Iran. Persian monarchs of the Sassanian dynasty combined with the Turks in A.D. 567 to overthrow the Ephthalites.

The quarrel between the two branches of the Turkish confederation which ensued almost immediately allowed the Sassanians to
push the frontier of the Persian empire to the Oxus river once
again, thus reuniting the eastern marchlands with the rest of the
Iranian lands.

Weakening of the Roman empire. The Romans, however, were
not so successful. During the first prolonged and bitter crisis of
civil war and invasion (A.D. 235–84) the Roman imperial government had become an undisguised military despotism. Such a regime
was not very popular since officials often behaved in a violent and
tyrannical fashion. Moreover, the will of the soldiery was fickle. A
general, elevated to supreme power through a soldiers' revolt,
might find himself deposed without warning if, for any reason, he
proved incapable of pleasing the armies that put him in power. Fictitious election to office by the "Senate and people of Rome" no
longer meant anything more than ceremonial validation of naked
military usurpation.

The Emperor Constantine (ruled A.D. 312–337) changed Roman government in two important respects. He established a new
capital at Byzantium, which he renamed Constantinople, and he
made Christianity a favored state religion. The new capital was
well situated both for trade and for defense, since it was relatively
easy to supply the city from the far-flung coastlands of the Black
and Aegean seas. The uninterrupted survival of Roman (often
called Byzantine) imperial government until 1204 was made possible by this fact.

Christianity also lent important support to the imperial Roman
government from Constantine's time onward. Most of the Christian bishops proved eager to co-operate with the emperor, and regarded Constantine and his successors as chosen by God for their
imperial office. Here was a simple but persuasive idea that could
really clothe the nakedness of military usurpation with the garment
of legitimacy. The Emperor Theodosius (d. A.D. 395) carried the
alliance between throne and altar to its logical conclusion by pro-
hibiting all rival faiths, thus making Rome officially Christian.

Yet this commitment raised another acute problem, for Christians did not all agree on details of doctrine. Soldier emperors and

JUSTINIAN'S EMPIRE c. 565

◻ East Roman Empire c. 530

▨ Extent of Justinian's reconquest to 565

Volga R.

Dnieper R.

Danube R.

GEPIDS from 450
AVARS after 567

AVARS 559-567

Scale of Miles

0   500

SLAVS

THRACE

Black Sea

Constantinople

SASSANIDS

EAST ROMAN EMPIRE

Antioch
SYRIA
Jerusalem
Red Sea

EGYPT
Nile R.
Alexandria

Athens

Mediterranean Sea

SICILY

SARDINIA

Rome

CORSICA

KDM. OF THE VANDALS

Carthage

KDM. OF THE EAST GOTHS

Ravenna

Milan

KDM. OF BURGUNDY

Rhône R.

Rhine R.

KDM. OF THE FRANKS

BRITAIN

ANGLO-SAXONS

BASQUES

SUEVES

KDM. OF THE WEST GOTHS

MAURETANIANS

A F R I C A

Atlantic Ocean

politic bishops found it hard to handle such issues in an age when abstruse questions of theology became popular rallying cries around which all sorts of discontents against constituted authority quickly gathered.

Most of the Germanic kingdoms of western Europe confronted similar problems. Nearly all the German kings accepted a variant form of Christianity which made them foul heretics in the eyes of most of their Roman subjects. The emperor Justinian, therefore (A.D. 527–65), had good ground for hoping that if he could overthrow the German kings' military forces he could expect a majority of the local inhabitants to rally to his side. He accordingly launched a series of campaigns into the western Mediterranean, seeking to re-establish the unity of the Roman empire. He was only partly successful; and nearly all the gains he won in north Africa, Spain, and Italy had to be given up immediately after his death, when new invaders attacked the Roman frontiers.

Reactions to the barbarians in China and Iran. The differing degrees of success with which the Chinese, Iranians, and Romans re-established the unity and security of their states in the sixth century provide an index of the adequacy of their political and military institutions in the face of the barbarian challenge.

China had the advantage that her traditional imperial institutions had themselves been shaped in the days of the Han to cope with the barbarian threat offered by the Hsiung-nu. Hence the Sui emperors and their successors of the T'ang dynasty were able to conform faithfully to ancient imperial precedent while re-establishing an effective frontier guard against the Turkish confederacy. Diplomacy, subsidy, and the use of Chinese commanders to control barbarian mercenary troops guarding the frontier, all came into play. Behind the reconstituted defenses, the Sui organized an efficient, rather ruthless, bureaucratic regime, whose greatest accomplishment was the completion of a canal linking the Yangtse with the Yellow river. This canal speedily became a major artery of China's imperial economy. Products from the fertile south could be sent north via the canal to the imperial capital where officials and soldiers stood ready to consume the enlarged supply that thus be-

WEI CHINA
398-580

JUAN-JUAN

Kanchow

Yellow R.

Yangtze R.

Nanhai

SUI CHINA
580-618

EASTERN TURKS

Kanchow

Yellow R.

Grand Canal

Yangtze R.

Kwangchow

RESTORATION OF CHINA'S UNITY

L. Baikal

Amur R.

MANCHURIA

L. Balkhash

Jaxartes R.

WESTERN TURKS   EASTERN TURKS

552-748

Oxus R.

EPHTHALITES

Kashgar

Khotan   Silk Route

Kanchow

Great Wall

Yellow R.

JAPAN

KOREA

Grand Canal

SASSANIAN EMPIRE TO 650

Indus R.

HIMALAYAS

T I B E T

Lhasa

Ch'angan

Wu

Pacific

Ganges R.

Brahmaputra R.

TAIWAN

Pataliputra

Yangtze R.

I N D I A   BURMA

Salween R.

Kwangchow

Ocean

T'ANG CHINA
618-906

South China Sea

Mekong R.

Scale of Miles

0   500

194

came available to them. Closer control of the entire Yangtse valley and a far greater concentration of goods at imperial headquarters became possible after the opening of the Grand Canal, as this waterway was called. Hence the reconstituted imperial China was stronger than in Han times, able to mobilize more men and material for warlike or peaceful enterprises than ever before. Barbarian raiding, therefore, quickly lost its terrors in the face of the organized imperial might of reunited China.

The Iranians had a rather more complex problem. No new resources lay easily at hand, as in China, to reinforce the imperial, central power. To be sure, the technology of heavy armored cavalry was familiar enough. The difficulty lay in creating a system of society that could support a sufficient number of suitably armored and trained cavalrymen near enough to the frontier to provide effective and continual protection against steppe raiding. The Parthian monarchs had allowed (perhaps they even encouraged) the growth of a military class of landowners who equipped themselves as heavy cavalrymen and were perpetually on the alert to protect their own lands from destruction. But the Parthian monarchs never solved the problem of exerting anything like an effective central power over the Iranian baronage. The Parthian royal government seems to have favored cities and towns, whence came their supply of ready cash. But the towns of Iran and Mesopotamia failed to supply enough money to the king to permit him to maintain a strong enough standing force of heavy cavalry to be able to overawe his powerful subjects. Hence the price of an effective frontier guard against the steppe had been a continual welter of local rebellion and disobedience which enormously weakened the central authority of the Parthian government.

The Sassanian empire. In A.D. 226 one such rebel, Ardashir, supplanted the Parthian regime entirely. The Sassanian family to which Ardashir belonged remained on the throne of Persia and Mesopotamia until A.D. 651. Sassanian royal power underwent many spectacular crises during these centuries, and not all the kings followed the same policy. Nevertheless, the principles laid down by Ardashir (reigned A.D. 226–241) were never abandoned for long. For the founder of the Sassanian state based his power squarely on the Iranian baronage. He cultivated a consciousness of the Persian imperial past, and in particular supported and was supported by a reconstituted Zoroastrianism. Appeal to Persian imperial greatness and to the faith of Zoroaster apparently had the effect of persuading most of the barons of the countryside to support the Sassanian monarchs, at least in times of crisis. The central power therefore remained alive and vigorous, a formidable rival for the Roman empire.

Zoroastrian doctrine depended on local traditions that had been treasured by priestly and aristocratic families like that from which Ardashir himself had sprung. But there were embarrassing divergences from shrine to shrine. The Sassanian kings therefore ordered that a canonical version of the Zoroastrian scripture, the *Avesta*, should be established. They further decreed that the Zoroastrian heritage should be enriched by suitable borrowings from Greek and Indian authors. But the revamped faith, despite the coherence and completeness with which its scriptures were thus endowed, never took root in the cities of the Sassanian realm. The baronage, however, appears to have been well enough pleased, since rebellion, usurpation, and royal assassination — which constituted the order of the day in Rome — remained comparatively rare in Persia. Throne and altar, in other words, appear to have made an effective alliance in Sassanian Persia almost a full century before Constantine inaugurated a similar alliance within Roman boundaries.

The real importance of the Sassanian experiment lay not in details of doctrine, which were lost soon after the Moslem conquest cut off Persian cultural independence. Rather, it was the fact that the supernatural sanctions invoked by official religion and an organized priesthood effectively reconciled the conflict of interest between militarized landowners and the central royal authority. A numerous and formidable fighting class of heavy armored cavalry could thus protect the land from raids without at the same time threatening to tear civilized society apart through incessant civil war. No other part of the civilized world was so successful at inventing new institutional forms. The Sassanian example, therefore, had a powerful effect on Byzantium, and through Byzantium on western Europe.

Sassanian religion. Nevertheless, the alliance of king, barons, and Zoroastrian priesthood was not without its cost. The cities of Mesopotamia, from which the Parthian rulers had drawn their strength, were more or less excluded from the Sassanian scheme of things. Perhaps for this reason, the Sassanian period was one of unusual religious effervescence in Mesopotamia. The greatest figure was the prophet Mani (*c.* A.D. 216–77). King Shapur I (reigned A.D. 241–271), son and successor of the founder of the Sassanian dynasty, appears to have looked favorably upon Mani, perhaps hoping to balance the proud rural Zoroastrianism of his father against Mani's new revelation which appealed mainly to the urban inhabitants of his realm.

Mani was a most self-conscious prophet. He set out to purge all existing religions of the corruptions which time had worked in the divine message, which, he held, had everywhere been the same, even when delivered through such diverse lips as those of Jesus, Buddha, and Zoroaster. To guard against similar corruption of his own revelation, Mani personally wrote his message down and emphatically prohibited careless copying of his sacred texts. As a result, Manichean scripture always remained scarce, and modern scholars cannot reconstitute Mani's texts from the scraps and paraphrases (often emanating from religious rivals) which alone survive. Mani's precautions against corruption thus backfired. So did the excessive precision with which he established his church and organized missionary enterprise. Having foreseen and prohibited all sorts of errors and vulgarizations, Mani in effect limited his doctrine to an elite of specially trained and disciplined souls.

Despite this limitation, during his lifetime Mani met with wide acceptance in Mesopotamia and in other commercial centers, both east and west. Yet at home, the Zoroastrian priesthood was not kindly disposed to a prophet who accused them of having corrupted the truth originally entrusted to them by Zoroaster. Hence, when Shapur I died (A.D. 271) Mani was exposed to the anger of outraged Zoroastrian orthodoxy. As a result he spent his last years in prison and his followers suffered severe persecution. This did not prevent the survival of the faith, but did make the Manicheans into opponents of the regime.

Three hundred years later a more definitely revolutionary faith was preached in Persia by a prophet named Mazdak. An emphatic egalitarianism seems to have been central to Mazdak's message, although details cannot be recovered from the shocked denunciations of his opponents who accused the Mazdakites of advocating community of property and of women. For a while, Mazdakism enjoyed royal tolerance; but when Chosroes I (reigned A.D. 531 –79) came to the throne, he embarked upon a policy of violent suppression which extirpated all of the sect's overt manifestations.

As it happened, none of these Iranian-Mesopotamian religious movements led to the establishment of a world-girdling faith. Instead, Islam invaded Iran and gave the Sassanian world a religion suited to urban needs and at the same time able to over-awe the countryside. Because of this, not much is known about Sassanian religion or cultural life at large. Yet, if one remembers that despite its late start, Manicheism constituted the most formidable competitor Christianity had to face in the Roman empire, and realizes that the oases of central Asia as far as the Chinese frontier became outposts of Sassanian religious and cultural life, then the strength and vitality of the Sassanian civilization can be better appreciated.

Art also offers some indication of the importance of the Sassanian accomplishment. Some of the features of Byzantine architecture appear to have originated in Sassanian Persia. But unfortunately the piles of dusty brick which alone survive today can give us no real idea of what the royal palaces were like. Their exteriors may never have been particularly impressive, but the domed and vaulted interiors, where glazed bricks once made the light shimmer in brightly colored patterns along the walls, must have been splendid indeed.

The Byzantine empire. Other things too the Romans borrowed or adopted from Persian models. Royal state, for instance — crown and scepter — and rituals of court ceremonial were deliberately borrowed by Diocletian (reigned A.D. 284–305), in the hope of clothing his person in an aura of mystery that would inhibit the sort of squalid assassination that had met so many of his predecessors. Most important of all, after the time of Constantine, the Romans also made heavy armed cavalrymen the backbone of their imperial field army. No other kind of force was capable of meeting Persian attack on the one hand and barbarian harassment on the other.

The Romans, however, were unwilling to adapt their social structure to the Sassanian "feudal" style. An elaborate body of legal principles and practices that had grown up piecemeal across the centuries inhibited any really drastic alteration of the urban-centered social and political order. Justinian's (A.D. 527–65) codification of Roman law was therefore not merely a matter of administrative convenience; it also constituted a reassertion of continuity with a distinctly Roman and fundamentally urban antiquity.

To solve the immediate military problem of defense the Byzantine emperors tried to keep a standing force in being, preferably near their own persons, ready at a moment's notice to travel to any threatened frontier or revolted province and there enforce the imperial will. But tax income was not sufficient to maintain a large force of expensively equipped and armored cavalrymen. When Justinian attempted to reconquer the lost provinces of the western Mediterranean, for example, he resorted to the practice of allowing his great general Belisarius to raise a company of 5000 heavy cavalrymen privately, in the expectation of paying them from booty and plunder. Belisarius' long campaign in Italy (A.D. 535–548) therefore involved ruthless and prolonged plundering, which turned out to be more damaging to local inhabitants than any of the previous barbarian invasions had been.

Inevitably, when the principal armed force of the state remained near the imperial person, the frontiers were seriously exposed. Time and again small-scale raids from beyond the Danube, for instance, went scot-free since the imperial bodyguard could not leave Constantinople to chase down every little band of marauders. As a result, the Balkan hinterland lay at the mercy of small bands. Only a few coastal cities, strong behind their walls, remained safe. Nothing remotely resembling the vigorous Sassanian local defense system protected Roman frontiers.

The exposure of the borderlands to barbarian raids and infiltration was, in a sense, the price paid by the urban populations of the empire for their continued dominance of society. An armed, rural aristocracy would have challenged that dominance, as had happened in Iran and Mesopotamia with the establishment of the Sassanian empire. The emperors and people of Constantinople opted instead to let the remote and barren inland regions of the empire go, if need be, while defending the vitals of the state with a small mobile standing army, technically equipped in the Persian manner, but maintained by taxes and booty rather than by grants of land.

Heresy and orthodoxy. The urban, and in certain basic tenets also democratic, character of Christianity reflected and sustained this emphasis within late Roman and early Byzantine society, just as the aristocratic Zoroastrianism of Sassanian Persia did for the militarily more successful regime of Iran. Thus, in refusing to imitate the Sassanian military model in its entirety, the Byzantines asserted the socio-political difference between their sea-centered empire and a purely land power such as Persia. The development of Christianity and clearer definition of church organization and doctrine also underlined the differences between the two rival empires.

Even before Constantine made Christianity a legal religion, teachers in Alexandria had tried to organize Christian doctrine into coherent form. The great pioneer was Origen (d. *c.* A.D. 251), who, inevitably, when attempting to speak about ultimate realities fell back upon the vocabulary of Greek philosophy. Thenceforward, argument about points of Christian doctrine was couched in a philosophic, and sometimes extremely abstruse, Greek. As soon as the pressure of official persecution was removed (A.D. 312) a series of bitter disputes broke out among Christians. Donatism in North Africa and Arianism in Egypt attracted Constantine's personal attention; and when remonstrance failed to bring reconciliation among the warring theologians, the Emperor summoned the first ecumenical council of the Christian church at Nicaea in A.D. 325. There the doctrine of Arius concerning the relation between Father and Son of the Trinity was anathematized, and a concise creed

(The Apostles' Creed) was approved as orthodox. This did not suffice to convince Arian Christians, however. Subsequent councils, summoned to deal with yet other heresies, succeeded only in defining orthodoxy more and more precisely, and in expelling those who thought otherwise on disputed points.

The major and enduring doctrinal splits that developed among Christians tended to conform to deep-seated ethnic and cultural lines of demarcation. The Coptic church in Egypt and the Syriac church in western Asia voiced secular and ethnic as well as theological dissatisfaction with rule from Constantinople. Disaffection was so widespread that when Moslem Arabs invaded Egypt and Syria, they were often greeted as liberators from a heretical and oppressive yoke.

Relations between Greek- and Latin-speaking Christians were more complex. Rome was the seat of the pope, i.e. the bishop of Rome. Tradition held that the church of Rome had been founded by the Apostle Peter. The popes therefore considered themselves to be successors to Saint Peter and claimed primacy over the entire Christian church on the ground that Peter had been specially appointed by Christ as prince of the Apostles. Other major bishoprics of the Christian world resisted the pope's claim and preferred to rely on a council of all the bishops to settle matters of common concern. When the Council of Chalcedon (A.D. 451) accepted Pope Leo the Great's formulation of trinitarian doctrine (thereby repudiating a theological view popular in Egypt and Syria) a headlong collision between the two theories of church government was postponed but not, of course, resolved.

Debate over points of doctrine and church discipline occasioned a great outpouring of polemical and expository works, together with numerous commentaries on scripture and a few ventures into speculative theology. The bulk of this literature was written in Greek, where it gave exhaustive definition both to orthodoxy and to its opposing heresies. In the Latin world, the role of the church fathers was different, for they were less concerned to refute heresy than to make the truths and basic documents of Christianity available to Latin readers. St. Jerome (d. A.D. 420), for example, translated the whole Bible into Latin — the so-called *Vulgate*, which became a canonical version for later generations of Latin Christians. His contemporary, St. Augustine of Hippo (d. A.D. 430), produced a shower of sermons, biblical commentaries, and apologetic writings. His greatest work, *The City of God*, sketched a universal Christian history, extending from creation to the day of judgment, which remained fundamental to the world-view of western Europe. His *Confessions* offered a vivid autobiography of his conversion to Christianity and ended with a penetrating philosophic inquiry into the nature of time and eternity. Taken together, Augustine's works gave later Latin Christians a theological and philosophic statement of their faith and imparted a distinctly Platonic coloring to it.

As the Germanic invasions and attendant disorders (A.D. 375–525) disrupted the urban centers of the Latin West, monasteries became the most active centers of Christian piety, education, and culture. Latin monasticism received its lasting and individual character when St. Benedict of Nursia (*flor. c.* A.D. 529) drew upon his personal experience as abbot of a monastery at Monte Cassino to create his *Rule* for the governance of the monks' daily lives.

With the decay of imperial administration in the western, Latin-speaking provinces of the empire, the church inevitably assumed a fairly independent attitude vis-à-vis secular authorities, who were more likely to appear as ravaging plunderers than in any other guise. The conversion of Clovis, king of the Franks, to the orthodox form of Christianity in A.D. 496 did bring the most powerful German kingdom officially within the pale of papal Christianity; but the conduct of Clovis and his successors was barely tinged by Christian precepts. Impoverishment and political chaos in Italy attendant upon Justinian's long-drawn-out wars of conquest weakened the authority the pope was able to exert outside of Rome itself. By contrast, the Eastern church under the administration of the patriarch of Constantinople remained closely in touch with the imperial authorities. In many cases the Greek church operated almost as an arm of the government, yet in other instances, patriarchs boldly opposed imperial decrees as heretical.

A Christendom so deeply divided between Greek, Latin, Syriac, and Coptic churches was clearly in no very favorable position to withstand the assault of Islam, especially since the Arab conquest from the south coincided with renewed attacks from the north where disturbances on the steppe once again set whole peoples in motion across Christendom's ill-defended frontiers.

The changed balance of the world resulting from the explosion of Islam will be the theme of the next chapter.

XIII

The Rise of Islam

IN A.D. 636 an Arab army defeated the Roman (Byzantine) garrison of Syria and Palestine, and permanently eliminated Roman power from those two provinces. Shortly thereafter, other Arab expeditionary forces overran Mesopotamia (A.D. 641) and Egypt (A.D. 642), and by A.D. 651 Iran had also been annexed to the new Islamic empire created by these victories. The fervor of fresh religious revelation vouchsafed to the prophet Mohammed (d. A.D. 632) inspired these extraordinary victories. Even more remarkable was the fact that the religious conviction Mohammed aroused enabled crude Arab conquerors and their descendants to weld a new and distinctively Islamic civilization from the various and often discordant elements Middle Easterners had inherited from a past that reached all the way back to the first beginning of civilization.

The life of Mohammed. In Mohammed's time, Arabia was divided between warlike tribes, some nomadic and some settled at agricultural oases or in trading towns. Judaism and Christianity had made some inroads into Arabia, but Mecca, the city of Mohammed's birth, remained pagan. As a young man, Mohammed probably traveled with caravans carrying goods to towns along the Palestinian border. Then at about the age of forty he began to fall into trances and hear voices, which he presently recognized as visitations from the angel Gabriel, instructing him in obedience to the will of Allah. Under the impulsion of these experiences, Mohammed began to preach the unity and omnipotence of Allah, the impending day of judgment, and the necessity of complete obedience to Allah's will. He summed up his message under the rubric "Islam," that is, "submission" to Allah. Prayers five times daily, alms-giving, pilgrimage to Mecca at least once in a lifetime, abstention from wine and pork, and a month-long fast from sun-up to sun-set every year were the principal obligations Mohammed imposed upon the faithful. Obedience to Allah, the Prophet revealed, would be rewarded by a place in Paradise, whereas idolaters and other wicked men were destined to suffer eternal fiery torment. Bodily resurrection on the Last Day was another point upon which Mohammed put much emphasis.

Initially, the Prophet assumed that Jews and Christians would recognize his preaching as the last and most perfect revelation of God's will. For Allah, Mohammed believed, was the same deity who had spoken to Abraham, Moses, Jesus, and all the other Hebrew prophets. Since Allah could not contradict himself, differences between Mohammed's own revelation and the tenets of the older religions were explained simply as the result of human error or corruptions of the authentic divine message.

A few Meccans accepted Mohammed's warnings, but the great majority declined to give up their traditional worship, which Mohammed denounced as idolatry. Then, in A.D. 622, Mohammed fled from Mecca to Medina, where he had been invited by strife-torn factions of that oasis city in the hope that an outsider could adjudicate their quarrels. From this time onward, Mohammed became a political leader and lawgiver. At Medina, Mohammed had his first direct encounter with Jews, who declined to accept his authority. Mohammed therefore attacked them, and took their land for his own followers. A little later, Mohammed subjugated another Jewish oasis. This time he left the inhabitants in possession of their land on condition that they render tribute in the form of a head tax. These first encounters were of great importance because they became binding precedents, defining the relation between Moslem rulers and their Jewish (and also Christian) subjects.

While at Medina, Mohammed attracted a steady flow of new recruits and converts. As a result, the community of the faithful was soon hard pressed to find a livelihood in the narrow confines of the Medinan oasis. An obvious solution was to raid caravans owned by the Meccans. The first raids were successful; others soon followed until resistance in Mecca crumbled. Mohammed returned in triumph and then went on to unite all of Arabia under the banner of Islam, partly by war, but mainly by diplomacy and negotiation.

Scarcely had this been accomplished when Mohammed died (A.D. 632), leaving no son to succeed him. One of the Prophet's old friends and close companions, Abu Bakr, was chosen as caliph (i.e. successor) to lead the Moslem community. He immediately had to face a widespread withdrawal of allegiance by Arab chieftains, who felt that their submission to Mohammed did not obligate them to the community of the faithful as a whole. But when it came to fighting, the enthusiasm and conviction of the hard core of Mohammed's converts once again prevailed, and the Arabian chieftains were forced to unite once more behind the banner of the new faith. Abu Bakr died as soon as this crisis was past (A.D. 634). Leadership passed next to Omar (caliph from A.D. 634–644), who proved himself not only pious and devout, but also a very successful general and administrator.

Arab conquest and the Ommayad caliphate. The consolidation of all Arabia prefaced the amazing series of Arab conquests that brought the whole of the ancient Middle East (except for Asia Minor) as well as the desert region of the lower Indus valley (by A.D. 705), North Africa and even Spain (by 711) under Moslem control. No military change accounts for these victories. Arab armies were neither very numerous nor particularly well equipped, but the conviction that God was with them, the belief that death in battle assured a blissful life in Paradise, and Omar's effective leadership sufficed to give the Arabs superiority over their enemies.

After A.D. 715, however, easy victories stopped. The city of Byzantium withstood a hard and prolonged siege (717–18). This major defeat was matched by failure in a series of frontier skirmishes in central Asia, where a Turkish force pushed the Moslems out of eastern Iran by 715. A little later, the Franks defeated a

RISE OF ISLAM
622-733

Under Mohammed (to 632)
Under Abu Bakr (to 634)
Under Omar and Ommayad Caliph (to 656)
Under Ommayad Caliph (to 733)

Scale of Miles
0   1000

ENGLAND

Atlantic Ocean

Tours 733 ✕

KDM. OF THE
FRANKS

Rhine R.

KDM. OF THE
WEST GOTHS

Cordova

SLAVS

AVARS

Danube R.

BULGARS

EAST

LOMBARDS

Rome

ROMAN

Constantinople (Byzantine)
EMPIRE
717-18

Black Sea

KHAZARS

Caucasus

Caspian Sea

Aral Sea

A   S   I   A

CHINA

KASHMIR

Indus R.

INDIA

Talas ✕ 751

FERGANA

712

Oxus R.

705

SIND

P E R S I A
(IRAN)

Baghdad

A R A B I A

Medina

Mecca

Red Sea

646

636

640

SYRIA

Damascus

PALESTINE

CYPRUS

Mediterranean Sea

643

Cairo

EGYPT

Nile R.

Kairouan

647

FEZZAN

700

A   F   R   I   C   A

ETHIOPIA

Arabian Sea

Indian Ocean

207

Moslem raiding party at the battle of Tours in central Gaul (A.D. 733).

These defeats, together with the inevitable waning of the first flush of religious excitement and conviction, created acute problems within the Moslem community. During the first generation or two, the Arab warriors had remained more or less insulated from their subjects. Omar set up special garrison cities, where the Arabs settled down under their tribal leaders. Each warrior received pay derived from the taxes collected from the population at large by traditional Roman and Persian bureaucratic methods. This system worked pretty well at first, and remained effective even when the leadership of the Islamic community passed into far less capable hands than those which had guided its first years.

The first test came in A.D. 644, when Omar was assassinated. A chieftain of the Ommayad family then succeeded to the caliphate and the office remained in that family until A.D. 751. The Ommayads made Damascus in Syria their capital. The power of the Ommayad caliphs depended upon maintaining a delicate balance between three very different roles. The caliph had first of all to mollify clashes among the rival Arab chieftains and tribes, who constituted the garrison forces of the empire. He had also to manage the bureaucracy inherited from his Roman and Persian predecessors and use it to tax the population at large. Then, in the third place, the caliph somehow had to serve as religious head of the community.

Of these three roles the one the Ommayads failed to fill adequately was the last. Serious and devout men, seeking to know the will of Allah and to do it faithfully, found no satisfaction in the spectacle offered by Ommayad administration. As long as military success continued uninterruptedly, such discontents were politically ineffective. But after A.D. 715, when the Moslems suffered their first serious defeats, the pious opposition, which demanded a worthy, God-chosen caliph, became a serious matter.

As administrators of the population at large, the Ommayads also ran into increasing difficulty. Numerous Christians and Zoroastrians and followers of other religions found the theological simplicity, legal precision, and practical success of Islam perfectly convincing. On principle, such converts were welcome to join the community of the faithful. But when conversion meant relief from taxation — as at first was the case — religious success meant acute fiscal embarrassment. Moreover, Arab custom had difficulty in fitting masses of newcomers into the tribal system into which the Moslem community was still organized. Arabs tended to look scornfully upon the new converts and treated them as less than fully equal members of the community of Islam, despite the plain injunctions of Mohammed's revelation.

All these strains came to a head in A.D. 744, when a disputed succession precipitated civil war. Fighting ended with the overthrow of the Ommayad regime and of the privileged position of the Arab garrison forces as well. The Abbasid victors set up their capital at Baghdad in Mesopotamia. The backbone of their military support came from the Persian converts. It is not, therefore, surprising that Abbasid policy from the start smacked strongly of Sassanian precedent. Arab tribal groups, which had been so important before, disintegrated because tribal garrisons no longer received pay through their chiefs, as in Ommayad times. In Arabia proper, where the old style of nomad life continued, tribal ties remained unchanged. But in the settled parts of the empire the Arabs blended into the general population, usually as landowners or in other privileged positions, and soon forgot their tribal identity and discipline. Instead, bureaucracy of the familiar imperial model took over all ordinary administration, while Iranian and Turkish or other mercenaries more and more constituted the core of the caliph's armed forces.

These reversions to very ancient imperial precedents met the demands of the non-Arab converts to Islam, who were now, like everybody else, the distant subjects of a secluded and somewhat unapproachable caliph. But these changes did nothing to meet the demands of the pious Moslems who were bent upon realizing God's will on earth in all its specificity. The solution Abbasid statesmen found for this difficulty was of fundamental importance for all subsequent Islamic society. Instead of trying to combine religious authority with military and political leadership as previously, the Abbasids tacitly agreed to transfer jurisdiction in all matters of religious importance to an informal body of experts in the lore of Islam — men known collectively as *ulema*.

Moslem scripture and sacred law. The *ulema* had developed spontaneously. Pious men, confronting a problem of conduct, wished to know what God's will in the matter might be. The way to find out was to seek for precedents in the words or deeds of the Prophet. But ordinary men were not familiar with these deeds and words, and had to ask experts who were. As the first generation of the Prophet's companions died, this called for systematic study. Naturally enough, Medina was the first seat where the details of Mohammed's career were studied. Here his inspired utterances were collected and committed to a canonical order just a few years after the Prophet's death. The resulting scripture, the *Koran*, has ever since constituted the ultimate repository of religious authority for Moslems.

Many matters for which the *Koran* offered no direct guidance had somehow to be coped with also. For answers to such questions, experts in the lore of Islam resorted at first to reports about Mohammed's uninspired words and deeds emanating — really or fictitiously — from companions of the Prophet. When this failed, the conduct of men closely associated with Mohammed might be helpful. When even these "traditions" could not be brought to bear on a case, the *ulema* admitted the use of analogy to decide a difficult point. If analogy failed to offer convincing guidance they fell back ultimately upon the consensus of the faithful, arguing that Allah would not permit the entire community to err, however faulty individual judgments might be.

Using these methods, the learned men of Islam rapidly built up an elaborate system of law, which they believed expressed the will of Allah. The sacred law was, of course, unchangeable, since Allah did not change. It was also rather detailed and specific, since the whole effort was aimed at making unambiguously clear what Allah wished men to do in particular situations. As a result, the sacred law of Islam later proved a heavy burden for Moslem society to carry, since it could neither be repudiated nor altered.

Under the Abbasids, however, the sacred law still glistened like newly minted gold. Allah's will for men seemed surely there revealed, and it behooved the faithful to bend every effort to conform to its clear and definite prescriptions. This was not hard to do since learned men, respected for their exact knowledge of the

Koran, the Traditions, and the details of the Sacred Law, sat in the market place of every considerable town, ready to pass judgment on matters of conscience brought before them. Much of the business of government affecting private persons and individual lives was thus transferred to the jurisdiction of these religious experts. Pious Moslems could therefore feel that in everything that really mattered, the best and wisest men were in control. By comparison with this, who happened to be running the central government, collecting taxes, guarding the frontiers, and enjoying the luxuries of palace life did not matter so very much.

The early ideal of the totally holy community, led by a worthy successor to the Prophet and dedicated solely to obedience to Allah, was thus somewhat reluctantly surrendered by the majority of Moslems. But not by all. Some stubborn idealists clung to the original vision and thereby became heretics. Many of them came to hold that only descendants of Ali, the son-in-law of the Prophet, were worthy of heading the community of the faithful. When Ali's direct line died out in the twelfth generation, some argued that the true successor to the Prophet had withdrawn from an irremediably wicked world but would return in the future and turn his terrible avenging wrath against those who had betrayed the truth and been false to Allah's commands. Extreme sects split into numerous sub-groupings, harboring a truly revolutionary intolerance for Abbasid, or indeed for any other constituted authority that fell short of their utterly unyielding ideal. Such groups are termed Shi'a. The majority, who were willing to seek holiness within the framework accorded by Abbasid policy, are known as Sunni Moslems.

The Sunni–Shi'a split has continued to run throughout Islam right down to the present day. Equally, the restrictions the Abbasid compromise placed upon the jurisdiction of secular government have continued to affect the policy of all Islamic states ever since.

An important corollary of the autonomous administration of the Sacred Law was that Moslem political authorities expected the leaders of other religious communities to guide and legislate for their flocks in all personal and religious matters just as the *ulema* guided the lives of Moslems. Far-ranging autonomy for Christian and Jewish communities was thereby assured.

A second important implication of the Moslem legal code was that a man had to accept Islam in its entirety or reject it utterly. No halfway house was possible. Either Mohammed was Allah's latest and most perfect prophet, and the Sacred Law in every jot and tittle was the veritable expression of Allah's will for men, or else these claims were false. No middle ground could be found in logic, and very little was discovered in fact. Islam, in short, shared the doctrinal intolerance of its Judaic and Christian forerunners to the full.

The religious aspiration that found expression in Islam very soon set a powerful stamp upon the daily lives of millions of men in the Middle East and north Africa. Cultivation of the Arabic language as the necessary vehicle for all religious discourse became part of piety. As a result, a rather rapid linguistic shift went hand in hand with the propagation of Islam, as Arabic displaced Greek and/or Aramaic as the everyday speech of the Middle Eastern peoples. Persian, however, retained its currency in Iran, although for a while it ceased to be used for literary purposes.

Arabic court life and culture. Poetic records of tribal and individual prowess were an important part of the culture of pre-Islamic Arabia. Mohammed had looked with disfavor upon these rivals to the poetry of his own inspired utterances. Nonetheless, Arab warriors continued to cultivate a taste for poetry and rhythmic prose in spite of the Prophet. The warrior's ideal expressed in such poetry was reinforced by the ease and leisure the first Arab generations experienced, when they could live upon the taxes collected from their new subjects. As a result, a courtly style of gentlemanly life developed among Arab fighting men which stood in conscious opposition to the ideals of the pious Moslems. Wine drinking, for example, was part of the gentlemanly code of behavior despite Mohammed's prohibition. More generally, a warm appreciation of the sensory joys of the world, refinement of manners, and delicacy of sentiment in matters of pride, hate, and love, accorded but ill with the pious drive for complete obedience to Allah. Only in high political circles, pre-eminently in the court of the caliph himself, could this secular, lei-sured, and essentially aristocratic style of life flourish freely.

A second element inherited from the past also stood stubbornly in the way of energetically pious champions of Islam. The specu-lative habit of mind, so persistently cultivated among the Greeks, could not be entirely suppressed. In matters of religion, to be sure, the *ulema* resolutely and on the whole successfully resisted tempta-tion by refusing to entertain questions of speculative theology. They held it to be a self-evident truth that everything a man needed to know was provided by the *Koran* and Traditions.

Nevertheless, there were two professional services the Moslems — or at least the rich among them — were not prepared to do without: the prediction of the future by astrologers and the curing of illness by doctors. Astrology and medicine were, of course, deeply imbued with Greek thought. In taking these professions over, the Moslems, therefore, inevitably imported into their own learning a generous share of the Greek inheritance. And once Mos-lem minds began to reason about things, it was hard to call a halt. Before long, curiosity spread to other matters not directly related to either medicine or astrology. Some of the Abbasid caliphs even became patrons of learning and organized systematic translation of Greek and Indian works of science and philosophy. In this way much of Greek knowledge and some Indian learning (e.g. the decimal-place notation system) passed into Arabic and fired the curiosity of a handful of courtiers and professional men.

The most fruitful direction in which this curiosity turned was toward alchemy. Many of the ideas and some of the skills alchem-ists acquired seem to have originated among Taoists in China. But the Arabs took up the search for the philosophers' stone with en-thusiasm and tried long and hard to transmute base metals into gold. In the process, devices for distillation, heating, dissolving, and in other ways altering the physical state of matter were invented or improved; and a number of chemical compounds were synthesized successfully, despite radically erroneous ideas about how chemical reactions occur. A second science in which Arab work surpassed anything known to the Greeks was mathematical optics — a result of the skill the Moslems acquired in grinding lenses of glass to fit a mathematical curve. But such improvements did not shake the general authority of such authors as Galen in medicine and Ptolemy in astronomy. Arab science remained always faithful to the Greeks in fundamentals and departed from their authority only in detail.

The Abbasid empire. Under the Abbasids, therefore, the traditions of Greek rationalism and science, the aristocratic warrior ideal cherished by pre-Islamic Arabic tribesmen, and the radical striving for holiness characteristic of pious Moslems, all found shelter under the roof of an imperial bureaucracy and armed establishment that drew its main inspiration from Persian prototypes. The amalgam created a richness and complexity of civilization that surpassed anything then known in Europe and rivaled the efflorescence of T'ang China far to the east.

Two points of weakness remained. At home, the dissent of Shi'a groups, feeding upon ethnic and perhaps also upon economic divisions within Moslem society, let to recurrent revolt. After A.D. 861, various break-off states that drew some of their strength from just this sort of religious-social discontent began to eat into the imperial structure. Secondly, along its northern frontier the Abbasid empire was not able to cope for long with the perennial pressure from the steppe. As a result, Turkish mercenaries gradually took over political control, even though they continued to cloak their usurpation of effective authority by putting members of the Abbasid family on the throne until 1252. Long before that time, however, the combination of provincial rebellion and palace *coup d'état* led to the breakdown of imperial control even in the Mesopotamian-Syrian heartland of the empire.

Thereafter, new strands within Islam, arising from the infolding of Turkish tribesmen from the steppe and the increased scope allowed to mystic seekers after forms of religious enlightenment for which early Islam had made no room, gave the Moslem world a markedly different character. The date A.D. 1000 roughly accords with the onset of these transformations and corresponds also to important alterations in relations between the Moslems and their Hindu and Christian neighbors. But before pursuing these matters further we must retrace our steps in time to survey the reactions of other civilized peoples to the rise of Islam and to the new style of civilization that Islamic conquerors so successfully created at the ancient Middle Eastern crossroads of the Old World.

XIV

China, India, and Europe

A.D. 600–1000

ECAUSE Islam quickly became a coherent and legally defined way of life, neighbors had either to accept or reject it *in toto*. This tended to divide the civilized world into more nearly watertight compartments than had been true in earlier times when dogmatic religions had not played so central a part in civilized life. Nevertheless, stimulus across cultural frontiers remained negatively important. In resisting Islam both Hindustan and Christendom had to define their own distinctive traits more emphatically than before.

A second general characteristic of the centuries between A.D. 600 and 1000 was the spread of semi-civilized styles of life throughout broad borderlands both north and south of the earlier zone of civilization. In the Far West, for example, Celtic, Germanic, and Slavic tribes were all brought within the fold of Christendom by the year 1000. With Christianity came at least the rudiments of high culture and civilized social order. In eastern Europe and central Asia, Turkish tribes entered the penumbra of civilization at the same time. The best-organized Turkish states did not accept a religion established already among their civilized neighbors, but preferred Judaism (in the case of the Khazars) or Manicheism (in the case of the Uighurs). They thus retained greater spiritual and cultural independence vis-à-vis their civilized neighbors.

The fact that traditional pastoralism, war, and caravan trade continued to dominate the life of Turkish tribesmen of the steppes made it easy for them to keep religiously apart from their civilized contemporaries, who were all fundamentally agriculturalists. Further west, however, there was no such gap between barbarian and civilized communities. Instead, a major improvement of agricultural techniques permitted German and other barbarian peoples to transform the forests of the north European plain into fields. As a result, civilization could now penetrate the forested lands of the Far West in a fuller sense than was geographically or socially possible on the steppe grasslands. The key change was that German cultivators invented a new type of heavy mouldboard plow, capable of draining wet low-lying lands and strong enough to penetrate even the heavy clay soils that covered much of northern Europe. This mouldboard plow made it possible to cultivate for the first time lowland forested areas where the light, scratch plows familiar to Mediterranean and Middle Eastern farmers had been completely ineffective. No comparable technical change came to the steppe to transform the conditions of life in that region. Hence the northward extension of civilization to German and Slavic peoples involved far more radical changes than did the simultaneous northward movement of familiarity with aspects of civilized life which occurred among the Turkish tribes living to the east of them.

In the Far East the situation was again different. A slow, painstaking extension of the garden-style of cultivation, which had been developed by the Chinese centuries before, continued. Nameless pioneers ditched and diked and pumped and piped water from innumerable little streams into new fields. No technical innovation was involved, just a vast expenditure of human effort. And while the Chinese slowly brought the Yangtse valley to the south into high cultivation, Koreans and Japanese, on the northeastern flank of the original center of Chinese life, painstakingly carried through another geographically substantial expansion of the area of Far Eastern agricultural civilization by raising the cultivation of their respective homelands to the Chinese level.

Like their Uighur contemporaries, the Korean and Japanese peoples maintained their cultural distinctiveness vis-à-vis China by sticking to their separate languages and by espousing a religion different from that prevailing in the center of the civilization with which they were in contact. Thus the Koreans made Buddhism into a state religion and clung to it all the more emphatically after the Chinese officially outlawed Buddhism in A.D. 845. Japan, on the other hand, was far enough away from China not to feel the risk of complete absorption into the Chinese culture sphere. Hence, between A.D. 600 and 1000 the Japanese welcomed Buddhism, Confucianism, and every other aspect of Chinese culture they could import. They did so with an energetic enthusiasm for things foreign, which, recurring in later times, gives Japanese history a jerky character all its own. Thus during the Nara period (646–794) the Japanese imperial court very quickly and systematically created a miniature model of the great T'ang court in China. The precocious sensibility of Japanese courtly life is delightfully illustrated by Lady Murasaki's delicate love story, *The Tale of Genji*, written soon after A.D. 1000. But it was a much cruder style of life, sustained by baronial patrons in their provincial castles, that really nourished Japan's cultural independence. As the political and military power of such warlords grew at the expense of the imperial administration — a feature of Japanese life that became very prominent after 1000 — the unique nature of Japanese cultural development came to be assured.

On the southern flank of the civilized world a similar string of new peoples and states arrived at a level of life properly termed civilized during the same period of time. Yunnan became a cultural satellite of China as Annam (modern North Viet Nam) had done earlier. Tibet took advantage of its intermediate position between China and India to combine elements from each, taking its religion from India and secular aspects of culture mainly from China, but retaining always a strong local individuality. Tibet's religion, for example, mingled native "Bon" rites with Buddhist motifs to create what is known as Lamaism. On the southern flank of the Himalayas, Bengal and Kashmir became important frontiers of Indian culture, where powerful local states arose that dominated the political life of the north Indian plains, although neither was ever able to unite the Ganges and Indus valleys into a new "universal" empire.

Arabia's sudden eruption into the Middle East we have already studied. Across the Red Sea, Ethiopia and Nubia in east Africa and Ghana in west Africa became seats of local states that boasted many of the trappings of civilization. Ethiopia and Nubia accepted a form of Christianity (monophysite) declared heretical in Rome and Constantinople. Ghana remained pagan.

The enormous geographic expansion of civilized styles of life and the increased variety of local blends and combinations of disparate cultural elements that occurred all along the northern and southern flanks of the civilized world after A.D. 600 recapitulated, but on an enlarged scale, the development of regional sub-cultures and variants around Mesopotamia that had occurred when civilization first became attuned to survival on rain-watered land about 2000 B.C. The intrinsic attractiveness of civilized accomplishments was of course centrally responsible for both spreads. In both cases, also, a much enhanced export of commodities from the civilized world in the form of plunder and tribute as well as trade made it possible for barbarian chieftains, kings, captains, and potentates of every description to initiate the exposure of their peoples to the seductions of civilization. After A.D. 600 the various civilized communities of the Old World were in a position to export more goods than before because their own internal economic and technical development everywhere underwent significant advance in the course of what has traditionally been called the "Dark Age" of Europe's history.

To appreciate better the increasing reach of civilized societies, we shall consider each in turn.

China. Not long after the reunification of China (A.D. 589) by the Sui dynasty, a brief round of war brought a new dynasty, the T'ang, to power (618–907). The T'ang, in turn, after a longer interregnum were succeeded by the Sung (960–1260). Actually, the realities of Chinese government do not precisely correspond to the traditional dynastic pattern. Within the four centuries (600–1000) with which we are concerned, strong central government lasted only until 755 and was followed by a period of weakened imperial power, local war-lordism, and dependency upon a powerful Turkish confederacy headed by the Uighurs of central Asia. The overthrow of the Uighurs in 840 simply substituted other barbarian masters, who took over direct administration of north China during the later decades of the T'ang rule. The Sung dynasty failed to displace these barbarian rulers from the northern tier of Chinese provinces.

Yet the disruption of central power after 755 did not seriously check the economic development of China. Particularly in the south the labor of millions of peasants gradually extended their rice paddies up the hill slopes from the river edges to make a continuous carpet of fertile and carefully tended fields, producing rice in quantities great enough to maintain a much enlarged urban population of craftsmen, landlords, and officials. Trade was often in foreign — especially Uighur and Arab — hands. Confucian doctrine held merchants to be social parasites anyway. Hence, despite a substantial growth of foreign trade and of interregional exchanges within China, the urban classes did not challenge the traditional dominance of the landowning gentry. Instead, the ingenuity and skill of Chinese artisans and of foreign and Chinese merchants were directed mainly toward satisfying the tastes of the landlord-official class, whose members, being educated in classical Chinese learning, strove to practice the arts and decorum appropriate to gentlemen.

The gentlemanly idea underwent considerable elaboration in the T'ang and early Sung periods. Painting, for example, which became the principal fine art of China, assumed classical forms in this period, although no authenticated works survive. Poetry also assumed its classical form with the work of Li Po (A.D. 701–62) and Tu Fu (A.D. 712–70) whose verse patterns elaborated rhythms of popular songs and snatches, and in doing so established conventions that became binding for subsequent generations. The freshness and autobiographical poignancy characteristic of Li Po's verses was more difficult to imitate than his prosody, so that those who are capable of judging agree that Li Po was not only the pioneer but also the greatest of Chinese lyric poets.

Buddhism assumed an almost official status in early T'ang times, but ran into systematic persecution after A.D. 845. The emperor's desire to confiscate the lands that Buddhist monasteries had accumulated from gifts of the pious may have triggered these persecutions. But the basic factor was the distrust, indeed antipathy, Confucians felt toward an alien faith that taught disregard of all the obligations and duties Confucians held to be central to the good life. After the persecutions of the ninth century, Chinese Buddhism survived only in comparatively humble walks of life — in remote provinces where the official writ ran only weakly, and among humble village folk who perhaps found a secret attraction in a faith that was so much out of favor among their social superiors.

Yet Buddhism contributed a great deal to Chinese culture. Confucians, for example, learned from the Buddhists how to read new meanings into old texts by analogy and symbolic interpretation. Moreover, many of the new meanings they discovered in the classics of the Confucian canon dealt with metaphysical and eschatological questions which had first been brought to Chinese attention by Buddhist teachers. For their part, the Taoists chose to combat Buddhism by borrowing not merely aspects of doctrine but the pattern of monastic organization and a system of schooling from their rivals. Hence even in its official defeat, Buddhism left a large heritage behind — a fact nicely illustrated by the manner in which later Chinese painters used representational and narrative techniques which had been brought to China by Buddhist artists in order to illustrate secular and Confucian subjects.

The elaborated and philosophically sophisticated reinterpretation of the classics is called Neo-Confucianism. Its full development came after the period we are now considering, but the school was well launched before A.D. 1000. The policy of the early Sung rulers, who enthusiastically championed everything they felt to be authentically Chinese and rejected consciously all that was felt to be foreign, assured the victory of Neo-Confucianism in official circles. Gentry dominance of society went hand in hand with this cultural policy. By operating together, these factors gave China a remarkably uniform cultural history, as compared with the stormier developments of western Asia and Europe.

India. Islam offered no direct military challenge to the Chinese. There were skirmishes in central Asia, but the loss of a few distant oases to Moslem warriors after A.D. 751 (Battle of Talas) was of no great importance. In the decade immediately following this defeat, disasters far closer to home disrupted the T'ang imperial power; and soon thereafter the Uighur Manicheans interposed themselves as an effective cushion between the Moslem and Chinese worlds. India was far more exposed. Moslems conquered Sind in northwest India by 705 and soon thereafter seized primacy on the seaways of the Indian Ocean as well. Hence it came to pass that followers of Mohammed, who regarded Hinduism, at least in principle, as abominable idolatry, cut India off from her erstwhile cultural dependencies in southeast Asia.

The caste organization of India, with the political-military weaknesses that inevitably resulted from such a system of society, meant that Hindus were unable to repel the Moslems by force. Their response was therefore peaceable, aimed at conserving the Hindu heritage that Moslems found so offensive. On the one hand, a handful of Indian philosophers set out to systematize the intellectual tradition of the Upanishads. This allowed the learned to rebut effectively Moslem reproaches against the idolatrous practices traditional to Hinduism by explaining that all such rites, if properly understood, helped simple men along the path to a pure and transcendent theological monism. The philosophic system created by Shankara (*flor. c.* 800) became classical for later Hinduism. Shankara justified even the crudest traditional religious practices by claiming that they encouraged humble intellects to reach toward knowledge of the Absolute residing behind every sensory experience. As a good Hindu, he was even prepared to argue that Moslem rites had value for those who could see no further into the Truth than Mohammed had done.

Turning the tables on Moslem teachers in such a dexterous fashion was all very well in theoretical discussions. At the more practical everyday level Indian sentiment hardened against foreigners. Like the Chinese of later T'ang and Sung times, popular Indian culture set out to reject systematically everything felt to be of alien inspiration and to defend and acknowledge all that seemed autochthonous. In the process, much that had been hidden and primitive in Indian life entered the literary record for the first time. In particular, extremely varied cult practices known collectively as

Tantrism came into the open and underwent vast elaboration. Tantric adepts sought to achieve the supernatural powers popularly attributed to holy men and ascetics by using magic charms and incantations. Tantrism therefore constituted a short cut to salvation, allowing quite ordinary men to attain the ascetic's goals without undergoing the pains and tribulations of ascetic discipline. Such a bargain had wide appeal and tended to undercut all forms of asceticism.

Tantrism was always a mainly private system of rites, although small groups might make magic together. On the more public side, temple services supplemented by occasional spectacular festivals in honor of one or another deity of the Hindu pantheon continued as before, and may even have become more elaborate. In Gupta times, the court provided patronage and an audience for writers and artists. After the collapse of the Gupta imperial peace, no comparable courtly center arose. Temples therefore took over first place. The more secular, intellectual aspects of Hindu civilization suffered from this transformation. In particular mathematics, which had made such a promising start in the Gupta age, simply fell into oblivion having no function in a temple-centered high culture. Courtly poetry like that of Kalidasa was supplanted by anonymous hymns which sometimes celebrated the love between God and his worshippers in vivid and very fleshly language. Dancing and hymn singing amid crowds of onlookers and participants could and did generate high emotional excitement and public catharsis. Hinduism thus retained deep roots in popular feeling, making it pretty well proof against the arguments of Moslem (and later of Christian) missionaries.

Information about the social and economic life of India in this age, and even about the political units into which the land was divided, remains very imperfect. A generally high level of activity certainly continued, and in such border regions as Bengal and the high Himalayan valleys of Kashmir, important geographical expansion of Indian society occurred. In these regions, jungle and swamp, hillside and forest, gave way to cultivated countryside. The total mass of Indian society therefore continued to increase, despite the loss of the border provinces along the Indus to Islam.

Yet these continued successes do not suffice to counterbalance the fact that in general the Indian reaction to the Moslem threat appears to have been an indrawing of sensibilities, concentrating upon what was clearly and unambiguously Indian, rejecting alien stimuli, and in so doing abandoning or de-emphasizing some of the more active and successful endeavors of the preceding Gupta age.

Europe. Europeans, too, remained on the defensive until the very end of the period we are here considering. But the European defensive was military first and foremost, and only in a secondary sense intellectual and emotional. Thus, in contrast to India, the primacy of politics over other bases of human association which classical Greece had first so emphatically declared was reasserted by the warlike barbarians and struggling Christians of Europe's "Dark Age."

It is useful to group the disturbed events of Europe's political history during this age into three successive waves of barbarian invasion, separated from one another by two periods of short-lived stabilization. We considered the first wave in Chapter XII. This was the movement of peoples triggered by the Hunnic invasion of central Europe that brought Goths, Burgundians, Vandals, Franks, Anglo-Saxons, and other Germanic peoples to Roman soil between A.D. 375 and about 450. The consolidation of a Frankish monarchy in Gaul under the descendants of Clovis (d. 511) and the reassertion of Roman administration in North Africa, Italy, and parts of Spain by the emperor Justinian (d. 565) constituted a precarious stabilization of civilized (or in the Frankish case semi-civilized) administration in the wake of this first great barbarian advance.

A second wave developed immediately after the death of Justinian, when a new band of nomads, known as Avars, drove westward from southern Russia into the Hungarian plain, and like Attila before them, began to raid far and wide into the agricultural lands lying south and west of their new headquarters. Avar power was near its height when the Moslems besieged Constantinople in the years 717–18. Yet the walls of Constantine's capital on the Bosphorus held. A new emperor, Leo III, the Isaurian (717–41), came to power and proceeded to reorganize and strengthen the Byzantine armed establishment. He did so by making extensive land grants to fighting men who undertook to guard the frontiers in return for the lands thus assigned to them. In Asia Minor this policy soon rolled back the attacking Arabs and proved capable of checking them permanently at about the line of the Taurus mountains. In Europe, however, Leo and his successors failed to stem a massive Slavic infiltration which gradually transformed all the northern and central regions of the Balkan peninsula into a predominantly Slavic-speaking countryside. In a similar fashion, after 568 the German tribe of Lombards displaced the Byzantines from control of all the inland parts of Italy.

Stabilization of a sort came to Europe with the recovery of Byzantine power in Asia Minor (after 718) and the consolidation of two barbarian states: the first Bulgarian empire on the lower Danube (after 679) and the Carolingian empire in the Far West (after 687). The Bulgar kingdom folded Slavic manpower into a Turkish war-band organization. It proved powerful enough to become a serious military rival to the Byzantine empire. In the process, attributes of civilized government and administration penetrated among the Balkan Slavs, even before the Bulgar khan's conversion to Christianity (865) opened the floodgates to civilization in its Byzantine form.

Among the Franks a somewhat similar pattern of events unfolded. The kingdom had become officially Christian in the time of Clovis (A.D. 496). Despite savage quarreling among his descendants (the Merovingians), traces of old Roman life remained precariously alive in Gaul. Then in 687 Pepin of Heristal won effective control over both the halves into which Clovis' kingdom had divided. Pepin came from the eastern and more purely Germanic (Austrasian) portion of the Frankish lands. He granted extensive new estates in the more Romanized parts of Gaul to his own followers and supporters on a scale sufficient to constitute a second wave of Germanic invasion. In 751 the power of Pepin's family was officially recognized when the pope crowned his grandson (also named Pepin) king of the Franks. In the next generation Charlemagne brought the power of the newly constituted Carolingian dynasty to its peak. He conquered all of Germanic and Roman Europe, save for Scandinavia and England. He converted

CAROLINGIANS
800-900

KHAZARS

Volga R.

SLAVS

SWEDES

LITHUANIANS

SWEDES

DANES

ENGLAND

London

IRELAND

Vikings 870

Vikings
800-900

NORMANDY

BRITTANY

Aachen

Paris

Rhine R.

EAST-FRANKISH

Elbe R.

Regensburg

KDM.

CENTRAL

KINGDOM

OF THE

FRANKS

W. FRANKISH KDM.

Lyon

Rhône R.

KDM.

Rome

Venice

CROATS

Carpathian Mts.

HUNGARY

KIEVAN RUSSIA
(after 862)

Kiev

Dnieper R.

MAGYARS, 895

Danube R.

BULGARIANS

BULGARIA
(895)

Constantinople

Black Sea

BYZANTINE EMPIRE

SYRIA

MOSLEMS

CYPRUS

CRETE

Mediterranean Sea

Tunis

MOSLEMS

EMIRATE
OF
CORDOVA

Tagus R.

Ebro R.

ASTURIAS

Atlantic Ocean

Scale of Miles

0   500

226

Saxons and other pagan German tribes to Christianity by main force. He destroyed the Avar camp in Hungary and asserted a somewhat shadowy control over a fringe of Slavic lands in central Europe. In recognition of his power, in 800 the pope crowned Charlemagne Emperor of the Romans. A few years later, the imperial master of Byzantium ratified the pope's action, thus in legal form reconstituting a Roman empire in the west to match the Roman (Byzantine) empire in the east.

Co-operation between Byzantines and Franks was never close. Political distrust was exacerbated by persistent religious friction, centering on the proper role of images in Christian worship. Emperor Leo III, the Isaurian, having saved Constantinople from the Moslems by breaking the siege of 717–18, wanted to purge the Christian church of image worship. He therefore banned icons. He may have been responding to Moslem reproaches of idolatry; but undoubtedly there were many Christians who believed that the military setbacks they had suffered at Moslem and barbarian hands were due to God's displeasure at idolatrous practices. The pope in Rome and many ecclesiastical leaders in Constantinople resisted the emperor's iconoclastic policy. Each denounced the other as heretical. It was at a time when the pope was at odds with the imperial government in Byzantium that he crowned Pepin king of the Franks, thus finding in the half-barbarian monarch of the north a substitute for the imperial protector on the Bosphorus who had turned heretic.

Even when the iconoclastic controversy ended with a final capitulation of the imperial government to popular practice (843), the gap between the eastern and western portions of Christendom continued to widen. As a result of the Slavic infiltration of the Balkan hinterland, Latin all but disappeared from the streets of Constantinople after Justinian's time (d. 565). Long before, Greek had been forgotten in the west, where knowledge of Latin itself was only precariously maintained in a few monastic and cathedral schools. Popular speech was evolving rapidly away from classical forms, toward the various Germanic and romance languages of medieval and modern times.

It was therefore a culturally and politically divided Christendom that met the third and last wave of barbarian invasion. Once again, a new war band, fleeing from southern Russia, penetrated to the Hungarian plain and began raiding from that base. This time the invaders were named Magyars or Hungarians. They crossed the Carpathian passes in A.D. 895. A little later, Moslem states in north Africa abruptly reversed the balance of power in the Mediterranean by almost destroying Byzantine naval strength. A series of large-scale piratical raids followed, directed against the entire northern coastline of the Mediterranean. A similar and even more ruthless harassment was simultaneously launched by Viking pirates, whose base of operations lay in Scandinavia.

A fundamental reversal of western Europe's relations with its neighbors occurred about A.D. 1000. This was signalized by the rise of Italian shipping which presently was able to exchange blow for blow with the Moslems in the Mediterranean, and by the conversion to Christianity of Russia (989), Hungary (1000), and the three Scandinavian kingdoms of Denmark, Sweden, and Norway (between 831 and 1000). In every case, conversion signified the emergence of an ambitious royal authority which welcomed Christianity as an aid in taming the unruliness of subordinates and in establishing such necessary adjuncts of civilized life as literacy and organized religions among their still barbarous subjects.

The beginnings of feudalism. The taming of the northern barbarians by spontaneous acts of conversion was at least in part a tribute to the much enhanced effectiveness which Europe's institutions began to demonstrate under the hammer blows of Magyar, Viking, and Arab raids. In the east, the Byzantine empire at length transformed itself in the fashion pioneered so long before by the Persians. A feudal system developed, whereby princely landowners maintained retinues of heavy armed cavalrymen along the frontiers of the state, ready for local self-defense against raiding neighbors of whatever sort. The risk involved in this transformation was real enough. The greatest Byzantine conqueror, Emperor Basil II (ruled A.D. 989–1025), who finally succeeded in overpowering the Bulgar empire and was able to push his frontiers to the Danube and the upper Euphrates, was twice nearly toppled from his throne by rebellions of local magnates. Moreover, the emergence of great

EUROPEAN
COUNTER-OFFENSIVE
1000–1100

Scale of Miles

0   500

Roman Church
Greek Orthodox Church
Boundary of the
Holy Roman Empire
Trade routes
from Italian centers

Atlantic Ocean

NORWAY

SWEDEN

ESTONIANS

LITHUANIANS

PRUSSIANS

SCOTLAND

ENGLAND

IRELAND

WALES

Hastings X
1066

DENMARK

Hamburg

"KNIGHTHOOD"

GERMANY

Mainz

Rhine R.

POLAND

Vienna

HUNGARY

CROATS

SERBS

Danube R.

BULGARIANS

BURGUNDY

FRANCE

MERCHANT
TOWNS

Genoa

Pisa

Venice

ITALY

Rome

NORMAN
SICILY
c. 1097

SPAIN

Barcelona

MOSLEMS

Mediterranean Sea

MALTA

GREECE

Constantinople

Black Sea

BYZANTINE EMPIRE

Route of
First Crusade
(1096–1099)

Manzikert X
c. 1071

SELJUK TURKS

Antioch

SYRIA

Euphrates

MOSLEMS

Jerusalem

KIPCHAKS

RUSSIA

Kiev

Novgorod

KHAZARS

Caspian Sea

GEORGIA

warrior-landowners in the countryside eroded urban dominance of society as a whole — a fact perhaps related to the eclipse of Byzantine sea power which had unleashed Arab raiding in the Mediterranean.

In the west, central administration did disintegrate. Charlemagne's empire proved quite incapable of defending itself from Viking and Magyar raids. Instead, military and political leadership passed into the hands of a rough-and-ready body of local lords and men-at-arms, who equipped themselves as heavy armored cavalry, or knights. But Western knights differed in one very important respect from heavy armored cavalrymen of other parts of the world. Apparently from the time when this sort of expensive armament was first introduced into the Far West, i.e. in the time of Charles Martel (ruled A.D. 714–741), Frankish knights relied upon a fundamentally new tactic. Instead of shooting arrows at opposing troops as their Persian and Byzantine prototypes had done, the Franks relied upon a heavy lance. By charging headlong against the foe, they could put the full momentum of horse and rider behind the lance point and thus exert a comparatively enormous force that could easily break through any other sort of military formation.

Stirrups were essential to this invention. Without stirrups to stand in, leaning the entire body forward at the moment of impact, the shock of contact would sweep the rider ignominiously from his horse's back. Unfortunately, the origin and diffusion of stirrups is quite unclear. But it does seem certain that early in the eighth century the Franks combined stirrups, armor, big horses, and a heavy lance to produce a style of fighting man whose equal, man for man, could be found nowhere else. As long as their numbers remained very few the newfangled knights were unable to stop barbarian raiding. But need for local defense was acute and pressing. Consequently, partly by legal grant from the king or from some other public authority (duke, count) and partly by local usurpation and informal arrangement, more and more agricultural land was assigned for the support of knights. As a result, well before the year 1000 most villages of western Europe had come under the control of a professional fighting man who was equipped with a horse, lance, and armor, and a generous store of brute ferocity. The knightly class which thus came into existence proved able not merely to turn back attack but quickly took the offensive across every frontier of western Christendom.

Two other fundamental changes gave additional reach and power to the emerging medieval system of society. One was the spread of the heavy mouldboard plow, mentioned earlier (see p. 217.) Agriculture based on such a plow provided the economic support needed to maintain enough knights to make Europe truly formidable. The second was the development of trade in Europe's northern seas. Pirates and sea rovers quickly discovered that trade might be advantageous when ravaging was no longer safe. Bands of itinerant merchants, seamen, and part-time pirates often found it convenient to settle down at some more or less permanent headquarters, wherever lines of communication and safe harborage created a suitable site. In this way the kernel was fashioned from which medieval town life later arose in northwestern Europe. It was most significant for the future development of Western civilization that the first European townsmen were accustomed to running their own affairs and defending themselves against all comers. This gave the middle classes of northwestern Europe a very different, more assertive ethos than was habitual among townsmen of the other civilizations, where deference to social superiors and polite catering to landowners and officials prevailed.

The combination of knighthood, the heavy plow, and a morally independent not to say aggressive mercantile population gave the Far West a set of local institutions and techniques that were both new and quite distinct from any contemporary civilization.

The decay of learning. In this sense the "Dark Age" of European history was in fact very fruitful. Yet in another sense the age deserves its traditional name. On the European mainland, men were too busy struggling against one another to devote much energy to literature or art. In Ireland and Great Britain, however, a remarkable upsurge occurred which, under other circumstances, might have developed into an independent civilized style of life. The first landmark of this history was the conversion of Ireland to Christianity by St. Patrick (d. A.D. 461). Thereafter, in a number of Irish monasteries a traditional Celtic oral literature was fertilized by Latin and even Greek letters and learning. Missionaries sailed to Scotland and England; thence others visited the mainland, where they played a conspicuous part in converting the Germans, and everywhere brought a higher level of intellectual culture to the scene than anything preserved in Gaul or Germany itself. The Venerable Bede (d. A.D. 735), whose greatest work was an ecclesiastical history of England, represents one of the finest flowers of this tradition of learning. Soon after his death, Vikings destroyed the monastery where he had lived and worked. The same fate befell all the other centers of Irish and British learning, so that by the year 900 almost nothing remained. Ireland, together with the rest of Celtic Europe, relapsed into the status of a marginal and backward participant in the wider European world.

Summary. If one tries to compare Chinese, Indian, and European responses to Moslem and barbarian pressures, it seems clear that by far the most radical changes came within Europe. China, in effect, was untroubled in essentials and went its own way, returning, after a Buddhist interlude, to a restored and enriched Confucian antiquity. India was more deeply affected, but reacted by withdrawing within its indigenous religious tradition. Europe, on the contrary, fought back, and in doing so transformed its most fundamental institutions and improved its techniques in a fashion that proved capable of sustaining even greater future achievements. At the time, however, Islam, China, and India far surpassed the level of European civilization, as measured by almost any conceivable standard. The Far West had in fact sunk back toward barbarism, retaining only tattered shreds of classical learning, literature, and art. Fresh creativity in these fields came only after A.D. 1000.

XV

The Impact of Turkish and Mongol Conquests

1000–1500

LOSER ties between steppe nomads and the civilized world had been a prominent feature of the centuries before A.D. 1000. During the ensuing five hundred years, this eventuated in a series of infiltrations and conquests that brought Turkish and Mongol rulers to China, the Middle East, India, and eastern Europe. Civilized victims and subjects reacted in different ways.

The Moslems altered the emphasis and internal balance of their society and civilization in a far-reaching and strikingly successful fashion. In effect, the Moslems captured the military energy of the steppe peoples for themselves. The new cutting edge that Turkish and (much less important) Mongol recruits imparted to Islam established it as the ruling faith in all of India and in eastern Europe. Simultaneously, merchants and itinerant holy men carried the religion of Mohammed to southeast Asia and through east and west Africa as well, and even penetrated some of China's western provinces.

The Chinese found nothing to admire in the novelties brought to their attention by Mongol conquerors, and at the first propitious moment they rallied to cast off what was always felt to be an alien and barbarian yoke. Hence the episode of Mongol rule (the Yuan dynasty, 1280–1368) left remarkably few traces behind, unless an enhanced determination to value old and authentically Chinese culture can be attributed to the energy with which the Ming dynasty (1368–1644) repudiated the Mongol rule.

The great majority of Indians and orthodox Christians who found themselves under the government of Islamized Turks remained faithful to their respective religious traditions. Nevertheless, prolonged geographical intermingling provoked a good deal of interchange between the rival religious communities, despite official efforts by guardians of the faith on each side to maintain the purity of their respective versions of theological truth.

The Turkish infiltration. Before examining civilized reactions in more detail it will be well to recapitulate the course of world events. In A.D. 1000 Turkish-speaking tribes lived throughout the middle reaches of the steppe, from the Altai mountains as far west as southern Russia. In eastern Iran, extensive interpenetration between Moslem towns and cultivators and Turkish nomads had already occurred, and many Turkish tribes had accepted Islam, usually in a somewhat casual and superficial fashion. The Iranian barons who for so many centuries had held the steppe nomads at bay ceased to be effective after about 850 or 900. The reasons are obscure, but it seems possible that many moved into towns, acquired a far richer culture than their forefathers had known, and in the process lost their taste for war and hard knocks, leaving that role to Turkish mercenaries, who presently found themselves in a position to hold urbanized Iranian and other Moslem societies up for ransom.

When, therefore, Turkish mercenaries and tribesmen started everywhere to dominate the political life of Islam (after about A.D. 900) the newcomers already knew a good deal about Persian, Arab, and Moslem culture. Yet the Turks maintained their own languages and a certain sense of military camaraderie against the rest of Islamic society. Their rule was disorderly. Detribalized military adventurers competed with the unstable power of clan leaders, whose followers regularly deserted ancient discipline after a few years in a civilized environment. Rivalries and alliances among such precariously situated rulers were unusually fragile and created an endless political kaleidoscope throughout the heartland of Islam.

Nevertheless, the newcomers extended Moslem frontiers very substantially. Penetration deep into India began with massive raids launched by Mohammed of Ghazni in the year 1000. Within three centuries only the southern part of that sub-continent had escaped Moslem conquest; and in 1565 the south capitulated also when the empire of Vijayanagar fell before a coalition of Moslem princes. Turkish successes against Christendom were also very great. After the battle of Manzikert (1071) the Byzantines lost control of the interior of Asia Minor to Seljuk Turks. Simultaneously other Turkish tribes (Kipchaks) pressed across what is now the Ukraine, where they cut off easy communication between Byzantium and freshly Christianized Russia. These heavy blows helped to precipitate the First Crusade (1096-99); but despite some successes, this and later crusades failed to check the Turkish advance. On the contrary, when the Fourth Crusade actually attacked Constantinople and captured and sacked the city (1204), the weakness of the Byzantine state was advertised to all the world. Partial recovery — there was a Greek emperor again in Constantinople after 1261 — was not sufficient to check the force of Italian commercial exploitation on the one hand and Turkish military assault on the other. The Ottoman Turks reaped the ultimate victory. They won their first foothold in Europe in 1326 by crossing the Dardanelles and seizing the peninsula of Gallipoli. After 1389, when they defeated the Serbians at the battle of Kossovo, the Turks won military supremacy in the Balkans. Not until 1453, however, when they conquered Constantinople and made it the capital of their empire, was the last trace of Byzantine power erased from the face of the earth.

The Mongol conquest. This vast tide of Turkish advance into India and Europe was punctuated in the thirteenth century by a sudden storm emanating from Mongolia. The founder of Mongol greatness was Genghis Khan (ruled 1206-27). In his youth an all but helpless refugee from local enemies, Genghis succeeded in welding together a vast military confederacy among the peoples of the steppe. He then raided successfully in every direction — southward into China, westward against the Moslems of Iran and Iraq, and against the Christians of Russia as well. On his death the empire was divided among his four sons. They transformed the massive raiding of Genghis' time into a somewhat more stable form of political rule. For some time, there continued to be effective co-operation between the separate parts of the vast empire. Leadership rested, according to Mongol custom, with Genghis' youngest son and that son's heirs. They ruled Mongolia and China and commanded nearly the whole of the Mongol army.

In Genghis' time the Mongol tribesmen were pagan shamanists. They treated their human victims much as they treated their animals — tending or slaughtering them as convenience might dictate. But once encamped amid more cultivated peoples, the Mongols did what every other nomadic conqueror had done: they quickly took on the color of their subjects' civilization. In the Middle East and Russia this meant the acceptance of Islam. In China, matters were different, for the Mongol emperors could not afford to see the armed forces upon which their power depended dissolve into the Chinese mass. The effort to hold themselves aloof from the Chinese led the Mongols to accept Tibetan Lamaism as the preferred religion of state, although a grand mélange of faiths — Christian, Moslem, shamanist, and others — continued to be represented at court. Yet the penalty of remaining distinct from the Chinese was vulnerability to native reaction, which brought the Ming dynasty to power only a century and a half after Genghis had launched his raids.

Mongol rule therefore constituted no more than an episode in China's long history. In the Middle East and Russia almost the same was true, for after an initial period of hesitation the Mongols not only accepted Islam (Russia, 1257; Persia, 1295) but rapidly assimilated themselves to the Turkish community, which was already dominant everywhere on the central and western steppe. There were too few Mongols and their culture was too crude to permit any other result. Hence in the fourteenth and fifteenth centuries Islamized Turkish warriors, often led by captains who claimed descent from Genghis Khan, again pressed forward against Christendom and Hindustan. The Moslem world had by then fully recovered from the temporary set-back wrought by the pagan Mongol conquest of the thirteenth century.

The Ottoman empire. By far the most durable and most important of the new states that arose in the course of this renewed
Turkish offensive was the Ottoman empire. It originated as a small
frontier principality in northwestern Asia Minor. Turkish warriors
flocked to the service of the Ottoman sultan from all over the Moslem world, because his raids against Christian territory made religious merit and heroic exercise of violence coincide as was true
nowhere else in the Moslem world. Under these circumstances territorial advance became rapid, especially after 1354, when the
Turks made their first permanent lodgment across the straits in Europe. Presently, the Sultan faced difficulty in commanding the loyalty and obedience of his followers, who had been assigned lands
from the conquered territories on the usual feudal pattern. The Ottoman rulers met this difficulty by expanding their personal household into a standing army, staffed by men who were legally classed
as slaves, but who as the Sultan's agents and soldiers of the janissary
(i.e. "new troops") corps actually commanded Moslem landowners and warriors in battle. Personnel for the imperial slave family
came partly from Constantinople's slave markets and capture in
war. But when really large numbers of men were needed for the
incessant campaigns of the fifteenth and sixteenth centuries, the
sultans fell back upon rough-and-ready conscription among the
Christian villages of the remote Balkans. Thus it happened that
young men born as Serb, Greek, or Albanian peasants in the western mountain zone of the Balkan peninsula provided a strategically
decisive element in the military and administrative cadres of the
Ottoman empire.

No other Moslem state achieved such a remarkable and effective
internal organization; and none played anything like the role in
world affairs that the Ottoman empire was to do.

We shall now examine a little more closely the reactions of each
of the major civilized communities to Turkish and/or Mongol rule.

Islam—the Sufi movement. The Abassid caliphs had become
mere puppets and playthings of Turkish mercenary captains long
before the Mongols, in capturing Baghdad (1252), put an end to the
caliphate and to the pretense of a single jurisdiction over all Mos-

lems. Under such circumstances, the principles and compromises upon which classical Islam rested lost their plausibility. What, indeed, was the use of the entire effort to shape a society in accordance with Allah's express will and command as revealed to Mohammed and his companions if brutal chicane and impiety brazenly flaunted themselves in the seats of the mighty? The private sphere remained, and here the doctors of the Sacred Law continued as before to guide personal conduct by giving opinions on difficult cases in accordance with the elaborate precedents they so carefully gathered and studied. But in all this effort there remained a gaping hole: for the Sacred Law could no longer be stretched by any feat of the imagination to legitimize the political chaos that prevailed almost everywhere in the Moslem world.

Such a logically imperfect and increasingly routine approach to holiness could not sustain the authentic fires of conviction which had fueled the first Moslem centuries. Instead, seekers after holiness increasingly drifted into mysticism. A great variety of holy men — or Sufi as they were termed — cultivated the beatific vision of God. They adhered to diverse disciplines. Followers gathered round a man of unusual holiness and sometimes thereby founded a dervish order that might last for centuries and spread over wide regions of the Moslem world, and in other cases disbanded again, leaving no trace. But organizational fuzziness did nothing to obscure the vision of God which, when experienced personally by scores of thousands of men, gave the Sufi movement an emotional force and vivacity which "official" Islam had lost.

Conversion to Islam became comparatively easy when the first step was reverence for and imitation of Sufi holy men who walked familiarly with God. It was no longer the case that acceptance of an elaborate law code and radical changes of private life were needful before becoming a Moslem. Instead, the remodeling of private life to accord with the Sacred Law came gradually and only after Sufi mystics had brought initiates into the Moslem fold. The success with which Asia Minor was made into a Moslem land, the geographically far more extensive conversion of the western and central steppes to Islam, the substantial penetration of India by Islamic sects, the annexation of large parts of east and west Africa to the

Moslem world, and, not least, the conversion of nearly all the Christians remaining within the Syrian and Egyptian heartland of Islam all resulted from the new momentum Sufi mystics imparted to Mohammed's creed.

Previously, Islam had been a city religion. Indeed, some of the ritual prescriptions of the Sacred Law could not be met in rural isolation. But when reverence for "saints," homage at their tombs, and a spectator's part in their ecstasy-inducing rituals became the first step toward membership in the Moslem community, then simple country folk could share the faith with urban sophisticates. In other words something like the gradation and variety of religious practice and outlook which had long characterized Hinduism permeated Islam. Indeed, insofar as the mysticism of the Middle East retained traces of Indian origins, one may describe the triumph of the Sufi path as an Indianization of Islam.

Sufism also worked important changes within the fabric of Islamic high culture. Its greatest success was in suffusing the gentlemanly and courtly ideal of early Islam with the delicate ambiguity of heavenly as opposed to carnal love. Persian poetry became the supreme vehicle of this semi-religious, semi-secular sensibility. The three great poets were Rumi (d. 1273), founder of an important Sufi order; Sa'di (d. 1291); and Hafiz (d. 1390). They, with some lesser luminaries, created a body of poetry which soon became part of the education of all cultivated Moslems. Persian thus displaced Arabic as the leading poetic language of the Moslem world. Arabic, however, remained supreme for all sacred matters, while Turkish was reserved for war and administration.

In the intellectual sphere, the impact of Sufism was less happy, though no less great. Men who themselves saw God in visions were not much interested in mere human reasonings. Kings and successful captains continued to need the services of doctors and astrologers, and these professions therefore continued to flourish. Systematization set in with men like ibn-Sina (d. 1037), who wrote a widely used *Canon* of medicine, and al-Biruni (d. 1046), who deliberately sought to synthesize Indian, Greek, and Moslem thought, in the hope of thereby mastering all knowledge. Perhaps the systematizers were too successful. What after all remained for any doctor of medicine to investigate once so comprehensive a professional handbook as that of ibn-Sina had been compiled? Or perhaps, by fastening attention upon mystical penetration of reality the Sufi adepts deprived mere scientific investigation of any attraction for men of sensitive intelligence. Whatever the reasons, Moslem science withered after about 1200.

Disinclination from and distrust of reason found its own systematic expositor in the person of al-Ghazali (d. 1111), who used Aristotelian logic to demonstrate the impossibility of discovering the truths of theology by human reasoning. His book, *The Destruction of Philosophy*, as its title implies, expressly repudiated the value of logic as a path toward truth. Yet, mystics could not entirely refrain from talking and writing about their supra-rational experiences. From such discussion there emerged a complex analysis of the stages and nature of mystical reality which had many of the characteristics of a reasoned, theologico-philosophic system. This sort of Sufi learning hardened toward fixed forms after about 1200, in much the same way as the Sacred Law of Islam had done about 350 years before.

As this occurred, Moslem minds encased themselves in twin (and mutually quite incompatible) mausoleums. By remarkable ill fortune, they did so just as men of western Europe were beginning to embark upon the restless investigations and inquiries of medieval and modern times. Thus, by a striking paradox, such rigorous and challenging thinkers as the Spanish Moslem ibn-Rushd (Averroës, d. 1198) and the Egyptian Jew Maimonides (d. 1204), both of whom found central inspiration in the philosophy of Aristotle, were almost disregarded in the Moslem world, whereas they both had powerful influence upon the emerging Scholastic philosophy of Paris.

In summary, we may say that Sufism succeeded in merging the rationalistic tradition inherited from the Greeks, the genteel tradition inherited from Arab and Persian aristocrats, and the sacred tradition inherited from Mohammed into a single, and far more coherent, whole than had been achieved in Abbasid times. When one adds to this the fact that Sufi missionaries introduced Islam to an area more than twice the size of the Abbasid empire, something of the magnitude and success of the movement can be appreciated, even by those for whom the mystic path has no attraction.

Fine arts. The Sufi movement was matched by the rise of impressive and distinctive Moslem styles of architecture and painting. Among Moslems architecture was always more important than painting, since religion itself required the construction of mosques and other public buildings. But because nearly all the important centers of Islamic life have been continuously inhabited to the present, details of the architectural past are often unsure. Buildings have been repaired and remodeled from time to time, and old ruins have sometimes been buried under structures which cannot be disturbed by the archaeologist's spade. Nevertheless, where careful study has established dates and the sequences of style — as, for example, in Cairo — it is clear that the size, magnificence, skill of workmanship, and accuracy of detail, together with the artistic success of the structure over-all, tended to increase throughout the five centuries with which we are now concerned. Islamic architects were no longer, as in the first days of Ommayad rule, dependent on Greek or Persian models, but had a style of their own in which "arabesque" linear decoration played a prominent part.

Pious Moslems always disdained the art of painting since portrayal of the human figure invited idolatry. Nevertheless, a school of illuminators arose in Persia whose miniatures usually illustrated manuscripts of the great Persian poets. The bright colors, minute detail, and linear elaboration of these paintings rank them among the most sophisticated and perfect of the world. The best such work, all anonymous, was done in palace ateliers between 1400 and 1600. Other arts — carpet weaving for example — reached a comparable level of refinement and allowed the rulers of the land to surround themselves with a splendor that amazed and impressed the first crude European intruders who encountered it.

India — changes in Hinduism. The Moslem conquest of India had a serious impact upon Hinduism. To be sure, the conquerors fitted into the Hindu social system without straining it unduly, becoming another caste, just as earlier conquerors had done. But Islam, being a universal and missionary faith, systematically resisted encapsulation within the Indian caste system. Moslem doctrine held that all men were equally puny before the omnipotence of Allah and equally precious in his eyes. Hence, it is not surprising that itinerant Sufi holy men, preaching Islam, met with considerable success in attracting low-caste urban Hindus to the faith of Mohammed. Along the frontiers of Indian society also, especially in eastern Bengal, newcomers to Indian civilization tended to prefer Islam with its equalitarian emphasis to Hinduism, which placed them near the bottom of the caste hierarchy. Moreover, the reproach of idolatry which Moslems leveled against traditional Hindu piety was not easy to meet, even after refined philosophical systems had been devised to explain and justify India's age-old multiplicity of cult practices.

Hence the Islamic community in India came to be divided between a thin layer of rulers, warriors, and landowners — many of them Persian in culture and Turkish in origin — and a much more numerous company of poor and humble local peoples, who inevitably brought with them into Islam much of their peculiar local cultural heritage. As a result, Indian Islam remained always distinct from the Islam of Arabic-speaking Moslems of the Middle East.

Hinduism itself altered in three main directions under Moslem rule. First of all, Moslem invaders pillaged the temples around which Hindu cult practices had begun to crystallize. Moslem rulers usually refused to allow such idolatrous structures to be rebuilt. Hence only in southern India do Hindu temples survive with anything like the splendor and elaboration they once attained all over the land. Driven from the ruined temples, Hindu religious ceremonies took on a more public and plebeian character, often taking place in a public square or forming processions that wound their way through town and village streets. Holy men, enjoying an ecstatic communion with Vishnu, Shiva, or some other member of the Hindu pantheon, became the charismatic figures of Hinduism. Inasmuch as Hindu saints saw God with the same vividness as Sufi mystics, Islam enjoyed no emotional superiority over Hinduism on Indian ground. Hence, in general it was only the fringes of Indian society that were attracted to Islam.

Secondly, a few individuals found the intellectual challenge of Islam too immediate to be passed by merely on the strength of

Chinese, Mongol, Persian, and Mughal Painting

Ma Yüan. Two Sages and an Attendant Under a Spreading Plum Tree, Sung dynasty.
Museum of Fine Arts, Boston.

CLASSICAL CHINESE PAINTING

This and the three plates following have been chosen to suggest the wide variety
of effects Chinese gentlemen were able to achieve with the restricted means they
chose to employ: paper, brush, and ink. All these works date from the Sung dynasty
(960-1260), when Chinese painting attained its classical forms. Authentic earlier work
scarcely survives, and subsequent artists were nearly always content to work within
one or other of the genres established by the Sung masters. They sought refinement
and perfection and eschewed the ostentatious vulgarity of personal innovation. As
a result, the history of Chinese art lacks sharp changes of style. Delicate economy of
means devoted to maintaining an elegant and multifold stability made Chinese
painting a faithful mirror of the structure of traditional Chinese society.

PLATE 25

Ma Fen (attributed). The Hundred Geese, Sung dynasty,
section of the scroll. Honolulu Academy of Arts, Hawaii.

PLATE 26

Liang K'ai. The Poet Li T'ai-po, Sung dynasty.
Formerly Count Matsudaira Collection, Tokyo.

Mu Ch'i. Persimmons, Sung dynasty.
Ryūkōin Temple, Kyoto.

PLATE 27

Tung Yüan. Clear Weather in the Valley, Sung dynasty,
section of the scroll. Museum of Fine Arts, Boston.

THE IMPACT OF CHINESE ART ON PERSIA: I

The hunting scene opposite illustrated a Persian poem—a subordination of art to literature entirely strange to Chinese practice. Moreover, the innumerable tiny patches
of brilliant color that irradiate the original (but must here be left to the imagination)
contrast utterly with the low tints characteristic of Chinese painting. Nevertheless,
the mountain in the upper left of this picture is clearly Chinese (compare above) and
attests the impact of Chinese styles—first brought to Persian attention by the Mongols,
who ruled both lands in the thirteenth century—upon an already highly skilled school
of palace art.

PLATE 28

Bihzād. King Darius Reproved by His Herdsman, from a "Būstān" MS, 1488, Iran.
Royal Egyptian Library, Cairo.

PLATE 29

THE IMPACT OF CHINESE ART ON PERSIA: II

Comparison of the tree shown here with the plum tree of Plate 25, and of the leaves with the bamboos of Plate 26, shows once more how Persian artists picked up motifs from Chinese masters and put them to their own—sometimes incongruous—uses. Contrast the partial and controlled use of Chinese motifs by these Persian artists with the wholesale appropriations of foreign styles characteristic of barbarian peoples, illustrated above in Plates 4-7 and 21-24.

Courtesy, The Art Institute of Chicago

Serpent, from a "Manafi Al-Hayawan" MS, Mongol, c. 1300, Iran.
The Art Institute of Chicago.

PLATE 30

Illustration from the Romance of Amir Hamzah, Mughal, 16th cent.
The Metropolitan Museum of Art, New York. Rogers Fund, 1923.

FROM CHINA TO INDIA BY WAY OF PERSIA

The Mughals carried their Persian culture with them into India, as demonstrated by
this painting, which was produced during the first part of the reign of Emperor Akbar
(1556-1605). By that time in Persia itself religious reformers had stamped out all
figure art as dangerously idolatrous; but this did not prevent motifs that had originated in China some five hundred years before from appearing now in India. In
the process of transmission we see (compare Plate 28) that what had been mighty
mountains dwarfing humanity have shrunk so small as to become a strangely shaped
peacock perch. Yet, however misunderstood by the Mughal artist, the odd and eye-
arresting shape of the Chinese original unmistakably survives.

PLATE 31

Prince Dara Shikuh and His Son, Mughal, 16th cent. Staatliche Museen, Berlin.

THE POMP AND SPLENDOR OF IMPERIAL ISLAM

Three great empires, ruled by the Ottoman, Safavi, and Mughal dynasties, consolidated their control over most of the Moslem world during the sixteenth century. These mighty states found it relatively easy to expand their power at the expense both of a squabbling Christendom in Europe and of a disorderly Hindustan in India.

These political facts find faint echo in this painting of a magnificently caparisoned elephant, gay yet stately, whose mighty tread dwarfs the landscape. The scene may also be read as an indication of how Persian ways (the carpet and riders' dress) mingled with older Indian traits (the elephant's anklets) to produce a new and distinctive Mughal style, both of art and of life.

PLATE 32

warm emotional attachments to the Hindu pantheon and rituals. Venturesome thinkers attempted to synthesize Hinduism and Islam, repudiating what they felt to be false in each system and retaining the common core of truth that each of the rival faiths had buried under false accretions. The most famous such religious innovator was Kabir (c. 1450), whom the Sikhs of modern India claim as their founder.

In the third place, the Sanskrit integument in which Hinduism had wrapped itself so enthusiastically during the Gupta age was generally discarded. Vernacular tongues — Hindi and others — came into use for all religious purposes. Sanskrit sank back toward being the precious possession of a learned few; while popular Hindu piety almost lost sight of its ancient Sanskrit base.

These changes all had the effect of bringing Hinduism closer to the population at large, while cutting away courtly and priestly elaboration. This surely helped to assure the survival of Hinduism. It also cost Hindu civilization a great deal, for all the more costly and official aspects of culture became Moslem. From an architectural point of view, India became a province of the Islamic world, nothing more. And without royal and princely patronage, Hindi literature failed to develop a secular counterpart to the hymns and other religious texts which dominate (perhaps disproportionately) our record of India's past.

Orthodox Christendom. It is a striking and not entirely accidental fact that only Orthodox Christendom succumbed to Moslem rule. The separation between the two halves of Christendom achieved formal and lasting definition in 1054, when the pope and the patriarch of Constantinople anathematized each other, thus creating a schism which has endured until the present. The occasion of the quarrel was a difference of opinion about the proper phrasing of the Apostles' Creed; but the distinction between the two halves of Christendom ran very deep, and the gap widened when a new and vigorous civilization began to arise in western Europe, in which the Greek Orthodox had no real share. Instead, as the Latin west increased in wealth, power, culture, and self-confidence, eastern Christendom became one of the victims of Latin expansive energy.

The Orthodox world's loss of Asia Minor and of southern Russia to Turkish invaders was noticed above (p. 234). This two-pronged assault coincided with a similar double thrust from the west. Italian merchant traders came by sea; Norman knights seized Sicily and southern Italy from the Byzantines (by 1065) and then crossed the Adriatic to march overland against Constantinople. Byzantine diplomacy was able to parry this first thrust from the west by diverting the formidable "Franks" to the Holy Land, where they could expend their ferocity on Byzantium's other dangerous enemy, the Turks. The result was the First Crusade, 1096–99. Later, however, the Greeks were less fortunate. The climax came in 1204 when the Fourth Crusade actually captured the city of Constantine, and left behind a short-lived Latin empire of the Levant.

From the point of view of Orthodox Christians, Moslem Turks were definitely preferable to Latin Christians. The Latins insisted on trying to force the Orthodox Christians to accept their version of Christian doctrine at the expense of the immutable truths of Orthodoxy. The Moslems, on the contrary, were prepared to allow Christians of whatever persuasion to continue to follow their accustomed rites. Moreover, the theologians of the church officially classified Islam as Christian heresy: hence Moslem error was really no worse theologically than Latin schism. In addition, the Ottoman Turks, when they first appeared in the Balkans, were much less oppressive tax gatherers than their Christian predecessors had been. The Turks, indeed, in accordance with the Sacred Law gave their Christian subjects far wider local autonomy than they were likely to enjoy under any Christian ruler. Every consideration, therefore, predisposed the Orthodox Christians to opt for Turkish Moslems against Latin Christians if and when choice between the two became necessary. The option expired in 1453 when Constantinople fell to the Turks. Nearly the same factors applied further north in the Russian forests, where such a ruler as Alexander Nevsky (d. 1263) resisted Latin conquest heroically and then tamely submitted to the Mongols.

Before succumbing to the Ottoman Turks, however, the Greek Christians launched a rather vigorous Hellenic renaissance. Memories of classical Greece and of the pagan age of Rome had never entirely disapppeared, but after about A.D 1000 Byzantine artists and literary men began to cherish the past glories of paganism as never before. Art imitative of classical models and literary composition in every mode established by the ancient Greeks were deliberately revived, with varying degrees of success. The *Alexiad*, a history written in verse by Anna Comnena, daughter of the emperor Alexis (reigned 1071–1118), is one of the most distinguished products of this effort. Very different was the rough border balladry, recounting the deeds of heroes fighting against the Moslems, which provided the raw material for the anonymous epic, *Digenes Akritas*, whose rude heroic spirit appeals to modern taste more strongly than does the somewhat artificial learning of the Byzantine upper classes. The Turkish conquest of Constantinople in 1453 abruptly throttled all varieties of secular Byzantine literature; but echoes of the Hellenic renaissance were felt in Italy, and constituted a significant stimulant to the far more fruitful Italian renaissance, which lagged about two centuries behind the Byzantine revival.

In the ecclesiastical sphere, an interesting change occurred within the Greek Orthodox church just after the Turks established themselves in Europe. A monkish party of mystic visionaries, the Hesychasts, overthrew the "Politicians" who had previously controlled the patriarchate and other high offices of the church. Thenceforward, bishops and all other high ecclesiastical dignitaries were recruited exclusively from monasteries, a practice which was not followed in the Latin church. The victory of the monkish party — inspired by personal visions of God — created a popular, emotionally powerful spirit within the Orthodox community at the time when the Turks took over control of most of the Balkan hinterland. As a result, conversion to Islam, which had occurred very generally in Asia Minor and had begun to occur also on the European side of the straits, came almost to a halt, thus assuring the survival of a Christian majority in the Balkans.

The northern offshoot of Orthodox Christendom, Holy Russia, underwent a slow but very significant development during the period of Mongol rule (1241–1480). Agriculture crept deep into the

MOSLEM DOMINATION OF ORTHODOX CHRISTENDOM to 1453

Venetian possessions

■ Trading centers under control of Genoa

- - - Italian trade routes

SWEDEN

DENMARK

Baltic Sea

ORDER

TEUTONIC

HOLY
ROMAN
EMPIRE

POLAND

• Vienna

HUNGARY

Danube R.

SERBIA

Kossovo
1389 ✕

• Rome

KDM. OF
NAPLES

• Venice

• Novgorod

C H R I S T E N D O M

M O S C O W

• Moscow

Volga R.

TURKS AND MONGOLS
(1237-1408)

LITHUANIA
(1263-1386)

Kiev
Dnieper R.

K I P C H A K S

O R T H O D O X

Black Sea

Adrianople
•

Constantinople
✕ 1453
♦ Brusa

OTTOMAN   EMPIRE

Manzikert
1071 ✕

Tigris R.

TURKS (from 1071)

ASIA
MINOR

M e d i t e r r a n e a n

CRETE

S e a

CYPRUS

SYRIA

Euphrates R.

PALESTINE

MAMELUK

S U L T A N A T E

ARABIA

EGYPT

Nile R.

Red Sea

Scale of Miles

0   500

forest, back from the river banks where the population had first congregated. Little by little great areas of ground were cleared for farming. This allowed a comparatively numerous, though extremely poor, peasantry to establish itself despite the inhospitable soil and severe climate.

Politically, the Mongols were content to farm out taxes, first to corporations of central Asian merchants and then to native Russian princes, of whom the Grand Duke of Moscow became the chief. As agent for a harsh though distant taskmaster, the Grand Duke of Moscow created an administrative bureaucracy of tax gatherers. The result was that in 1480, when Ivan III repudiated Mongol suzerainty, he had a ready-made administrative machine at his command. Moscow thus became the only great and independent Orthodox state. Russian churchmen soon developed the idea that Moscow was the Third Rome, succeeding to Constantinople as Constantinople had succeeded the first Rome on the Tiber, because only in Russia had Orthodoxy remained pure and undefiled. Ever since then the notion that Russia was uniquely chosen for the special mission of guarding the true faith on earth has never ceased to play a part in Russian public life, not least since the Communist revolution of 1917.

China — the triumph of tradition. As already explained, the outward appearance of Chinese civilization was remarkably little affected by the episode of Mongol domination. Neo-Confucianism attained its full development under the later Sung, when the greatest philosopher of this school, Chu Hsi (1130–1200), flourished. But the whole effort of Chu Hsi and his fellow literati was to remain faithful to the ancients, as Confucius himself had tried to be. Hence innovation was never consciously admitted whether in thought or in art, in manners or in government.

Nevertheless, during the Mongol period important socio-economic development put considerable strain upon the traditional frame of Chinese civilization. In the end, the old Confucian forms triumphed decisively, but this should not blind us to the importance of the forces which nearly transformed Chinese society. The late Sung and Mongol periods saw a great development in trade and commerce, based upon regional specialization within China and upon far-ranging export and import up and down the coast. Fukien and adjacent parts of the south China coast were among the most active centers of this development.

Early in the Ming period (1368–1644) official organization was brought to the maritime enterprise of south China. Results were spectacular. Between 1405 and 1433 a court eunuch named Cheng-ho launched a series of expeditions into the Indian Ocean, in the course of which truly imperial fleets of several hundred vessels visited all the strategic gateways to the southern seas — Malacca, Ceylon, Calicut, and even Hormuz at the mouth of the Persian Gulf — and temporarily established Chinese control over most of these places. Then the Ming emperor ordered the expeditions stopped, and forbade Chinese subjects from building sea-going vessels or leaving the country. Court intrigues between rival cliques may have had something to do with this decision, so pregnant for the future commercial and imperial balance of power in Asia. But basically the Ming rulers, from their capital at Peking near the ever-dangerous Mongol border, felt that imperial resources should not be squandered on such distant enterprises when the need for protection against the nomads required all the strength the government could muster.

This deliberate abdication from an active role in the southern seas condemned Chinese overseas colonies to speedy decay. Mastery of the seas passed to Japanese and Malay pirates, who soon made the coasts of China unsafe for peaceable shipping. From time to time they even succeeded in interrupting transport on the Grand Canal by penetrating inland along China's numerous waterways.

Merchants had always, of course, ranked as social parasites in Confucian estimation, whereas Mongols and other steppe peoples accorded them a much more dignified place in society. The trading community, which had prospered under barbarian protection, was therefore particularly disadvantaged by the Ming restoration of Neo-Confucian orthodoxy. Yet the failure of the mercantile interest to hold its own after the really great advances made in Sung and Mongol times seems, at least to a Westerner, to require further explanation. The fact that Chinese agriculture also underwent a very great development may help to explain why the conservative Confucian ideal prevailed. About A.D. 1000 new varieties of rice were introduced that could ripen quickly enough to permit double cropping on well-watered land, and — even more important — could mature successfully on hilly ground where irrigation could be had only during a short period of the spring run-off. The total agricultural productivity of China was thereby greatly enlarged, especially in the far south, where hilly ground, previously unsuited to rice growing, prevailed. Hence, as trade and commerce prospered, so did the landowning gentry. Their numbers and weight in society presumably increased more or less equally with the increase in the importance of merchants and artisans. Then, with the overthrow of the Mongol rulers who had been special patrons and protectors of merchants (witness Marco Polo), the stage was set for the native Ming dynasty first to organize and then officially to throttle China's overseas trade.

The social dominance of the gentry class meant that even such potentially disturbing inventions as gunpowder (reported in Chinese sources from about 1100), printing (invented 756), and the magnetic compass (first mentioned early twelfth century) were kept under control and used simply to strengthen the existing social order. Printing, for example, widened the circle of Confucian literati; it was not employed to bring unorthodox novelties to public attention as happened so dramatically in Reformation Europe. Gunpowder, similarly, made suppression of local warlords easier than before and allowed the imperial government to maintain a more or less effective central control over all of China (with only a few brief periods of breakdown) from the time the Ming dynasty completed the expulsion of the Mongols until 1911. Nothing could be more traditional. The equally traditional, high-handed yet effective, fashion with which the Ming court warded off the distraction of sea-borne enterprise, which use of the compass and other navigational improvements permitted, has already been mentioned.

Chinese culture and institutions had, in short, attained such inner perfection and balance that nothing short of wholesale social breakdown of a sort that did not occur in China until the twentieth century, sufficed to make more than superficial, transitory impression upon the bearers of the Chinese learned tradition. The myth of immutability, so eagerly accepted by nineteenth-century Europeans, fed upon this fact, overlooking earlier times and aspects of Chinese society which continued to alter, even when the government and official culture remained frozen to the ideal of Confucian propriety.

XVI

Medieval Europe and Japan

THE self-transformation and expansion of Islam was the most dramatic and conspicuous shift in world history that took place between A.D. 1000 and 1500. A second change, even more significant for the future, was the rise of two new civilizations on the extreme flanks of the civilized world, in northwestern Europe and in Japan.

Both were closely related to adjacent, older, and more sophisticated civilizations: Japan to China and western Europe to Byzantium. Both Japan and Europe also exhibited a pronounced militarism, which penetrated all ranks of society in a fashion elsewhere unknown among civilized peoples. This imparted a degree of formidability vis-à-vis their more polished neighbors that allowed both Europeans and Japanese to borrow whatever they felt good from these same neighbors without surrendering their sense of superiority and cultural individuality by doing so. Unusual flexibility and capacity for growth resulted, so that by about 1500 both medieval Europe and Japan had arrived at a level of culture and style of civilization that in most respects could bear comparison with any other in the world.

Medieval Europe. By the year 1000 the inhabitants of northwestern Europe possessed a comparatively numerous knightly class whose armament and training gave them man-to-man superiority over any other military force in the world. Manorial agriculture,

EXPANSION OF
MEDIEVAL EUROPE
to c. 1492

Boundary of the
Holy Roman Empire
Venetian possessions

War of the Roses
1455-1485

SCOTLAND
IRELAND
ENGLAND
London
Paris
LATIN CHRISTENDOM
FRANCE
BURGUNDY
Rhine R.
Rhône R.
Avignon
Savoy
Swiss.
Conf.
GERMANY
Branden-
burg
Bohemia
Silesia
POLAND
LITHUANIA
Prussia
GERMAN
ORDERS
Estonia
Livonia
Novgorod
1491
Moscow
Volga R.
Dnieper R.
Kiev
KHANATE OF KAZAN
R U S S I A
GOLDEN
HORDE
(until c.1480)
CRIMEAN
KHANATE
Black Sea
Constantinople
Anatolia
CYPRUS
CRETE
OTTOMAN
EMPIRE
Greece
Bulgaria
Wallachia
1480
Danube R.
HUNGARY
Buda
Pest
Bosnia
Croatia
1460
Venice
PAPAL
STATES
Rome
NAPLES
Genoa
CORSICA
SARDINIA
KINGDOM OF ARAGON
Mediterranean Sea
GRANADA
(to Spain, 1492)
Madrid
PORTUGAL
MOSLEMS
Atlantic
Ocean
NORWAY
SWEDEN
DENMARK
Vienna
Moravia
1466
1420

Scale of Miles
0
500

252

based upon the mouldboard plow, provided an adequate economic support for society as a whole. There was a further advantage in that it could readily be enlarged by clearing additional woodlands, which everywhere lay close at hand. Finally, energetic and enterprising townsmen and a church which had inherited an elaborate theological doctrine from antiquity, stood ready to organize and advance economic and cultural life.

Western Europe's improved posture was demonstrated most dramatically by geographical expansion across every frontier confining Latin Christendom. The effective incorporation of Scandinavia and the western Celtic fringe into the European body social was an affair of centuries, but the conversion of Norway and of Iceland (1000) together with the invasion of Wales (1081) and Ireland (1171) by Anglo-Norman knights made the ultimate upshot clear. In an eastward direction, German knights conquered and colonized a broad belt of territory across the Elbe river; others used ships to leap-frog along the Baltic coast, conquering Prussia, Livonia (modern Latvia), and Estonia, but failed (1241–44) in an attempt to penetrate and subdue the Russian interior. Poland and Hungary withstood the German pressure only by imitating the armament of German knights and by importing German (and Jewish) townsmen to provide essential artisan and mercantile services. In so doing, of course, these outposts of Latin Christendom became far more firmly incorporated into western European society than before.

The most significant frontier for Latin Christendom lay to the south and east, for here Moslem and Byzantine neighbors had something more than barbarian hardihood and backwardness to contribute to European civilization. The Norman conquest of southern Italy and Sicily (1059–78) brought formerly Byzantine soil under papal and "Frankish" rule.* A long-drawn-out advance of Christian power in Spain and Portugal also rolled back the Moslem frontier bit by bit, until Granada, the last Moorish stronghold on the European side of the straits, was overrun in 1492. These

---

* All Latin Christians were called "Franks" by Byzantines and Moslems. The term is useful as an indicator of the cultural watershed separating them from their eastern and southern neighbors.

conquests were more lasting than the spectacular crusading ventures to the Holy Land, the Aegean, north Africa, and Egypt, which led to the establishment of Europe's first overseas empires. These empires, nonetheless, weathered innumerable ups and downs across the centuries until the last of them disappeared in 1797 with the extinction of the Venetian republic by Napoleon Bonaparte.

Geographical expansion abroad was matched by a great work of consolidation at home. Consolidation proceeded in every walk of life, and won spectacular successes, yet never quite sufficed to fix European institutions and cultural patterns in an enduring mould. The incessant mutability of European (more recently of Western) civilization is, indeed, its most salient characteristic. No sooner had the restless West worked out a potentially "classic" style of life, as happened for the first time during the medieval period, than with great tribulation that particular ordering of society and culture was discarded. Then, after a time of troubles, another potentially "classic" mould emerged only to encounter the same fate. No other civilization of the world has undergone spontaneous and repeated mutation in this fashion, though as we shall see, the sudden turns and shifts of Japanese cultural history have been quite as drastic and a good deal more abrupt than anything in European experience. The difference lies in the fact that the major shift of Japanese history came in response to circumstances others had created, whereas Europeans responded mainly to dilemmas and opportunities of their own making.

The geographical reversal which came with the opening of the oceans to commerce, whereby what had before been remote and isolated extremities of the civilized world became instead strategically open to every sort of foreign sea-borne influence, does much to explain the recent instability of European and Japanese history. Deep-seated discrepancies, producing internal polarities and tensions within the two civilizations, also help to account for what happened.

Europe's economic consolidation. Clearing of forest, founding of new villages, and expansion of the cultivated fields surrounding old ones went ahead rapidly from about A.D. 900 until the middle of the fourteenth century. Then, at least in some parts of Europe, the ravages of the Black Death (1348–50), together with more obscure changes in markets, rents, and taxes, halted or even reversed agricultural expansion. By that time, nearly all the easily cultivated land of Europe had been put to the plow. Further agricultural improvements required new crops, ditching and draining, or other expensive innovations which, for a while, were not forthcoming.

Town life exhibited the same general curve. Very rapid upthrust occurred between 1000 and about 1300. Thereafter, growth slowed, or stopped entirely, save in certain special regions, such as along the Baltic coast of Germany or in central and northern Italy, where vigorous commercial exploitation of the new Baltic and Levantine "empires" that had been created by German and Frankish knighthood continued to sustain important urban development until after 1400. Thereafter major economic innovation tended to concentrate more in central Germany and the Low Countries, where mining and the herring fisheries gave a special fillip to increasingly large-scale capitalist enterprise.

The outstanding characteristic of European commerce was the great importance of rude and vulgar commodities. Articles of rather wide consumption, like woolen cloth, grain, herring, and iron, entered interregional trade. Luxuries and fine articles designed for the rich constituted only a minor part of the stream of European commerce. In most of the civilized world, transport was so costly that long-distance trade was pretty much confined to articles of high value in proportion to their bulk. Europeans could afford to move much less valuable goods to distant markets because intrusive seas and long, slow-moving streams made water transport available to very large parts of the European countryside. Shipping was of course immeasurably cheaper than transport overland, which, in the absence of well-maintained roads, had to be conducted by animal pack trains.

Neither India nor the Middle East had as dense a network of natural waterways as Europe, but China's canals and rivers and Japan's indented coastline offered facilities for water transport about as good as those of the Far West. Nevertheless, as we saw in the preceding chapter, the social structure of China was so dominated by officials and landlords as to inhibit the free development of shipping and trade. As for the Japanese, they did not take to the sea on a large scale until after 1300. Then, early in the seventeenth century, after a heroic period of sea roving, the government, as in China, forbade all naval enterprise. Hence it was only in Europe that an aggressive merchant class confronted the technical potentialities of sea transport in a geographically propitious environment without being hampered by hostile officialdom.

From about 1000, Europeans were therefore in a uniquely favorable position to exploit their natural waterways to bring articles of common everyday consumption to market. To be sure, improvements in ship building and navigation were necessary before the stormy and tide-beset waters of northwestern Europe became reasonably safe for shipping. Critical improvements in seamanship were made during the Viking age, when, for example, the much more efficient stern rudder supplanted the steering oar. Thereafter as shipping grew and flourished, all the advantages of economic specialization, which Adam Smith was later to describe in his *Wealth of Nations*, accrued to medieval Europe. Trade and commerce affected almost every rank of society, since peasants as well as townsmen and landowners could afford to buy some of their tools and other necessities from petty traders, artisans, or shopkeepers. In other words, the market penetrated deeper into the tissues of European society than it did in land-fast Asian communities. Correspondingly European manufactures catered to a cruder level of taste and a cheaper market than was usual elsewhere.

Political consolidation. Throughout the Middle Ages a confusing variety of overlapping jurisdictions competed for sovereignty. The Pope in Rome and the imperial heirs and successors of Charlemagne each claimed universal leadership over all Christendom — meaning, in practice, over Latin Christendom alone. National monarchs, feudal princes, local landowners of every degree, as well as towns and (on the fringes of Europe) even clans and free villages, all competed with one another for authority, rights, immunities, and jurisdictions.

We can distinguish three phases of medieval Europe's political evolution. During the first period, the emperor (i.e. the ruler of Germany whose title derived from Charlemagne's usurpation) supported by most German and some Italian bishops sought to keep all more local sovereignties in check. In practice the kingdoms of France, England, Spain, Scotland, Scandinavia, Poland, and Hungary were always free to go their own ways. The emperors had more than enough to do in trying to rule Italy and Germany. During the second period, beginning in 1059, the papacy took the lead in seeking to purify and reform the Church. Among other matters, this reform deprived the emperor of his customary right to appoint the bishops of Germany and (parts of) Italy. A long struggle ensued, in the course of which the popes allied themselves with the new-sprung Norman kingdom of southern Italy and with Italian towns of central and northern Italy, in order to find the military strength needed to resist sporadic invasions from the north launched by a succession of indignant German emperors. By 1252, however, the imperial power had utterly collapsed and the papacy was left as the only claimant to the universal government of Latin Christendom.

Papal authority soon collided with the national monarchies of France and England, both of which had before usually stood in loose alliance with the papacy as a form of insurance against the German emperor's claims to supreme authority over Christendom. In 1302 the new balance of power was dramatically demonstrated when agents of the French king kidnapped Pope Boniface VIII, yet met with neither divine nor human retaliation. Soon thereafter the popes and kings of western Europe struck a bargain whereby the papacy gave up its claims to appoint bishops without consulting the king, while the king in return agreed to allow the pope's agents to collect specified taxes and dues from the prelates of the realm. In effect, kings and popes collaborated in reducing the powers and independence of lesser local jurisdictions, specifically seeking to diminish the rights and powers of local nobles, both lay and ecclesiastical.

In Germany and Italy, however, city-states and various princely jurisdictions acquired most of the attributes of sovereignty. In 1272, after a long interregnum, Rudolf of Hapsburg was elected emperor. Thereafter, with only a few exceptions, members of the Hapsburg family continued to occupy the imperial office until 1806, when it was abolished. Their power, however, rested not so much on the imperial title as upon hereditary lands, which centered around Austria in southeastern Germany.

Soon after the empire thus limply revived, its victorious rival, the papacy, suffered a serious set-back. Pope Clement VII and his successors set up their residence at Avignon in southern France (1207), thereby becoming the close allies and at times almost the agents of the French king. Efforts to remedy this situation resulted in the establishment of rival popes in Avignon and Rome (1378–1417). Unity was restored only by means of a general council of bishops, summoned to meet in the Swiss city of Constance by the Emperor Sigismund (1414–18). Nothing resembling universal papal monarchy could survive such an experience.

Before turning attention to the cultural consolidation of medieval Europe, a word should be said about the development of representative and parliamentary government. This distinctive political institution had two principal roots. On the one hand, canon law held that bishops should be elected by the clergy of their cathedral church, and that matters of general concern should be settled by meetings of church leaders, whether in a local synod or in a general council. Particularly during the fourteenth century, when rival popes claimed supremacy over the Church, ecclesiastical reformers developed elaborate arguments in favor of settling the question through a council. Some went on to argue that all legitimate authority derived from consent of the governed, expressed through designated or elected representatives. Such ideas were readily transferrable to secular government, where the traditional relationships between a ruler and his followers provided a second root from which parliamentary institutions grew. Princes of every degree had to consult their subordinates and servants from time to time, particularly before undertaking any important new enterprise. Originally such consultation served two main functions: the settlement of quarrels among the prince's followers, and deliberation about whether to undertake a particular military campaign. To this was presently added the grant of "aids," i.e. of money payments needed by the prince for some public undertaking.

Aids tended to become more and more important as time passed. Many knights or holders of knights' fiefs (e.g. the young son of a dead knight not yet of age) preferred to pay someone to fight in lieu of making a personal appearance when summoned to war. Knight service was thus sometimes commuted to a fixed money payment. This allowed the king to gather round himself a body of salaried fighting men who were, in the nature of things, more obedient to the royal will than a levy of landholders, scattered far and wide across the kingdom, could ever be.

But as soon as money matters became a major subject of consultation between the prince and his followers, it seemed sensible to bring representatives of the towns to court also, for the townsmen were, of course, the most fertile source of cash. Representatives of the towns usually sat apart from the noble landowners in a separate house or "estate." The upper clergy also constituted a separate estate, since, being also under the pope, they had a special legal relationship to secular authorities. In this somewhat haphazard fashion, it became customary in every important European state for the prince or king to consult representatives of all the major interests of the realm — about tax payments first and foremost, and about other matters of general concern too, since representatives easily discovered that they could withhold approval of a new tax levy until the prince redressed their grievances — or promised to do so.

By means of such representative institutions, important conflicting interests within each European state found more or less effective voice. Peasants were seldom represented and town artisans were likewise left out. But property holders and taxpayers were heard in public matters that most concerned them.

Europe's political consolidation therefore involved the enfolding of the most active elements of society into the political process in a fashion that had no real parallel in other civilized lands. Relatively close collaboration between rulers, landowners, and merchants was thus assured. It is hard to believe, for example, that any European government could have overridden the interests of such a massive group of shipowners and seamen as existed in south China at the time the Ming emperor forbade the further construction of seagoing vessels. A somewhat stumbling but generally effective sensitivity on the part of public administrators to the economic interests of the subjects was built deeply into the fabric of European government. In this sense, therefore, European governments, like European trade and commerce, were unusually vulgar, and by the same token unusually apt to accommodate themselves to new forms of economic enterprise — particularly if the innovation seemed likely to produce additional tax revenues.

Cultural consolidation. For more than two centuries, from the time when Europe's recovery commenced until about 1200, eager appropriation of everything that appealed to Western men in the Arabic and Byzantine cultural traditions, together with bold and vigorous creativity, imparted a youthful brilliance to medieval culture that can only be compared to the ancient Greeks' similar period of apprenticeship to and emancipation from the cultural model of the ancient Middle East.

Both in Spain and in southern Italy, scholars organized systematic translation from Arabic into Latin. A large literature of professional handbooks and encyclopedic information was thus added to the Latin inheritance, which had previously been almost exclusively ecclesiastical. The translation of Aristotle's works into Latin proved particularly influential. Western men found in Aristotle's pages a reasoned, complete, and persuasive view of the entire universe which was, however, pagan. The task of reconciling Aristotelian doctrine with Christian truth became critical for those — and they were many — who refused willingly to surrender any part of their intellectual inheritance, whether it be the new Aristotelian logic or the old Christian faith.

Another dimension of European culture — the inheritance from the barbarian world generally, and the knightly style of life in particular — also called for integration into a Christian mould, for the rough brutality and violence of the tenth century had next to nothing in common with Christian love, hope, and charity.

These challenges were initially met in a spirit of reckless abandon. St. Anselm (d. 1109) and Peter Abelard (d. 1142), for example, seem to have felt that human reason and Christian doctrine would be sure to support one another if reason were resolutely and rigorously pursued. Thus, St. Anselm found it possible to prove the logical necessity of the Incarnation, and Peter Abelard launched a critical inquiry into the conflicts among Christian writers on points of doctrine. Simultaneously, in the field of law the monk Gratian (c. 1140) weightily argued the pros and cons of discordances within the laws of the Church, while Irnerius (d. c. 1130) began the systematic study of Roman law in hope of finding a key wherewith to unlock the prevailing confusions that plagued the local, customary law of Europe. To such men, nothing was too difficult to try.

Monumental stone building in the style known as Romanesque dates from these same years. Western architects expressly repudiated the Byzantine architectural style, which had previously found a modest footing in western Europe, and preferred a style based upon ancient Roman basilicas and early Christian church structures. With the same sort of sublime confidence, barbarian violence was at last partially Christianized through such enterprises as the Crusades (beginning 1096) and by the development of a knightly ideal that asked men-at-arms to aid the weak, serve womankind, and protect Mother Church.

Between about 1200 and 1300 the initial *élan* of medieval Europe's cultural upthrust developed a more complex and troubled yet richer texture. Tensions between Christian faith, ecclesiastical order, and naïve acceptance of the authority of the past on the one hand, and men's rational, secular, and critical faculties on the other, became acute. Yet in diverse and conscious ways these tensions were for a while effectively resolved, thus producing the great climax of medieval culture — the synthesis of the thirteenth century — toward which an important company of sensitive Westerners have ever since nostalgically looked back.

In the field of thought, faith and reason were resolutely reconciled by theologians like St. Thomas Aquinas (d. 1274) and St. Albert the Great (d. 1280). Aquinas' *Summa Theologica* arrayed authoritative opinions and carefully reasoned answers to a vast number of questions of faith and morals. His book very soon came to be recognized as a semi-official statement of Christian doctrine. Aristotelian logic and some of Aristotle's conclusions were thus skillfully harnessed to the task of upholding Christian truth, in accordance with the general principle that while faith and reason could never contradict one another, there were points of theological truth that were simply not accessible to unaided reason and had therefore to be imparted to mankind through divine revelation. Yet Aquinas was not without his critics. The most influential of these distrusted long chains of logical proofs, and preferred the certainty of things divine that came from mystical experience, and the knowledge of things mundane that could be achieved by careful attention to information supplied by the senses. Such thinkers as St. Bonaventura (d. 1274) and Roger Bacon (d. c. 1292) represented this loosely Platonic (and Franciscan) intellectual tradition, which they consciously opposed to the Dominican Aristotelianism of Aquinas.

In the field of action, diversity and discrepancy were more apparent than synthesis; but opposing tendencies and ideals were balanced against one another in such a way as to give scope to a wide spectrum of human impulse and diversity of character. Thus, for example, Christian knighthood was countered by a "romantic" ideal that emphasized courtly (i.e. extra-marital) love and a code of manners that risked sensuality in the pursuit of sensibility. Or again, heresy which spread widely among weavers and other artisan groups met a counterpoise in the piety of Franciscan and Dominican friars. Unlike monks, the friars lived and worked among laymen, preaching, caring for the sick, aiding the poor and helpless, and in other ways offering a practical demonstration of Christian idealism. St. Francis (d. 1226), founder of the Franciscan order, and St. Dominic (d. 1221), founder of the Dominican order, were the most important leaders of this fresh outpouring of Christian feeling. Yet here too lay a difficulty, for the very intensity of St. Francis' pursuit of holiness pushed him to the verge of heresy. Some of his followers, who criticized the pope and bishops of the Church for failing to imitate Christ and the Apostles by leading lives of poverty (as the friars in principle undertook to do), passed beyond the verge at which their saintly founder had always called a halt. After a long legal process these "Spiritual Franciscans" were condemned as heretics, despite (or because of) the intensity of their piety.

The literary activity of the thirteenth century gave voice to all these diverse strands of thought and feeling, and did so partly in Latin, partly in vernacular languages. Popular tales, often scurrilously anti-clerical, and naïvely pious "miracle" plays based on Biblical stories reflected the diversity of life in the towns. Romances and troubadour songs did the same for the aristocracy. The greatest literary figure of the age was Dante, the Florentine exile (d. 1321). His love sonnets, political writings (*De Monarchia*), and above all his Christian epic, *The Divine Comedy*, set forth a world view that more nearly captured the multifaceted life of thirteenth-century Europe than any other man came near to doing.

The history of art shows the same headlong rush toward multiplicity and variety. Gothic cathedrals of the thirteenth century achieved a complex, subtle, and enormously successful solution to the problem of enclosing a large space for Christian worship. Yet the Gothic style quickly evolved toward greater and greater decorative complication, until encrusted tracery obscured the structural simplicity of rib, buttress, and pier. This flamboyance matched the complication and occasional triviality of later Scholastic philosophy and may have corresponded also to a certain weakening of Christian conviction and increased delights in display and luxury which gave point to the "Spiritual" Franciscans' attacks upon the worldliness of ecclesiastical dignitaries.

A general fraying out of the medieval cultural synthesis was characteristic of the period after 1300. In the fourteenth and fifteenth centuries, the competing ideals of holiness and human satisfaction in this world failed to find any really satisfactory resolution. During this time, developments in Italy diverged significantly from the climate of opinion north of the Alps. Italy became the seat of a conscious renaissance of classical antiquity, meaning, in practice, the Roman rather than the Greek past. Many educated Italians discovered that study of the pagan Latin poets and of Cicero offered not only models of literary excellence but fresh and valuable insights into the question of how men should live and conduct themselves. Humanists, as men who cultivated these concerns were proud to call themselves, seldom broke explicitly with Christianity. Indeed, humanistic literary and artistic values often were shared by prelates of the Church, who ranked among the most important patrons of the movement.

In the milieu of the Italian towns a new art style was born. Like the humanists' Ciceronian Latin, it was deliberately modeled on ancient example. Architecturally, pillars, pilasters, and round arches constituted the elements from which the "renaissance" style was derived. In painting few ancient examples were available, and perhaps in consequence, a more profound originality developed. Aerial and — from about 1430 — linear perspective gave the Italian painters a systematic, remarkably rational, and optically persuasive technique for arranging objects in an illusory space. The result was to create a powerful and unique style of painting which matured shortly before 1500. It endured as the fundamental frame for European painting until the end of the nineteenth century.

North of the Alps no such successful and venturesome assertion of novel humanistic and naturalistic interests came to expression. Instead, something of a stalemate between the discordant elements of the European cultural inheritance set in. Florid court chivalry accorded ill with the brutal reality of the Hundred Years' War (1337–1453) between France and England, when bands of mercenary soldiers robbed and burned their way across the fertile fields of France. Popular discontents found expression in a rash of peasant revolts and in the rise of new heretical movements like the Lollards of England and the Hussites of Bohemia.

The medieval frame of European culture was clearly in difficulty, but its eventual repudiation was a painful and prolonged process, decisively launched only by such great events as the opening of the oceans to European shipping and the nearly simultaneous outbreak of the Reformation. Discussion of the genesis of modern Europe will, however, be reserved for the third part of this book.

Japan. The precocious courtly culture of Japan did not entirely disappear even when the imperial power had become no more than a shadow. But border barons who pioneered the expansion of Japanese society northward through the archipelago were not in a position to share or admire the refined and anti-militaristic cultural ideal which the first Japanese courtiers had imported wholesale from T'ang China. Instead, they developed a code of manners and a warrior ideal of their own, emphasizing courage in battle, loyalty to a chosen leader, and the infrangible personal dignity of each and every fighting man, no matter how poor he might be or how desperate his cause. In time the code of the *samurai*, as the Japanese warriors were termed, became strict and binding, and even attained written codification. It arose from the discipline and spirit of successful war bands, recruited by individual captains for their own and their followers' aggrandizement. A successful band of course took possession of a piece of territory and collected dues in kind from the peasant inhabitants. Hereditary possession became usual, but continual vigilance and ready capacity to demonstrate individual and collective prowess in battle were always required to maintain what had been won. Constant local wars were the result, for any quarrel between members of different bands could only be adjudicated by the sword, and, for that matter, it was not always possible for members of a single band to settle differences among themselves peaceably.

Japanese feudalism, therefore, closely resembled the feudalism of early medieval Europe. Even the survival of an ineffective imperial suzerainty in Japan resembled the vague deference paid to the imperial idea by Europeans. In detail there were important differences. For example, the Japanese samurai grouped themselves into clans (real or fictitious), whereas European knights were governed by contractual relations — homage and fealty — not by kindreds. Moreover, the style of agriculture which sustained the Japanese fighting class was entirely different from that of Europe. As in China, a garden type of intensive cultivation prevailed in Japan. Accordingly a densely settled peasantry, producing a smaller food surplus per family than European peasants could do, constituted a very poor but extremely hard-working mass base for Japanese society as a whole.

After about A.D. 1300 a third element began to achieve greater prominence in Japanese society — to wit, townsmen and sailors.

Important improvements in naval architecture, pioneered by the Chinese, permitted this development in Japanese society. The compass, adjustable centerboard, keels, cloth instead of slatted bamboo sails, and a general increase in size and strength of ship construction all spread from China to Japan. This made sea voyaging practicable up and down the Japanese coasts, and across the sea to China, to southeast Asia, and to the nearer islands of the Pacific as well. Fishing soon developed into an important industry. Then, when the Chinese withdrew from the seas in the 1430's, the Japanese rapidly took over naval primacy throughout the southwest Pacific region.

In these circumstances, piracy and sea roving offered a very promising career for poverty-stricken samurai who lacked enough land or had been dispossessed in some local struggle. Japanese pirates, therefore, quickly became the scourge of the China coast. They brought back rich hauls of booty to their home ports, where town life burgeoned. An extensive interpenetration between merchants and warriors produced a warlike, self-reliant middle class, whose only analogue in the civilized world was in Europe, where piratical origins had also helped to define the townsman's ethos.

The rise of towns in Japan meant also the appearance of new social milieux in which the polarity between Chinese civility and Japanese reality could work itself out and generate a more elaborate Japanese high culture than the spartan idea of rural samurai allowed. Drama based on episodes from struggles among samurai clans and war bands was one of the products of this interaction. The development of a Japanese style of painting, related to yet distinct from Chinese styles, was another. The refinement of samurai manners by such elegancies as the "tea ceremony" and the use of silk clothes was still a third.

Japan's religious history reflects the same development toward local independence of Chinese examples. Zen Buddhism was initially imported from China, but on Japanese soil Zen became intertwined with the samurai ideal in a fashion totally alien to Chinese precedent. Aged or defeated samurai not infrequently retired to Zen monasteries, where they found in the metaphysical doctrine of sudden enlightenment a needed supplement to the bleak militarism of their secular life. From about 1200, Pure Land Buddhism became prominent in Japan. This sect appealed to a wider public. It was organized on congregational lines and expressly repudiated reliance upon priestly or monkish mediators between ordinary men and salvation. Both Zen and Pure Land Buddhists occasionally resorted to violence. Zen monasteries, indeed, were often important landholders and therefore found themselves compelled to defend their property like a samurai clan. Pure Land Buddhists, on the other hand, provoked a number of large-scale peasant risings. These broke out after 1400, but were nowhere successful for long.

The cult of the Sun Goddess from whom the imperial family claimed descent underwent an important transformation in the fifteenth century. Previously this cult had been almost entirely confined to the imperial court and family, and had been assimilated to Chinese patterns of ancestor worship. After 1400, however, priests of the Sun Goddess's principal shrine began to develop allegorical interpretations of traditional myths, thus equipping the cult with a metaphysical theology comparable to Buddhist doctrines. This remodeled cult, or Shinto, could and did appeal to an emerging Japanese sense of national identity and uniqueness — a sense greatly stimulated by the enlarged contacts with the outside world their successful sea roving inaugurated.

By 1500, therefore, Japanese society and culture had become comparable in complexity, formidability, and sophistication to other civilized communities of the Old World. A comparatively small and isolated geographical range and the comparatively great ethnic homogeneity of the bearers of Japanese culture cramped the full development of this new civilization. Or perhaps one should rather say that before Japanese civilization had time to spread beyond the confines of the Japanese islands and attract other peoples (e.g. the Filipinos and Amerindians) into its ambit, rival sea-borne civilizations, to wit, the Islamic and European, pre-empted the ground and effectually fenced Japanese culture in, so that it could not spread among new peoples in the way more favorably situated new civilizations had always done. Japan, nevertheless, achieved civilized status in time to preserve full cultural and political autonomy in modern times, as the less advanced peoples of Africa, Australia, and the Americas, whose cultural development we will glance at in the next chapter, were quite unable to do.

XVII

The Fringes of the Civilized World

to 1500

Y A.D. 1500 only a slender zone of tundra and
Arctic shoreline in the Old World remained un-
affected by the development of civilized styles of life. A few reindeer herders continued to carry on a traditional existence, and an
Eskimo culture, skillfully adapted to survival in the special environment of the Arctic shoreline, came into being without any percep-
tible or plausible relationship to what men had done in more favored regions of the earth.

South of the belt of civilized communities that extended all the
way across Eurasia, geographical conditions and cultural relationships were far more complicated. Yawning gaps remain in our information about the history of such a vast and varied region of the
earth as Africa, and what is known presents almost as many historical puzzles as it solves. Only a very tentative summary of what appear to be the main lines of development is possible in a book such
as this. The reader should be aware that much of what follows rests
on nothing more solid than shrewd guesswork.

In A.D. 1500 Africa south of about the Zambesi river, as well as
the whole of Australia and adjacent islands like Tasmania and New
Guinea, remained entirely untouched by civilization. Primitive peoples there pursued a Stone-Age life similar, so far as we can tell, to
that of the earliest human hunters.

Southeast Asia and the South Pacific. North of these two major refuge areas, however, the transforming force of civilized styles of life had everywhere been felt. In southeast Asia and the islands of Indonesia, societies familiar with root agriculture and adept in the arts of primitive seamanship existed before either Indian or Chinese explorers penetrated the river mouths of that part of the world. Then, as we have already seen, beginning about the Christian era, massive acceptance of Indian culture occurred. After about A.D. 600 links with India weakened, largely as a result of the replacement of Hindu by Moslem shipping in the Indian Ocean. The various Hindu (and some Buddhist) courts of southeast Asia were therefore thrown back upon their own local resources. The results were occasionally magnificent. Java, for example, became the seat of a Hindu empire which built the great temple of Majapahit, while the lower Mekong became the seat of a similar state, the Khmer empire, whose monument is the vast and impressive palace-temple-city of Angkor Wat.

Beginning about A.D. 1200 two outside forces attacked the Indianized court civilizations of southeast Asia. Thai tribes descended from the north, overthrew the Khmer empire, and substituted their own more warlike and more tumultuous dominion in the Mekong valley. Missionaries in time converted the Thai to a form of Buddhism bearing a Burmese-Tibetan rather than an Indian stamp. Simultaneously, Moslem missionary enterprise gathered headway as a result of the internal changes in the Islamic community which we have already noticed. Accordingly, Malaya, Sumatra, and presently Java and distant Mindanao in the Philippines became the seats of Moslem regimes. Sooner or later Hindu cults disappeared everywhere, save in the island of Bali, where something of the older life survived until modern times.

During these same centuries, Polynesian navigators were carrying their high barbarism far across the Pacific. Their culture was at least loosely related to the cultures of southeast Asia. Ancestors of the Polynesians probably came from somewhere on the Asian mainland, but their great dispersion occurred only after the invention of outriggers permitted a canoe made from a single hollowed log to travel in safety across the open ocean. When this critical breakthrough had been made (about A.D. 600) Polynesians spread across the vastnesses of the Pacific within a few hundred years — a fact attested by the close affinity of their languages in regions as distant from one another as New Zealand and Hawaii.

Sub-Saharan Africa. Africa was probably the original cradle of mankind, and that continent has preserved until our own time a greater ethnic variety than any other part of the earth. Peoples as widely different in their physical appearance as Bushmen, Hottentots, Dinka, and Masai cannot be found elsewhere. In times past some of these peoples held much larger territories than they do today, whereas other populations—Bantu-speaking Africans in particular— were once confined to a small portion of the ground they now occupy. The naïve idea that Africa is and has always been inhabited by a more or less uniform Negro population is completely unfounded; but the truth is too complicated and too ill-recorded to be easily reconstructed.

The Sahara desert effectually divides Africa in two. The northern coast shared in the classical and medieval history of the Mediterranean and does not concern us here. Sub-Saharan Africa, however, is far from uniform geographically. The Congo rain forest is bordered north, east, and south by savanna—that is, landscapes of grass dotted by occasional clumps of trees. But the mountains and great lakes of central east Africa interrupt the arc of the savanna, so that it is not a continuous belt, but divides into two major parts: west Africa, bisected by the curved course of the Niger river, and east Africa, running down the east spine of the continent all the way to the Cape of Good Hope. Scant pasture lands, fringing the southern Sahara, skirt the northern face of the mountain barrier. This miniature steppe therefore linked the two major productive regions of east and west Africa.

The geographical compartmentation of Africa helps to account for the restricted reach of ancient Egypt, whose influence does not appear clearly outside the Nile valley itself, and then only as far south as Nubia. About the Christian era, or perhaps shortly before, an important Indonesian component was brought into Africa. At that time, the island of Madagascar was colonized by a people who

AFRICA
c. 1500

Desert and
subdesert steppe
Tropical rainforest
Moslem influence
Caravan route

Scale of Miles
0   1000

arrived by sea from one of the islands of Indonesia, perhaps from
Borneo, where their closest linguistic relatives live in modern times.
Other Indonesian settlements probably once existed along the eastern coast. The surest evidence of this is that a number of root crops
native to Indonesia and therefore well suited for rain-forest cultivation established themselves as staples of African agriculture. The
new crops had their major impact on west Africa where cultiva-

tors began to penetrate into the vastnesses of the Congo rain forest about this time, perhaps because the new Indonesian crops first made agriculture in that environment practicable. The initial expansion of the Bantu-speaking peoples, whose original homeland and point of dispersion lay in west Africa, not far, perhaps, from the Bight of Benin, may have depended on their successful exploitation of the new Indonesian crops.

About A.D. 300 trans-Saharan camel trains began to bring influences from the Roman world to bear upon west Africa. On the strength of a growing caravan trade, whose main commodities were gold, salt, and slaves, Ghana, the first major west African state, began to take form, sometime between A.D. 300 and 600. Meanwhile in east Africa the kingdoms of Nubia and Abyssinia entered into much closer relations with the Roman world. Both became Christian at an early date, but Abyssinian and Nubian Christianity soon developed local idiosyncrasies. Abyssinia for a while controlled the straits of Aden and exercised considerable power in Arabia. But the rise of Islam and Mohammed's unification of Arabia drove the Abyssinians back across the straits. Thereafter, the Christian culture of Abyssinia was always on the defensive. Islam quickly planted itself in east Africa and Moslems soon took over all the coastline, confining the Christians to the highlands, where they still exist.

The Arab conquest of Egypt (A.D. 641) and of all north Africa (by 711) gave both east and west Africa, Moslem instead of Christian neighbors. The further fact that Moslem shipping speedily took over primacy on the Indian Ocean meant a further exposure of Africa to Moslem infiltration. Until after the year 1000, however, Islam made only modest headway south of the Sahara. Thereafter, its advance became much more rapid. Ghana, for example, was overthrown in 1076 by a Moslem conqueror. Thereafter Moslem states dominated west Africa. The most important of the early Moslem empires was Mali. The effort required to resist Islamic assault actually generated something of a "golden age" in Abyssinia's cultural history, but Nubia succumbed to Islam in the fifteenth century. After the conquest of Nubia Arab nomad tribes began to move all the way across the African continent, skirting the southern edge of the Sahara. When these migrants reached west Africa they actually rolled back the frontier of cultivation a considerable distance.

The history of east Africa south of Cape Guardafui is still quite unclear. At some time between 700 and 1400 large-scale gold mining occurred at several sites in what is now Rhodesia. Extensive rock-built ruins at Zimbabwe and nearby attest the scale of this enterprise. Another important event was the spread of cattle nomads southward. Once again, the pioneers were Bantu-speaking tribes who had presumably acquired the art of cattle rearing from some more civilized people — perhaps from Nubia. Bantu cattle nomads rapidly drove the Hottentot hunters southward. By 1500 the frontier of Bantu expansion had reached the Zambesi river.

Before Europeans circumnavigated the Cape of Good Hope, therefore, nearly all of Africa had felt the influence of more advanced societies in attenuated but unmistakable form.

The Americas. The Americas had meanwhile become the seat of complex societies that fully deserve the epithet "civilized." Generally speaking, the level of mastery over the environment attained in Mexico and Peru by 1500 seems very similar to what the ancient Mesopotamians and Egyptians had achieved by about 2500 B.C. A four-thousand-year lag was far too great for the Amerindians to make up when the Spanish conquistadors burst in upon their seclusion. Since the higher culture of the Aztec and Inca empires left only limited traces behind, we can afford to be quite cursory in our consideration of the Amerindian civilization.

Cultivation of maize, the fundamental food crop of the New World, dates back at least as far as 2500 B.C. About a thousand years later, settled village life developed in Mexico, presumably as better and more productive strains of maize evolved. Not long before the Christian era monumental cult centers began to take form in such places as the Guatemalan highlands (Mayas) and the central Mexican plateau (Toltecs). What archaeologists call the "classic" stage of the Amerindian cultures of Central America emerged by about A.D. 300 and lasted for about six hundred years. During this time, Mayan and Toltec temples attained vast size and systematic elaboration. The Mayas developed an accurate calendar and a form of writing which scholars today can partly decipher. Priestly control and management of society seem clear; but the details of the ideas and myths, religious principles, and administrative organization by which the effort of ordinary farmers was mobilized to raise the great temples, and how expert stone masons and other artisans were maintained, cannot now be known.

Peru may have lagged somewhat behind the Mexican and Guatemalan development, but the "classic" period of the three major cultures of Peru is thought to coincide fairly closely with the classic ages of the Mayan and Toltec temple states. Potatoes and the llama were important resources of the Andes slopes not available in Mexico. In addition, the Peruvian societies of the coastal area depended on a very skillful irrigation, whereas in Central America maize was grown on rain-watered land. At some date between A.D. 500 and 1000 all of the Peruvian valleys that plunge down to the Pacific were overrun by an art style originating in the high Andes at Tiahuanaco. Perhaps this attests military conquest, though it may represent some religious movement. Whatever its nature, centralization did not survive for long. When the Incas began to develop a new empire from a center in the high Andes, their expanding power met and overcame a series of local city and tribal states (fifteenth century). The Incas imposed a very strictly centralized regime upon all of Peru. Their empire was linked together by roads, officials, and a religion of the sun, of which the Great Inca was chief priest. The resemblance to the religio-political centralization of ancient Egypt is striking.

The Mexican area was more various and may be compared in this respect to ancient Mesopotamia. About A.D. 900 Mayan and Toltec priest-led communities broke down. The reasons are not clear. In the central valley of Mexico it seems probable that barbarian invasion from the north brought down the Toltec regime. Further south, traces of military assault are lacking, and it is possible that some withdrawal of belief, whereby the Mayan farmers ceased to find it necessary to support the priestly centers in order to assure the fertility of their maize fields, accounts for the abandonment of the temple sites. Nevertheless, more militaristic regimes did come to

NORTH

AMERICA

Atlantic

PUEBLO
INDIANS

Mississippi R.

IROQUOIS

CHEROKEES

Ocean

FLORIDA

Cortez, 1519-1520

Columbus 1492

Tenochtitlan
(Mexico City)

Mayapan

Chichen
Itza

CUBA

HISPANIOLA

AZTECS
(TOLTECS)
from c.500 A.D.

YUCATAN

WEST

MAYAS
from c.100 B.C.

Caribbean   Sea

INDIES

P
a
c
i
f
i
c

EQUATOR

CHIBCHAS

Pizarro, 1531-1535

SOUTH

O
c
e
a
n

Amazon R.

INCAS
from c.1200 A.D.

A
N
D
E
S

AMERICA

Lima

Cuzco

L. Titicaca

Tiahuanaco

M
T
S.

**AMERINDIAN
CIVILIZATION
c.1500**

ARAUCANIANS

 Civilized influence

Scale of Miles
0   400   800

the Mayan lands. First Chichén Itzá in Yucatán and then Mayapan seem to have created a sort of loose empire among the Mayans, but by the time the Spaniards arrived, even this sort of political unity had vanished. Despite their past, attested by the great temple centers, Mayan agriculturalists were living in simple village communities when the Spaniards first appeared and had no elaborate military, political, or even priestly organization.

Further north a number of waves of invasion may have occurred before the Aztecs asserted a loose hegemony over all of central Mexico. Aztec military operations were directed toward the capture of prisoners whose hearts were then offered to the gods daily throughout the year. We may presume that the victims were not pleased with their fate. No really effective loyalty or political unity therefore existed among the millions of inhabitants of the central Mexican valley when Cortez led his handful of ruffians to Montezuma's palace.

Other Indian societies had begun to move toward agricultural elaboration before the European discoveries. In the southeastern United States, for example, cult centers had begun to arise, simpler than those of Mexico but influenced by them. Similar proto-civilizations existed in what is today Colombia and Chile. Still further afield, the Indians of Virginia and New England knew how to raise maize, and a people like the Iroquois had begun to construct a formidable political-military confederation even before they came into contact with white men.

A much debated issue is whether or not Amerindian cultures owed anything important to trans-oceanic voyagers, whether from across the Atlantic or the Pacific. Some striking resemblances between a few art motifs in Central America and southeast Asia, together with the pre-European distribution of cultivated plants in the Pacific islands, suggest that some sort of relationship existed among the cultures on the two sides of the Pacific from a fairly early time. Nevertheless, many scholars emphatically deny that Amerindian civilizations profited significantly from contact with the rest of the world. The matter must remain open and cannot be firmly settled without more careful archaeological study than has yet been made.

As I conceive world history, the entire span of time between 500 B.C and A.D. 1500 belongs together, as a sort of inflated "Middle Ages," sandwiched between the constitutive age of civilization-building and the age of Western dominance that set in after 1500. Such a classification runs counter to the traditional periodization of our history, which divides what is here treated together, at about A.D. 400, into a classical and a medieval segment. The traditional chronological pattern fits the histories of other parts of the world very awkwardly, however, and it therefore seems best to list titles by region alone, and not to undertake any chronological ordering.

EUROPE. Most classical authors have been translated into English and published in the Loeb Classical Library, with opposing pages in the original Greek or Latin. In addition, the more important authors have been translated elsewhere and often, and I lack sufficient knowledge to be able to recommend a particular edition of authors like Aeschylus, Sophocles, Aristophanes, Herodotus, Thucydides, Plutarch, Livy, Tacitus, Plato, Aristotle, Cicero, and others of similarly enduring popularity. Any curious student should, however, be invited to turn to these authors at once, for they constitute one of the tap roots of Western civilization.

Among the moderns, choice becomes arbitrary and difficult. Two fine, standard texts are: J. B. Bury, *History of Greece to the Death of Alexander the Great*, 3rd ed. (London, 1951), and Max Cary, *History of Rome down to the Reign of Constantine the Great*, 2nd ed. (London, 1954). Gisela M. A. Richter, *Sculpture and Sculptors of the Greeks*, rev. ed. (New Haven, 1950), is another standard authority; and Moses Hadas, *History of Greek Literature* (New York, 1950), surveys his subject gracefully. For economic history, see F. M. Heichelheim, *Ancient Economic History*, 3 vols. (New York, 1958); M. I. Rostovtzeff, *The Social and Economic History of the Hellenistic World*, 3 vols. (Oxford, 1941); the same author's far more impassioned *Social and Economic History of the Roman Empire*, revised by P. M. Fraser, 2nd ed., 2 vols. (Oxford, 1957); Tenney Frank, et al., eds., *An Economic Survey of Ancient Rome*, 5 vols. (Baltimore, 1933-40); and A. H. M. Jones, *The Greek City: From Alexander to Justinian* (Oxford, 1940). On special aspects of military and political affairs the following are particularly interesting: A. R. Burn, *Persia and the Greeks: The Defence of the West* (New York, 1962); H. W. Parke, *Greek Mercenary Soldiers* (Oxford, 1933); A. H. M. Jones, *Athenian Democracy* (Oxford, 1957); and Sir Ronald Syme, *The Roman Revolution* (Oxford, 1939). Two other books that can be warmly recommended are: Marshall Clagett, *Greek Science in Antiquity* (New York, 1956), and W. W. Tarn and G. T. Griffith, *Hellenistic Civilization*, 3rd ed. (London, 1952).

Early Christianity is a subject by itself. Two excellent works by classicists are C. N. Cochrane, *Christianity and Classical Culture* (New York, 1944), and Arnaldo Momigliano, ed., *The Conflict Between Paganism and Christianity in the Fourth Century* (Oxford, 1963). Good general treatments of early Christian history are: Kenneth Scott Latourette, *A History of the Expansion of Christianity*, I: *The First Five Centuries* (New York, 1937); Robert M. Grant, *Historical Introduction to the New Testament* (New York, 1963); and Rudolf Karl Bultmann, *Primitive Christianity in Its Contemporary Setting* (London, 1956). More specialized themes of interest are dealt with by A. D. Nock, *Conversion: The Old and the New in Religion from Alexander the Great to Augustine of Hippo* (London, 1933); J. M. Allegro, *The Dead Sea Scrolls and Origins of Christianity* (New York, 1957); and Jean Doresse, *Secret Books of the Egyptian Gnostics* (New York, 1960). Salo W. Baron, *A Social and Religious History of the Jews*, 2nd ed., 8 vols. (New York, 1952–58), is a very useful counterpart to the study of early Christianity.

Medieval histories divide almost always between the Latin and Greek halves of Christendom, and Slavic Europe often constitutes still a third compartment. Similarly, relationships with Islam are neglected or treated in isolation from general narrative. The result is to emphasize, more than perhaps the facts really warrant, the compartmentalization of relationships in the medieval period within Europe — not to mention Eurasia as a whole. Hugh Trevor-Roper, *The Rise of Christian Europe* (London, 1965), transcends this sort of narrowed vision; so do Gustave E. von Grunebaum, *Medieval Islam: A Study in Cultural Orientation*, 2nd ed. (Chicago, 1955), and Lynn White, Jr., *Medieval Technology and Social Change* (Oxford, 1962).

Recent work on medieval economic history has turned very largely upon the "Pirenne thesis," as set forth in Henri Pirenne, *Mohammed and Charlemagne* (New York, 1955), and reaffirmed in a larger context in his *Economic and Social History of Medieval Europe* (New York, 1937). *The Cambridge Economic History of Europe*, 3 vols. (Cambridge, 1941–63), reflects expert consensus; and C. S. and C. S. L. Orwin, *The Open Fields*, 2nd ed. (Oxford, 1954), bring practical experience with farming to bear upon elucidation of the much disputed matter of manorial land patterns.

In matters political it seems best to settle for a list of the books that are more interesting or important than most: Marc Bloch, *Feudal Society* (Chicago, 1961); Carl Stephenson, *Medieval Feudalism* (Ithaca, N.Y., 1942); Sir Steven Runciman, *A History of the Crusades*, 3 vols. (Cambridge, 1951–54); Charles Homer Haskins, *The Normans in European History* (Boston, 1915); Geoffrey Barraclough, *The Origins of Modern Germany*, 2nd. ed. (Oxford, 1947); and P. H. Sawyer, *The Age of the Vikings* (New York, 1962).

A similarly arbitrary principle for cultural history suggests the following:

Christopher Dawson, *The Making of Europe* (London, 1932); Johan Hui-
zinga, *The Waning of the Middle Ages* (London, 1924); L. J. Daly, *The
Medieval University* (New York, 1961); Charles Homer Haskins, *The
Renaissance of the Twelfth Century* (Cambridge, Mass., 1927); C. H. Mc-
Ilwain, *The Growth of Political Thought in the West* (New York, 1932);
David Knowles, *The Evolution of Medieval Thought* (London, 1962); Ernst
Kitzinger, *Early Medieval Art in the British Museum*, 2nd ed. (London,
1955); Erwin Panofsky, *Gothic Architecture and Scholasticism* (Latrobe,
Pa., 1951); Paul Oskar Kristeller, *Renaissance Thought: The Classic, Scho-
lastic and Humanist Strains*, rev. ed., 2 vols. (New York, 1961); and Ernst
Cassirer, et al., eds., *The Renaissance Philosophy of Man* (Chicago, 1948).

Eastern Europe has less in English, but the following can be recommended:
Archibald R. Lewis, *Naval Power and Trade in the Mediterranean, A.D.
500–1100* (Princeton, 1951); Sir Steven Runciman, *Byzantine Civilization*
(London, 1933); Norman H. Baynes and H. St. L. B. Moss, eds., *Byzantium*
(Oxford, 1961); O. M. Dalton, *East Christian Art: A Survey of the Monuments* (Oxford, 1925); N. P. Kondakov, *The Russian Icon* (Oxford, 1927);
and George Vernadsky, *A History of Russia*, 4 vols. to date (New Haven,
1943–   ).

THE REALM OF ISLAM. This is an elastic term because Islam continued to
make converts and expand its territorial base throughout its first thousand
years, and in fact continues to do so today. Moreover, it is convenient to
consider the Parthian and Sassanian empires under this general heading, since
in many respects they were precursors of the Abbasid caliphs. In general,
studies of Iran are few. Two brief general works are Richard N. Frye,
Heritage of Persia (Cleveland, 1963), and Roman Ghirshman, *Iran from the
Earliest Times to the Islamic Conquest* (Penguin, 1961). Neilson C. Debevoise,
A Political History of Parthia (Chicago, 1938), has no English language
equivalent for Sassanian times. Arthur Christensen, *L'Iran sous les Sassanides*,
2nd ed. (Copenhagen, 1944), exists for those who read French. Roman
Ghirshman, *Persian Art, The Parthian and Sassanian Dynasties* (New York,
1962), and Arthur Upham Pope and Phyllis Ackerman, eds., *A Survey of
Persian Art*, 7 vols. (London and New York, 1938–39), are excellent. On
religious history, F. C. Burkitt, *The Religion of the Manichees* (Cambridge,
1925), and two books by Robert Charles Zaehner, *The Dawn and Twilight
of Zoroastrianism* (New York, 1961), and *Zurvan: A Zoroastrian Dilemma*
(Oxford, 1955), are available.

Among the numerous general accounts of Islam, the following are es-
pecially good: H. A. R. Gibb, *Mohammedanism: An Historical Survey*, 2nd
ed. (London, 1953); Bernard Lewis, *The Arabs in History* (London and
New York, 1950); Gustave E. von Grunebaum, *Medieval Islam: A Study in
Cultural Orientation*, 2nd ed. (Chicago, 1955); T. W. Arnold, *The Caliphate*
(Oxford, 1924), and T. W. Arnold, *The Preaching of Islam*, 2nd ed. (Lon-
don, 1913). On Mohammed's career, Tor Andrae, *Mohammed: The Man and
His Faith* (New York, 1956), W. Montgomery Watt, *Muhammad at Mecca*

(Oxford, 1953), and W. Montgomery Watt, *Muhammad at Medina* (Oxford, 1956), are excellent. Many translations of the Koran exist; none seems to capture in English the literary power of the original, and I lack the capacity to choose which is best. Eric Schroeder, *Muhammad's People* (Freeport, Me., 1955), is a very striking pastiche of translations from Arabic poetry, mostly pre-Islamic. Utterly different in tone is Ibn Khaldun, *The Muqaddimah: An Introduction to History*, tr. Franz Rosenthal, 3 vols. (New York, 1958); and *The Faith and Practice of Al-Ghazali* (London and New York, 1953), an autobiography by a famous Moslem theologian, translated by W. Montgomery Watt, offers an insight into still a third dimension of Moslem civilization.

For the great change that came to Islam with the Sufi movement, A. J. Arberry, *Sufism: An Account of the Mystics of Islam* (London, 1950), and Reynold Alleyne Nicholson, *Studies in Islamic Mysticism* (Cambridge, 1921), may be recommended. Edward G. Browne, *A Literary History of Persia*, 4 vols. (London and Cambridge, 1902–24), is a classic deserving its reputation; and T. W. Arnold, *Painting in Islam* (Oxford, 1928), is useful. No satisfactory general account of Islamic art is known to me.

More specialized themes are capably handled by: George Fadlo Hourani, *Arab Seafaring in the Indian Ocean in Ancient and Early Medieval Times* (Princeton, 1951); W. Barthold, *Turkestan down to the Mongol Invasion*, 2nd ed. (London, 1928); Paul Wittek, *The Rise of the Ottoman Empire* (London, 1938); J. K. Birge, *The Bekashi Order of Dervishes* (Hartford, 1937); and Marshall G. S. Hodgson, *The Order of Assassins* (The Hague, 1955).

CENTRAL ASIA AND THE STEPPE. The Eurasian steppe has not usually been treated as a whole. In French there is René Grousset, *L'Empire des steppes: Attila, Gengis-Khan, Tamerlan* (Paris, 1939), one of the few books that does try to link happenings East and West into a single conspectus. William M. McGovern, *The Early Empires of Central Asia* (Chapel Hill, 1939), and Owen Lattimore, *The Inner Asian Frontiers of China* (New York, 1940), treat the eastern portions of the steppe. W. W. Tarn, *The Greeks in Bactria and India*, 2nd ed. (Cambridge, 1951), and A. K. Narain, *The Indo-Greeks* (Oxford, 1957), deal with a particularly dramatic episode of central Asian history. No comparable work on the Kushan empire is known to me, nor is there any satisfactory treatment of the Sassanian penumbra that spread through Central Asia in the time of the Uighur Manichees. Sir Mark Aurel Stein, *On Ancient Central Asian Tracks* (London, 1933), records his finds but fails to weave the record into a history.

The westerly portions of the steppe are better treated by historians. M. I. Rostovtzeff, *Iranians and Greeks in South Russia* (Oxford, 1922), and Tamara Talbot Rice, *The Scythians* (London, 1957), were mentioned in the bibliographical essay for Part I. Mortimer Wheeler, *Rome Beyond the Imperial Frontiers* (New York, 1955), E. A. Thompson, *A History of Attila and the Huns* (Oxford, 1948), and D. M. Dunlop, *The History of the Jewish*

Khazars (Princeton, 1954), cover major phases of steppe history very satisfactorily as far as relations with Europe are concerned. Two books about the Mongols are particularly good: H. Desmond Martin, *The Rise of Chingis Khan and His Conquest of North China*, ed. Eleanor Lattimore (Baltimore, 1950); and Christopher Dawson, ed., *The Mongol Mission* (London and New York, 1955).

INDIA AND SOUTHEAST ASIA. A. L. Basham, *The Wonder That Was India*, rev. ed. (New York, 1963), is by far the best general introduction to Indian civilization. K. A. Nilakanta Sastri, *A History of South India from Prehistoric Times to the Fall of Vijayanagar*, 3rd ed. (Madras, 1966), and E. H. Warmington, *Commerce Between the Roman Empire and India* (Cambridge, 1928), present interesting data on the inter-relations of the Mediterranean and Indian Ocean worlds.

For Indian thought and letters, standard works are: Surendranath Dasgupta, *A History of Indian Philosophy*, 5 vols. (Cambridge, 1932–55); A. B. Keith, *A History of Sanskrit Literature* (London, 1928); and A. B. Keith, *The Sanskrit Drama in Its Origin, Development, Theory, and Practice* (Oxford, 1924). Indian art is well portrayed by Heinrich Zimmer and Joseph Campbell, *The Art of Indian Asia*, 2nd ed., 2 vols. (New York, 1955), and Benjamin Rowland, *The Art and Architecture of India* (Penguin, 1953). Among available translations from Indian literature, V. R. R. Dikshitar, ed. and tr., *The Lay of the Anklet (Silappadikāram)* (Oxford, 1939), Johannes A. B. van Buitenen, *Tales of Ancient India, translated from the Sanskrit* (Chicago, 1959), Franklin Edgerton, tr. and ed., *The Bhagavad Gita, translated and interpreted*, Harvard Oriental Series (Cambridge, Mass., 1944), and N. A. Nikam and Richard P. McKeon, eds. and trs. *The Edicts of Asoka* (Chicago, 1958), are particularly interesting.

Southeast Asian history may be pursued with help from: D. G. E. Hall, *A History of Southeast Asia* (New York, 1955); John F. Cady, *Southeast Asia: Its Historical Development* (New York, 1964); H. G. Quaritch Wales, *The Making of Greater India: A Study in Southeast Asian Culture Change* (London, 1950); J. C. van Leur, *Indonesian Trade and Society* (The Hague, 1955); and B. H. M. Vlekke, *Nusantara: A History of the East Indian Archipelago* (Cambridge, Mass., 1943).

THE FAR EAST. L. C. Goodrich, *A Short History of the Chinese People*, 3rd ed. (New York 1959), is the best narrative history of China in English. George B. Sansom, *Japan: A Short Cultural History*, rev. ed. (New York, 1962), plays the same role with respect to Japan. No really satisfactory history of Korea is known to me, but M. Frederick Nelson, *Korea and the Old Orders in Eastern Asia* (Baton Rouge, 1945), and Homer B. Hulbert, *The History of Korea*, rev. ed. by C. M. Weems, 2 vols. (Hillary, N.Y., n.d.; first published, Seoul, 1905), are available. E. O. Reischauer and John K. Fairbank, *A History of East Asian Civilization*, I: *East Asia, the Great Tradition* (Boston, 1961), treats the Far East as a whole.

Special themes in China's long political and social development are dealt with by: Derk Bodde, *China's First Unifier: A Study of the Ch'in Dynasty as Seen in the Life of Li Ssu* (Leiden, 1938); J. K. Shryock, *Origin and Development of the State Cult of Confucius* (New York, 1932); Arthur F. Wright, *Buddhism in Chinese History* (Stanford, Cal., 1959); Wolfram Eberhard, *Conquerors and Rulers: Social Forces in Medieval China* (New York, 1952); Edwin G. Pulleyblank, *The Background of the Rebellion of An Lu-shan* (London, 1955); and J. J. L. Duyvendak, *China's Discovery of Africa* (London, 1949).

Chinese art and thought may be approached with the help of Osvald Sirén, *Chinese Painting: Leading Masters and Principles*, 7 vols. (New York, 1956–58); Lawrence Sickman and Alexander Soper, *The Art and Architecture of China* (Penguin, 1956); and Fung Yu-lan, *A History of Chinese Philosophy*, tr. Derk Bodde, 2 vols. (Peiping, 1937). Joseph Needham, *Science and Civilization in China*, mutivolume (Cambridge, 1954–   ), and T. F. Carter and L. C. Goodrich, *The Invention of Printing in China and Its Spread Westward*, 2nd ed. (New York, 1955), are the best authorities for their respective subjects. China's two most famous historians may be studied through Burton Watson, *Ssu-ma Ch'ien, Grand Historian of China* (New York, 1958), and Homer H. Dubs, tr. and ed., *The History of the Former Han Dynasty by Pan Ku* (Baltimore, 1938). Two of Arthur Waley's translations also deserve special mention: *The Poetry and Career of Li Po, 701–762 A.D.* (London, 1951), and (from the Japanese) *The Tale of Genji*, by Murasaki Shikibu (Boston, 1935).

AFRICA. Roland Oliver and John D. Fage, *A Short History of Africa* (Penguin, 1962), is now standard. Regional accounts of general interest include: Zoë Marsh and G. W. Kingsnorth, *An Introduction to the History of East Africa*, 2nd ed. (Cambridge, 1961); John D. Fage, *An Introduction to the History of West Africa*, 2nd ed. (Cambridge, 1960); E. W. Bovill, *Caravans of the Old Sahara: An Introduction to the History of the Western Sudan* (London, 1933); J. Spencer Trimingham, *A History of Islam in West Africa* (London, 1962); and A. H. M. Jones and Elizabeth Monroe, *A History of Ethiopia* (Oxford, 1955; a reissue of *A History of Abyssinia*, 1935).

THE AMERICAS. Gordon R. Willey, *New World Prehistory*, Smithsonian Institution Report for 1960 (Washington, D.C., 1961), and H. E. Driver, ed., *The Americas on the Eve of Discovery* (Englewood Cliffs, N.J., 1964), are good general introductions to the Amerindians. G. H. S. Bushnell, *Peru*, rev. ed. (New York, 1963); J. Eric S. Thompson, *The Rise and Fall of Maya Civilization* (Norman, Okla., 1954), and G. C. Valliant, *The Aztecs of Mexico* (Penguin, 1950), are also useful. On the disputed question of trans-Pacific contacts with the New World before Columbus, see M. W. Smith, *Asia and North America: Trans-Pacific Contacts*, Society for American Archaeology, Memoir No. 9 (1953), and Andrew Sharp, *Ancient Voyagers in the Pacific* (Wellington, N.Z., 1956).

Part III

THE DOMINANCE OF THE WEST

The year 1500 serves better than most historical landmarks as a divide between modern and pre-modern times. This is true in European history, for the great discoveries, quickly followed by the Reformation, gave the *coup de grâce* to medieval Europe and inaugurated a century and a half of desperate effort to achieve a reasonably stable new pattern of thought and action. As a result of these efforts, a new pattern for European civilization attained a hazy sort of definition after 1648. The year 1500 marks an important turning point in world history also. The European discoverers made the oceans of the earth into highways for their commerce and conquest. They thus created a new cultural frontier along every habitable coast that rivaled, and in the end eclipsed, the importance of the land frontiers where the civilizations of Asia had for centuries stood guard against steppe nomads.

Little by little all the non-Western peoples of the earth found it necessary to do something drastic about the intrusive Europeans with their restless, disturbing ways. The rise of the West to this position of dominance all round the globe is, indeed, the main theme of modern world history.

Nonetheless, changes such as these take time to ripen. For a full two hundred years after Christopher Columbus (1492), Vasco da Gama (1498), and Fernando Magellan (1522) imprinted their wakes upon the oceans of the earth, the old established civilizations of Asia reacted sluggishly to the new sea-borne challenge consti-

A.D.	AMERICAS	EUROPE	RUSSIA

AGE OF RECONNAISSANCE (left vertical margin)

Ivan III repudiates Tatar rule

Columbus

1500 — E U R O P E A N .... O C E A N I C

RENAISSANCE   **REFORMATION**

Cortez
Pizarro

Leonardo da Vinci   Luther
Machiavelli

Empire of Charles V

Henry VIII

Hawkins brings first
African slaves

Catholic reformation   Calvin
Michelangelo   *Copernicus*   Loyola
Dutch   *Vesalius*   Xavier
    revolt
      Philip II of Spain
Montaigne

Ivan IV captures

Livonian war   Russians

1600

Virginia, Quebec,
New Amsterdam,
Massachusetts
established

Shakespeare   Henry IV of France   *El Greco*
Bacon
Cervantes   *Kepler*
Galileo   **THIRTY YEARS' WAR**
    Cyril Lukaris

Time of Troubles
Polish assault

sugar plantations fix Negro
slavery upon New World

Dutch driven from New
Amsterdam

English civil wars
Milton   *Descartes*   *Rembrandt*
Harvey   Louis XIV
Glorious revolution   *Molière*
Newton   *Spinoza*   Frederick the Great
Locke   *Hobbes*   decay of Swedish
       empire

NIKON AND
CHURCH REFORM

PETER THE GREAT

1700

Leibniz   rise of Austria
Mabillon
    Bach
Voltaire
Rousseau   **SEVEN YEARS' WAR**

Newcomen's engine
South Sea Bubble

St. Petersburg new
capital (DYNASTY)

British gain Canada
abolition of trade
monopoly in
Spanish empire

AMERICAN WAR
OF INDEPENDENCE   *Mozart*   partition   of   Poland
    Watt's engine
Adam Smith   **FRENCH REVOLUTION**   *Linnaeus*
       Hume
       Kant

nobles exempted from
state service
CATHERINE   Russo-
THE GREAT   treaty
Pugachev revolt (ROMANOV)

1800

Latin American
independence

Hegel   **NAPOLEON**
    Congress of Vienna
    Herder

Alexander I
Pushkin
Nicholas I

C R I M E A N   W

United States
Civil War

1848-49 revolutions
Darwin
railroad building *Marx*
    Napoleon III
Nietzsche
automobile
radio   rival alliance systems

Cavour
Bismarck
Papal infallibility

abolition of serfdom

Dostoyevsky

railroad building

1900

Panama Canal
Wilson   airplane

Einstein   *Freud*   *Picasso*
W   O   R   L   D
D E P R E S S I O N

Russian revolution
1905   W A R
**RUSSIAN REVOLUTION
OF 1917**   LENIN

CONTEMPORARY

F. D. ROOSEVELT   *Atomic energy:*   CHURCHILL   HITLER   MUSSOLINI
P-   W *Fermi*   O   R   L

STALIN

ISLAM	SOUTH ASIA	EAST ASIA	PACIFIC AND AFRICA
		Cheng-ho	
capture of Constantinople			
V O Y A G E S		**O F**	
ISMAIL SAFAVI	da Gama		Magellan
Ottoman-French alliance	Moslem control of Java	**D I S C O**	
SULEIMAN THE LAWGIVER	Babur ———▶ India		
	Chaitanya	**V**	Portuguese ———▶ Japan
Kazan, Astrakhan		Macao founded	**E R Y**
			Spanish ———▶ Philippines
	fall of Vijayanagar to		
conquer Sibir	Moslems		
	AKBAR, MUGHAL		
Shah Abbas the	EMPIRE	Hideyoshi invades Korea	
Great	Dutch and English East	Ricci ———▶ Peking	Dutch ships ———▶ Japan
	India companies	Russians reach Pacific	
Taj Mahal *Tulsi Das*		*Tibetans convert Mongols to*	Japan closed to
		Lamaism	foreigners
		MANCHU CONQUEST	West African slave trade
Kiuprili revival of Ottoman		OF CHINA	
empire	Aurangzeb, last strong		
second seige of Vienna	Mughal emperor	treaty of Nerchinsk	
treaty of Karlowitz; loss of			
Hungary		*rites controversy*	Bering's
		treaty of Kiakhta	voyages
Nadir shah			
		Chinese control in Tibet,	
Abdul Wahhab	battle of Panipat	Mongolia, Turkestan	Captain Cook's
	British expel French from		voyages
	India		Spanish
Turkish war			found San
of Kutchuk Kainardji			Francisco Australia
			colonized
Serbian and Greek revolutions	Consolidation of British	abolition of East India	New Zealand
Mohammed Ali of Egypt	control in India	Company monopolies	colonized
defeats Sultan and Wahhabis	British-Afghan wars	opium war	Perry opens Japan
A R			
Suez Canal	*Ram Mohan Roy*	Taiping rebellion	Livingstone's explorations
	Sepoy mutiny		Meiji restoration
		Europeans capture Peking	colonial
		Sino- Japanese war	scramble
		Boxer rebellion ——— Russo-Japanese war	in Africa
I		Chinese Republic Japan rules Korea	
		Sun Yat-sen	
Mustapha Kemal	GANDHI	Japanese in Manchuria and	
ibn-Saud	**W A**	North China	African
L U T I O N	Indian independence **R**	Chinese Communists **II**	states become
		to power	independent

tuted by Europe's growing wealth and power. In the Americas, and in the less highly developed lands of northern Asia, the European impact was much more drastic. Local cultures withered when confronted by the missionary spirit and technical superiority of European pioneers in both these great regions of the globe. As a result, a European type of society expanded both east and west from its original focus and center in northwestern Europe, penetrating deep into Siberia and across the Atlantic into the New World.

After 1700, however, the Islamic peoples together with the Hindus and Buddhists of Asia found themselves unable to stave off the Europeans. Old institutions and attitudes hallowed by centuries of religion could no longer stand up to the new power western European peoples had been able to generate. Successive demonstrations of this fact in India, the Balkans, and the Middle East caused a stunned paralysis to descend upon nearly all Moslems and most Hindus. Yet decisive breakdown of traditional ways and institutions did not occur before about 1850, when with an extraordinary suddenness the Ottoman, Mughal, Manchu, and Japanese empires within a single decade either collapsed or found themselves compelled to venture forth from the shelter of familiar ways in the hope of being able to beg, borrow, or steal from the Westerners the secrets of their strength.

This effort at conscious modernization or Westernization still continues to command the central place in the aspirations of all the non-Western peoples of the world. The pace of social change accelerates steadily, and the effort to manage society so as to achieve goals set by some directing clique or party seems to gain force with every passing year.

After 1500, however, divisions of European history do not match the bench marks of world history very closely. This is no more than what we should expect, for if it is correct to say that the main theme of modern history is the rise of the West to dominance over the globe, there should be a time lag between successive stages of Europe's own development and the impact upon other peoples and distant continents.

Hence it seems well to bracket the history of the non-Western world down to 1700 with Europe's domestic history until 1648 as a period when the Far West first decisively and definitely challenged all the other cultures of the earth by demonstrating important superiorities in such fields as military organization and technology, natural science and inquisitiveness. The period of world history between 1700 and 1850 may similarly be bracketed with Europe's Old Regime, 1648–1789, when a potentially classic reorganization of European civilization emerged from the struggles and confusion of the preceding period. By the same logic, world history since 1850 may be paired with Europe's history since 1789, when the twin movements of industrialization and democratization began to transform Western institutions fundamentally, and imparted to them the irresistible force to which the other civilizations of the world bowed only after 1850.

The chapters that follow are therefore arranged in three tiers: A survey of Europe's self-transformation 1500–1648 precedes discussion of the development of each of the major regions of the world in the period 1500–1700. Then chapters on Europe's Old Regime and on the colonial expansion of European society in the years 1648–1789 set the stage for a second tour of the rest of the world, surveying its development in the period 1700–1850. Then, third, remarks about the West's transformations since 1789 are followed by a survey of how different parts of the non-Western world have reacted to Western superiorities since 1850. The awkwardness of such a plan will, I believe, be counterbalanced by the fact that its chronological irregularity underlines and illuminates the central reality of modern world history.

XVIII

The Great Discoveries

and Their World-Wide Consequences

RINCE Henry of Portugal (d. 1460), nicknamed "the Navigator," prepared the way for the
dramatic voyages of oceanic discovery that opened the entire cir-
cuit of the habitable globe to Europeans within a time span of no
more than two generations. What he did was to bring the best available theoretical knowledge into contact with traditional rule-of-
thumb seamen's and shipbuilders' skills, in order to improve the sea-
worthiness and navigability of his ships. Prince Henry had in view
the rounding of Africa, hoping thereby to link up with the half-
mythical Christian champion, Prester John, and thus outflank and,
hopefully, overwhelm, the realm of Islam. Profit from trade in
slaves and other commodities to be picked up along the African
coast helped to sustain the enterprise, but this was not a central
motive.

Navigation remained inexact, for until the invention of a satisfactory marine chronometer (1760) no precise method for determining longitude (east-west) was known. Latitude (north-south)
could be measured by finding the angle of the sun above the horizon at noon. With the help of tables of the sun's declination at
known latitudes for each day of the year, a sea captain could establish his position north or south of the equator within some thirty
miles or so, even when using comparatively crude sighting instru-

ments. The trick lay in compiling accurate tables. This task Prince Henry assigned to specially selected astronomers and mathematicians who, after lengthy calculation, provided Portuguese sea captains with the necessary information. By guessing how far east or west they had gone, explorers could then make charts of the African coast, permitting later navigators to travel long distances across the open ocean and yet steer their ships toward an expected landfall at a precisely established latitude. In 1497, for example, Vasco da Gama spent ninety-seven days out of sight of land, and yet steered accurately for the Cape of Good Hope, despite the fact that the Cape had not been visited by any European since it had first been discovered by Bartolomeo Diaz sixteen years before.

European shipbuilding made equally important advances. The Portuguese took the lead, multiplying the number of masts and fitting at least the larger central masts with more than a single sail. This allowed sailors to trim their canvas to fit different conditions of wind and sea, and made the ship much more maneuverable and seaworthy. This in turn permitted the construction of larger vessels; but large vessels required stouter hulls. As a result, by 1500, the mighty keel, heavy ribs, and double oak planking of a European vessel were able to withstand the recoil from heavy cannon. Vessels of lighter construction, such as those familiar in the calmer waters of the Indian Ocean, could not fire such weapons without shaking themselves apart.

These developments of European shipbuilding entirely outmoded prevailing methods of sea fighting. Ramming and boarding — standard tactics of earlier times — could seldom be brought into play against vessels capable of smashing enemy ships with cannon fire at a distance of as much as 200 yards, and capable also of rapid and agile maneuver to bring enemy ships under fatal bombardment. Hence, when Columbus, Vasco da Gama, Magellan, and numerous less famous but no less daring captains opened the oceans of the entire globe to European navigation, their ships enjoyed a crushing technical superiority over vessels built elsewhere and designed for less stormy waters than those of the North Atlantic. Chinese and Japanese junks offered the only competition. They usually lacked enough heavy guns to come near to matching European ships. Gun metals remained comparatively rare in the Far East, whereas Europe's cruder but much larger-scale metallurgical industry allowed Europeans to arm their vessels much more lavishly than Far Eastern shipbuilders could ordinarily afford to do.

These technical facts help to explain the rapidity of Europe's initial expansion along the seaways. Vasco da Gama completed the first round trip to India in 1499. Ten years later the Portuguese defeated a numerically much superior Moslem fleet off the port of Diu in the Arabian Sea, and thereby fastened their naval supremacy on the Indian Ocean. Without delay they established naval stations at the key strategic points of Goa (1510), Malacca (1511), and Ormuz (1515). A Portuguese expedition penetrated the Spice Islands themselves in 1511–12, and an individual merchant reached Canton in 1513. A generation later, regular missionary and trade relations were opened with Japan (1545) and a permanent Portuguese settlement was established along the south China coast in 1557 at Macao. Here Portuguese expansion lapped up against the rival imperial power of Spain, which fastened itself upon the Philippines via Mexico in 1571.

As far as the Asian civilizations were concerned, Europe's naval supremacy after 1500 did not make much difference. From the point of view of the Chinese imperial government, for example, it was not in the least important whether or not sea trade passed into the hands of a new set of barbarians. Moslems from southeast Asia, Japanese pirates, or the beak-nosed "south sea barbarians" from Europe seemed all alike to Peking. In India also the rulers of the land were little concerned with mercantile matters and after the defeat at Diu (1509) made no concerted effort to oppose the Portuguese presence. Instead, Moslem trading vessels evaded Portuguese patrols, which always remained scant because of the vast distances from the homeland. Light, small ships soon were able to conduct trade almost as before. The occasional loss of a vessel to the Portuguese became for Moslem traders and shipowners a mere inconvenience.

In the Americas, however, the arrival of Spanish conquistadores in Mexico (1519–21) and Peru (1531–35) brought sudden and irreparable disaster to the Amerindian high cultures. The complete collapse of the Aztec and Inca regimes opened the way for the creation of a vast land empire, ruled by Spaniards and dedicated both to the saving of Indian souls and to the export of silver and gold from the American mines. With remarkable docility, the Amerindians submitted to Spanish leadership. Earlier religious and cultural ideals survived only at the village level, or in remote regions of the rain forest, mountain, and desert, where Spanish power and missions failed to penetrate. Thus a new type of society, Spanish in form and Catholic in religion but based upon the labor of millions of almost mute Amerindians, arose in the New World.

Europe's new naval supremacy had no remotely comparable result in the Old World. Nevertheless, three major consequences of the opening of the world's oceans to European shipping affected every civilized society and transformed conditions of life for many barbarous and primitive peoples as well. These were (a) the price revolution resulting from the flow of massive quantities of silver and gold from the Americas, (b) the spread of American food crops, and (c) the spread of diseases. Each of these deserves a little elaboration.

The price revolution. The price revolution affected Spain first and most drastically, but spread to other parts of Europe with only small delay and modest diminution of its force. The Ottoman empire in the eastern Mediterranean was affected too, and so was distant China, where Mexican silver provided a far more abundant coinage than had been available before. As for India, nothing is known. The economic and social consequences of the price revolution in Turkey and China have not been studied, and may not have been as important as they were in Europe, which felt the first and strongest impact, since it was to European — specifically to Spanish — ports that the treasure first came. Careful investigation has shown that within a century, prices in Spain multiplied about four times over. Less drastic price rises occurred elsewhere in Europe, but everywhere the changes were enough to disturb traditional economic relations profoundly. Persons with fixed incomes suffered severe loss of status, while those engaged in business often prospered, since the prices of their goods tended to increase while their debts did not.

All the certainty inherent in an established routine of life defined by traditional socio-economic relationships crumbled in an age when prices changed as sharply as happened in Europe between 1500 and 1650. Governments universally found their accustomed sources of income insufficient, and were compelled to find new devices for raising revenue. Even the humblest artisan or the poor peasant selling his few eggs in the market place felt the force of the price revolution. No one of course understood the relationship between increased supplies of silver and increased prices. But when all society was affected, so that some prospered while many were deprived and everyone — rich or poor — suffered from uncertainty as to the future, most men concluded that greater greed and wickedness were loose in the world than ever before. This pervasive sense of grievance intensified the extraordinary bitterness of religious and political controversy which set this age off from both earlier and later periods of European history.

American food crops. American crops were botanically altogether different from those familiar in the Old World. Some of them proved to be extremely valuable supplements to what European, Asian, and African farmers had previously known. American corn, or maize, for example, spread rapidly to southwestern China, Africa, and southeastern Europe. In China the potato proved to be less important than the botanically unrelated sweet potato, which flourished abundantly on hillsides and other previously waste lands, where rice could not be grown. In Europe the relationship was reversed, for a cooler climate suited a plant native to the high Andes, whereas European summers were not warm enough to allow sweet potatoes to mature.

The reception of American food crops increased local food supplies, and usually provoked a corresponding increase in population. This certainly occurred in south China. American crops also permitted a dramatic multiplication of population in Africa, especially in west Africa, whence came most of the millions of slaves who worked the plantations of the New World in the seventeenth and eighteenth centuries.

Details of the American food plant migration are not well established, and it is likely that the major impact of the new crops came after rather than before 1650. This was certainly the case in Europe, where it took time for illiterate cultivators and tradition-bound peasantries to discover the advantages of and to learn how to raise the new crops.

The spread of diseases. The spread of disease did not wait upon human initiative, but proceeded, like the price revolution, despite human intention and without being understood at the time. Indeed, all details remain obscure, since the records of pestilential attacks, whether among Indians in America or in some city of Europe, are so imprecise as to make accurate medical diagnosis impossible. In general, however, it is clear that as ships began to ply the oceans they carried germs as well as goods from one port to another. Consequences for human life were sometimes important. European vessels, for example, transferred a number of diseases — including in all probability such scourges as yellow fever and malaria — from the Old World to the New, where these mosquito-borne infections made much of Central and South America almost uninhabitable. In addition, diseases long established among the populations of Europe proved devastating when loosed upon the Amerindians who had no inherited or acquired immunities to such infections as small-pox, measles, or chicken pox. Perhaps the Amerindians reciprocated by transmitting syphilis to the Old World, although the American origin of syphilis is not certain.

Despite these ignorances, we may discern some of the over-all consequences of the diffusion of disease germs by ocean-going ships. First of all, previously isolated populations suffered drastic losses. It has been calculated, for example, that the population of the central plateau of Mexico decreased from about 11 million when Cortez first invaded in 1519 to a mere 1.5 million in 1650, and this despite Spanish immigration! Similarly drastic depopulation occurred in small islands of the Pacific and elsewhere, whenever new diseases encountered locally dense, previously isolated and therefore unresistant populations.

Civilized populations, however, had long been exposed to a wide variety of infection. Indeed — with the possible exception of syphilis — no important new disease seems to have found large numbers of victims awaiting its ravages among the civilized inhabitants of the Old World. On the contrary, diseases that had been known previously in epidemic form gradually became endemic. As a result, by 1700 epidemic pestilence ceased to play any important role in checking population growth. Very likely the modern upward spurt of civilized populations dates from this change in the nature and incidence of diseases. Available statistics certainly seem to show that in Europe, China, India, and in at least some regions of the Middle East, population growth set in at previously unheard-of rates from some time between 1600 and 1650. By then the epidemiological effects of oceanic shipping had had time to make themselves felt and American food crops had begun to come into their own. Modern scientific medicine on the other hand had little influence upon demography before about 1800 even in Europe, much less in China or India, and cannot be held responsible for the early phase of modern population growth.

Clearly, the effect of the new oceanic dissemination of diseases redounded strikingly to the advantage of Europeans. Their home populations suffered no irreparable loss and soon began to multiply at a hitherto unparalleled rate, while in the Americas, and in other remote parts, the sudden ravages of disease crippled native resistance to European dominion. Even in the Old World the destruction (1757) of the last nomad confederacy in central Asia successfully to oppose civilized arms was the work not of guns but of smallpox.

European knowledge and inventiveness. On an entirely different plane, too, the consequences of the great European discoveries worked strongly in Europe's favor as against all the rival cultures of other parts of the earth. For new skills and knowledge garnered from all over the habitable world became available to enrich and enlarge European technology and culture. As was the case with their forefathers of the feudal age, when the techniques of knightly warfare had given western Europeans a short-lived military superiority on land, naval supremacy in the early modern age imparted such a sense of security to European seafarers that they found it possible to examine all they met with a naïve yet confident curiosity, eager both to know and to discover, and ready to borrow anything that pleased them in the tool kit of others. An upsurge of Eu-

ropean inventiveness and ingenuity, feeding upon their enlarged
knowledge of the world and its variety, both natural and human,
was the inevitable and admirable result.

No other civilization responded to the new possibilities opened
by ocean travel with anything remotely resembling European ven-
turesomeness. Toying with foreign novelties did occur, most notably in the Far East, but nothing inimical to ancient and well-estab-
lished tradition ruffled the mind of Chinese mandarins for very
long. Moslem and Hindu reaction was even more emphatically
negative. Anything conflicting with ancient truths was simply repudiated and neglected — or not noticed at all.

How different was Europe's response, where the convulsions of
the age of Renaissance and Reformation shook European society to
its core and shattered the medieval frame of European civilization
entirely! The stimulus of the discoveries, and their subsequent exploitation, was not the sole cause of this transformation of Europe.
Deep-seated and long-standing tensions within European civilization contributed at least as much as anything from the outside. To
an examination of these internal forces and their interplay we must
therefore devote the next chapter.

XIX

Europe's Self-Transformation

1500–1648

DESPITE tremendous complication in detail, it is not difficult to discern the main thrust of European development in the field of politics between 1500 and 1648. As compared with the tangle of overlapping jurisdictions that had prevailed in medieval times, power tended to concentrate at relatively few centers. The European landscape came to be partitioned into a series of well-consolidated states, each controlled by a central and usually monarchical government. Within the borders of each successful state, the powers of government expanded radically. Matters which had once been strictly local came within the cognizance of agents of the central government. Kings and princes also acquired authority in matters of ecclesiastical administration and patronage, even in countries that remained Catholic and continued to recognize papal headship of the church. Noble rights and immunities together with town and village autonomies suffered drastic curtailment. Every sort of local authority based on inherited personal status crumbled before demands made in the name of a distant sovereign by officials whose power depended on royal or princely appointment.

This process of political consolidation may be looked at in a number of different ways. In one sense, it amounted to the application north of the Alps of techniques of government which had been first worked out in Italian city-states. Thus, for example, the merging of noble and burgher classes into a single (if tumultuous) body politic had been pioneered in Italian cities like Florence about two hundred years before French and English kings began to make much progress in that direction. Or, again, the use of standing professional armies to back up the will of the sovereign was commonplace in Italy long before 1500, but became practicable in Spain and France only after that date. In the important instances, of course, state-building north of the Alps proceeded on a much enlarged territorial scale as compared to anything Italy knew. With this territorial enlargement the effective power of the leading European governments increased enormously, and the whole scale of interstate politics underwent corresponding magnification.

From another point of view, however, the complex overlapping jurisdictions of medieval political life were dissolved far more by the violent deeds and emotions connected with the Reformation than by slow seepage of Italian political practices north of the Alps. Assuredly, the effort to renew the church and make it holy had an enormous and immediate impact upon politics. Sustained and serious effort to make human life conform to God's will as revealed in the Bible changed men's minds and altered their behavior. Wholesale violence sanctified by dogmatic differences quickly erupted, and for more than a century Europe was convulsed by wars fought in the name of Christian truth — though scarcely in accordance with its dictates.

Amid all the violence and bloodshed, secular sovereigns unceasingly inched their power forward. In the principal states that became Protestant the government took over most of the properties formerly owned by churchmen, and acquired the right to appoint, or at least to approve the appointment of, leading clergymen. Almost the same fate befell the church in countries that retained their allegiance to the pope. The fact that land and other property was not confiscated outright did not prevent Catholic rulers in Spain, France, and Austria, for example, from appointing the dignitaries and taxing the lands of the church within their domains.

From still a third viewpoint, the consolidation of political power in a comparatively small number of centers reflected the rapid

elaboration of military technology. As weapons became more sophisticated, the exercise of organized violence became prohibitively
expensive for local rulers, and impossibly complicated for universal
authorities. The medieval knight, once he acquired a horse, armor,
and training was almost self-sufficient, or, more accurately, wherever he went he could find what he needed in the way of food and
minor repairs to his equipment without much difficulty. If threatened by some superior force he could retire behind castle walls,
where, if the castle were well provisioned, he could wait safely
enough until the enemy went home. But when artillery and infan-
trymen armed with pikes and guns drove the knight first from his
castle and then from the battlefield — a process lasting from about
1350 to 1550 — military organization became vastly more complicated. Supplies of powder and shot, transport for heavy guns, the
arts of discipline, and money to pay for everything an army needed
were not within the reach of most merely local authorities and, as it
proved, were too disparate for any universal monarch to muster
effectively across the whole of Europe.

Dependence upon a growingly complex system of land armaments also tied governments to the sources whence such complicated devices came: that is, to artisan shops and manufactories,
mining and metallurgical entrepreneurs, capitalists, bankers, and
generally, to the urban element in society which alone could assemble the necessary raw materials, produce the weapons, and deliver
them to the soldiery in the right assortment and at the right time.
Hence, really powerful governments were those in whose territories a sufficient urban development had occurred to sustain the
complex demands of the new military technology, whereas territorially great states like Poland, for example, in which such a development failed to occur, were unable to take advantage of their size
to become correspondingly powerful.

Each of these three points of view is surely valid. Their interplay
over a century and a half, acting amidst the innumerable unpredictable acts of individual men who found themselves in critical situations facing new and unparalleled choices, gives the political history of this period an unusually intense, chaotic quality.

At the time, the eventual victory of the royal and princely governments over both local and universal rivals for sovereignty was far from obvious. In some of the eastern and northern parts of Europe, for example, aristocrats and clan chieftains retained or even enhanced their liberties. This was done both in the name of Calvinist reform of church and state, as in Hungary and Scotland, and in the name of a restored and reinvigorated Catholicism, as in Poland and Lithuania.

In the Dutch provinces and in England similar political developments proceeded from very different causes, for there the royal power was dismantled by townsmen and commercial farmers who found in legal precedent and Calvinist doctrine suitable justification for their defiance of the centralizing authority.

The Dutch revolt against Philip II of Spain began in 1568 and attained definite success by 1609, when a truce was concluded that ended large-scale campaigning. The rebel provinces worked out a loose federal union in the face of the exigencies of the war against Spain. The union survived the war, and, despite recurrent friction between urban and rural elements, sufficed to make the Dutch into a world power of the first rank.

In the next generation the English civil wars (1642–48) also ran counter to the trend toward monarchical absolutism. It was the parliamentary opponents of modern, efficient royal bureaucracy who prevailed. Like the Reformation itself, the parliamentary cause was radically reactionary, for it rested as much on a reaffirmation of the traditional liberties of Englishmen (Magna Carta and all that) as upon relentless Puritanical striving after a government of saints. But like other successful revolutionaries, the Puritans in power were compelled to betray their program. English liberties and a government of saints degenerated after the execution of King Charles I (1649) into an open military dictatorship under Oliver Cromwell (d. 1658). His earnest efforts to re-establish a parliamentary form of government ran afoul of the stubborn fact that the vast majority of Englishmen repudiated the Puritanical ideal that inspired Cromwell's armies. After Cromwell died, King Charles II's restoration (1660) resolved the impasse; but the new king did not attempt to build up royal power as Charles I had done. Sovereignty remained with Parliament; and the English Parliament managed to balance local and national interests in such a way as to make the central government reasonably responsive to changing circumstances.

Yet, however pregnant English parliamentarianism and Dutch federalism may have been for later times, they were exceptional and entirely atypical of the age. By giving political expression to the stubborn localism of landowners and burghers, the English and Dutch governments seemed to be defending a lost cause. Only the fact that their formidability vis-à-vis other states rested on naval rather than on land forces explains how it was that these two maverick nations were able to play roles as great powers without submitting to the bureaucratic centralization which in other lands proved to be the price of military strength, or indeed of political survival.

International politics. The most spectacular aspect of European politics between 1500 and 1648 was not the incessant wearing down of local jurisdictions by representatives of some central authority. However important, administrative centralization proceeded by means of innumerable petty local quarrels and decisions. Far more dramatic was the conflict at the other end of the political scale, which pitted the two great universal institutions of Latin Christendom — papacy and empire — against the emerging territorial sovereigns of western and central Europe. It seems clear, at least in theory, that Renaissance rationalism and the Reformation effort to apprehend and enforce a complete truth that could save men from uncertainty and error might both have been harnessed to support a universal state and a single church — if any single sovereign had been able to exploit the increasing technical complexity of warfare in order to organize a power so strong as to overwhelm all political rivals and hunt down all heretics.

Nothing of the sort happened. Yet in 1519, when Charles V of Hapsburg added the title and powers of Holy Roman Emperor to his already magnificent inheritance, it certainly seemed that universal monarchy might indeed prevail. For through a fortunate marriage alliance, Charles V inherited not merely his family's lands in Austria and nearby regions of Germany, but a magnificent Bur-

gundian inheritance as well that extended southward from the Low
Countries in an irregular strip of territory lying between France
and Germany. In addition, he fell heir to the Spanish crown in
1516. To this was soon added the vast new empire of the Americas,
which emerged before Europe's startled eyes as first Cortez (1521)
and then Pizarro (1535) unlocked the dazzling wealth of the New
World. As though this were not enough, Charles's brother Ferdinand, whom he entrusted with the administration of his Austrian
possessions, inherited the crowns of Bohemia and Hungary in
1526, when his brother-in-law, the Hungarian king, died without
heirs when fleeing the Turks after the disastrous battle of Mohacz.

Charles's enemies were as numerous as his subjects, however, and
his subjects never united for any sort of prolonged common effort.
The result was therefore first stalemate, and eventually evisceration
of the imperial power, even in Germany. But a long and stormy
passage intervened between the time of Charles's coronation as
Holy Roman Emperor (1519) and his descendants' reluctant ac-
knowledgment in the Treaty of Westphalia (1648) of the sovereignty of local German princes.

The king of France and the sultan of Turkey were the most
consistent opponents of the Hapsburg imperial power. (Their
treaty of alliance, 1536, though seldom effective in the field, was a
constant reproach to the Most Christian King of France.) In addition, at the beginning of his reign Charles tangled violently with
the papacy, and his soldiers sacked Rome in 1525. Later on, after
Spanish arms and Spanish piety had invaded Italy, captured the papacy, and inspired the Counter Reformation, the popes began to co-
operate with the Hapsburgs. The resulting alliance between empire
and papacy proved very strong and effected the reconversion of
nearly all the Austrian, Hungarian, and Polish lands which had
briefly proved hospitable to Protestantism.

In Germany, however, the Reformation enormously strengthened and intensified the opposition of local princes to any consolidation of the imperial power. After initial hesitation, Charles V declared himself firmly against Martin Luther and his followers; but
wars with the French and Turks, fought mainly in Italy and the
Mediterranean, kept him so busy that he never had time to marshal

his full force against the Lutherans. In 1556 Charles abdicated, transferring Spain and its empire together with the Burgundian lands to his son, Philip, but endowing his brother Ferdinand with Austria and the imperial title.

Yet even this division of the inheritance did not, in the end, permit consolidation of either part. Germany remained divided and its princes nursed a lively suspicion of Hapsburg imperial ambitions. For a long time Ferdinand and his heirs followed a cautious policy, while the greater power of Spain under Philip II struggled vainly first to consolidate and then to hold dominion over the Low Countries. The success of the Dutch revolt (1568–1609) and the English victory over the Spanish Armada in 1588 did not prevent the Spaniards from retaining the rest of the Burgundian lands in Europe and dominating most of Italy while staving off the Turks in the Mediterranean, establishing their empire over a vast region of the Americas, and even, for a while, annexing Portugal and the Portuguese empire (1581–1640).

Only after Philip's death (1598) did Spanish predominance begin to fade. France had been distracted by a series of religious wars which pitted rebellious Protestants against the royal authority, but emerged again as a strong and united state under Henry IV (1589–1610). Meanwhile industrial stagnation or even retrogression diminished Spain's capacity to equip the armies and navies needed to maintain her imperial position. The weakening of Spain coincided with the accession of Ferdinand II (reigned 1619–37) to the Austrian inheritance and imperial title. Ferdinand II was a far more energetic and ruthless monarch than his predecessors had been. His agents set out in the name of Catholic restoration to overthrow local rights and immunities. The result was to fan a local revolt in Bohemia (1618) into thirty years of violent war that convulsed most of Europe. The collision between Protestant and Catholic doctrines envenomed the conflict, but just as much at stake were the conflicting princely and imperial claims to sovereignty. When Ferdinand's forces seemed likely to win, first the Danes, then the Swedes, and finally the French intervened against the Hapsburg imperial cause. Brutal devastation of parts of Germany ended with the Peace of Westphalia (1648), which guaranteed the emptiness of the imperial title by recognizing the sovereignty of the separate German princes. Thenceforward, for more than two hundred years, Germany remained divided among scores of local rulers whose courts and governments imitated but could not rival the really great power that emerged from the Peace of Westphalia — that is, France.

European colonization and trade. The upshot of Europe's political, military, and religious history between 1500 and 1648 was, therefore, almost as confused as the events themselves. Plural sovereignties still divided the landscape, and their relations were complex and changeable as ever. Papal power remained real in much of Europe; Spain retained most of her empire both in the Americas and in Europe; and even the imperial power of the Austrian branch of the Hapsburg family found ample scope in consolidating and strengthening its administrative control over hereditary lands in Austria, Bohemia, and Hungary. The French dominance that emerged in 1648 was therefore very limited, even on the continent of Europe. When one considers naval power and overseas empire, French preponderance disappears, for England and the Dutch had both become formidable sea powers, superior to the French. They used their ships to encroach upon the Spanish and Portuguese overseas empires, dispatching interlopers to the Indian Ocean and colonists to the Americas.

The establishment of the Dutch and English East India companies (1600, 1601) gave a lasting and effective mercantile organization to the enterprises of these two nations in Indian and Far Eastern waters. At first it was the Dutch who won the most spectacular successes. From an initial venture in 1594, within a mere fifty years they drove the Portuguese from Malacca and Ceylon and established their power in Java, thus becoming the masters of the spice trade. Early English lodgments along the west coast of India were relatively modest.

In the Americas, however, the balance was reversed, for the English colonies in Virginia (founded 1607) and Massachusetts (founded 1620) soon outstripped the Dutch colony at New York (founded 1618). French colonization of Canada started almost simultaneously at Quebec (founded 1608). By far the most lucrative European ventures across the Atlantic in the seventeenth century were directed toward the smaller islands of the Caribbean, where sugar plantations, worked by slaves imported from Africa, provided a commodity in high demand at home. By the 1640's, English, French, and to a lesser extent Dutch entrepreneurs had taken the lead in this trade, overtaking the Portuguese and Spaniards, who had first experimented with sugar along the Brazilian and Caribbean coastlines.

This very rapid expansion of European settlement and trade attested the restless growth of European power vis-à-vis other less volatile peoples and civilizations. All the futilities and confusions of European politics, the brutal clash of arms, and the impassioned struggle after theological certainty which constituted the stuff and substance of European experience in these years were not entirely in vain. Men seldom accomplished what they desired, but their struggles did very greatly increase Europe's capacity to mobilize wealth, manpower, and ingenuity for political and economic purposes. The consolidation of sovereignty and the expansion of the scope of governmental activity constituted one important aspect of this evolution. The rise of joint stock companies like the Dutch and English East India companies — and of other large-scale business enterprises — was another. Equally, in the intellectual and artistic realms, a reckless pursuit of truth and of beauty, enhanced and sometimes stimulated by advances of technology (e.g. printing, the telescope), imparted to European culture a greater variety and toughness than the comparatively parochial outlook and limited knowledge of the medieval age had allowed. We must consider these changes next.

The Renaissance. The twin yet rival movements of Renaissance and Reformation emphasized different aspects of the European cultural inheritance. Men inspired by the ideal of giving rebirth to the knowledge, skills, and elegance of pagan antiquity magnified the Greco-Roman constituent of Europe's past, whereas believers anxious to reform religion on Biblical lines drew their main inspiration from the Judeo-Christian component of Western civilization. A few single-minded advocates in either camp sought to repudiate the other entirely; yet this was unusual, for a complex cross-play always existed between the two movements. Some of the greatest reformers were skilled classical scholars and found the techniques which had been developed for establishing the correct texts of pagan authors applicable to Biblical studies too. Similarly, the artists and men of letters of the Renaissance remained deeply concerned with religion and questions of theology, not least, when, as with Machiavelli (d. 1527), they expressly renounced the Christian faith.

The Renaissance had, of course, taken form in Italy, from about 1350. A return to antiquity, with its memories of Roman greatness, naturally had strong appeal to Italians. More than that, Italian towns harbored secularly minded commoners and princely patrons who deliberately turned their attention toward things human and away from things divine.

The Italian Renaissance reached its peak just about the year 1500. Leonardo da Vinci's (d. 1519) restless probing of the natural world through his art and through minute observation of men and things, together with Niccolò Machiavelli's ruthless analysis of the nature and use of political power based upon personal experience and study of classical authors, well represents its culmination. Only a little later, Michelangelo Buonarroti (d. 1564) and Nicholas Copernicus (d. 1543) — who though he died in Cracow drew his intellectual stimulus from the University of Padua where he had been trained — gave up the radical reliance on human rationality which seems implicit in the work of both Leonardo and Machiavelli. Michelangelo suffered torments of doubt about practically everything, even about the value of his art; and Copernicus' heliocentric system of astronomy, which assumed a circular instead of an elliptical orbit for the planets, was inspired by neo-Pythagorean number mysticism and actually flew in the face of observational data.

The attractions of the Renaissance ideal of beauty as created by human skill and of truth to be discovered by untrammeled exercise of human faculties were not lost on the rest of Europe. Aristocratic and courtly circles were particularly receptive north of the Alps; but wherever urban growth had created a substantial middle class

— as in Holland, the Rhineland, England, and France — commoners, too, were soon attracted by local efforts to imitate or surpass Italian models. The result was the development of distinct national schools of literature and to some extent also of painting. Thus, for example, Miguel Cervantes' *Don Quixote* (1605–15) and the plays of Lope de Vega (d. 1635) gave literary definition to the Spanish language. Modern French acquired its literary form through the labors of three utterly diverse men: François Rabelais (d. 1553), who mocked what he could not alter, John Calvin (d. 1564), who strove relentlessly to reform and sanctify all human life, and Michel Eyquem, seigneur de Montaigne (d. 1592), who recommended an aloof moderation in the face of human shortcomings. English owes its literary definition to Elizabethan writers — William Shakespeare (d. 1616) above all — and to the King James Bible (1611). Modern literary German is the creation of Luther's translation of the Bible. Most of the other tongues of Germanic Europe (Dutch, Danish, Swedish) took form also as a by-product of Protestant translations of the Bible into the vernacular.

The Reformation. The other leading characteristic of Europe's cultural life in this age was the reassertion of religious concerns despite the charms of rampant secularism toward which the thought and sensibility of Renaissance Italy seemed to be moving.

Reform and reinvigoration of the Christian Church had been undertaken repeatedly in medieval Europe. By their very nature such movements challenged constituted ecclesiastical authorities, who were always tempted to declare their critics heretical. This had been the fate of John Wycliffe (d. 1382) in England and Jan Hus (d. 1414) in Bohemia, each of whom nevertheless attracted a considerable body of followers. The healing of the Great Schism in 1417 through the restoration of papal monarchy at the Council of Constance made it harder for heresy to flourish in the following century. In Spain, particularly, religious conformity and political loyalty tended to coincide. The crusading spirit, fanned by centuries of war against the Moors (driven from Granada only in 1492), continued to inspire the Spanish imperial effort both in Europe and overseas. A uniquely close relationship between church and state resulted. Elsewhere, pope and monarch usually collaborated in taxing the clergy, but were otherwise as often at odds as in alliance.

The papacy itself claimed sovereignty over part of Italy, and some popes allowed their pursuit of political advantage in the peninsula to outweigh the spiritual headship over Christendom their predecessors had so vigorously asserted. Elsewhere in Italy and Germany bishops and abbots often followed the pope's example.

Amidst such a religious scene, Martin Luther's (d. 1546) burning conviction, based on poignant personal experience of how a sinful man might still win through to salvation, flashed like the sword of an avenging angel. Luther initially challenged the validity of the sale of indulgences. Sales of these documents which purported to relieve suffering souls from the torments of Purgatory, had been organized in a thoroughly commercial spirit as part of a campaign to raise money to build a new St. Peter's cathedral in Rome. According to the conventions of traditional Scholastic debate Luther publicly denied the value of indulgences by posting 95 theses on the church door at Wittenberg in 1517. But instead of remaining a matter of academic controversy, Luther's views spread like wildfire through Germany. Public debates with champions of the papacy rapidly drove Luther toward more radical and complete exposition of his convictions. Three eloquent pamphlets written in 1520 — *An Appeal to the Nobility of the German Nation*, *The Babylonian Captivity of the Church*, and *The Freedom of a Christian Man* — defined the heart of Lutheranism. Subsequent controversy developed innumerable differences in doctrinal formulation between Catholics, Lutherans, and other kinds of Protestants. At the center of this theological strife was the question of the source of religious authority. Luther rested his case on the Bible and his own personal experience of what he felt to be the freely given grace of God. He further denied that the clergy had any necessary mediating role between the individual sinner and God, and boldly proclaimed the priesthood of all believers.

The printing press spread Luther's views rapidly and widely through Germany and adjacent lands. His protest speedily gathered other discontents behind the banner of church reform. Luther's attack on the papacy, for example, attracted many in Germany who felt aggrieved at being taxed and exploited by foreigners; but this nascent expression of German nationalism was soon stifled by the refusal of the emperor, Charles V, and of other important rulers in Germany to become Lutheran.

Instead, therefore, of becoming German, the Protestant movement became pan-European, particularly after John Calvin established his headquarters in Geneva (1536) and made it the center of a vigorous propaganda that affected almost every country of Europe. England, for example, broke with the pope in 1534, but the Church of England became Protestant in doctrine only by degrees, very largely under stimulus from Geneva. Simultaneously the Dutch and Scots made Calvinism dominant in their countries. In France, on the contrary, the government remained Catholic. French Protestantism, after a promising start, lost its *élan* about 1600. In Italy, Protestantism never commanded wide support and withered quickly when the force of revived Catholicism became apparent. Scandinavia, on the other hand, became Lutheran, along with almost half of Germany. Local nationalisms, which were beginning to emerge all over Europe, played important parts in determining each of these results.

Social and economic revolution also made a brief appearance in Lutheran dress. But when rebellious peasants took Christian liberty to mean relief from dues and rents, Luther denounced them violently (1525). Thereafter, social unrest and religious radicalism passed into Anabaptist and other channels, where it survived persecution only among small secret or semi-secret groups.

The drastic nature of the social and economic changes that came to Europe between 1500 and 1648 contributed powerfully to religious controversy. Yet it would be wrong to forget that the search for an absolutely certain religious truth gathered enormous energy behind it simply because of the inherent attractiveness of a definite and coherent world view. Peace of mind required authoritative and adequate answers to the uncertainties that daily experience thrust so remorselessly upon a large proportion of Europe's population. Luther was sure about how he himself had gained God's grace. This was one of the secrets of his success, since others wished desperately to achieve a similar state of inward grace and assured salvation. When a man did achieve certainty, he naturally wished both to communicate the saving truth to others and to denounce error in all its guises. A great outpouring of preaching and writing, aimed at such explication, was soon supplemented by systematic schooling in carefully drawn-up catechisms. Defenders of the papacy presently developed Roman Catholic counter-propaganda. All across Europe a far greater knowledge of Christian doctrine and an emotionally deeper commitment to chosen or inherited forms of the faith resulted.

One of the ironies of Protestantism was its tendency to split into sects and sub-sects. The reformers never abandoned the ideal of a single Catholic church embracing all Christians. But the Bible — their sole source of religious authority — was capable of diverse interpretation. Truths that seemed self-evident to one man did not always seem so to others who were just as sincere and equally eager for the certainty of salvation. In such a case each was compelled to denounce the other as a preacher of false doctrine, and often did so with more vigor than charity. Yet as the white heat of the first generation of reform receded, efforts to build a church organization and enforce doctrinal conformity met with success in most parts of Protestant Europe. In England the process was more drawn out. Piecemeal reform under the Tudors (1534–1603) failed to satisfy a powerful group of rigorists, or Puritans. Their effort to make over all human life in accordance with God's will did not exhaust itself until after the utter failure of the government of saints under Oliver Cromwell (1658).

The Roman church reacted slowly to the Protestant challenge. At first many hoped that reconciliation could be achieved, and the most pious Catholics, who were best capable of meeting the Protestant movement on its own terms, often hesitated to divide Christendom even more deeply by counter-attacking against the Lutherans. Yet the passionate drive for theological certainty which armed the Protestants could also be harnessed to the Catholic cause. St. Ignatius Loyola (d. 1556) did so. After a conversion experience as poignant as Luther's, he set out to preach the truth as a soldier of the pope. He soon collected a group of like-minded young men around himself and then organized them into the Society of Jesus, which speedily became a most effective agent for the defense and

REFORMATION AND
COUNTER-REFORMATION

- - - - Stabilized Religious Frontier
→ Protestant Reform
➤ Catholic Reform

Scale of Miles
0   500

propagation of Catholicism, both in Europe and overseas. When the Jesuit order was still in its infancy, the Council of Trent (1545–63) assembled. After lengthy and thrice-suspended sessions, it succeeded in decreeing a number of practical reforms and defined disputed points of doctrine in a firmly anti-Protestant sense.

Thereafter the initial ambiguity of the appeal for church reform faded, and men everywhere in Europe were confronted by the spectacle of a comparatively well-organized, united, and reformed Roman Catholic church locked in combat with an equally determined but not nearly so tightly organized Calvinist movement, while Lutherans and conservative churchmen in England looked on with a general distaste for both of the protagonists. Eventually, the failure of pope and emperor in the Thirty Years' War (1618–48) and the almost simultaneous failure of the Puritan revolution in England (1640–60) turned many men's minds away from religious controversy, which, in the course of both conflicts, had often become a transparent disguise for ignoble political and economic interests.

The growth of science. As a matter of fact, throughout the Reformation period a small but important company of men had not permitted the quest for theological certainty to eclipse other, more mundane concerns. Galileo Galilei (1564–1642), for example, lived through the height of Europe's religious conflicts, yet found it preferable to devote himself to physical and astronomical investigations. His defense of Copernican astronomy on the basis of telescopic observation and mathematical reasoning, and his ingenious efforts to give mathematical expression to carefully recorded observational data inaugurated lines of inquiry which physicists and astronomers have not yet exhausted. René Descartes (d. 1650) was another who deliberately turned his back on theological controversy and instead set out to create a mathematically rigorous philosophy which would, with sublime impartiality and on the basis of reason alone, provide answers to metaphysical as well as to all other questions about which men had quarreled so bitterly and desperately since the time of Luther and before.

Other intellectual traditions were active and fruitful too. Paracelsus (1541), Andreas Vesalius (d. 1564), and William Harvey (d. 1657) successfully challenged the authority of Galen in medical matters, as much on mystical and neo-Platonic grounds as upon the basis of more exact observation of human anatomy. Similarly, a superstitious mystic, Johannes Kepler (d. 1630), strove vainly to discover the harmonic ratios among the orbits of the planets, but did, after vastly laborious computation, discover a mathematical formula that exactly described the elliptical motions of each separate planet in its orbit — thus, incidentally correcting Copernicus and removing one of the most important objections to the Copernican hypothesis. Still another tradition, optimistic and empirical, was represented by Francis Bacon (d. 1626), who argued that careful observation and systematic collection of information would allow men to unlock nature's secrets without the help of either religious revelation or mathematical reasoning.

Invention of a number of new instruments, particularly the telescope (*c.* 1608) and the microscope (*c.* 1590), the pendulum clock (*c.* 1592), thermometer (*c.* 1592), and barometer (*c.* 1643), gave the observations and experiments of the small company of natural philosophers much greater precision than had been possible in earlier ages. This, together with the vast influx of miscellaneous information flooding into Europe from overseas, provided a rich diet for those who preferred such studies to the controversies of theologians. Hence, when (after 1648) hostile religious camps came to be widely discredited among reflective men, the natural philosophers were ready and primed to offer a world view less complete perhaps but scarcely less fascinating than the rival theologies that had dominated the attention of earlier generations.

Yet it would be wrong to suggest that science supplanted religion. On the contrary, the Reformation age left behind a heightened religious concern in all walks of life. Science and other secular inquiries did not expressly oppose the claims of religion, which had been pitched so very high by reformers of both Protestant and Catholic persuasions. Rather, secular investigation grew up and throve in the interstices of knowledge which were treated as matters of indifference by theologians. Later, after about 1650, scientific investigation attained enough respectability that scientists and men of learning no longer had seriously to worry about how (or even whether) their discoveries might fit into the frame of official theology.

Emergence of cultural pluralism. Thus the upshot of Europe's long travail between 1500 and 1648 was strangely contrary to what almost all the great men of the age had desired. Instead of discovering and enforcing a universal truth, Europeans discovered that they could agree to disagree. Intellectual pluralism established itself on European soil more flagrantly than ever before. No official hierarchy of knowledge provided a complete scheme for understanding the world — as had been the case, in theory if not in practice, in medieval times. Each separate church, nation, and profession was in a position to pursue truth according to its own lights. Such diversity assured the continued and very rapid development of European thought down even to our own time.

Art and letters also exhibited an increasing pluralism. The rise of the vernacular which had occurred at the beginning of our period created separate national schools of literature. Painting, too, tended to diverge from the pattern established by the great Italians, so that Spanish (Velasquez, d. 1660; El Greco, d. 1614), Dutch (Rembrandt, d. 1669), and Flemish (Rubens, d. 1640) schools, each with distinctive traits, developed within the general European tradition. Architecture remained less variable. In all of Catholic Europe a baroque elaboration of Renaissance styles prevailed, whereas in most Protestant lands variations upon Gothic held the ground.

The trauma of emergence from the medieval mould was enormous. Never since have Europeans faced more agonizing or more pervasive uncertainties. Yet the severity of the experience called forth human genius and individual achievement on a most unusual scale. Columbus and Cortez, Luther and Loyola, Leonardo da Vinci and Descartes, Copernicus and Galileo — to name only a few of the greatest — were makers of the modern world in a more profound sense than were men of earlier or later generations who did not confront, as these men did, the challenges of a new world — both literally and metaphorically — opening before their startled eyes. The surpassing success with which these and scores of thousands of other Europeans rose to meet this unprecedented opportunity is best attested by the subsequent career of Western civilization, of which we and all the world are heirs.

XX

Europe's Outliers: Russia and the Americas

1500–1648

A T a time when China, India, and the Middle East found it unnecessary to make more than trifling accommodation to the European presence along their shores, Russian and American populations were already deeply entangled with western Europe. Paralyzing collapse came to Amerindian higher cultures, and the new institutions planted on American soil by the conquistadors in every case derived directly from Spain. Russian institutions were much tougher and did not crumble like Amerindian institutions at the first approach of armed strangers. Yet Russia, too, found it hard to shift from resisting traditional pressures from the steppe to resisting the quite novel challenges coming from western Europe. Severe strain in both church and state registered the difficulties of this about-face, which was quite as profound as western Europe's simultaneous struggle to emerge from its medieval chrysalis.

The rise of Moscow. Until 1480 most of the Russian lands remained under the formal suzerainty of the Khan of the Golden Horde, whose capital was at Kazan on the Volga river. In fact, the khan entrusted tax collection to the Grand Duke of Moscow, who did not always find it necessary to remit what he collected to his suzerain. Hence when Ivan III formally renounced his allegiance and assumed the title of tsar (1480), the act had more symbolic than practical significance. The really important fact was that the Tatars were unable to do anything about it. Military supremacy no longer rested securely with the cavalry archers of the steppe. The Kremlin, a citadel impregnable to anything short of prolonged siege, secured Moscow from capture. The artillery pieces defending it announced with their every discharge that the end of steppe nomad supremacy was at hand.

One should not, however, exaggerate the rapidity with which the new technical possibilities of warfare could be applied effectively on the ground. As late as 1571, for example, an unusually large Tatar raiding party burned the outskirts of Moscow. By that time infantry fire power had already become decisive on the battlefield, but the problem was how to bring elusive raiders to battle. Not until a string of fortified frontier posts had been constructed, manned by horsemen (Cossacks) as fleet as the Tatars themselves and better equipped with weapons than they, could steppe raiding be entirely halted. This occurred only after 1648.

Yet while satisfactory frontier defense against hit-and-run raids continued to exceed Russian military capability, the central fact remained: from about 1500, horse archers could no longer overcome well-equipped infantry. The trading and agricultural society of Russia could and did equip infantry regiments with guns, the master weapons of the age, whereas the nomad societies of the steppe, which had for so long enjoyed a fundamental military superiority over settled agriculturalists, could not. The radically new balance of power which resulted was not long in manifesting itself. In 1552, Ivan IV, the Terrible, captured Kazan. Six years later his soldiers completed the conquest of the lower Volga by taking Astrakhan. An enormous territory thereby came under Moscow's rule, and a line of river communication with Persia by way of the Caspian opened up. Russia's southern flank still remained exposed to raids by the Tatars of the Crimea. But their power depended on political alliance and commercial relations with Constantinople. A fully independent nomad empire could no longer survive in the face of civilized musketeers.

In the next generation, Russian pioneers crossed the Urals, overthrew the Moslem khanate of Sibir, and by 1587 had established themselves along the middle reaches of the Ob river. Once across the Ural mountains, their long-established skill as river boatmen (in winter, sleighdrivers) allowed Russian adventurers to cross the easy portages separating one Siberian river system from the next. As a result, in 1638 the first Russian explorers reached the Pacific at Okhotsk. Native hunters and gatherers who inhabited the grim and forbidding Siberian swamps and forests were few in number and politically weak. Hence, when Russians demanded tribute in furs, they set their hunting and snaring skills to work for their new masters and soon provided them with a commodity that was in great demand both in Europe and in China. Income from the export of furs was, in fact, especially important to the Russian state, since it allowed the import of European armaments and other manufactures on a scale that would have been impossible otherwise.

Withdrawal of the long-standing pressure exerted by the military superiority of the steppe peoples had, however, its disruptive side. As long as the Grand Duke of Moscow had to appease a distant but terrible suzerain in Kazan by delivering tributes punctually, the Russian people saw the necessity of obedience and submission to the Grand Duke's tax collectors. But, after the Tatar danger had gone, emigration into the new lands along the Volga or in the Ukraine became a practicable alternative to paying taxes; and many restless young men did in fact escape into the wilds. Rudely egalitarian Cossack communities in the Ukraine and along the lower Don recruited their members in this way. Farther east, in the Volga and Ural regions, individual settlers and pioneers broke away even from the loose discipline of Cossack life and developed a style of isolated small-family existence very similar to that familiar on the North American frontier.

This sort of leakage extended Russian settlement to new ground rather rapidly. Loss of manpower could be borne by the central authority so long as most peasants and townsmen remained behind to pay taxes. The discontents of the noble (boyar) class were far more dangerous. The fact that right next door in Poland-Lithuania, great nobles enjoyed effective independence from any sort of royal administration was a constant reminder of how easy it would be to live without the Muscovite autocracy. Religious distaste for the Catholicism of their western neighbors, was, perhaps, the strongest factor inhibiting a mass transfer of loyalty to Lithuania. The Muscovite autocracy, however, did not view treason lightly. Ivan IV acquired his sobriquet, the Terrible, through the bloody violence with which he attempted to destroy boyar opposition to his rule. He did, in fact, kill off so many of the old families as to make the creation of a noble republic on the Polish-Lithuanian model impossible. This became evident during Russia's Time of Troubles (1605–13), when despite breakdown of political legitimacy the old boyar families proved unable to seize and hold power in the name of aristocratic liberty on the Polish model. Instead, by common consent, autocracy was soon restored.

Western influence — political turmoil. The main reason that the Muscovite centralized and autocratic regime survived was the appearance of a new foreign threat, coming this time from the west rather than from the steppe. Western pressure had two dimensions: military-political and religious-cultural. Militarily, Ivan IV had found it impossible, despite very strenuous efforts, to avoid losing territory to Sweden and Poland. Ivan began the Livonian war (1558–82) with high hopes of matching his new-won Caspian coastline with a window on the Baltic. Instead, the war strained Muscovy to the limit and ended in failure. A generation later, during the Time of Troubles, when usurpers ruled and civil strife spread all through the Russian lands, the Westerners took the offensive. A Polish army occupied Moscow in 1608 and set up a puppet government. But a great revulsion against the foreigners soon developed among all classes of Russians. Simultaneously, civil disturbances in Poland weakened the invaders. In 1613, accordingly, the invaders withdrew and the Patriarch of Moscow was able to proclaim his nephew, Michael Romanov, tsar. The Romanov dynasty remained on the Russian throne until 1917.

Autocratic Russia's military and political survival — helped, incidentally, by the diversion of Swedish power into Germany during the Thirty Years' War and by Polish concern for the outcome of that struggle — remained precarious as long as Russian technology and wealth lagged conspicuously behind the levels attained farther west. Yet, by a supreme irony, deliberate and strenuous efforts to close the gap and overtake the West required wholesale resort to force. This, in itself, emphasized differences already dividing Russian from Western institutions and social relationships. Ivan IV's secret society of aides, bound to the service of the autocrat by common participation in orgies and crimes, constituted a strange caricature of Western bureaucracy, even though the "service nobility" he created performed the same functions that Western officials and army officers performed for their sovereigns. Moreover, at the bottom of Russian society serfdom was being fastened upon the peasantry precisely at the time when in more westerly lands peasants (along with the rest of society) were beginning both to suffer from and to enjoy greater personal freedom and independence.

The reason for this development is clear enough. In Russia the tsar lacked enough money income to pay salaries to officials and army personnel. He had, therefore, to reward his servants with grants of land. But land without peasants to work it was useless. To prevent peasants from running away, it seemed therefore necessary to pass laws authorizing landholders to chase after and capture runaways. By 1649, when a new law code systematized previous enactments, a theoretically rigid frame had been imposed upon Russian society, whereby each man was required to remain at his post, in the place and walk of life to which he had been born. Russian reality never conformed to this legal prescription. Runaways continued to make good their escape to the frontiers, pushing the fringe of Russian society and settlement ever deeper into Asia and the Ukraine. Others, who happened to catch the eye of some powerful man, might rise from humble beginnings to the very top of officialdom — but always by exception.

Western influence — cultural change. The abrasive effect of contact with Westerners upon Russian religious and cultural life was almost as troublesome as these military-political tribulations. Russians badly needed a sense of national mission in order to be able to counterattack and devalue the all-too-evident superiority of Western wealth and technique.

After the fall of Constantinople to the Turks in 1453, therefore, the Russians easily convinced themselves that their branch of the

Orthodox church was the last stronghold of true Christianity. This flattering view came under severe attack after 1568, when Jesuit missionaries established themselves in Poland and, having quickly routed their Protestant opponents, turned serious attention to the task of converting Orthodox Christians to the papal obedience. At that time, the Polish-Lithuanian state embraced a broad band of west Russian lands whose Orthodox inhabitants recognized the ecclesiastical jurisdiction of Kiev. When, therefore, in 1596, the Metropolitan of Kiev together with most of his subordinate bishops accepted the papal definition of Christian doctrine, the shock in Muscovy was sharp. The fact that the Ukrainian or "Uniate" church was permitted to retain a Slavonic ritual for church services did nothing to diminish Orthodox consternation.

Yet effective rebuttal to Jesuit arguments for Roman Catholic doctrine was difficult. Russian church books were not everywhere precisely the same, and some copyists' and translators' errors had crept into the most familiar of all sacred texts, the ritual phrases of the eucharist. As long as no unfriendly critic called such anomalies to their attention, Russian churchmen had found no trouble in adhering to traditional formulas, despite minor local variations. But once Jesuit scholars had pointed an accusing finger at such irregularities, how, indeed, could Orthodox Russia's claim to a monopoly of Christian truth be sustained? Worse yet, how could the real truth, the authentic sacred phrase, be recognized amid the confusing textual variants that in fact had been inherited from the past? The traditional learning and piety of the Russian church was quite unable to cope with this problem.

Nevertheless, the Russians could fall back on one undoubted fact: Greek Christianity was older and therefore presumably more authentic than the Latin Christian tradition so ably represented by the Jesuits. Yet, to alter Russian liturgical books in order to bring them into accord with Greek models constituted a confession of past error, which the Russian church found hard to stomach. Salvation itself, they felt, depended on correct ritual. Error — or at least its admission — endangered the whole structure of Orthodox dogma.

Religious scholarship and propaganda were not, of course, the only guises in which western European cultural achievements came to Russian attention between 1500 and 1648. Ivan III initiated the importation of Italian workmen and architects to beautify and dignify Moscow with buildings of stone. Italian stone-masonry and decorative motifs when crossed with older Russian styles of wooden church architecture, and livened also with a dash of Persian elegance, produced the famous Cathedral of St. Basil, which adorns Moscow's Red Square. This amazing and remarkably successful structure was built for Ivan IV to celebrate his victory over the khanate of Astrakhan in 1558.

Russian icon painting, also, reached its climax during this period. The artists harnessed painters' skills derived from Italy and Byzantium to the expression of the mystical piety that sustained the Russian Orthodox church through the long decades when its spokesmen could find no effective reply to Western criticism. Until 1648, this emotion allowed Russian Orthodox civilization to remain spiritually independent, despite constant contact with the parts of Europe where the cultural mutation of early modern times was proceeding so powerfully.

Spanish America. The traumatic experiences of Holy Russia arising from its uncomfortable proximity to a restlessly ambitious western Europe were slight in comparison to the shocks suffered by Amerindians who had to confront the same challenge with a far weaker cultural inheritance of their own upon which to rely. As a matter of fact there was almost no organized, overt struggle to preserve the pre-Columbian ways of life. Instead, a catastrophic collapse of Amerindian cultural leadership allowed the Spaniards — almost unobtrusively — to substitute themselves for the vanished priests and warrior clans of the Aztec and Inca realms. Within little more that a generation, all the important inhabited locations of Mexico and Peru had become at least superficially Christian. Soon thereafter, wherever the needful labor power and architectural skill could be mobilized, huge baroque churches arose. In details of decoration they sometimes betray the hand of an Indian artist only imperfectly familiar with European prototypes; otherwise they look as though they had been translated bodily from Spain.

In cities and towns, legal forms and relationships were promptly recast in a Spanish, as well as Catholic, mould. The mines, too, whence came the flow of silver that so disturbed the world's price system, were promptly organized along European technical lines. But the great peasant majority at first lived much as before. The new masters with their religion and laws played the same limited role in their lives that the vanished rulers of the Aztec and Inca past had done. This simple relationship was soon upset by the fact (see p. 294) that diseases cut deeply into village manpower. As depopulation proceeded, the old subsistence agriculture broke down, for the Spaniards badly needed the village labor that did remain to feed the towns and to work in the mines. If Indian farmers could be induced to accept a loan, extra-legal force was seldom required. Energetic enforcement of debtors' obligations sufficed to put Indian labor legally at the disposal of Spanish creditors. Thus, despite official policy intended to preserve Indian village society, a commercial system, built at least in part on the European model, speedily established itself on ground which had formerly been dotted by more or less self-sufficient rural settlements.

After the first rush of gold-hungry conquistadores subsided, Christian missionaries took over their role as pioneers along the frontiers of the Spanish domains. Jesuits, Franciscans, and others labored both to save souls and to civilize their charges by teaching them the useful arts of Europe. A remarkable mission society arose in Paraguay, for example, where Jesuit priests exercised a truly benevolent despotism to create a large and prosperous Indian community among tribes that had previously been quite primitive. Skillful management, indeed, made the mission pay for itself through export to European markets of the product of the Indians' labor. Before long the Jesuits were in fact able to make substantial profit from their enterprise.

Other European colonists. Benevolent efforts within the framework of a mission society to transform native behavior along rational economic lines were interestingly intermediate between the paternalistic and protective policy officially adopted by Spanish authorities toward the Indian villages of Mexico and Peru, and the radically rational plantation economies that soon began to develop along the Caribbean and Brazilian coasts and in some of the Caribbean islands. In these regions, the native Indian population died away quite rapidly. But labor power was needed; slaves imported from west Africa filled the gap. An Englishman, John Hawkins, piloted the first slave ship to Spanish waters in 1562–63; but until sugar cultivation became firmly established (after about 1630) Negro slavery and agricultural plantations were not of great importance. After that date this inhumane mode of exploiting the land of America with the labor of Africa rapidly assumed a vast scale, and directed to the New World a stream of migration from Africa almost as large as the migration from Europe itself.

The entrepreneurs of the slave economy in the New World were mainly Portuguese, English, French, and Dutch, not Spanish. With their arrival on the scene, the Amerindians confronted considerably more ruthless intruders than the Spaniards had been. Missionary concern for the welfare of the bodies as well as the souls of their converts had always been a real factor in limiting Spanish exploitation of their Amerindian subjects. No comparable inhibitions checked the behavior of Portuguese, English, and Dutch settlers and traders. The French, like the Spaniards, attempted to organize missions and to protect the Indians of Canada from the ill effects of too rapid exposure to European civilization. Success was small, because unlike the situation in Paraguay, where the Jesuits maintained a strict quarantine against any but authorized movement into and out of their domain — to control spiritual rather than bacteriological infection — the Canadian missions were not proof against destructive epidemics of smallpox and similar diseases. Hence French benevolence, as much as English and Dutch indifference, had the effect of disrupting and destroying pre-existing Indian societies along the east coast of North America. In Brazil, the Portuguese lodgment, which dated from 1530, had similar consequences.

Until after 1648, of course, European settlement in North America as well as in Brazil remained very near the coast. The vast interiors of the two continents were only indirectly affected by the arrival of white colonists. But indirect effects could be important, as, for example, the development and spread of a Plains' Indian culture across the North American prairie. This nomadic, hunting style of life was based upon the use of horses to hunt buffalo — horses which had, of course, first been introduced into America by the Spaniards.

Thus, even in regions where European settlement had not yet penetrated and in parts of the continent where no European foot had yet trod, the impact of the West's civilization was sometimes felt. Just as the Russians could no longer afford to disregard the stimuli and challenges emanating from the lands that lay across their western frontier, so also the Americas had clearly become an outlier of the civilization of western Europe. In 1648, no other parts of the world had yet suffered anything like so drastic a shift of cultural climate.

XXI

The Realm of Islam, with Its Hindu and Christian Subject Communities, 1500–1700

OCAL and temporary set-backs notwithstanding, the realm of Islam had tended steadily to increase ever since Mohammed first established the holy community of the faithful at Medina. This age-old process did not come abruptly to a halt after A.D. 1500, despite the Far West's new dominion of the seas. On the contrary, India, southeast Asia, Africa, and Europe all continued to be theaters for Moslem expansion. Indeed, if one estimates millions of square miles or numbers of new subjects brought under Moslem rule between 1500 and 1700, these two centuries would certainly rank among the most successful of the entire Moslem era.

In India, for example, a flow of refugees and adventurers from north of the mountains supplied Moslem rulers with enough fighting manpower to allow them to overwhelm the last important independent Hindu state in south India, the empire of Vijayanagar, in 1565. And just at the close of our period almost the whole of Peninsular India was brought under the single sovereignty of the Mughal emperor Aurangzeb (1659–1707).

In southeast Asia, a coalition of Moslem coastal states combined to overthrow the Hinduized empire of Java between 1513 and 1526. Both before and after this coup, successful missionary activity, conducted by merchants and itinerant Sufi holy men, continued to spread Islam throughout the ports and coastal districts of southeast Asia as far as Mindanao in the Philippines and Borneo in Indonesia. Penetration of Africa continued, operating overland rather than by sea, and substituting caravans for ships. In both these great regions, the development of trade and market relations went hand in hand with an acceptance of Islam by those elements in the local population that were most active in the new sorts of economic activity such trade provoked. Subsequently, military operations and administrative pressures were often applied to bring the countryside and remoter parts into the Moslem fold. Thus a series of imperial Moslem states arose in west Africa — Timbuctoo, Kano, Bornu, and Morocco — whose policy toward pagans resembled that which Charlemagne had followed in northwestern Europe nearly a thousand years before when he converted the stubborn Saxons to Christianity by force.

In Europe itself resistance to Islam was better organized than in India, Africa, or southeast Asia. Yet there too, Moslem power advanced at the expense of Christendom. By 1543 most of Hungary came under Turkish administration. Thereafter recurrent border wars tended, as late as 1683, to favor the Turks as against both the Poles and the Hapsburgs in Austria. Ottoman military inferiority vis-à-vis the Europeans first became unmistakable during the long war, 1683–99, which began with the second Turkish siege of Vienna and ended with the transfer of most of Hungary from Ottoman to Austrian hands. Yet a provincial variant of Ottoman society continued to expand and consolidate itself in Roumania long after 1699, though it is true that Turkish power in this region of the empire was exercised only indirectly through Greeks of Constantinople.

In the western and central steppelands of Eurasia, Islam did suffer permanent territorial setback before 1700. Russia's advance at the expense of the Moslem khanates of Kazan, Astrakhan, and Sibir has already been mentioned. Farther east on the steppe, Islam suffered another equally serious defeat. Between 1550 and 1650 a revivified Tibetan Lamaism (the "Yellow Church") forestalled Islam in Mongolia and displaced it in the regions of central Asia around the Ili river.

EMPIRES OF ASIA c. 1600–1700

The steppe, however, was in itself poor and unpromising country. When trade routes ceased to run across the grasslands (being diverted north along the Siberian rivers and through the southern oceans), Moslem merchants and holy men, who had long been the principal propagators of Islam, simply ceased to frequent these lands. The remarkable missionary successes of Tibetan Lamaism on the steppe therefore owed something to the withdrawal of Moslem competition.

Inroads of European commerce. On the seas, matters were more complex. On both the Mediterranean and the Indian Ocean, Spanish and Portuguese fleets challenged and in critical battles defeated Moslem sea power. Yet the naval resources of the two Iberian states were never great enough to allow them to drive Moslem shipping from the seas. Hence a long series of Mediterranean struggles ended in 1578 with Turkish sea power dominant in the eastern Mediterranean, just as it had been in 1511 when the contest began. In the Indian Ocean, also, small and light Moslem ships recovered most of the trade they had lost to the Portuguese. Before the end of the sixteenth century the Portuguese even decided to admit Moslem vessels to ports under their control because they needed revenue from harbor tolls.

After 1600, however, a new regime began to assert itself upon the seas. Dutch, English, and French vessels supplanted Spanish and Portuguese as the principal merchantmen of the Indian Ocean and Mediterranean Sea. In the short run, this shift certainly looked like a victory for the Moslem cause. In each case the newcomers established their first footholds by virtue of special treaty arrangements with Moslem rulers, and refrained from any sort of Christian missionary activity. This represented a sharp change in policy. Missions had been as important as trade for the Portuguese and Spaniards; whereas the new Dutch, English, and French traders left the field of religious propaganda exclusively to the Moslems.

Nevertheless, the economic activities of the newcomers proved in the long run a much more powerful solvent to traditional Moslem styles of life than Iberian religious propaganda had ever been. Moslem minds, after all, were effectively closed against even the most eloquent and learned Christian missionary by the assurance, central to all Islamic learning, that Mohammed's revelation had corrected and therefore superseded the partial and distorted truths of Christianity. But Moslem society was by no means proof against economic rationalization and the expansion of market relations, especially when repercussions of the European price revolution lapped over into the realm of Islam.

Inland regions were, of course, least affected. At any great distance from salt water, age-old patterns of caravan trade and artisan production, peasant-town exchanges and interregional trade in luxury objects, remained almost unaffected by the business practices, organization, and energy of Europeans. But along the coasts far-reaching changes had begun to manifest themselves by 1700. In the Ottoman empire, for example, commercial agriculture made rapid advances, based in part on maize and tobacco brought from the Americas and on cotton come originally from India. The peasantries of Roumania, Bulgaria, Thrace, and Macedonia, together with others living in Anatolia, began to feed themselves and their animals on maize, and were able to export much larger quantities of wheat and cattle than before because the new American crop was so much more productive than older crops had been. The coastal lands of the Black Sea and the north Aegean were the main theaters of this development.

The rise of commercial agriculture in the Ottoman empire did not stimulate manufactures. Artisan guilds clung to traditional processes. They possessed powerful allies in the janissary corps, whose members intermingled with the artisans of all the main cities of the Ottoman empire after 1572 when these formidable soldiers were first legally permitted to marry. Entrepreneurial energy was diverted from industrial and commercial channels by the superior gains to be had by tax farming and making loans at high interest rates to aspirants for high office. Officials repaid such loans by mulcting the public in a variety of legal and extra-legal ways. Thereby, of course, they made new industrial or commercial ventures nearly impossible, since anyone who could afford to invest in a new enterprise became an obvious target for illegal "squeeze" at the hands of local officials. The absence of technical advance in manufactures and the restrictions upon entrepreneurial energy in trade meant that Ottoman exports tended to become almost exclusively agricultural. This resembled what had happened in the last centuries of Byzantine independence, when Italian cities took over the commerce of the Levant. The parallel surely augured ill for the economic health of Ottoman society.

In the Indian Ocean, European merchants also began to alter Asian economies by their systematic and organized pursuit of profit. The great European trading companies were under constant home pressure to export more goods to India and thus reduce the outflow of specie. But woolen cloth and other European manufactures were generally too coarse to command much sale in the warm climates that prevailed on the shores of the Indian Ocean. Dutch and English merchants had, therefore, to try to develop profitable carrying trade between Asian ports, for this alone would allow them to pay for the goods of Asian origin that they brought back to Europe without having to ship large quantities of gold and silver to India in exchange. They did so with very considerable success.

The English, for example, organized cotton cloth manufacture in western India by advancing small sums of money to the spinners and weavers. In return, they specified the sort of cloth they wished to have produced, and by regulating the scale of such advances could also affect the amount of cloth reaching the market. The "calicos" thus made to English specification were sold up and down the African and Asian coasts, wherever purchasers could offer anything of commercial value in exchange. This sort of trade stimulated rapid development of many parts of the southeast Asian coastlands, where relatively simple, subsistence societies had previously dominated the scene. Under such a regime, the coasts of Burma and Siam, for example, and the Philippine Islands, together with Java and Sumatra, underwent very rapid commercial development — mainly agricultural. East Africa, however, found it easier to export men. The African coast became the seat of a series of slave-raiding principalities and port cities supplying slaves to the Moslem world on a scale that rivaled but never equaled the west African slave trade with the Americas.

The areas of the spice islands which fell under Dutch control witnessed an even more intensive and systematic economic transformation. For the Dutch early embarked upon a policy of military conquest, and found it possible to pay the costs of administra-

tion by compelling local princelings to deliver specified quantities
of agricultural commodities that could be sold on the world
market. In this way the Dutch made local notables into plantation
overseers, and reduced the cultivators to a sort of semi-serfdom.
New crops were systematically introduced. Coffee from Arabia,
tea from China, and sugar cane from India were all imposed upon
the Javanese by the imperious demands of the Dutch, whose policy
was based on calculations of how to maximize profit by securing
the best assortment of commodities to suit an ever-changing market
demand.

Moslem political sovereignty, exerted in India and southeast Asia
through traditional administrative forms, was obviously far less important for the lives of Indian weavers and Javanese cultivators
than was the new, market-oriented, capitalistic enterprise directed
by English and Dutch agents of impersonal companies whose headquarters were in London or Amsterdam, and whose owners were
identified only by the possession of pieces of embossed paper called
stock certificates! Yet, in 1700 this was not easy to recognize. A
Moslem statesman or religious expert could very reasonably con-
gratulate himself upon how successfully the tried and true institutions of Islam had withstood the Iberian crusade which, at the
beginning of our period, had seemed as serious a threat as the
medieval Crusades had been in a still earlier time. In both cases, the
crusading movement had been blunted and then turned back successfully, while the realm of Islam had continued to expand. What
better proof of Allah's favor and of Islam's superiority to all other
faiths could be asked?

The Shi'a revolt. The smug self-satisfaction which such a frame
of mind induced was the more remarkable because at the very beginning of the sixteenth century Islam had experienced a profound
religious shock. Moslem lands had long been hospitable to various
religious sects, divided into the two general camps of Sunni and
Shi'a. Many Shi'a groups conformed outwardly to Sunni forms of
piety, but taught a secret doctrine to trusted initiates that was
sometimes, as among the Bektashi order of dervishes, fundamentally
subversive of all forms of organized religion. Most Moslem rulers

supported the Sunni position officially and tolerated dissenting groups as long as they made no overt attack upon the official religious establishment.

This *modus vivendi* was rudely shaken in the year 1500, when, after a series of rapid victories, a fanatical Shi'a sect of Turkish tribesmen saw their leader, Ismail Safavi, crown himself shah in Tabriz. In quick succession Ismail conquered Baghdad (1508) and then secured his eastern flank by administering a crushing defeat to the Uzbeks of Bokhara. In 1514 his forces met the imperial muster of the Ottoman empire at Chalderon; but despite defeat in the field Ismail had the satisfaction of seeing the victorious sultan withdraw because the Ottoman janissaries refused to press forward.

Shah Ismail's military career was not so very remarkable in itself, for Tamerlane (d. 1405) and other central Asian captains had previously been able to create great states almost as speedily. What made the establishment of the Safavi empire so disturbing to the Moslem world was that the shah's unlettered followers thought him to be Allah incarnate; and even his more learned and theologically erudite adherents, in whose ears such a claim was sacrilege, argued that as a descendant of the seventh of the twelve legitimate rulers of Islam, Shah Ismail was rightfully the head of the entire Moslem community.

Such claims, advanced with the full fanaticism of complete conviction and sustained by a series of striking military victories, introduced a profoundly disturbing element into the realm of Islam. For if the Safavi claims were correct, all other Moslem rulers were of course usurpers. In many parts of the Moslem world there were important groups of Shi'a sectarians who were prepared to listen sympathetically to such ideas. Indeed, Shah Ismail's supporters provoked a large-scale rebellion in Anatolia in 1514, defying Ottoman authority with fanatical zeal.

The Ottoman response was swift and effective: the sultan, Selim the Grim (ruled 1512–20), defeated the rebels of Anatolia and mercilessly hunted down remnants of the disaffected communities afterwards. This discouraged other Shi'a groups in other parts of the Ottoman empire from open revolt. He then pressed forward against Ismail himself, but as we have seen failed to destroy the root of the trouble because the janissaries refused to march onward against the heretical shah. In subsequent campaigns Selim annexed Syria, Egypt, and Arabia, thus forestalling an alliance between Ismail and the rulers of these lands and gaining control over the religiously strategic centers of Mecca and Medina. His successor, Suleiman the Lawgiver (ruled 1520–66), concentrated upon combatting Shi'a heresy by organizing Sunni orthodoxy at home. He instituted state support for Sunni religious colleges and state control of religious functionaries in all the important towns of the empire. Such a policy would have excited the liveliest resistance in earlier ages; but the Sunni doctors accepted Suleiman's regulations without demur, partly because of the attraction of state salaries, and partly because they feared the fanaticism and disorder that Shah Ismail's religious revolution threatened to spread throughout Islam.

From about 1514, Shah Ismail himself found that the fires of religious revolution needed control. He summoned doctors of Shi'a law, of the Twelver sect, from all over the Islamic world, and with their help set out to purify his lands of all traces of erroneous belief. In pursuit of this end he persecuted Sunni and dissenting Shi'a groups and confiscated their properties. Simultaneously, the vigorous popular propaganda upon which Ismail's power had originally been based was directed into more nearly orthodox channels. Doctrinally precise equivalents of the "shorter catechisms," which Protestant teachers were simultaneously imprinting upon the minds of their followers, spread familiarity with the tenets of the Twelver sect among nearly all of Ismail's subjects.

The duel between the Sunni and Shi'a versions of Islam, embodied so spectacularly in the collision between the Safavi and Ottoman monarchs, presented all the other Moslem states and peoples with an often embarrassing choice. Everywhere long-standing and traditional local arrangements between Sunni and Shi'a sects threatened to erupt into bitter struggles. Religious principles tended to become an index of political loyalty. The Mughals of India were particularly embarrassed. At low points in their fortunes, both Babur (d. 1530), the founder of the Mughal dynasty, and his

son Humayun (ruled 1530–56) publicly professed the Shi'a faith
in hope of securing much-needed aid from the shah. Later when
their position in India seemed more secure, they proclaimed their
independence of the Safavis by renouncing the Shi'a form of Islam
in favor of Sunni doctrine. Akbar (ruled 1556–1605), under
whose administration Mughal power became for the first time securely established, preferred to claim independent religious authority for himself. He experimented with Hindu and Christian as
well as Moslem forms of piety, to the agonized scandal of Roman
Catholic missionaries, who convinced themselves more than once
that the emperor was on the point of conversion.

Under Shah Abbas the Great (ruled 1587–1629) the power of the
Safavi state reached its peak, but the fires of religious conviction
had dimmed — at least in court circles — by that time. Ottoman
fears correspondingly relaxed, and in 1639, the sultan's government
concluded a lasting truce with their erstwhile enemy. Religious
tensions were, indeed, so much reduced that after 1656, when a reform administration achieved power in Constantinople, the new
Grand Vizier, Mohammed Kuprili, actually allowed crypto-Shi'a
groups to operate freely again in Ottoman society. One interesting
result was that for the first time in more than two hundred years
conversion from Christianity to Islam again assumed an important
scale in Crete, Albania, and southern Bulgaria, where dervish communities became especially active.

Intellectual retreat and artistic advance. The cultural repercussions of the Sunni-Shi'a split within Islam were as far-reaching as its
political-military consequences. Persian poetry dried up at its
source, since delicate ambiguities between divine and human love
upon which that poetry turned were anathema to the stern sec-
taries who followed Ismail. More important, perhaps, the learned
men of Sunni Islam failed, in a fundamental sense, to fulfill their
social responsibility. The doctors of Sunni Islam did not meet the
Shi'a challenge on its own terms — that is, as a religious doctrine
claiming to be true. Instead, they fell back on the secular arm and
everywhere repressed their rivals and critics by force. When,
therefore, at a later time European ideas and knowledge clearly
outstripped traditional Moslem lore, the learned class of the Otto-

man empire was in no position to investigate the new ideas responsibly. Having avoided one challenge by sheltering behind the police power of the Ottoman state, the experts in the Sacred Law also declined to grapple seriously with the second challenge, perhaps for fear of exposing their flanks to religious attack from within the Islamic community while trying to cope with Christendom's intellectual novelties. Better, they felt, to repeat the *Koran* and to memorize commentaries upon the Sacred Law and thus assure Allah's good favor. As long as Moslem military power remained great enough to meet all comers on equal terms, such resolute conservatism and anti-intellectualism was, of course, a tenable posture. Its eventual costs became clear only after 1700, when Moslem state power everywhere proved unable to resist new-sprung rivals.

Intellectual stultification, induced very largely by official policy, did not imply artistic decay. On the contrary, the rise of great empires in the Moslem world assured ample and comparatively stable patronage for architects and artists of all varieties. Isfahan, for example, was constructed as a garden city by order of Shah Abbas the Great. It is one of the most impressive monuments of architectural and city planning in the world. On a smaller but still very grand scale, the Taj Mahal of India was built to suit the Mughal emperor's taste between 1632 and 1653. Persian art, likewise, continued to flourish into the seventeenth century. In India new growth occurred when painters applied Persian techniques to Hindu religious themes. Such paintings appealed to "Rajput" landowners, whose Persianate culture and service to the Mughal empire did not wean them from the Hindu faith of their forefathers.

Indeed, by any standard except that set by the contemporary pace of cultural development in western Europe, Islam was in a flourishing condition between 1500 and 1700. Not decay, therefore, nor yet stagnation, but vigorous growth is the right phrase with which to describe Islamic society in this period. It is ironic to reflect — with benefit of hindsight — that precisely during these years of success Islam failed to grapple with or even to notice vital challenges which Europeans were beginning to present both on the economic and on the intellectual level.

Other religions under Moslem rule. Before turning from the Moslem to the Far Eastern cultural domain, something should be said about the history of the Hindus and Buddhists who found themselves under Moslem rule or on the edges of an expanding Islamic world. Likewise, the fate of the Orthodox Christians of the Balkans, who constituted an important part of the Ottoman body politic, deserves attention.

Between 1500 and 1700 Hinduism underwent a revival in India. Moslem conquest deprived Hinduism of state support, though the new rulers tolerated most traditional rites. This in effect forced the religion into the streets, where a company of holy men and poets provided India's ancient and amorphous faith with vibrant new foci of adoration.

The saint and revivalist, Chaitanya (d. 1534), was believed by his devotees to be a living incarnation of Krishna. He gathered around himself a substantial following which repudiated caste distinctions and other outwardnesses of religion in favor of intensely emotional public ceremonies. In Bengal, where Chaitanya spent most of his time, the new sect effectively stopped conversion to Islam. This meant that as Indian society slowly advanced eastward and tamed the jungles beyond the Ganges delta, conversion to Hinduism rather than to Islam became again the hall mark of incorporation into civilized society. The present-day division of Bengal between Pakistan and India is, of course, the direct result, for, as we saw, Islam had previously met with solid success along this frontier.

Two important poets, Sur Das (d. 1563) and Tulsi Das (d. 1627), did even more than Chaitanya to revivify Hinduism, since their influence was not confined to a single sect. Both used Hindi verse to develop themes from the rich tradition of Hindu mythology. They thus created a stock of chants and hymns suitable for religious celebrations that could be understood by the general public of northern India where Hindi was spoken. Tulsi fastened attention on the figure of Rama, Sur preferred Krishna: but both these deities were viewed as avatars of Vishnu. Thus there was no clash of doctrine between the two great renovators of Hindu piety. Save for the followers of Chaitanya, there was not even any repudiation of ancient Sanskrit piety or of Brahmanical ritual. But

Sanskrit was relegated to professionals. Daily religion found expression in the Hindi vernacular. The warm emotion generated by the adoration of a divine yet human deity, with whom the pious devotee could enter into mystic union in moments of public religious excitement, made popular Hinduism entirely proof against the arguments of both Moslem and Christian missionaries. Political eclipse after 1565 therefore altered the form but entirely failed to destroy the spirit of Hinduism. The overwhelming majority of Indians remained, as always, true to the protean religion of their ancestors.

Buddhism survived among three smaller peoples as a religion of state: the Singhalese of Ceylon, the Burmese of Burma, and the Thai of Siam. In each case Buddhism served as a national identity marker, protecting each of these peoples against the encroachment of polyglot, cosmopolitan faiths: first of Islam, then of Christianity. Those nations welcomed Christians at first, partly at least as counterweight to long-standing Moslem pressures, but as soon as the European presence seemed to threaten traditional ways in any important fashion, each instituted a policy of isolation and withdrawal. Not until the nineteenth century did the barriers thus erected against outsiders fall before a renewed European thrust.

The Orthodox Christian subjects of the Ottoman empire inevitably shared many of the experiences of their Turkish masters. Prejudice against the Latin west was as deep among Greek Orthodox Christians as among the Moslems themselves. Hence it is not surprising that when the Patriarch Cyril Lukaris (d. 1636) inaugurated doctrinal discussion of issues raised by Calvinists and Catholics from the west, his efforts met with suspicion and hostility. The effort died with him. Thereafter, the Orthodox hierarchy gave scope to the ambition of place hunters, but allowed both learning and piety to decay.

An important change in the relationship between the Ottoman government and the subject Christian communities came when the Sultan ceased to recruit members of his slave family from Christian villages of the Balkan wild west. As long as the highest officials and military leaders of the empire spent the first twelve to twenty years of their lives as peasant boys in remote, usually impoverished, mountain villages, a modicum of sympathy for the Christian peasantry pervaded the Ottoman administration. A very different bias prevailed when these posts came to be filled by the sons of placeholders — a transformation that came about gradually between 1572, when legal marriage was first permitted within the sultan's slave family, and 1638, when recruitment from Christian villages was discontinued.

When the high officials of the empire came to be city folk, born and bred, they began to exploit the villagers and to connive in the dubiously legal actions of others who sought to use peasant labor to establish commercial farming. Radical worsening of the villagers' lot was often the consequence. The cost was a widespread disaffection among the Christian populations.

A deep alienation between town and country — a fissure which approximately, but only approximately, coincided with the religious line between Christian and Moslem — had thus become a serious and fundamental weakness for Ottoman society by the end of the seventeenth century. Yet peasant disaffection was normal in most Christian states, and of itself should not be exaggerated into a sign of inevitable decay. It was the unwillingness — nay the inability — of Moslem minds to modify traditional attitudes and institutions to take account of challenges from within and from without that presaged decay, despite all the outward splendor of Moslem art, the complexity of Moslem learning, and the might of the Ottoman, Safavi, and Mughal empires.

XXII

The Far East, 1500–1700

IN 1513 when the first Portuguese merchant visited the south China coast, the Ming regime was already beginning to show the ills typical of decaying Chinese dynasties. Heavy and inequitable taxation together with court and clique intrigues provoked sporadic uprisings in the provinces, and raids from the steppe and from the sea were becoming serious. The Ming armies were numerous and well enough equipped. When well led they were capable of giving a good account of themselves. Between 1592 and 1598, for example, Ming troops helped Koreans to halt two formidable invasions from Japan, despite the best efforts of the Japanese war lord Hideyoshi. On the sea, Ming naval forces also won some notable victories, even over Portuguese ships. Yet the land-minded administration in Peking never authorized the creation of a permanent naval force, and disbanded sailors inevitably gravitated toward piratical enterprises, thus justifying the inveterate official distrust of seamen.

The final collapse of the Ming government came in a thoroughly traditional way. Acting in concert with a Ming general, a powerful and well-disciplined barbarian war band from Manchuria entered Peking in 1644 under the pretext of helping suppress a domestic rebellion. Once in possession of the capital, the Manchus refused to obey agents of the Ming emperor any longer, and instead proclaimed their own leader the Son of Heaven, thus founding a new dynasty, the Ch'ing. It took more years of war before the Manchus consolidated their hold over all of the Chinese mainland. Taiwan, the last refuge of a self-styled champion of the Ming cause, did not submit to Peking's authority until 1683.

The Manchus already had a fairly intimate acquaintance with Chinese civilization when they entered China as conquerors. No alien taint from western Asia, such as had colored Mongol culture at the time of their victories over the Chinese, prevented a smooth and rapid appropriation of all outward trappings of Chinese civilization by the new masters of the land. Nevertheless, the Manchu emperors distrusted the loyalty of native Chinese, and sought to keep military power in the hands of their own people. Garrisons of Manchu soldiers were therefore stationed at strategic points all over China. They maintained their own distinctive native dress and manner, for it became a matter of policy to keep the soldiers from mingling too freely with the Chinese population. The civil administration, however, employed Chinese as well as Manchus, and traditional methods of recruitment to the bureaucracy by state examinations based upon knowledge of the Confucian classics continued in force without more than local and temporary interruption.

Such a smooth transition from one dynasty to the next had seldom occurred before in China's long history. Moreover, the behavior of the Manchu emperors was completely traditional. They directed their main attention and the bulk of their forces to securing the land frontier of China against the steppe nomads and such restless neighbors as the Tibetans. In this they were extremely successful, thanks to the growing superiority civilized armament had over the old-fashioned horse archers of the steppe. Yet there was a novel aspect to the Manchu pacification of China's land frontier, for they had to deal not merely with nomad tribes but with the expanding agricultural empire of Russia as well. Russian fur traders, it will be recalled, had extended their operations right across Siberia in the early seventeenth century, reaching the Pacific at Okhotsk in 1638. Russian agents then sought, not without some success, to enter into relations with the steppe peoples lying southward of the Siberian forests. In addition, they had opened a trade in furs with China, where ermine was as much admired as it was in Europe.

After some sparring for advantage, in 1689 the two civilized nations agreed to the Treaty of Nerchinsk. According to this treaty the main portion of the steppe, in Outer Mongolia and farther west in central Asia, was to be a no man's land, insulating the two empires from one another. The treaty also provided for a regulated caravan trade, built around the exchange of tea and silk for furs. This settlement was unstable, however, because the Mongols and the Kalmuks, who inhabited the buffer zone, were not willing to play the neutral and passive role China and Russia had assigned to them. Instead, they entered into religious and diplomatic relations with Tibet. This aroused Chinese fears of a new barbarian league, potentially as dangerous as the never-to-be-forgotten hosts of Genghis Khan. To forestall such a possibility the Chinese embarked again upon a forward policy, and, since the Russian armies were then deeply engaged against the Ottoman Turks, the tsar's representative had to stand quietly by while the Chinese, after some severe fighting, conquered Outer Mongolia and Chinese Turkestan. Tibet then came obediently to heel. These campaigns were not completed until 1757, when the Kalmuk confederacy collapsed before Chinese armies and a smallpox epidemic. The remnant secured asylum in Russian territory and was planted near the Volga where their descendants still exist. Thirty years previously, in the Treaty of Kiakhta, the Russians had formally registered their acquiescence in this very substantial advance of Chinese power across almost half of the Eurasian steppe.

The Manchu emperors were equally successful in settling the problem of sea defenses. In 1638, for reasons of its own, the Japanese government forbade its subjects to sail the high seas, and stopped the construction of ocean-going vessels. This cut off the main source of the piratical raids that had plagued the China coast for more than a century. Agreement with the Europeans, concluded informally between local representatives of the Chinese administration and no less haphazardly appointed spokesmen for the Portuguese merchant community, had the effect of taming the ravages and controlling most of the illegal activities in which the first European merchant ships had freely engaged. Hence, the need for any departure from traditional methods of guarding the sea coast disappeared just when governmental stability returned to China. As was to be expected, therefore, the Manchus did nothing to build a navy or to improve their coastal defenses. They saw no need for such steps, and in fact there was none.

Prosperity and conservatism in China. The restoration of peace and regular administration throughout the vast Chinese mainland provided propitious conditions for a great upthrust of prosperity. Population began to grow rapidly. The new American crops — especially sweet potatoes and maize — allowed the agricultural community to expand *pari passu* with the growth of artisan manufactures and the expansion of commercial activity. Trade with European merchants became brisk. Portuguese ships long enjoyed an effective monopoly of the carrying trade between China and Japan, since neither government allowed its nationals to construct sea-going vessels. In addition, export of tea and porcelain and of a host of other Chinese wares to distant European drawing rooms steadily increased in scale. To supply these markets, Chinese entrepreneurs developed mass production of certain cheaper types of porcelain. But such changes merely strengthened traditional China by increasing its already enormous bulk without in the least straining the traditional articulations of society.

Cultural life demonstrated the massive conservatism of Chinese society. Nothing in the Chinese experience between 1500 and 1700 failed to fit into the frame of inherited learning and sensibility. To be sure Europeans brought some intriguing novelties to the attention of the learned world. New geographical information, improved astronomical skills, and such delightful devices as pendulum clocks were accorded the recognition they deserved. In 1601 a Jesuit mission headed by a learned Italian, Matteo Ricci, was even admitted to the court at Peking, but only after the Christian missionaries had acquired a decent veneer of Confucian learning so as to be able to communicate with the scholars of the court. The change of dynasty did nothing to disturb the Jesuit position in Peking. On the contrary, between 1640 and 1664 the head of the mission, Adam von Schall, established a remarkable friendship with the young Manchu emperor, and exercised some influence upon the conduct of the imperial government. Yet for all their position at the imperial court, the Jesuits seem to have made remarkably little impression upon the circle of learned mandarins with whom they associated, and their efforts to evangelize the population at large met with small success.

Instead, Chinese scholars and gentlemen fastened their eyes resolutely upon the classics and sought, by using the most careful critical methods they could invent, to establish the true meanings of old Confucian texts. A sparer, more philologically rigorous "Han school of learning" thus came into vogue, discouraging the bold flights of allegorical interpretation in which earlier generations of Neo-Confucianists had freely indulged.

No explanation is needed to understand why the Chinese declined to take seriously the learning and alien modes of thought professed by the "south sea barbarians" from distant Europe. When home institutions were working well, why indeed should wise, sober, and responsible men waste time on such trifles? And when the empire was formidable abroad, peaceful at home, rich, cultivated, and elegant, organized according to the principles of Confucian teaching, and properly decorous toward those who had spent long years of hard labor mastering the classics — when all this was true, why indeed should anyone pay more than passing attention to things foreign? Almost without exception, therefore, the Chinese followed the dictates of sound common sense, and took no more than casual notice of the novelties the Jesuit missionaries brought to China.

Hideyoshi and the Tokugawa shoguns of Japan. Japan's history during these two centuries was totally at variance with the majestic continuity of Chinese life. At the beginning of the period, Japan was in the throes of endemic civil war. Local samurai, monkish strong-arm bands, urban-based pirates, and footloose adventurers of every stripe, fought and double-crossed one another incessantly, under the fiction of an imperial administration. The arrival of the Portuguese in the 1540's brought a significant change to the scene.

The Japanese were impressed by many aspects of European civilization. A vogue for European styles of dress and for baptism into the Christian religion spread rapidly and widely through the islands. Not all of course approved such novelties, but few failed to

recognize the uses of European guns. Local lords eagerly traded
supplies of metals and other valuables for arms imported by the
Portuguese. But just as in Europe, when cannon and muskets became the decisive instruments in war, the increased cost of armaments meant that only large territorial sovereigns could afford what
it took to win victories. Rapid political consolidation was the result. Within less than half a century after the first Portuguese ship
touched at Japan, the entire Japanese archipelago had been effectively united under a great war lord, Hideyoshi (d. 1598).
Hideyoshi's authority was based upon successful leadership in the

field, for he was of humble birth and had served as a groom when a boy. His government rested upon alliances between a number of samurai clans, whose members were assigned income from particular villages in return for military services to their immediate chief, and through him to Hideyoshi himself.

Having consolidated his power over all Japan, Hideyoshi attempted to turn Japanese military energies outward. He organized two great attacks upon Korea, intending, if his manifestos are to be believed, to conquer the entire world! But, as we have seen, Hideyoshi's troops failed to win decisive success on the mainland, and when he died, the Japanese withdrew, since a fresh outbreak of civil war threatened. After a single battle, one of Hideyoshi's companions, Ieyasu of the Tokugawa family, succeeded in asserting his supremacy.

Japan's new ruler was a much less reckless and expansive character than Hideyoshi had been. He abandoned all thought of overseas conquest and instead set out systematically to guard himself against real or potential domestic rivals. This meant, first of all, controlling the sea rovers, for a samurai clan leader, disposessed in the wars at home, might always recoup his fortunes by a successful piratical cruise, and might even return home rich enough to try his hand at regaining what had been lost in earlier struggles. Such risks the Tokugawa shoguns — as Ieyasu and his successors are called — were unwilling to face. Accordingly, they first regulated and then forbade sea roving entirely, with the happy consequences for China's coastal security that we have already noticed.

The substantial Christian community of Japan also seemed dangerous to the shoguns. Hideyoshi himself had issued an edict in 1587 banning foreign missionaries from Japan, but had not seen fit to enforce his own decree, perhaps because he feared that the Portuguese would retaliate by breaking off trade with him. After 1609, when Dutch ships first appeared in Japanese waters, the Japanese had an alternative channel through which they could supply themselves with whatever they needed from Western arsenals. It therefore became safe to launch sporadic persecutions against the Japanese Christian community. Then in 1637 a Christian revolt broke out in Kyushu, and the shogun determined upon their entire destruction. A full year was required before the last Christian stronghold was taken. The struggle was to the death. All captured Christians, whether Europeans or Japanese, were executed out of hand. A few secret conventicles survived, but they were weak and without influence. Almost the entire Christian population of Japan was destroyed, bringing to a bloody and disastrous end a venture that had been by far the most successful mission in any civilized Asian country.

For more than two hundred years thereafter the Tokugawa shoguns continued to rule Japan. Yet for all the outward rigidity of their government, important changes in the economic and cultural life of the country continued to keep Japanese society and civilization under severe though hidden strain, far different from the serene stability Chinese life seemed to have attained by 1700. The core of the problem was that the samurai found themselves without a meaningful occupation as soon as warfare ceased. They could waste time in a genteel way by elaborating the code of the warrior, engaging in approved ceremonies appropriate to their station in life, while waiting endlessly for the summons to action which never came. Or else they could plunge into the expensive delights of town amusement quarters, where a vigorous, sensuous, and entirely unofficial cultural life quickly developed.

Many samurai in fact went bankrupt and sold or mortgaged their legally assigned right to collect rice from the villages. Merchants who bought such rights usually transported the rice they had acquired to town markets. Consequently, a bustling market economy insinuated itself between the peasant and landholding classes, and reached far down into the interstices of Japanese society, affecting almost the entire population. Against such forces, the best efforts of the shogun's government to reinforce traditional patterns of samurai life met with very imperfect success. Instead Japan presented the spectacle of a profound duality between the vigorous vulgarity of the towns and the austere decorum of official culture.

Yet this seemingly antithetical duality continued to prevail in Japan as long as the shogunate lasted. Perhaps the two modes of life were really complementary, the attractions of the one remedying the deficiencies of the other.

XXIII

The Old Regime in Europe

1648–1789

THE volcanic passions loosed in Europe by the Reformation and Counter Reformation subsided after 1648. Leaders of both church and state recoiled from the attempt to enforce total conformity to theological or any other sort of truth. Carefully skirting both the heights and depths of human passion, the leaders of European society preferred to rely on the competence of trained professionals, whose grasp on truth could only be partial and whose temper was seldom fanatic. Tepid professionalism therefore found new scope in all the strategic loci of society: in barracks, pulpits, law courts, universities, schools, government bureaus, and even in the offices of such new-sprung instruments of power as chartered companies and banks. By providing a secure niche and useful function for these and still other specialized professions, European society opened wide the door for pluralism of thought and sensibility as never before. Each profession, pursuing its own limited vision of the truth, advanced and elaborated upon the work of earlier generations, and felt no pressing need to erect or conform to any overarching grand synthesis of all truth and knowledge. So long as their own professional autonomy and dignity were not flouted, Europe's men of affairs found it perfectly possible to let others in other walks of life think and, within limits, act as they pleased.

Pluralism and compromise had of course been present in European as in every other civilized society from the time civilization first began. Indeed, one definition of civilization is a society in which occupational specialization exists. What was new in the second half of the seventeenth century in Europe, therefore, was not so much the fact as its recognition, and a willingness to tolerate discrepancies and divergencies which the most strenuous reforming efforts of preceding generations had been unable to remove. Moderation, balance, manners: these could replace the impassioned striving after metaphysical certainty which had for so long inspired Europeans to denounce and destroy one another. Logic certainly suffered from such compromise, but common sense and the fact that it worked supported the new professionalized piecemeal approach to problems of truth and morals.

Limited wars. Moderation, balance, and manners even infected interstate relations. Something approaching a code of professional conduct for diplomats and soldiers defined itself in the decades after the close of the disastrous Thirty Years' War. Formalization of warfare reached its peak, perhaps, at the battle of Fontenoy (1745), when French and English officers courteously offered one another the privilege of firing first. Thereafter, the intensity of European warfare tended again to increase. Weapons became more destructive and the political stakes larger, until French revolutionary leaders once again armed and unleashed popular passions upon the battlefield.

Between 1653 and 1689 France enjoyed a definite superiority over her rivals. In his boyhood, King Louis XIV (1648–1715) witnessed the failure of the last aristocratic effort to assert noble rights against the king by armed rebellion (the so-called Fronde, 1648–53). As a grown man, he set the victorious royal armies the task of winning for France the "natural boundaries" of the Rhine and Pyrenees. His initial successes at the expense of the tattered Spanish empire ground to a halt when the Dutch and English (1689) entered into alliance with the Hapsburgs to check French aggression. Thereafter, England and France conducted a series of wars in which dominion over North America and India were at stake, while on the continent the Austrians reaped the major fruit of the final dismemberment of Spain's European empire by taking over Spain's position in Italy and the southern Netherlands (Wars of the Spanish Succession, 1700–1713). By 1763 England (became Great Britain in 1707) won decisive victory overseas in India and Canada — a success only partly undone in the next generation when French aid (1778–83) allowed rebellious British colonists to make good their effort to establish an independent nation in North America.

While western Europe experienced these tumultuous yet limited actions, eastern Europe witnessed a more drastic realignment of power. After 1648, Poland and Sweden, like the Dutch in western Europe, ceased to be able to defend their status as great and imperial powers. Instead, Austria, and a new-sprung German state, Brandenburg-Prussia, competed with Russia for Swedish and Polish territories (1648–1721) and completed the job toward the close of the century by partitioning Poland between them (1773–95).

Central Europe remained a sort of bridge (and not infrequently a convenient theater of war) between Europe's western and eastern balances of power. The small states into which Italy and Germany had been divided by the Treaty of Westphalia continued to incline either to a French or to an anti-French alliance, depending on local conditions and rivalries, dynastic ties, and — at least sometimes — upon straightforward sale to the highest bidder.

Balancing intranational interests. Within each of the sovereign states of Europe, the government recognized no legal limits to its freedom of action in matters of foreign policy. Yet in fact calculations of the balance of power restricted any one ruler's freedom of maneuver within rather narrow bounds. Similarly, each European monarch, even when claiming absolute power over his subjects, was in fact limited by a tangle of countervailing interests and privileges, traditionally distributed among different groups and classes. Moreover, these diverse interests usually had some sort of corporate organization that could and did give them effective political weight.

Thus the stately grandeur of Louis XIV's court and his proud boast, "*L'état, c'est moi,*" disguised a very different reality. Even in Louis's youth, when energetic officials in his service sought to carry through a systematic centralization of French administration, the countervailing force of corporate immunities, some of long standing (e.g. the provincial representative assemblies or "Estates" of France), and others newly established (e.g. the French East India Company), severely limited the practical success French bureaucrats achieved. Nevertheless, royal policy attained its central aim: the taming of the aristocracy. But King Louis XIV secured this end as much through a judicious distribution of pensions and court offices, as by direct suppression of noble rights and privileges.

After Louis XIV's death, the French aristocrats set out to reclaim some of their vanished independence, but did so by legal process and argument rather than by attempting, as their forefathers had so often done, to resort to force. Military and civil administration had advanced to such a point that any other course had become wildly impractical. For ordinary men, the consequent reduction of violence and the establishment of a regimen of law in the countryside were the central and basic achievements of the Old Regime in France, and in other west European countries.

The precise equilibrium between competing interests and corporate groups varied from state to state and from time to time, creating an ever-changing pattern. Generally speaking, the Hapsburg lands both in Spain and Austria, lagged perceptibly behind the French. In these lands the centralizing drive of bureaucratic reform, seeking to reduce or eliminate local differences, found its main expression in the eighteenth century. The Church retained far greater independence in the lands under Hapsburg jurisdiction than was the case in France, where Gallicanism — that is, the doctrine that there was and should be a separate French church within the Roman Catholic fold — had prevailed from medieval times. In practice, Gallicanism meant a close subordination of bishops and other dignitaries of the French church to the royal government.

English parliamentarianism. Toward the outer edges of western Europe, two quite atypical governments assumed distinctive form between 1640 and 1688. By a remarkable coincidence it was pre-

EUROPE 1648-1789

——— Boundary of the Holy Roman Empire, 1648
··········· Boundary of the Ottoman Empire, 1648

RUSSIA

Black Sea

OTTOMAN EMPIRE

Constantinople

POLAND

Dnieper R.

Kiev

Danube R.

VISTULA R.

SWEDEN

DENMARK

BRANDENBURG

To Prussia
1742

SILESIA

BOHEMIA

AUSTRIAN HAPSBURGS

AUSTRIA

Vienna

HUNGARY

To Hanover
1719

GERMANY

HOLLAND

Rhine R.

SWITZ.

Po R.

ITALY

Rome

NAPLES
(Aust. 1714–
Sp. 1735)

Adriatic Sea

SARDINIA

CORSICA

SICILY

GREAT
BRITAIN

London

IRELAND

Paris

FRANCE

Rhône R.

PYRENEES

SPANISH HAPSBURGS
(1735)
(1700)

Mediterranean Sea

Madrid

SPAIN

Gibraltar
(Br. 1713)

PORTUGAL

*Atlantic
Ocean*

Scale of Miles

0   500

351

cisely during these years that English parliamentarianism on the
one flank and Prussian militarism on the other achieved their decisive formulations. The English civil wars (see above) were the
crucible from which parliamentary sovereignty emerged; but a
workable adjustment between old-fashioned localism (so vigorously represented by the squires and burgesses of the House of
Commons) and the requirements of national policy was made only
after the Glorious Revolution of 1688. During the reigns of
Charles II (1660–83) and his brother James II (1683–88), the restored Stuart monarchs not unnaturally found it difficult to trust
Parliament, and, in fact, accepted subsidy from France to allow
them to get along without too slavish a dependence on parliamentary grants. Successful national policy could scarcely be conducted
under such conditions.

Circumstances changed abruptly with the Glorious Revolution
of 1688, which brought the Stadtholder of Holland, William of
Orange, to the English throne. William's interests focused on the
continent, where he became leader of the diplomatic-military coalition forming against Louis XIV. He was perfectly prepared to
leave the government of England to Parliament, if parliamentary
leaders would supply him the necessary means for keeping Louis
XIV in check. Thereafter, until George III mounted the throne in
1760, no English monarch attempted to evade or control parliamentary leaders, who thus developed the habit of and created the
needful institutions for governing the country with a nice respect
for the competing demands of local, national, and international
concerns.

To meet these requirements, English politicians and parliamen-
tarians developed cabinet government. The cabinet was appointed
by the crown, to be sure, but was responsible to Parliament. The
cabinet's ability to pass legislation by securing the votes of a parliamentary majority was based upon a loose but real clique-and-party
system of alliances among the members of Parliament. Despite occasional fumbling and frequent rumblings of dissatisfaction on the
part of the worsted party, this system of government had the virtue
of being able to register incessant changes in the assortment of interests represented in Parliament. No centralized bureaucracy of

the eighteenth century could adjust so sensitively to social changes. In this lay the essential superiority of parliamentary government as practiced in eighteenth-century England. It was not in the least a democratic regime, for the unpropertied majority together with religious dissenters had no representation at all, and rotten boroughs and political patronage allowed men of wealth and birth to dominate Parliament completely.

Brilliant success against the French in the Seven Years' War (1756–63) proved how formidable such government might be. Correspondingly, the failure of King George III's effort to control Parliament by developing a King's party that would rise above petty and selfish interests was sealed by his embarrassing defeat in the War of the American Revolution (1776–83). Hence, by piecemeal and entirely unsystematic evolution, the pattern of English (after 1707, when Scotland and Ireland were united with England, British) government diverged increasingly from the norm of bureaucratic monarchy which prevailed on the continent. Particularly after 1763, there were Frenchmen and others on the continent who came to believe that British parliamentarianism, which had seemed an archaic and disorderly survival from a medieval past in 1640 and 1688, might in fact provide a useful model for the reorganization of their own more rigid governmental system.

Prussian militarism. Prussia's development was very different. Under stern and unremitting prodding from Frederick William, the Great Elector (ruled 1640–88), the scattered territories he had inherited from his Hohenzollern ancestors were welded together into a tightly centralized and strictly disciplined state. The drastic experience of the Thirty Years' War, when Brandenburg (which lay at the heart of the Hohenzollern possessions) had been repeatedly subject to devastation by Swedish and other foreign troops, disarmed local resistance to the Great Elector's policy. He aimed to achieve sufficient military strength to repel attack and was prepared to pay almost any price. The cost was certainly high, for his lands were poor and not very thickly inhabited. Yet, he was able by severest parsimony and unremitting care to create a standing army powerful enough not only to defend, but to enlarge his territories. His successors carried on the same policy, with no less success though with an increasingly relaxed temper. At his death, Frederick II, the Great (reigned 1740–86), left a much enlarged and territorially consolidated state, the kingdom of Prussia, which had become one of the great powers of Europe, rivaling Austria in the Germanies and dealing with Russia, the colossus of the east, on even terms.

Hohenzollern policy evinced systematic concern for economic development. Prussia's kings well knew that manufactures and population provided the sinews of victory in war. So successful were they in developing the unpromising sandy soils and limited mineral resources under their administration that Prussia began, by the end of the eighteenth century, to assume more of the social complexity familiar to more westerly lands. Artisans, merchants, professional men, and other urban classes became more numerous and influential. As this occurred, the barracks atmosphere, which had been so distinctive in the time of the Great Elector and his immediate successors, receded. Yet it did not disappear from Prussian life. It merely retreated within the narrower circle of the professional officer corps, which was recruited mainly from among younger sons of the landowning squirearchy ("Junkers") of East Prussia and adjacent Baltic lands.

Advances in agriculture and technology. Europe's economic life underwent continued rapid escalation throughout the period of the Old Regime. Agriculture remained basic, and the great majority of the population continued everywhere to work as farmers, even in the most highly urbanized countries. In wide regions customary patterns of cultivation continued. Wherever the manorial style of collective cultivation had rooted itself, there were great obstacles to making any important changes in familiar routines, since overlapping property rights were likely to require unanimous (or nearly unanimous) consent for any important alteration. Nevertheless, even within old rhythms of work great increases of harvest could come from such simple procedures as systematic seed selection, or by improvements in plow design.

Some important departures took place in westernmost Europe.

New crops like clover and turnips came into use, providing adequate winter fodder for horses and cattle — always the vulnerable
point of medieval husbandry. In addition, turnips required careful
cultivation, which eliminated weeds from the fields (as could not
be done when only grain was planted); and clover helped to improve soil fertility by the fixation of nitrogen on its roots. The
spread of potatoes was, however, the single most important change
in European agriculture, for this very greatly enlarged food-
producing capacity. On the sandy soils and in the cool climate of
Baltic Germany, for example, as much as four times the number of
calories could be had from a crop of potatoes as from grain. This
permitted a dramatic upthrust of German population and prosperity, which began to manifest itself from about 1750, when potatoes
first became important in central Europe. Maize played a similar
role in the Balkans and in Hungary; but northern Europe was too
cool for maize to thrive, and western Europe too wet.

Manufactures and communications saw a similar improvement.
France took the lead in developing all-weather roads and a system
of canals that linked all the important river systems of the country
into a single network. Only after 1750 did the English begin to
catch up. In manufactures, however, the relationship tended to be
reversed, for private enterprise and empirical inventiveness found
freer scope in Britain than in the more tightly regulated economies
of the continent. In addition, English coal fields were abundant and
easily exploited. The invention of coking (c. 1709) permitted the
use of coal for smelting iron ores. Then in turn, a more abundant
supply of iron and steel allowed the substitution of metal for wood
in the working parts of many machines.

The most significant departure, however, was the development
of powerful engines, using steam pressure derived from the burning of coal to produce mechanical energy. As early as 1712
Thomas Newcomen invented a crude steam engine to pump water
from mine shafts. It depended on atmospheric pressure working
against a partial vacuum produced by the condensation of steam. In
1769 James Watt patented a much-improved engine, which used
live steam to drive a piston in a closely fitted cylinder. Since Watt's
engine did not require alternate heating and cooling as New-

comen's had done, it was vastly more efficient. Very quickly it was put to work providing power for factories and mines, and before long, for transportation too.

Among the most spectacular uses for Watt's steam engine was the driving of textile machinery, whose size and complexity had grown rapidly throughout the eighteenth century. The result was a tremendous increase in the amount of cloth that could be produced in a given period of time and the rapid cheapening of the final product. By 1789, indeed, English mills using cotton grown in India and imported to England around the Cape of Good Hope were able to undersell the Indian handweavers in India itself! No more startling demonstration of the technological advance brought by England's eighteenth-century success in harnessing coal, iron, and mechanical ingenuity could be conceived, for the skill of Indian weavers and the cheapness of their labor had previously excelled all rivals in the entire world.

Changes, sometimes small, sometimes fundamental, came to nearly all the traditional crafts of Europe. In addition, new crafts were created by systematic and deliberate imitation of the products of other lands. The most spectacular instance of this enrichment of European skills was the way in which craftsmen, scientists, entrepreneurs, and government officials collaborated to duplicate Chinese porcelain. The Chinese guarded their trade secrets well, and it was only after prolonged trial and error that Europeans learned how to produce porcelain almost indistinguishable from the Chinese.

At least as important as any of these technical improvements was the simultaneous development of organizational forms that permitted Europeans to mobilize greater and greater resources for undertakings requiring long exertion and the co-operation of large numbers of persons for successful results. The importance of joint stock companies for European overseas operations was mentioned above. In addition, such important fiscal devices as central banks and national debts were introduced during the Old Regime, thus beginning to free economic relations from restrictions imposed by limitations on the supply of gold and silver, and introducing an initially ill-understood and very violent cyclic fluctuation into the price system. Indeed, the first runaway credit boom (South Sea Bubble, 1718–20) so discredited joint stock companies that they were made illegal in all leading European countries — a situation that continued to prevail until the nineteenth century.

Europeans also explored the potentialities of another powerful device for co-ordinating industrial processes by learning how to supplement craftsmen's manual skills with the precision of mathematical measurement. The boring of cannon and of musket barrels required close accuracy, if the finished weapon were to fire properly. Equally, Watt's steam engines required a close fit between pistons and cylinder walls, and a general matching up of gear wheels, screw threads, bearings, and other moving parts. Clocks, watches, telescopes, and microscopes could only be made by specialists who were able to cut parts to specified dimensions so that the separate pieces could be assembled into a whole that really worked. This required dexterity of hand and eye, but also depended on a more and more precise mathematical definition of each task and accurate measurement of the product at each stage of manufacture.

These aspects of European economic organization remained rudimentary in 1789, and found their major application only later. Nevertheless, the start had been made, the idea was known, its practicability had been demonstrated. The possibilities of radical rationalization of manufacturing processes had been adumbrated to Europe's enormous advantage and further enrichment.

Mathematics and sciences. During the second half of the seventeenth century, Europe's intellectual energies, which had been concentrated on religious debate for more than a century, shifted focus rather abruptly.

Mathematics had been undergoing rapid development throughout the Reformation age, when men like Johannes Kepler (d. 1630) and Galileo Galilei (d. 1642) had been active. New notations helped to broaden and simplify calculations and induced new concepts. In particular, the sciences of geometry and algebra, which had been studied separately since the time of the Greeks, began to merge, thereby creating analytic geometry. Analytic

geometry in turn gave rise to "fluxions" or the calculus, which enlarged the scope and refined the power of mathematical reasoning,
as well as having important applications in the study of physics.

So great was the vogue for mathematics that many men felt sure
that appropriately rigorous and careful application of the techniques of mathematical reasoning to any and all questions of the
human condition might reach true and universally acceptable conclusions. René Descartes (d. 1650) was the first influential man to
make this bold attempt. His deductive reasoning from axioms and
self-evident first principles, in the manner of the geometricians, was
so persuasive that a school of enthusiastic Cartesians rapidly developed in France and elsewhere. They vigorously popularized and
defended Descartes's views. Others were fired by the same vision
of mathematical certainty, but, alas, came to different and mutually
incompatible conclusions. Baruch Spinoza (d. 1677) in Holland
and Thomas Hobbes (d. 1679) in England and France were
among the most famous of these philosophers. In the next generation, Gottfried Wilhelm Leibniz (d. 1716) nourished the same
ambition.

These philosophers lacked any satisfactory way of settling their
differences, for there was no empirical test by which disinterested
experts could choose between their rival views. The matter was
otherwise with the magnificently elegant analysis of physical and
astronomical motions developed by Isaac Newton (d. 1727) in his
book *Philosophiae Naturalis Principia Mathematica,* published in
1687. Like his predecessors, Newton sought to reduce observed
multiplicity to mathematical order. To explain the behavior of
moving bodies, both in the heavens and on earth, he hypothesized a
mysterious force — universal gravitation. This he supposed operated in space according to an absurdly and delightfully simple
mathematical formula — diminishing between any two bodies with
the square of the distance.

Some of Newton's contemporaries boggled at the mystical implications of a force acting at a distance. Newton's efforts to clarify
the issue by speaking of an ethereal substratum and, in another
passage, of space as "the mind of God," did not help much to re-

lieve such anxieties. But what did convince almost everyone was the fact that Newton's theory could be tested empirically. Newton's laws of motion had originally been generated through his effort to express mathematically the motion of the moon. But there were innumerable other moving bodies that could be used to test the accuracy of his formulas. On the basis of such observations and measurements it soon appeared that the formulas did work. Reality in fact conformed to Newton's laws of motion.

In our own time, scientific prediction and the operation of natural law are usually taken for granted. It requires, therefore, an act of the imagination to understand how extraordinary and exciting such discoveries were when they were new. Men who had been brought up to conceive the universe as ruled by a very active, personal God, who might intervene in any situation at any moment to work a miracle of conversion or to forgive a past transgression, found the Newtonian vision of the universe both liberating and frightening. God, it appeared, was a mathematician and had chosen to create the universe accordingly. In such a universe it seemed almost beneath God's dignity to work a miracle, for that would involve the local and temporary cancellation of his own decree, and a confession of the inadequacy of natural law to achieve all good and necessary aims. A starker contrast with the world view of Luther or Loyola, which turned upon an intensely personal and completely unpredictable relationship between God and each single human soul, could scarcely be imagined.

Yet most men, even after they had been persuaded to accept a Newtonian view of the natural universe, remained Christian. Newton himself wrote Biblical commentaries in which he attempted to discover hidden meanings in Holy Writ; and his long lifetime (1642–1727) was particularly prolific of new religious movements that emphasized personal relation with and experience of God. Within Protestantism, for example, the Quakers and Methodists of England and the Pietists of Germany got their start while Newton was still alive. Among the Roman Catholics, Jansenism and Quietism achieved their greatest influence in Newton's time. Official reprobation by the papacy resulted in the eventual disappearance of both these schools of piety, but the three Protestant movements, despite all intervening changes, continue to flourish today.

Other sciences proved rather less amenable to definitive mathematical formulation. Much was done to collect information about the various forms of plant and animal life, and new knowledge about distant human societies, both civilized and savage, poured into Europe as missionaries and other men of learning recorded their observations. Yet a mathematical formulation of the biological and social sciences failed to emerge from the cloud of new information. To be sure, a Swedish botanist, Carl Linnaeus (d. 1778), hit upon a system of classifying plants which has remained standard since, and a school of "physiocrats" in France, with Adam Smith (d. 1790) in Scotland, did attempt, with rather impressive success, to deduce what would happen to trade and industry if governments refrained from interfering with natural human propensities. On the assumption that men were motivated by rational self-interest they concluded that wealth as well as liberty would be advanced by such a policy. Unlike Newton's laws of motion, such laissez-faire theories were never put to the test of experience, since governments and men persistently declined to behave rationally.

Political theories, historiography, and empirical philosophy. Two other dimensions of social thought underwent very significant change. First, a new theory of political legitimacy had to be developed by men who no longer could take it for granted that God did intervene in everyday human affairs. A king claiming to rule by divine right was in fact a mere usurper unless God had in fact chosen him for his office from among all available candidates. Men who accepted the Newtonian view of the universe certainly found it hard to believe the older theory, particularly since so many kings seemed grossly unfit for their office. Solution to this problem was found in the idea of a social contract whereby tacitly or in some more active and definite way all the human beings living within a particular state were assumed to have reached agreement as to the forms and powers of government. Obviously, by assigning different terms to such a contract very different practical conclusions could be drawn. Thomas Hobbes, for example, ar-

gued that men, being nasty and brutish by nature, had been able
to establish civil society only by delegating unlimited power to an
absolute sovereign. John Locke (d. 1704) on the contrary held
that the contract lay between the public and the ruler, so that if the
ruler overstepped specified bounds the people were justified in re-
belling against his usurpation. In this way Locke was able to defend
the Glorious Revolution of 1688, which had evicted an undeniably
legitimate monarch from the English throne to the scandal of many
Englishmen who clung to old-fashioned ideas of Divine providence
and feared recrudescence of the recently concluded civil wars.
Across the Channel a far more radical view was propounded in the
next century by Jean-Jacques Rousseau (d. 1778), who held that
the social contract justified rebellion whenever the sovereign failed
to satisfy the people, in whose Common Will resided inalienable
and indefeasible sovereignty.

The other major change in men's view of themselves was a by-
product of the patient labors of numberless philologians, numis-
matists, historians, and other scholars. Their perseverance in sort-
ing out Europe's complex heritage of literary and historical
manuscripts, discovering how to translate dates from one calendri-
cal system to another, and arranging reigns, battles, and other
historical events into a reliable chronological sequence, gave a
depth and accuracy to historical knowledge which had never
before been approached. The greatest single figure in this world of
scholarship was Jean Mabillon (d. 1707), who established a sophisticated knowledge of the different types of handwriting used in
different ages and at different monasteries and royal chanceries in
the early Middle Ages so that it became possible to discover
— sometimes at a glance — where a given manuscript came from
and approximately how old it was. The same expertness of course
allowed detection of the numerous forgeries which had been in-
serted into the historical record at various times in the past for various purposes, and provided European scholarship with tools and
concepts which were later to be applied to the study of other civilizations. Just at the end of the eighteenth century, the first exciting
fruit of this venture came to public attention, when William Jones
(d. 1794) discovered that Sanskrit, the sacred language of India,

was closely related to the languages of Europe, and of such antiquity that it promised to provide an eager European world with fresh insight into the nature of their own most primitive ancestors!

These scholarly labors allowed men to write far more accurate and fuller histories than ever before. Edward Gibbon's *History of the Decline and Fall of the Roman Empire* (published 1776–88), is the most famous instance of what had become possible; but other historians, like Voltaire (d. 1778) and David Hume (d. 1776) were almost as popular at the time. By inserting between their own age and the time when Christianity had first been established a long and complex human history, with all its variety of episodes and personality, the ferocity of past quarrels and fluctuations of moral as well as of theological standards, the historians in their way also dampened the fires of religious controversy. For with a fuller vision of the historical past in mind, an immediate return to apostolic conditions in church and state — which had been the great hope of the Reformation age — ceased to seem possible or, perhaps, in view of the conduct of some of the Roman emperors, desirable!

While political theory and history flourished mightily, metaphysics passed through the needle's eye of empirical criticism and emerged strong and healthy, if a bit abstruse and far removed from day-to-day concerns. The confident deductive reasoning of Descartes and his fellow seventeenth-century philosophers came under the scrutiny of a group of English empiricists. First John Locke (d. 1704) and then David Hume (d. 1776) asked the embarrassing question of how sense experience is related to human ideas, and came up with the conclusion that certain knowledge about anything is impossible. Immanuel Kant (d. 1804) accepted Hume's conclusions, but turned his critical logic around by arguing that careful analysis of the structure and capacities of the human mind would give us accurate and necessary knowledge about the nature of all possible sensory experiences, since the unknowable thing-in-itself could only come to consciousness by conforming to human sensibilities and modes of thought. In this fashion Kant opened the door wide for nineteenth-century German philosophers to anatomize the Spirit, whose creative role in defining knowable reality Kant had so persuasively pointed out.

The arts, classical and romantic. By comparison with the progress of natural and social science, which inaugurated a new era in the second half of the seventeenth century, the fine arts, with the exception of music, remained conservative. Styles came and went, national schools rose to eminence or suffered comparative eclipse, and all along the way a tendency to add to an already richly various cultural inheritance manifested itself. But nothing as radically novel as the Newtonian world view emerged from such vigorous, but traditional, activity.

At the end of the seventeenth and the beginning of the eighteenth centuries, the prestige of French culture reached its apogee. Admiration for the power and grandeur of Louis XIV's government mingled with an equal or greater admiration for French literature, manners, taste. Classicism, which rested upon a belief that rules for artistic excellence could be discerned and should be followed, prevailed in both the visual and literary arts. In the hands of a great artist, such rules were no hindrance. Architect Christopher Wren (d. 1723) in London, or the three great classical dramatists of France, Pierre Corneille (d. 1684), Molière (d. 1673), and Jean Racine (d. 1699), for example, conformed with grand effect to rules of correctness, which in lesser hands became heavy baggage indeed.

In the eighteenth century, European music entered upon one of its greatest periods. New or newly perfected instruments and a physico-mathematical analysis of musical pitch gave musicians new technical range and variety. With so much that was new to digest, the "classical" rules of harmony and composition did not act as hampering limitations, as such rules sometimes did in literature, but instead stimulated creativity by focusing attention on a manageable range of variables. The work of Johann Sebastian Bach (d. 1750) and of Wolfgang Amadeus Mozart (d. 1791) established a norm for subsequent European music which became almost as fundamental, though not so enduring, as the norm created for European painting by the invention of linear and aerial perspective in the fifteenth century.

In literature the classical ideal tended to wear thin after the middle of the eighteenth century, particularly in Germany and England. Researches into the national and medieval past, and persuasive investigations of the palpitating flux of feeling nicknamed the human heart, combined to persuade many Germans and some Englishmen that true literary greatness could only be achieved by giving free reign to spontaneous impulse. This romantic point of view was associated with a new valuation for the language of the common folk and of the nation. Johann Gottfried Herder (d. 1803), for example, argued with passion that Germans could achieve national and literary greatness only by using German, not French. A similar interest in the national springs of literature inspired Thomas Percy (d. 1811) to compile and publish traditional English and Scottish ballads in his book *Reliques of Ancient English Poetry* (published 1765).

Yet it would be erroneous to put too much weight upon the traditional classification of Europe's cultural history into a classical followed by a romantic age. At all times a great diversity of taste and artistic creativity prevailed. In the history of English literature, for example, John Milton (d. 1674) wrote his great Christian epic *Paradise Lost* precisely when William Wycherley (d. 1716) was producing bawdy Restoration comedies; and toward the close of our period the artful simplicity of Robert Burns (d. 1796) confronted with equanimity the periodic sentences of Dr. Samuel Johnson's (d. 1784) sesquipedalian prose. Similarly, Luther's Bible and Shakespeare's plays never passed out of fashion in their respective countries, while the classical literatures of ancient Rome and Greece irradiated the separate national literatures of Europe by providing all educated men with a common stock of knowledge and range of sentiments upon which writers and artists could play, knowing that elliptical references and casual allusions to the Greek and Latin classics would be easily and immediately understood.

Roots of Europe's dominance. Richness, variety, vigor, and a readiness to grapple with any novelty that might swim within man's ken distinguished the cultural life of Europe in the days of the Old Regime. No other part of the world exhibited anything like such an adventurous spirit. For the first time, therefore, Europe began conspicuously to pull ahead of the other, more conservative civilizations of the Old World — not merely in matters technological and military, but in science, philosophy, history, and scholarship. Where unabashed and untrammeled application of reason to the matter in hand was not decisive — as in the realm of fine arts generally — Europe cannot be said to have enjoyed any clear and unmistakable superiority. Indeed, the refinement and stylistic coherence of Chinese and of Moslem artistry remained greater than anything Europeans ever managed to produce with their restless multiplicity of styles.

Yet the rise of the West to world dominance had clearly begun. In the following chapters we must trace the fashion in which Europe's new-found superiority undermined and in the end overthrew the cultural autonomy of other great civilizations of mankind.

XXIV

The Americas and Russia

1648–1789

IN 1648, colonial America together with Orthodox Russia were still outliers of Europe, and did not fully share in European civilization. By 1789 this was no longer true. The former outliers had become active participants in what we should no longer call European but rather Western civilization. A European-type of society had planted itself firmly in the Americas, and American ideas and institutions, proudly trumpeted to the world by the newly independent United States of America, threatened Europe's Old Regime as it had never been threatened before. In Russia, too, by 1789, the ruling clique had mastered the refinements of European high culture, and Russian state power had started to play a major part in European war and politics. Russia's enormous size and autocratic government also threatened the comparatively small and socially diverse states of western Europe. This threat, in its way, was no less real than that simultaneously presented by the American example of democratic revolution. Hence it seems better in this period to classify the two great offshoots of Europe as part of the expanding body social of Western civilization. The important peculiarities which still, of course, marked off both American and Russian society from that of the European heartlands did not indicate the emergence of separate civilizations.

Instead, increasingly intricate interaction across the Atlantic and across the Russian frontier tended to close the gap between western Europe and its Russian and American outliers.

The fundamental factor that distinguished society in both Russia and the Americas from that prevailing near the center of Western civilization was a comparative abundance of land and a shortage of manpower (or at least of trained and skilled manpower). In any such situation two responses are possible. All the elaborate interlocking of skills, ranks, services, and patterns of deference which holds civilized society together and provides a reasonable stability in relations between social classes and specialist groups may dissolve toward anarchic equality and cultural neo-barbarism. The Cossacks and many Siberian pioneers in Russia lived in just such a fashion. So did French *coureurs de bois* in Canada, English-speaking pioneers in the United States, Brazilian *bandieras,* Argentine *gauchos,* Australian swagmen, South African *voortrekkers,* and Alaskan sourdoughs. Unless restrained by some neighboring and hostile state, an expanding civilized society probably always tends to fray out toward just this sort of rudely equal, roughly violent neo-barbarism.

In other cases, however, an extreme polarization between masters and servants may arise in frontier societies. This is so because outside pressures — economic, political, and military — sometimes require a more elaborate social organization than that compatible with frontier equality. In such circumstances, no impersonal law of the labor market compels one man to work for another, and it is not physically difficult for a man at the bottom of the social scale to run away into the wilds and thus make good his freedom. Hence, only strenuous resort to force can prevent the social pyramid from eroding at its base. The slavery of the New World and the neo-serfdom of the Old were therefore quite as characteristic of the frontier as was the freedom and equality which a pious national tradition in the United States has tended to equate with frontier living.

On the whole, and with important exceptions, it is true that the equalitarian and libertarian option dominated the social and political development of North America and of parts of South America, whereas the repressive response to the frontier's labor shortage prevailed in Russia. Yet in the richest and most developed parts of America, those occupied by Spaniards, a sharply hierarchic society prevailed until long after 1789; whereas in Russia an anarchic, libertarian spirit has run (and continues to run) very near the surface of public life, despite recent Communist changes in the panoply of official repression. Seeming opposites, in other words, have much in common.

Competition for the Americas. As the tiny colonies established by French, Dutch, and British adventurers at the beginning of the seventeenth century took root and began to flourish, the Americas came to be divided into national spheres of influence. As a result, the wars of Europe were faithfully mirrored (and sometimes provoked) by colonial struggles, in which Indian warriors, European regulars, and colonial militiamen all took part.

The first decisive bench mark of these struggles was the exclusion of the Dutch from any leading part in American colonization. This occurred between 1643 and 1664, when the Dutch first lost Brazil to local insurgents who proclaimed their (somewhat conditional) loyalty to Portugal, and then New Amsterdam to the British, who renamed it New York. The second major turn came in 1763, when the French surrendered Canada to the British after an unprecedentedly severe, globe-encompassing war. This overwhelming success (the British simultaneously won supremacy in India) was quickly followed, however, by quarrels with the American colonists who felt aggrieved at being taxed by the British government. When danger no longer threatened from Canada, the colonists felt that British redcoats along with British revenue officers were clearly superfluous. The result was first controversy, then war (1775–83), won by the colonists with the potent help of the French, who took revenge for their earlier defeat by intervening decisively against the British between 1778 and 1783.

Along the Pacific coast of the Americas, Europe's international rivalries also affected events. Between 1728 and 1741, the Russian

Scale of Miles
0   1000

ALEUTIAN Is.
Bering Str.
ALASKA
RUSSIANS
Mackenzie R.
GREENLAND
ICELAND
Nootka Sound
(Sp. 1789-95)
Hudson
Bay
50°N
HUDSON BAY COMPANY
(British)
NEWFOUNDLAND
CANADA
Quebec
San Francisco
(Sp. 1776)
Missouri R.
LOUISIANA
NOVA SCOTIA
Boston
New York
Philadelphia
Santa Fe
Mississippi R.
UNITED
STATES
Pacific
NEW
Charleston
BERMUDA (Br.)
Atlantic Ocean
MEXICO
FLORIDA
Mexico City
SPAIN
BAHAMAS (Br.)
CUBA
HAITI (Fr.)
HONDURAS
(Br.)
JAMAICA (Br.)
WEST INDIES
(Br. Fr. Du.)
Ocean
Caracas
NEW
Bogota
Equator
GRANADA
(Dutch)(Fr.)
GUIANA
Amazon R.
Lima
PERU
Cuzco
BRAZIL
(Portugal)
(Dutch, 1630-54)
Recife
COLONIAL AMERICA
c. 1789
Potosi
PARAGUAY
LA
PLATA
Rio de Janeiro
Area of 13 original states
and boundary of U.S. in 1783
Spanish territory
Buenos Aires

369

naval captain Vitus Bering discovered Alaska as well as the strait
that bears his name. Russian fur traders soon followed this up by
establishing small settlements in the Aleutian Islands and on the
Alaskan mainland. This news stimulated the British Hudson's Bay
Company to explore and lay claim to all of Canada west of the
Rockies. This was accomplished by 1789. The Spaniards reacted to
the Russian advance by pushing farther up the coast, establishing
missions at San Francisco (1775) and Nootka (1789).

The net result, therefore, of Europe's power struggles was to
carve up all of the New World into more or less clearly delimited
imperial fragments. Social reality never caught up with claims of
course, for the advance of settlement in North America had barely
reached the Appalachian mountains at the time of the American
Revolution, and nowhere else had white men established a European type of society very far inland.

The magnificence of Spanish America. Given the economic and
political relations that prevail today, it is difficult for citizens of the
United States to keep an historically correct perspective on colonial times. Yet by almost any standard, the poverty and rustic simplicity of the Massachusetts backwoods or of the Virginia pied-
mont in the eighteenth century paled before the viceregal
splendors of Lima and Mexico City. Indeed, in 1793, the 100,000
inhabitants of Mexico City made it larger than any European city
except London and Paris.

The decay of the Indian population, which had been so precipitate in the sixteenth and early seventeenth centuries, came to a halt
about 1650. Thereafter, Mexico and other parts of the Spanish empire witnessed an increasingly rapid population growth. Presumably the initial vulnerability of Amerindians to European and African diseases had now been overcome. Growing populations, in
turn, provided the setting for a general upthrust of commercial
prosperity, particularly after the relaxation (1774–78) of monopolistic regulations which had long prohibited coastal trade among
the American ports of the Spanish empire, and had funneled the

Christ Pancrator, c. 1148. Cathedral at Cefalù, Sicily.

GOD INCARNATE, RULER OF ALL

The quest for certainty that can plausibly be read into late Roman sculpture (see Plate 8) has here come majestically to rest. Although this mosaic was made in Sicily when that island was under Norman rule, the style is Byzantine. In the restless West, however, even so powerful a style as this provided a chrysalis from which to emerge rather than a frame within which to exist, as the following pages will show.

PLATE 33

Giotto di Bondone, 1266-1337. The Resurrection of Lazarus. Arena Chapel, Padua.

PLATE 34

DEFINITION OF A FAR WESTERN ART STYLE

Between the fifteenth and twentieth centuries, mathematically exact perspective, creating an illusory third dimension, became the West's stylistic hallmark. Its emergence is illustrated here. Giotto's figures serenely inhabit a shallow depth in the foreground, but his landscape is on a different scale. A century and a half later, Piero della Francesca knew how to organize foreground and background into a single coherent illusory space. But his painting, too, is divided, for the resurrected Christ bespeaks the Christian past, whereas the foreshortened limbs of the sleeping soldiers both mock and proclaim mastery of a new, secular this-worldliness.

Piero della Francesca, 1416-1492. Resurrection of Christ. Galleria Comunale, Sansepolcro.

PLATE 35

Albrecht Dürer, 1471-1528. Self-Portrait. Alte Pinakothek, Munich.

MAN INCARNATE, RULER OF SELF

Albrecht Dürer's portrait of himself at age twenty-eight sufficiently resembles the traditional mein of Christ Pancrator (Plate 33) to make one wonder whether such a dip into the penumbra of blasphemy was deliberate. In any event, a proud self-consciousness and delight in technical virtuosity for its own sake (observe the contrasting textures of fur, hair, and beard) pervade the work. The humanist conception of the self as a work of art to be moulded to full manhood by conscious cultivation of the arts of life stares starkly back at us from Dürer's mirror.

PLATE 36

THE CHRISTIAN PILGRIMAGE THROUGH LIFE

Dürer's knight, averting his gaze from the menacing figure of death (with the hour-glass) and turning his back upon the Devil (here dressed up as the great beast of the Book of Revelation) is headed for the fair city high upon a hill in the background. The engraving is thus an allegory of the Christian life as understood in Germany on the eve of the Reformation. Like Luther the Christian knight of Dürer's engraving pursues salvation through the private heroism of an individual act of faith. Dürer here combines old sentiments—veritable clichés—and new techniques of realistic draftsmanship. With the same radical ruthlessness, Luther sought to recover old truths by applying the latest devices of humanist scholarship to the Bible.

The links and tensions between Renaissance and Reformation seem quintessentially summed up in the resemblances of and differences between these two products of Dürer's hand.

Albrecht Dürer, 1471-1528. Knight, Death, and the Devil.
Museum of Fine Arts, Boston.
Gift of Mrs. Horatio Greenough Curtis, in memory of her husband.

PLATE 37

St. Nicholas the Wonder Worker. School of Rublev, Moscow, 15th cent.
Collection, George R. Hann, Sewickley, Pennsylvania.

CONSERVATISM IN THE EAST

The reckless plunge toward modernity illustrated in the two preceding plates was
not shared everywhere and at once, even within Europe. Muscovy in the east clung
close to Byzantine tradition, and the Holy Orthodox Church remained immune from
catastrophic reformation until the seventeenth century. This icon bespeaks the conservative stability of Russian culture and society. Yet the stimulating presence of the
West may be glimpsed in details such as the use of shadow to give an illusory third
dimension to St. Nicholas's face and hand—a technique pioneered in Italy not long
before some anonymous monk painted this work.

PLATE 38

El Greco, 1541-1614. St. Jerome. The Frick Collection, New York.

CONSERVATISM IN THE WEST

In Spain, almost two centuries later, the stranger from Crete whom Spaniards called El Greco—that is, "The Greek"—painted in a style that preserved unmistakable echoes of the Byzantine icons he had known in his youth. But St. Jerome's elongated face and hands, his intense gaze, and the pyramidal garment he wears—elements deriving from Byzantine iconography—here appear decked out with the full virtuosity of Italian Renaissance technique. This is well illustrated by the way in which Jerome's hair and beard attain optical realism—at the expense, surely, of saintly otherworldliness. Incongruous juxtaposition of strictly traditional with radically new elements characterized Spanish society as a whole in the age of the conquistadors and of the Counter Reformation.

PLATE 39

Rembrandt van Rijn, 1606-1669. Syndics of the Cloth Guild. Rijksmuseum, Amsterdam.

THE OLD REGIME IN ART

Sober, serious, and self-satisfied burghers, careful of their money, jealous of their rights, and eminently capable of looking after their own interests, here confront a slender aristocrat, delightfully decorative and sweetly debonair. The two classes, whose contrasting styles of life find powerful expression in these paintings, dominated the Old Regime and by their prudent moderation gave Europe a modicum of stability after the wracking storms of Renaissance and Reformation.

PLATE 40

Jean Baptiste Perronneau, 1715-1783. Madame de Sorquainville. Louvre, Paris.

PLATE 41

Jacques Louis David, 1748-1825. Une Maraichère. Musée de Beaux Arts, Lyon.

PLATE 42

LIBERTY, EQUALITY, FRATERNITY

This pair of paintings gives visual shape to the conundrums raised in France between 1789 and 1815 by the resolute, revolutionary pursuit of a stubbornly elusive General Will, in whose undulating surge weak, wandering private wills ought (according to Rousseau) to find surcease from the pain of making practical decisions in a world where custom offered a less and less adequate guide to conduct in matters public as well as private.

Francisco Goya, 1746-1828. The Third of May, 1808. Prado, Madrid.

PLATE 43

Honoré Daumier, 1808-1879. The Third-Class Carriage. The Metropolitan Museum of Art, New York. The H. O. Havemeyer Collection.

PLATE 44

THE NEW REGIME

Daumier's painting on the left records the fact that nineteenth-century industrialism brought even peasant women to market and allowed them to mingle demurely with city folk while returning home third class. Thus at the lower end of the social scale, age-old distinctions between town and country diminished, while, at the other extreme, the dividing line between bourgeois and noble also blurred, as Sargent's portraits of a self-made businessman of London and his high-born wife suggest.

John Singer Sargent, 1856-1925. Asher Wertheimer and Mrs. Asher Wertheimer. Tate Gallery, London.

PLATE 45

Ben Shahn, 1898-   Liberation. Collection, James Thrall Soby, New Canaan, Connecticut.

PLATE 46

TWENTIETH-CENTURY LIBERATION

On the eve of World War I, a small band of iconoclasts deliberately repudiated the conventions of European painting which, despite all the intervening changes, had held up since the fifteenth century, when Italian artists first discovered the mathematical rules for creating illusory three-dimensional space in their pictures. Humanity at large quickly followed the artists' example by cutting adrift from tradition of almost every sort and in almost every society. Primitive impulse and abstract, depersonalizing intellectuality oddly collaborate in the uncharted landscape this wholesale liberation from the past opened up, as Miró's painting (below) may perhaps symbolize. Shahn's work commemorates both the destruction wrought by World War II and humanity's ruthless renewal amid the ruins.

Collection, The Museum of Modern Art, New York

Joan Miró, 1893-   . Person Throwing a Stone at a Bird. Collection, The Museum of Modern Art, New York.

PLATE 47

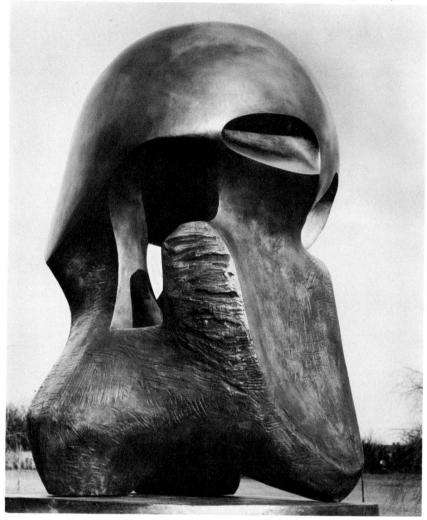

Henry Moore, 1898- . Nuclear Energy, photograph of a model. University of Chicago.

THE PAST IS PROLOGUE

This brooding presence, a monument in Chicago at the place where men first created a controlled and self-sustaining nuclear reaction, gives visual form to the hopes and fears with which we contemplate our fate—sentiments based today on new premises, yet presumably of no greater poignancy than in times past, since then as now life and death hung daily in the balance and no man knew (or knows) what the morrow will bring forth.

PLATE 48

movement of all colonial exports and imports through the single city of Cadiz, Spain.

Ancient universities and aristocratic traditions of culture allowed individual savants of the Spanish empire to participate in the cultural and intellectual life of Europe, even before the renewal of economic expansion in the late eighteenth century created a small but vivacious middle class of professional men, merchants, and officials who developed a lively interest in the latest fashions and ideas emanating from a newly "Enlightened" Spain.

Two features blunted the further development of Spanish American society despite such a palpable head start over anything yet achieved among English-speaking colonists farther north. First, the Indian peasantry, upon whose stolid labors the society depended, shared scarcely at all in the high culture of Spanish colonial life. Second, intellectual and moral sloth prevailed in the church and made its extraordinary economic dominance within colonial society indefensible. But when, as soon occurred, secular-minded liberals attacked the church they shook the only institutional link that gave the Indians an emotionally vital share in Spanish civilization and bound them to submission. Any serious move against the church therefore opened the door to Indian revolt and social chaos. Such a by-product of their convictions appalled liberal-minded men. Profound inner uncertainties promptly beset the Spanish elite—a state of mind that gave self-interested adventurers and political rakes unusually wide scope.

Such comments become plausible in the light of nineteenth- and twentieth-century developments in Spanish America. But up until the end of the eighteenth century, the future weaknesses of Spanish imperial society were not yet evident. Instead, like the Chinese empire on the other side of the Pacific, Spain's American empire towered like a great oak, standing high above all adjacent states, peoples, and cultures.

Backwardness versus precocity in the colonies. Brazil, on the Spaniard's southeasterly flank, remained politically chaotic even after the Dutch had withdrawn. The vigor of backwoodsmen's exploitation of placer gold, the ruthlessness of their attacks upon the Jesuit Indian preserve of Paraguay, not to mention the vitality of transplanted African cultures among the slaves of Brazilian plantations—all these seemed squalid when compared with the hierarchical dignity and hieratic pomp of the well-ordered, prosperous, peaceable, and reasonably well-administered Spanish viceroyalties.

The British colonies, too, could not rival Spanish grandeur. To be sure, in the ports of Boston, New York, Philadelphia, truncated replicas of the society and cultural life of England arose. Religious differences among the various colonies and, before long, within each colony as well, made enforcement of religious conformity impractical after 1700. Secularism perhaps found easier expression as a result of the breakdown of ecclesiastical authority; but the discomfiture of established religion also opened a path for emotional religious revivalism, which became a very prominent feature of colonial life.

In many respects the colonies lagged behind the contemporary development of Europe. But in some ways the evolution of American society outstripped that of the Old World. The American War of Independence gave by far the most important expression to this phenomenon. To be sure, the ideas which the colonists used to explain and justify their rebellion against King George III and the British Parliament drew heavily upon traditional definitions of the "rights of Englishmen." In addition, however, more radical definitions of the "Rights of Man" played their part and rescued the American Revolution from a merely parochial importance. Many Europeans actually persuaded themselves that the Rights of Man as realized in the United States of America constituted a model toward which benighted and backward peoples of Europe, like the French, might hopefully strive. Through its exemplary force, therefore, the American War of Independence and the constitutional settlement that emerged from the war entered powerfully upon the stage of world history. The liberal principles professed by men who had but lately ranked as poor and remote country cousins catapulted American affairs into the forefront of European politics.

The modernization of Russia. In joining the mainstream of European history, American colonists suffered no psychological wrench. On the contrary, they were recovering a fuller share in the cultural traditions their ancestors had left behind when they first emigrated from England. No conversion was called for. Russia, however, had first to repudiate its own special style of life, built around the Orthodox claim to monopoly of Christian truth, and upon obedience to an absolute tsar. To abandon such a past was difficult; yet this is what the Russians — or more correctly what the Russian rulers — did between 1654, when the Patriarch Nikon launched his official reform of the church's liturgical books, and 1725, when Tsar Peter the Great died.

Nikon sought to base the manuals used in all the services of the church upon authentic and indubitably correct Greek texts. Only so could uniformity be secured throughout Russia, and only so could the painful reproaches of Roman Catholic propagandists, who pointed to errors in existing Russian texts, be silenced. Leaders of secular government as well as of the church fully accepted this reasoning, so that even after Nikon had quarreled with the tsar (1658) and was dismissed from his patriarchal office (1666), his reform policy continued to prevail.

But many poor and humble Christians felt that official tampering with the familiar words of the church ritual had inaugurated the reign of Anti-Christ. Who else would dare to alter the sacred phrases necessary for salvation? As a result, communities of dissenters — the "Old Believers" of subsequent Russian history — came into existence and stubbornly, sometimes heroically, refused to submit to official coercion. Efforts to break up such communities by force occasionally led to mass suicide on the part of the beleaguered defenders of the old ways. Sometimes too, dissent ran into hidden channels so that peasants who outwardly conformed to the new order of church worship secretly listened to teachers who viewed the unholy alliance of a corrupted church with a secularized state as the work of Anti-Christ, tokening the imminent end of the world.

It is impossible to know how widely such opinions spread among the Russian people. It seems plausible to believe that massive peasant discontents which under other circumstances might have found political channels of expression were most effectually diverted into sectarian excitement, as secret and persecuted groups exhorted one another to await the miraculous opening of the skies that would announce the Second Coming of Christ. This psychological safety valve was probably what permitted Peter the Great and his immediate successors to revolutionize Russia as ruthlessly as they did without provoking a crippling revolt. For Peter's work was the work of a tiny clique that he created from among his personal acquaintances and boon companions, reinforced by captured Swedes and kidnapped Dutchmen, and by other flotsam and jetsam from the European world of the West that drifted within the tsar's reach.

Peter came to the throne in 1689 while still a boy, and did not begin his revolutionary assault upon old Russian life until after returning in 1696 from an anonymous (but well-advertised) trip to western Europe. Thereafter, he never rested from frantic and sometimes erratic efforts to build an army and navy as good as any in the world, supported by all the industrial, administrative, and intellectual skills that might be necessary. A vigorous and violent personality certainly helped Peter to achieve as much as he did, but his orders could only become effective through the actions of subordinates, educated to submit to his hectoring commands. He found these subordinates, in large measure, among the rank and file of the Guards Regiments, which he had personally created while still a mere stripling. Later he reinforced their ranks by requiring nobles' sons to enter the Guards Regiments as privates, where, if they did well, he might presently notice them and promote them, assigning them to any sort of task, civil or military, diplomatic or judicial, depending on the needs of the moment.

The system worked. Young men from the country houses of Russia came to court and there as members of the Guards Regiments were converted to a new set of manners, before being sent off to do the tsar's work in peace and in war. Philip of Macedon and the great Ottoman sultans had used the same device for creating an obedient military and administrative corps, capable, like

Peter's friends, of carrying through a revolution from above on the word of command precisely because each of them had first been cut off from his past by the seductive glitter of a radically novel style of court culture.

Peter's death in 1725 presented his associates with a serious problem, for they recognized no clear principle of political legitimacy. How then could succession to the throne be regulated, particularly since the revolutionary tsar had killed his own son and left no male heir? Resulting uncertainties bred intrigue and ugly palace *coups d'état.* The most spectacular of these put a German princess on the throne of Imperial Russia, in 1762, after the murder of her royal husband. She took the title Catherine II. Despite her dubious claim to power, Catherine ruled long and prosperously and, like Peter, soon earned the sobriquet "the Great." A stabilizing factor was that whenever quarrels and intrigues among the ruling clique threatened to get out of hand, all concerned drew back because they realized how few and weak they were when measured against the vast, resentful peasant mass of Russia. The further fact that the Russian economy experienced a prolonged boom with the opening of the Ukraine to commercial farming in the latter part of the eighteenth century also helped to maintain workable cohesion among the masters of the Russian land.

Russia arrives as a great power. In military and diplomatic matters Peter had met with incomplete success. He defeated the Swedes in a long and difficult war (1700–1721) and was able to secure a short coastline on the Gulf of Finland. With extraordinary ruthlessness, he then built a new city, St. Petersburg, on swampy land at the mouth of the river Neva, and made his new creation into the capital of Russia. Against the Turks, on the other hand, Peter fared much less well. Despite an initial success in 1701, he had to surrender all he had won ten years later. In the last year of his life, however, victory over his other Moslem neighbor, the shah of Iran, allowed the tsar to advance his frontiers to the southernmost part of the Caspian Sea.

Peter's successors regularly committed Russian troops to Europe's struggles. The most dramatic demonstration of Russia's power occurred during the Seven Years' War (1756–63), when a

change of ruler in Russia shifted Russian strength from one side to
the other, literally overnight, and saved Frederick II of Prussia
from what had seemed certain disaster. In addition, the Russians
fought two inconclusive wars against the Turks before Catherine
II, the Great, launched what proved to be a decisive campaign
against the sultan in 1764. To be sure, her grand plan for overthrowing the Turks and reinstituting a new Byzantine and Orthodox empire under her imperial protection was not realized. But
Russia did annex the Black Sea coast as far as the Dniester river,
and, as a sop for her restraint vis-à-vis the defeated Turks, the Prussians and Austrians agreed to permit Catherine to occupy a large
part of Poland in the first partition of that hapless country (1772).
In each of the two subsequent partitions, too, Russia secured a
share (1793 and 1795), advancing the Russian frontier west to the
Vistula.

While Russia thus became an active and respected member of
the exclusive company of the great European powers, at home the
progress of settlement southward into the Ukraine together with a
rapid upswing of manufactures and trade began to give Russian society a more European aspect. The peasant majority remained
"deaf and dark," living in a world apart from that of their masters,
who more and more imitated the manners and acquired the legal
rights possessed by the aristocracies of other more westerly lands.
In 1762, for example, the legal requirement that nobles must serve
the tsar was cancelled, and many did in fact withdraw to their
estates. By that time, enough men had been trained to fill and more
than fill available posts, and the government's tax income had become large enough to allow payment of modest salaries in lieu of
the land grants upon which Ivan the Terrible and Peter the Great
had mainly relied.

Serfs, whose legal obligations to the landowners were tightened
rather than relaxed, certainly felt deep grievance at the privileges
thus accorded their masters. Why should the poor and humble not
also be freed from the burden of forced service? A great uprising
led by Emilian Pugachev and centering in southern and western
Russia, where memories of the free frontier days were still fresh,

gave vent to these feelings. It was brutally repressed (1773–75). Thereafter peasant discontent reverted to religious sectarianism and addiction to alcohol. Most of the nobles, on the other hand, set out eagerly to try to equal or overtake France and the other great nations of Europe. For at least a generation after Catherine's time they found ample scope for their idealism and energies (as well as for self-interest) in forwarding the agricultural, commercial, and

administrative advance of their country. In spite of peasant disaffection, servants of the autocracy were sure that they were acting in the true interests of all, making Russia rich and great and
respected among the nations of the West.

XXV

Asian Reactions to Europe's Old Regime

1700–1850

N Moslem eyes, the Peace of Karlowitz (1699), whereby the Ottoman empire surrendered nearly all of Hungary to the victorious Austrians, ran completely against the grain of history. What was far more embarrassing, such a serious defeat also conflicted with fundamental theological principles, for ever since Mohammed's followers at Medina had attacked and overcome the scoffers of Mecca, victory in battle had been recognized as a sign and seal of divine favor. This being so, how could Allah favor Christian dogs and unbelievers, who were increasingly untrue even to their own mistaken faith?

The full force of this puzzle confronted the Moslem world only toward the end of the eighteenth century. Between 1768 and 1774 the Russians defeated Ottoman armies utterly and were prevented from capturing Constantinople and destroying the sultan's power more by the intervention of European diplomats than by any inherent strength of the Turkish regime. Even so, the treaty of Kutchuk Kainardji ("Little Fountain") ending the war was ominous for the future. It invited Russian intervention in Ottoman affairs by according the tsar a vaguely worded protectorate over Orthodox Christians under Turkish rule. The Russians also acquired important territories along the Black Sea coast, together with rights of unrestricted navigation on that sea and passage through the straits. The sultan's palaces and Constantinople itself thus came within easy range of Russian naval guns.

To be defeated by the Holy Roman Emperor, who ranked in Moslem eyes as the political leader of Christendom, was as nothing compared to defeat at the hands of a ruler whose predecessors had been obedient subjects to the Khan of the Golden Horde, and whose Orthodox Christianity classed them with the sultan's own Christian subjects in the Balkans. Moreover, by 1774, Moslem supremacy over India was also clearly in danger, and the Safavi empire had dissolved, turning Iran and Turkestan into a cockpit where rival military captains tore civil society apart.

To pious Moslems, who accept the principle that divine favor and military success are closely linked, world events since 1699 remain an unsolvable conundrum. Total apostasy seems the only alternative to blind faith — a faith that can only await the turning of the tide, when Allah's inexplicable reversal of the pattern of world history will in its turn be reversed. In the meanwhile, resentful passivity, supported by a doctrine of fatalism, has characterized Moslem reaction to Europeans throughout the period of Western ascendancy.

Some, however, were not content passively to await Allah's intervention. Two obvious remedies offered themselves: (1) to "spoil the Egyptians" by appropriating from the "Franks" the technical secrets of their military power or (2) to regain Allah's favor by purifying Islam from all traces of the corruptions that had crept into the lives of the faithful. Champions of each policy made their voices heard early in the eighteenth century; but it was Islam's misfortune — unlike, for example, the Japanese — that the two remedies seemed almost always diametrically opposed to one another. Reformers' efforts therefore tended to cancel out, leaving the mass of Moslem society more confused and frustrated than ever.

The Wahhabi movement. The most important champion of religious purification was Mohammed ibn Abdul Wahhab (1703–92), who lived in the Arabian desert and relied upon princes of the house of Saud to protect his followers and promulgate his teachings. Abdul Wahhab's aim was clear: to restore the faith of the

Prophet in all its pristine purity. This meant in practice a strenuous and unbending rejection of saint worship and other corruptions that Sufi holy men had insinuated into Islam. It meant also insistence upon strict observance of all the rules of personal conduct laid down in the *Koran*. Wine drinking, for example, and other religiously prohibited acts were sternly punished by the Wahhabis, who inclined, whenever a point of doubt legitimately arose, to adopt the severer and stricter view.

The Wahhabi community in Arabia grew from very small beginnings in almost exactly the same fashion as the original community of Islam had grown. By the time of Abdul Wahhab's death, his followers controlled most of Arabia, but soon thereafter the movement met a crushing military setback, when Egyptian troops, trained and equipped on the European model, collided with the old-fashioned warriors of the Arabian desert and defeated them decisively (1818). But defeat in battle did not destroy the Wahhabi movement. On the contrary, when Wahhabism ceased to be so closely tied up with the military-political fortunes of the Saud family, it actually widened its appeal by attracting pious and serious-minded Moslems in India and the Ottoman empire.

The delicate balance that had long prevailed in most Moslem lands between the legalism of early Islam and the mystical Sufi piety of later ages could not survive the corrosive effect of Western skepticism on the one hand and Wahhabi incandescence on the other. Intellectual somnolence, sheltering behind familiar phrases safely transmitted from generation to generation by rote memorization, had been characteristic of Sunni learning ever since the time of Suleiman the Lawgiver. Wahhabi zealots, by taking the words of the *Koran* with deadly seriousness and seeking to apply them anew to every condition of human life, made this sort of mindless conservatism impossible. Yet the heirs of Moslem learning and civilization knew more of the complexities of the world and its ways than was ordinarily vouchsafed to the Bedouin tribesmen among whom Abdul Wahhab found his first followers. Urban sophisticates therefore usually found it difficult to believe that all would come right again if only the faithful would conform exactly to Wahhabi prescriptions. Hence the Wahhabi movement failed to

provide the ground for resumption of vigorous and successful intellectual life within Islam, and, indeed, made departure from
ancient formulas and rules of conduct more difficult than ever.

The failure of reform. Reformers who sought to strengthen
Moslem states by borrowing European techniques met with small
success prior to 1850. In the eighteenth century, very few Ottoman officials took such an idea seriously. Moreover, any success in
the field had the ironical effect of reducing the apparent need for
further tampering with ancient practices. For example, after 1699 a
group of Ottoman officials did set out to reform and re-equip
Turkish artillery units with guns like those the Austrians had used
so effectively against Ottoman troops in the long war of 1683–99.
Later, after another disastrous war with the Austrians (1716–18),
military reform spread to a few infantry units as well. When both
Austria and Russia attacked the Turks, 1739–40, these new units
helped to administer unexpected defeats to the Austrians. The
Austrians soon withdrew from the war, whereupon the Russians
did the same. Yet this striking vindication of the policy of military
reform did not persuade the Ottoman government to persevere.
On the contrary, military victory was interpreted to mean that no
further military changes were needed, and, in fact, during the long
peace that ensued the new units were gradually allowed to wither
into ineffectiveness. When Catherine II of Russia attacked the
Ottoman empire in the war of 1768–74, the Turks therefore
found themselves hopelessly outclassed by the Russian troops
which had been freshly tempered and tested in the Seven Years'
War (1756–63).

This shattering defeat revived the effort to modernize Ottoman
armies, but not until 1826 did a decisive breakthrough come. The
reason was that the severity of the disaster which Russian armies
had inflicted seemed to demand a thoroughgoing reorganization of
all Ottoman institutions. In such circumstances conservatives felt
that the whole Islamic character of the state was in danger. Even
very modest steps toward reform of the armed forces therefore sufficed to rouse fanatic resistance. Not until a further series of military disasters had occurred, including successful revolt on the part
of the sultan's Serbian and Greek subjects, did the reforming cause

prevail. Even then it did so at enormous cost, for the sultan had to order his artillerists to mow down the rebellious janissaries and the Constantinople mob supporting them. Such a bloody and violent step did indeed destroy conservatism's armed strength but failed entirely to replace the old army with a new one capable of protecting the empire. Fresh humiliation therefore lay in store for the Ottoman empire at the hands of the European powers and of upstart rebels like the formidable tyrant of Egypt, Mohammed Ali (d. 1849).

By 1850, therefore, most Turkish officials and men of affairs concluded that aping European uniforms and guns was as ineffectual as standing fast. No solution seemed to offer itself, and the policy makers of the Ottoman empire relied instead on a certain low cleverness in diplomatic intrigue, seeking to divide the European powers and compel one or another of them to come to the rescue of the "Sick man of Europe."

British control of India. The Mughal empire survived in name until 1857, but only in name. No European balance of power came to its rescue. Instead, the struggle for trade and influence in India tipped decisively in favor of the British after 1763. Thereafter the turbulent political stage in India allowed — indeed invited — continued encroachment, so that after 1818 only the tribesmen of the remote northwest frontier remained truly independent of British authority.

The decay of Mughal power became apparent even before the Emperor Aurangzeb died in 1707. Although his conquests in southern Indian brought the empire to its greatest territorial extent, before he died a number of serious revolts had already begun to undermine the imperial authority. In particular, Hindu hillsmen in central India — the so-called Marathas — launched a guerrilla war which the slow-moving Mughal forces could not counter. Later, Sikhs also revolted and set up a territorial lordship in the northwest. In time many local governors made themselves independent of the central administration, until even the immediate environs of Delhi, the capital, sometimes ceased to obey the imperial command.

Under these conditions, the agents of the European trading companies found it necessary to protect themselves. They did so by enlisting Indian soldiers under European officers, equipping and training such forces in a European manner. Very soon it became evident that these troops were in fact superior to any other type of armed force known to India. Local rulers, and adventurers wishing to make good their claim to a piece of territory, obviously had deep interest in securing such troops for their own uses, and began

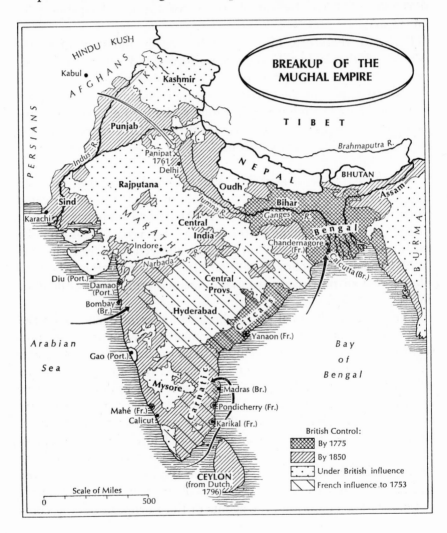

BREAKUP OF THE MUGHAL EMPIRE

British Control:
By 1775
By 1850
Under British influence
French influence to 1753

hiring Europeans to command "sepoy" armies. This in turn stimulated rivalries between the European powers, for a local European military commander could be assumed to favor the cause of his fellow nationals at the court of his employer. In the confusion which resulted, the French, who were seeking to build up a powerful India company, and the British, whose trading activities in the Indian Ocean dated from 1600, became the principal rivals. But the superior strength of the British navy meant that in case of war between the two countries, British forces in India could be moved to and fro by sea and be sure of supply from home, whereas the French, who risked being cut off, lost strategic mobility, save insofar as they could march their forces cross-country overland. When, therefore, all-out struggle was joined between France and Great Britain in 1756, it is not surprising that the British in India won decisive success, and after the end of the war (1763) effectually excluded the French from further participation in Indian political and economic affairs.

While the struggle between French and British companies was still in progress, an Afghan invading force ravaged northwestern India and administered a crushing defeat to the Maratha armies at Panipat, near Delhi (1761). From this time onward, therefore, the local princes of India found themselves caught between two equally aggressive foreign powers: the English coming from the sea and the Afghans coming from the north. When choice became necessary, most preferred the English. Without very much fighting, therefore, almost all Indian states had by 1818 concluded treaty arrangements establishing a binding alliance with the British. British control was usually exercised by a resident at court, who acted as a sort of watch dog to guarantee the faithful performance of treaty agreements. Part of India was directly administered by the British East India Company; but only when a native ruler stubbornly resisted offers of alliance or proved phenomenally incompetent did the company actually displace him from his throne.

The directors of the East India Company, sitting in London, almost invariably disapproved of territorial advance. They disliked military adventure on the ground that it interfered with trade. Their whole aim was to earn as much as possible as cheaply as possible. This meant, among other things, refraining resolutely from any attempts to convert Indians to Christianity or in any other way altering their accustomed ways of life and government. Indeed, many of the company's servants were convinced that a mere handful of Britishers could never govern India or maintain their favored position in the sub-continent by any other policy.

As long as genuinely independent states continued to exist in India this argument had considerable force. After 1818, however, when the last Maratha war ended in an easy British triumph, no military rival remained. Missionary pressure from home and the demand of a handful of Hindus for legal and humanitarian reform mounted. Moslems, on the other hand, whose quarrels and political-military weakness had invited the westerners into India in the first place, only wished to be left alone.

Iran and Turkestan. In Iran and Turkestan, too, Moslem political and economic life suffered humiliating decay, when measured against the mounting power of the West. To be sure, the military exploits of Nadir shah (ruled 1736–47), who deposed the last of the Safavis as a preliminary to invading India, and the no less spectacular career of the Afghan chieftain Ahmed shah Durani (1747–73), conformed admirably to the warrior tradition of their predecessors. The difficulty was that these great conquerors now encountered armies trained and equipped in the European fashion whenever they ventured far from home, and, in fact, depended themselves in no small measure on the import of guns, powder, and shot. Judicious distribution of subsidies by civilized neighbors who had access to abundant supplies of powder and shot could, under these circumstances, raise up a rival or bring down the mighty at the very zenith of his success. Hence, from the beginning of the nineteenth century, the political life of Iran and Turkestan began to turn less upon local factors than upon British and Russian subsidies and punitive raids, such as those which twice (1839 and 1842) brought British troops to the Afghan capital Kabul.

No Moslem could look with satisfaction upon the sad state into which the once proud realm of Islam had descended by 1850. No cultural rebirth or intellectual awakening relieved the somber political scene; while on the economic front, European machine-made goods had begun from about 1830 to reduce traditional artisan communities of the Moslem world to penury. Where, indeed, in such a world was Allah?

Hindu reform. Hindu and Christian subject communities of the Moslem world found the new order considerably easier to adjust to. Hindus could not get very excited at the spectacle of another invader destroying the equally alien Persian and Turkish dominion over India. Similar changes of master had occurred too often in the past for this to seem strange or particularly important. For a long time, therefore, the European presence in India provoked no very obvious repercussions within the Hindu communities. Hindus simply treated the Europeans as another caste.

Moreover, as we have just seen, official British policy sought to minimize shocks to established social institutions and relationships. Thus, for example, the language of administration remained unchanged until 1844, so that any young Hindu aspiring to a government job had to learn Persian, the language of his old Moslem masters, not English.

After the beginning of the nineteenth century, however, initiatives both from the British and from the Hindu side began to enlarge the range of interaction between Western and Hindu culture. Missionary colleges, established initially in open defiance of the British East India Company's policy, introduced an important new element onto the scene. A number of energetic missionaries, arriving privately in India, proceeded to translate European books into the vernaculars spoken in various parts of the country. This provided a powerful stimulant to the literary development of the modern Indian languages, as well as opening a window upon important aspects of Western culture to Indian readers.

Few Indians ever became Christians since Hinduism proved just as much proof against Christian as against Moslem preaching. But the widened access to knowledge of European civilization which missionary activity in India allowed did not fail to stimulate a few Indians to the effort of trying to understand the strange outside world inhabited by their British rulers. This effort was pioneered by Ram Mohan Roy (d. 1833), whose inquiries into Christian and Moslem religion convinced him that all world religions conveyed fundamentally the same message — ethical unitarianism. He and others easily convinced themselves, as well as a few eager disciples in the Western world, that Hindu philosophy had discovered these universal truths long before any other people. Hence, proud and pious Hindus could feel that even wholesale borrowing of European techniques might be acceptable, since Indians had such precious spiritual insight to give in return. Western scholars assuredly did have much to learn from the Upanishads and the Vedas and, especially in the early nineteenth century, showed a considerable enthusiasm in undertaking the task.

Energetic researches into early Indian texts, however, produced an unexpected backlash. Existing Hindu practices had little or no relation to the Vedas. This opened a door for Hindu reformers, who, by judicious selection from the vast religious literature of Hinduism, could find ample authority for the sorts of liberal and humanitarian reforms many of the Christian missionaries and a few of the company's servants had begun to advocate. The test case was the custom of *suttee*, i.e. the custom of burning the widow on the funeral pyre of her dead husband. There was no Vedic authority for this practice. Ram Mohan Roy launched a series of pamphlets condemning *suttee* and urging British authorities to prohibit it. In 1829 they did so. Six years later they also decided to introduce a school system for Indians that would be conducted in English and teach European subjects. This, too, had been advocated by Ram Mohan Roy as needful if Indian youths were to acquire knowledge of scientific truth.

Once such tampering with traditional customs and institutions had been started, there was no stopping. The British authorities soon found that each reform generated a demand for others. As a result, administrative action failed to keep up with demands for more and more resolute and radical transformation of the traditional social structure. A handful of educated Hindus were among those who clamored for faster action. The great majority, of course, remained passive, only vaguely aware of the concerns and aspirations of their reforming fellows. Nevertheless, the contrast with the Moslem community of India was fundamental, for Hindu leadership acquiesced when it did not demand reform, whereas Moslems of high and low degree were as one in deploring everything that was happening around them. This initial advantage remains until today, and has helped, more than anything else, to make India again a Hindu land.

The Christian Balkans. In the Balkans, on the other flank of Islam, the Christian populations also found it comparatively easy to welcome the decaying fortunes of their Ottoman masters. To be sure, there were groups of Christians in Constantinople who had benefited greatly from their position as bankers and advisers to the Turks and were not anxious to see the imperial fabric, upon which their wealth depended, fall to pieces. But strategically situated sophisticates — merchants and professional men in particular — fell under the spell of the secularized version of Western culture which goes by the name of the Enlightenment, and looked forward to change. Old theological quarrels about the wording of the Nicene Creed seemed irrelevant to readers of Voltaire and Rousseau. Moreover, civil liberties and natural rights had no announced geographical or cultural limits. Hence, insofar as Orthodox Christians of the Balkans took such ideas seriously, they not unnaturally aspired to create free and modern national states of their own to supersede the decaying Ottoman regime.

This spirit, combined with not a little old-fashioned Balkan banditry, gave the Serbian (1803–15) and Greek (1821–30) revolutions a character of their own, and made them the first step toward a more perfect incorporation of those nations into Western society. Difficulty soon arose from the fact that the Christian nations of the Balkans cherished conflicting territorial ambitions. But until after 1850 this was obscured by the confident anticipation of a future brotherhood of free men everywhere which infected revolutionary circles.

Christian missions in China. In the Far East, no events as dramatic as the British conquest of India or the Russian advance against Ottoman Turkey disturbed the calm of the Confucian world. Throughout the eighteenth century, China remained great and powerful and Japan persevered in a rigorous policy of isolation. After about 1775, however, changes in both countries began to undermine — at first imperceptibly — the basis upon which peace and prosperity rested. By the middle of the nineteenth century, therefore, when European powers began to surge against the Far Eastern citadel with an energy reinforced by the industrial and democratic revolutions, Chinese and Japanese capacity to resist had been drastically reduced.

Until the end of the eighteenth century, Chinese government remained so successful and so traditional as to require little description here. Europeans found much to admire in a society which lacked both revealed religion and hereditary aristocracy. Many "enlightened" spirits of the Far West advocated just these things in their own society, and easily persuaded themselves that the virtuous Chinese had already created a working model for the society of which they dreamed. The Chinese, however, did not return the compliment. Indeed they seem to have been rather less interested in European knowledge and skills during the eighteenth century than they had been when such matters were still novelties. This was partly due to the fact that a bitter "rites controversy" broke out among the Christian missionaries in China, discrediting Europeans generally, and, in particular, reducing the intimacy and scale of contact between learned men of the two cultures.

The issue at stake in the rites controversy was fundamental for Christian missions. The Jesuits, who had pioneered the penetration of China, followed a policy of accommodation to local customs and ritual observances insofar as such rites did not unmistakably conflict with Christian teaching. In China, for example, they had decided that rites honoring ancestors and Confucius were civil ceremonies not religious worship, and need not be forbidden to a Christian convert. Less politic missionaries, especially Franciscans, were shocked by this Jesuit policy and complained to the pope. Another point at issue was whether the Chinese word for "heaven" was suitable as an equivalent for "God," or whether its pagan associations were too close to make such a translation correct.

Clearly, the pope was in no position to decide how the term "God" should be translated into Chinese, and for a long time the papal court sought to compromise. This proved impossible, however, and eventually the papacy decided (1715) against the Jesuits. But the Emperor of China, to whom the question had also been referred, had already decided in their favor. The Son of Heaven, not unnaturally, felt that the papal decision flouted his authority in his own land. He therefore forbade any Christian missionary to enter China who did not subscribe to the Jesuit position. After 1715 an obedient Catholic could no longer do so. Missions therefore had either to close down or become illegal. Some illegal entry did occur, but the missionaries who succeeded in evading the imperial authority in this manner could appeal only to the poor and humble classes. Accordingly, Christianity ceased to be at home in the court and among highly educated Chinese, and became instead a small, seeemingly unimportant secret society, tinged with anti-governmental or even openly revolutionary sentiments. A handful of Jesuits remained at court as astronomers, and when the Society of Jesus was dissolved by the pope in 1773 this professional function was transferred to the Lazarist order. But the rites controversy had dramatized for the Chinese the extent to which Christian missionaries were agents of a foreign power. Loyal and obedient officials of the empire reacted by keeping the royal astronomers at a distance.

Opening China to European trade. Until the last quarter of the eighteenth century, China's political and economic order functioned so well that there seemed no reason for any concern with things foreign. After about 1775, however, the traditional signs of dynastic decay began to appear and multiply. Most fundamental was the fact that in many parts of China the population had grown so great that peasant farms had been subdivided into plots upon which a family could not produce enough to survive in a poor season. Indebtedness then led to dispossession from the land. Usurers thus tended to concentrate landed wealth in their hands, while peasant debtors accumulated grievances that burst out sporadically in violent risings. Serious rebellions began about 1775, and became increasingly widespread during the following decades, building up toward the catastrophic Taiping rebellion, which broke out in 1850.

These internal strains were accompanied by troubles across the frontier. Throughout the early nineteenth century, China's northwest frontier remained stable. The military power of steppe peoples had been completely broken in the eighteenth century by Chinese and Russian arms. But this unusual security was counterbalanced by the fact that novel and unprecedented difficulties arose on the southern coast, where trade with the "south sea barbarians" from Europe concentrated. This trade had long been conducted on monopolistic lines, between an association of Cantonese merchants on the one hand and the British East India Company on the other, which had largely supplanted its European rivals. In 1834, however, the British government abolished the East India Company's legal monopoly of the China trade, and sought to introduce at Canton the patterns of commerce normal to European ports. This the Chinese opposed, since the Chinese government was trying to tighten official regulation of trade. From the Chinese point of view indeed, the development of the Canton trade in the early nineteenth century was thoroughly deplorable. Large numbers of Chinese had begun to smoke opium, and the British and other Europeans gladly supplied the drug, which was produced mainly in India. When Chinese officials forbade the import of opium, European traders resorted to smuggling and bribery, so that trade began again to assume the extra-legal forms it had had in the first period of European activity along the China coast.

In 1839 a dispute about the administration of justice in Canton precipitated a war between Britain and China. To the surprise and dismay of the Chinese, British gunboats proved capable of overwhelming Chinese coastal defenses, and the Treaty of Nanking (1842), which ended the war, gave the British nearly all they asked. Four ports in addition to Canton were opened to European trade, Hong Kong was ceded to the British, and British consuls were admitted to all the treaty ports. Other Western nations soon demanded and received the same privileges, and indeed, improved upon the original British terms by demanding extra-territoriality for their nationals living on Chinese soil. The Chinese were enormously affronted by what had happened, but found themselves quite unable to do anything to drive the foreigners back.

China's decline from the heights of its eighteenth-century imperial grandeur was precipitous, yet quite in accord with ancient precedent. Other dynasties had also decayed in precisely the same fashion. Until after 1850 therefore, the old, traditional frame of Chinese life remained essentially intact. Foreign disaster, however unpleasant, was traditional too, and presumably required no more than traditional remedies.

Social tensions in Japan. Japan's history was very different. Japan remained at peace throughout the eighteenth and nineteenth centuries when Chinese armies were winning empire in central Asia. Japanese population remained about constant, thanks to infanticide, which checked excessive subdivision of peasant farms. And Japan escaped foreign harassment until 1854.

Nevertheless, Japanese society was in travail between 1700 and 1850. The samurai class had lost its traditional military occupation. Idleness induced extravagance; extravagance fastened a heavy load of debt on nearly all of Japan's military class. This introduced a persistent discrepancy between loci of political and of economic power. Japanese culture reflected the same sharp duality, juxtaposing the spare aesthetic of samurai ceremonial and a lascivious urban "floating world" of geisha girls and purse-proud upstarts.

The barriers between these two worlds tended to lessen as time went on. Samurai families sometimes adopted a merchant's son, thus refreshing their fortunes and admitting a few commoners to the ranks of the aristocracy. Intermingling of art styles, as artists experimented with elements from Chinese, Western, and Japanese autochthonous traditions, reflected a similar blurring of what had formerly been separated.

More significant for the future was the fact that a handful of Japanese intellectuals overcame great obstacles in order to study Western as well as Chinese learning. The Tokugawa regime had made Neo-Confucianism official, and even prohibited the study of other philosophies. But a few individuals, who felt disaffected toward the regime in greater or lesser degree, could not be prevented from pursuing the foreign learning which filtered into the country through the medium of books brought by the single Dutch ship that was officially allowed to enter Nagasaki harbor each year.

There were still other Japanese who opposed the Tokugawa re-

gime on Neo-Confucian and patriotic grounds. For if the supreme
virtue was obedience to superiors, as Neo-Confucians taught,
what was the proper relation between the shogun and the Emperor? No rewriting of the record could make the shogun's position look like anything but a usurpation, and some Japanese
scholars dared to say so, even at risk of their lives. Others
abandoned Neo-Confucianism in favor of the ancient Shinto, and
piously sought to elaborate that still somewhat inchoate body of
myths and rituals into a more systematic and impressive doctrine.

The really important fact about these currents of intellectual
dissent and opposition is that they tended to flow together and support one another. For Western learning could be valued not only
for its own sake but also because it pointed up hitherto unsuspected
deficiencies in Neo-Confucian doctrine. Thus, opposition to the
shogun, reverence for the emperor, Japanese patriotism, and enthusiasm for Western learning, all coalesced into a sort of intellectual
underground. Particularly in outlying parts of the Japanese
archipelago, where the so-called "Outside Lords" remembered the
time when their ancestors had been rivals, not subjects, of the
Tokugawa family, such ideas met with the protection of the powerful. Hence when in 1854 the shogun reluctantly decided to
abandon the policy of isolation, there existed in Japan a small but
vigorous body of men who had alternative policies for their nation
clearly in view.

The opening of Japan, in other words, was like the release of a
trigger. It did not of itself revolutionize the country. It did allow
opposition groups, who had long been maturing their thoughts and
aspirations to come to power, and in the name of a restored emperor and ancient legitimacy to initiate a wholesale appropriation
of Western technology. No other Asian people was anything like
so well prepared to take advantage of the opportunities offered by
contact with European civilization, for no other people had previously known the duality of culture and tensions between rival
ideals which prevailed in Japan throughout the Tokugawa period.

XXVI

The Transformation of Western Civilization by

the Industrial and Democratic Revolutions

1789–1917

NTIL about 1870, the industrial revolution had its primary seat in Great Britain. Then Germany to the east and the United States to the west began to catch up with British industrial technology. After 1789, the primary seat of the democratic revolution lay in France, where the defects of royal bureaucratic government and the critical temper of the public combined to provoke a long-drawn-out, impassioned, and deliberate effort to remake traditional political institutions in accordance with reason and the will of the people. Each of these great movements tended to spread from its primary center throughout the Western world, and, ere long, beyond the borders of Western civilization also.

As this occurred, older patterns of society, culture, and government were drastically altered — so much so that some observers are inclined to treat modern democratic and industrial civilization as different in kind from anything that went before, whether in Europe or anywhere else. On the other hand, one may regard this vast alteration in the way men live as the most recent in a long series of self-transformations of European (Western) civilization. Both views are plausible, and we of the twentieth century simply lack sufficient depth of time perspective to be able to choose firmly between them, if a choice must be made.

We begin, however, to be far enough removed from the interval between the outbreak of the French revolution in 1789 and the Russian revolution in 1917 to see some of the main lines of Western man's development during this period. The Western nations of Europe and overseas were able to expand their power and wealth enormously, partly by means of continued acceleration of technological improvements and partly also by changes in political and social organization that permitted mobilization of larger resources than ever before for greater and more prolonged enterprises. No other peoples underwent remotely comparable transformation. Hence the preponderance of the West as against other civilizations of the world, which had existed already under the Old Regime, became so great in the course of the nineteenth century that all traditional barriers against Western penetration collapsed. Westerners took advantage of their new-found power to surge into every part of the habitable globe. The world thus for the first time in human history entered upon an adventure in global cosmopolitanism, amid whose early phases we in the twentieth century still flounder.

It is convenient to analyze the transformation of Western civilization from the Old to the New Regime under three heads: (1) economic, (2) political, and (3) intellectual. But any such scheme is artificial and imperfect, tending to obscure relationships that run across these classifications. There is, for example, a sense in which both the industrial and democratic revolutions were simply applications of human reasoning power to economics and politics respectively. But, conversely, the industrial revolution provided a greatly increased margin of wealth which allowed more men to spend more time in intellectual and artistic pursuits than had been possible previously; and the democratic revolution, by breaking through status barriers, opened careers in business, politics, and the arts to anyone with requisite talent. Thus economic, political, and intellectual changes interpenetrated each other in a very complex and intimate fashion, so that all three aspects of the Western experience in fact constituted a single whole.

The industrial revolution. In the eighteenth century, spectacular technological innovation in Great Britain centered especially in the textile trades and, after 1769, when Watt's first patent was granted, in the development of steam engines powerful and versatile enough to drive the new machinery of textile mills. During the nineteenth century, radical technological changes not only spread to almost every established branch of manufacture, but also created vast new industries and products which had no traditional existence whatever.

There were two phases. Until about 1870, practical invention was mainly the work of ingenious mechanics and hard-driving entrepreneurs who relied more on common sense and traditional skills than on systematic research or theoretical science. This was the age of coal and steam, when the railroad conferred a new speed and efficiency upon overland transport, and when improvements in ocean shipping culminated in the substitution of steel hulls and steam-driven water screws for wood and sail. This was also the age when British leadership in every phase of technology and industry remained unquestioned. Textile machinery and steam engines, railroads and steamships, together with the coal and steel industries that provided the necessary basis for the new technology, all were first introduced or attained their earliest large-scale development in Great Britain.

The rise of the chemical industry, swiftly followed by the development of electrical technologies, announced a change in the character and direction of the industrial revolution. To be sure, the old sort of haphazard invention continued. In the United States, for example, Henry Ford introduced his automobile (1903) and the Wright brothers built an airplane (1903) after prolonged and ingenious tinkering. But this sort of isolated, individual invention more and more gave way to systematic research, conducted in well-appointed laboratories by staffs of engineers and scientists who kept in close touch with scientific theory on the one hand and with technological processes on the other.

Germany was the country where linkage between theory and practice first became habitual. The rewards were sometimes very great. By the beginning of World War I, for example, German chemists had made Germany the sole supplier of many industrial chemicals, and the German electrical industry likewise led the world in technological ingenuity and efficiency. Elsewhere, and in older, better-established industries, the idea that a firm should pay out good money to maintain a body of men whose job was to render obsolete the machinery and techniques on which the profits of the company depended still seemed quixotic in 1914. As a result, systematic, continual interplay between scientific theory and technological practice had barely begun to show its potentialities before 1914. Deliberate invention first came decisively into its own during the two great wars of the twentieth century, not before.

Nevertheless, the nineteenth-century rush of technical discoveries and improvements was tremendous when compared to changes occurring in any earlier time. Generally speaking, what happened was that hand processes were converted to machine production. Inanimate power — first steam and later electrical as well — was applied to machines that could produce goods equivalent or sometimes superior to hand-made articles. A vast expansion of scale was the first and most conspicuous consequence. Workshops gave way to factories. More power, more raw material, more end product, more waste, more transport, more clerks to keep track of the industrial and commercial processes, more consumers to buy and more salesmen to sell, and bigger firms with larger capital and larger work forces, all came rapidly into action. Older, simpler forms of manufacture were superseded by the cheapness and, sometimes, also by the improved quality of factory production.

Escalation of the scale of industry required enormous intensification of transport and communication. Distant supplies of raw materials and distant markets for the end products were vital to the success of machine mass-production. Improvements in roads and canals were important in many parts of Europe and the United States of America. But the construction of a railroad net, which got under way in the 1840's, reached boom proportions in the 1850's and 1860's, and continued to absorb large sums of capital until the eve of World War I (trans-Siberian railroad completed 1903; Berlin-to-Baghdad railroad under construction in 1914 and never since completed), far eclipsed all other forms of land transportation. The railroads opened up inland regions, and allowed transport of bulk materials like iron ore and coal across comparatively long distances. The coal fields of Silesia and of Pennsylvania were among the first to expand production because of the new possibilities opened by overland railroad transport. Other coal fields located deeper in the American and Russian interiors came into large-scale operation at somewhat later periods — a process continuing in central Asia as recently as the 1950's.

Revolution in oceanic transport came rather more slowly. Robert Fulton built the first successful steam boat as early as 1807, but for a long time their wasteful use of coal meant that steam vessels could not compete with sailing vessels on long ocean runs. Not until after about 1870 did better boilers and larger steel hulls allow steamships to come into regular use for transoceanic cargo carrying. One result was to flood Europe with grain raised on the broad and fertile plains of America, Argentina, and Australia, since railroads to carry the grain to the ports, steamships to cross the oceans, and farm machinery to plow, plant, and harvest grain on a hitherto unparalleled scale, all became available at about that time.

Air transport, on the other hand, was no more than an exercise of the imagination before 1917.

Communication was almost as important as transport in linking together the participants in the newly intensified industrial process. The establishment of the public penny post in Great Britain (1840) pioneered the development of modern mail systems. National mail delivery systems achieved trans-national integration as a result of the International Postal Agreement of 1875. The electric telegraph was invented in 1844. Since stringing wires from place to place required relatively modest expenditure, telegraph systems spread very rapidly throughout the Western world (first trans-Atlantic cable, 1866). Wireless telegraphy by radio also very rapidly achieved practical importance for long-distance communication after its first practical demonstration by Guglielmo Marconi in 1895. Improved communication provided a flow of news that sustained mass circulation newspapers, which came into being during the 1850's. This in turn affected politics and diplomacy, making it necessary or advantageous for statesmen to play upon and respond to public opinion as generated and expressed in the pages of newspapers.

Consequences of the industrial revolution. In general, the industrial revolution greatly increased the wealth of the Western world, and allowed fundamental improvement in standards of cleanliness, health, and comfort. In its initial stages, to be sure, the crowding of factory hands into new industrial towns and the rapid growth of older cities created social problems with which traditional institutions could not cope. This provided the basis for Karl Marx's (d. 1883) vision of a proletarian mass growing ever poorer in the midst of plenty — a view which was framed in essentials by regarding the harsh realities of early industrialism as insurmountable limits upon the future. In 1848, when Marx first clearly formulated his main idea, such a view was indeed plausible. Revolutionary violence, drawing its strength from the urban poor, had in fact been a decisive element in Europe's political experience since 1789, when a mob assault on the Bastille in Paris had ignited the torch of the great French revolution itself.

In 1848–49, however, a series of similar crowd risings ended in frustration. Soon thereafter, a variety of social inventions began to control and ameliorate the hardships and ugliness of early industrial society. Such an elemental instrument of modern public order as the urban police force came into existence only during and after the 1840's, for example. No less important were sewer systems, garbage collection services, parks, hospitals, health and accident insurance schemes, labor unions, orphanages, asylums, prisons, and a great variety of humanitarian and charitable enterprises aimed at relieving the sufferings of the poor, sick, and unfortunate. Throughout the second half of the nineteenth century these and other inventions came into operation almost as fast as the swelling towns created the need for them. As a result, revolutionary feeling tended to recede in the most highly industrialized countries, and remained vivid only along the expanding edge of industrialism — most spectacularly in Russia, where tsarist bureaucracy reacted slowly and unsympathetically to the needs of an industrializing society.

A second consequence of the industrial revolution was the accelerated growth of population. In Europe, for example, the population of the entire continent in 1800 was about 187 million. By 1900 it had increased to about 400 million, despite the fact that nearly 60 million had emigrated overseas during the nineteenth century and an unnumbered host had also crossed the Urals from European Russia into Siberia and central Asia. A drastically reduced death rate was the main factor promoting such rapid multiplication of population; and this in turn depended partly on improvements in medical science and public sanitation, partly on the enlargement of the food supply, and partly on a general improvement in the material conditions of life.

Before World War I only Great Britain saw a majority of its population leave the land and enter urban occupations. In every other important state the age-old tie to the soil and the rhythms of planting and reaping continued to govern the lives of the majority until after 1914. Nevertheless, the shift from field to factory and from village to city had made itself manifest everywhere in the Western world. This implied a shift away from a mode of life whose basic rhythms had been established in neolithic times, and toward a new pattern of life whose potentialities and limits we are still trying to discover.

It seems likely that the change in ordinary everyday human experience and habit implied by man's wholesale flight from the fields will alter society as fundamentally as it was altered when men ceased to be simple predators and began to produce their food. If so, it is difficult to overemphasize the historical importance of the industrial revolution and impossible to believe that the social organization and styles of life that will eventually prove to be best attuned to industrialized economies have yet clearly emerged.

The democratic revolution in France. The principle that governments derive their just powers from the consent of the governed and from that alone had been trumpeted to the world in 1776 by American rebels against King George III. This democratic notion continued to guide American constitutional experimentation during and after the war of independence. Such an idea had strong appeal in many countries of Europe — not least in Great Britain itself, where ever since 1688 parliamentary supremacy had meant the supremacy of a limited body of property holders. But it was in France that the new political doctrines stimulated dramatic revolution against royal absolutism.

During the eighteenth century, French government became hidebound. The king remained absolute in theory; but in fact almost all efforts at administrative reform were stopped in their tracks by the opposition of one or another special interest, operating usually from within the bureaucratic machine itself. Failures in war matched this dismal record at home; and when in 1778–83 the French did succeed in humbling British pride and helping the Americans toward independence, the result was to thrust the government into hopeless insolvency. This was not surprising, for in the absence of administrative changes, tax income remained inelastic whereas the expenses of warfare had multiplied with the elaboration of armaments.

Louis XVI (reigned 1774–92) sympathized in a small way with the idea of governmental reform, and agreed that a closer link between his government and the people at large would be desirable. When his efforts to increase tax receipts met with the usual crippling resistance, he therefore decided to revive the ancient representative assembly of France, the Estates-General, in hope of persuading that body to authorize new taxes and thus relieve the government's financial embarrassment. But when the Estates-General met on May 1, 1789, many of its members felt that before any new taxes were authorized far-reaching reform in government should be carried through. Their general aim was to make the French government responsible to the people, meaning, in practice, to property holders.

Reform sentiment was strongest among the representatives of the third estate, i.e. commoners. But a few clergymen and nobles favored the reform program also, and, in the absence of firm and consistent royal policy, this tipped the balance. Accordingly, during the month of June the Estates-General transformed itself into the National Assembly and undertook the task of preparing a constitution for the kingdom of France.

Advocates of reform soon generated widespread popular excitement. Rumors that the king was preparing to suppress the National Assembly precipitated a mob attack on the Bastille (July 14). This event was later celebrated as the birthday of the Revolution. Thereafter, Paris organized a revolutionary government — the Commune. Its leaders rested their power directly on the people of Paris, whom they summoned to mass demonstrations in times of crisis. The Paris crowd was frequently able to over-awe or frighten anyone who opposed or seemed to oppose the majesty of the people, with whose voice they claimed to speak.

From Paris, excitement spread to the countryside. During the months of July and August peasants began to burn noble châteaux and refused to pay traditional dues and rents. The National Assembly reacted to this phenomenon by annulling feudal rights and obligations on the night of August 4, 1789. This had the effect of winning a majority of the peasants for the cause of revolution — a fact of fundamental importance in the following years.

The task of making a new constitution for France proved difficult, and the Assembly had frequently to interrupt its work to deal with pressing immediate problems. In particular, the financial bankruptcy of the government called for remedy. The assembly decided to issue a paper currency — *assignats* — against lands confiscated from the church, with the idea that as these lands were sold the *assignats* would be retired from circulation. In fact, however, more and more paper currency was printed, and prices spiraled upward. Wages, as always, lagged behind. Real economic suffering thus gave a cutting edge to the crowd demonstrations in Paris, since it was easy to persuade poor wage-earners that higher prices were the work of "enemies of the people."

By 1791 the new constitution was ready. It established a limited monarchy, resting supreme authority in a Legislative Assembly, to be elected by all active citizens, i.e. those paying more than a certain amount of money annually in taxes.

The most enduring aspect of the constitution of 1791 was the abolition of innumerable local administrative anomalies which had long hampered the French government. Instead, France was divided into new geographical units of roughly equal size, called *départements*. Administrative, judicial, and ecclesiastical jurisdictions were made everywhere to coincide with the new and quite artificial *département* boundaries.

The most controversial aspect of the constitutional settlement of 1791 was the arrangement prescribed for the church. Bishops and priests were to receive salaries from the state, and were to be elected by the citizens of each diocese and parish, quite like any civil magistrate. The pope and most bishops and priests denounced this departure from canon law and demanded the return of confiscated church property. Thereafter the "Civil Constitution of the Clergy," as the laws affecting the church were called, divided Frenchmen sharply between those who supported the new ideas and those who adhered to the ancient traditions of the Roman Catholic church.

The constitution's greatest weakness, however, lay in the fact that it entrusted extensive powers (suspensive veto, appointment of army officers, etc.) to King Louis XVI, who had long since lost all sympathy with the revolutionary cause. He had, in fact, begun to conspire actively with foreign courts (Austria, Prussia) and with émigré nobles who had fled from France. War broke out in April 1792 and the French armies suffered initial reverses at Prussian and Austrian hands. This fanned suspicion against the king, until in August 1792 the Paris crowd intervened decisively again, and induced the Legislative Assembly to suspend Louis XVI from the exercise of his constitutional powers. A new assembly, the Convention, was summoned to make another constitution.

This inaugurated a second and much more radical phase of the Revolution. The Convention declared France a republic, executed King Louis, and instituted a reign of terror against "enemies of the people," in the course of which several thousand persons were summarily judged guilty and beheaded with a new efficiency and humanity, thanks to Dr. Guillotin's machine for cutting off human heads. Executive authority was concentrated in committees of the Convention, the most important of which became the Committee of Public Safety. Energetic efforts to enlist all able-bodied citizens for the defense of their country soon began to produce results, and French armies presently reached the Rhine, spreading revolutionary principles into Belgium and western Germany as they advanced.

Simultaneously, an impassioned and effective propaganda was organized within France as rival political cliques sought to justify and consolidate power. Until July 1794, the most successful of these groups was the Jacobin Club, where active and ambitious revolutionaries gathered to hear the impassioned oratory of Maximilien Robespierre (1758–94) and others who sought in the name of republican principles to inaugurate a reign of Virtue. Rival factions were not content to settle their differences by words and votes on the floor of the Convention. Mob demonstrations and the guillotine were called upon to assist Robespierre and his allies to defeat and destroy one group of "traitors" after another. But as the revolutionary armies rolled back the foreign invaders, justification for such high-handed violence faded. The members of the Convention demonstrated the new tone of public affairs in July (Thermidor by the revolutionary calendar) 1794, when an unexpected vote in the Convention led to Robespierre's arrest and execution. Though some at least of Robespierre's executioners had not intended it, the removal of the man who had become a symbol for revolutionary extremism quickly precipitated a widespread reaction, and the scale of revolutionary violence diminished sharply.

The Convention finally completed the task of drawing up a new constitution for France in 1795. The Directory, which thus came into existence, governed the country for the next four years. In 1799 a *coup d'état* brought a successful young general, Napoleon Bonaparte (1769–1821), to power. He engineered a series of constitutions, each of which gave him greater and more absolute authority than its predecessor. Nevertheless, Napoleon continued to claim that his power rested on the will of the people and he took considerable pains to prove his popularity by holding plebiscites to ratify each of his successive constitutions.

In fact, Napoleon was in many respects a true heir to the revolution. He completed the reorganization of the laws of France (*Code Napoléon*) which translated into everyday legal practice many of the principles enunciated in general terms by revolutionary orators, e.g. freedom of contract, civil marriage and divorce, and abolition

Scale of Miles

0   500

French Empire
in 1810

Under French
influence

Allied with France

**Napoleon's advance
and retreat, 1812**

**Boundary of France
at the beginning
of the Revolution, 1789**

Moscow

RUSSIA

Dnieper R.

Kiev

Black Sea

Constantinople

OTTOMAN EMPIRE

BESSARABIA

MOLDAVIA

WALLACHIA

Danube R.

PRUSSIA

DUCHY OF WARSAW

AUSTRIAN EMPIRE

Pest

Buda

Vienna

Berlin

Baltic Sea

SWEDEN

DENMARK

Hamburg

CONFEDERATION OF THE RHINE

Rhine R.

ILLYRIA

NAPLES

SICILY

ITALY

Milan

Rome

Mediterranean Sea

SARDINIA

CORSICA

SWITZ.

HOLLAND

AUSTRIAN NETH.

FRANCE

Paris

London

KDM. OF GREAT BRITAIN AND IRELAND

SPAIN

PORTUGAL

Atlantic Ocean

**EUROPE
UNDER NAPOLEON
1799-1812**

406

of legal discrimination between classes. The *Code Napoléon* offered a convenient model for other lands as they were brought under French influence by the victories of Napoleon's armies. Once such changes had simplified the daily routines of a region or country it proved practically impossible to restore the multiplicities and complications of the Old Regime.

Democratic revolution in the rest of Europe. Hence, even when Napoleon at length met with defeat at the hands of a coalition of almost all the powers of Europe (1812–15), traces of the revolutionary upheaval through which Europe had passed could not be removed. Indeed, by 1815 the revolutionary imprint had stamped itself upon Napoleon's most inveterate enemies. For it was only after the monarchs of Europe had learned how to stir patriotic enthusiasm by imitating the French and appealing to the sentiments and interests of their subjects that their armies and peoples became capable of meeting and overthrowing Napoleon's forces.

To be sure, the peace settlement that emerged from the Congress of Vienna (1815) failed to unite Germany, as many German patriots had hoped, and put a politically divided Italy under Austrian and papal influence once again. Prince Clemens von Metternich, chancellor of Austria and one of the principal architects of the Vienna settlement, tried to balance defeated France against insurgent Russia, whose tsar, Alexander I (ruled 1801–25), toyed with the thought of reorganizing Europe even more drastically than Napoleon had done. Metternich was successful in thwarting Tsar Alexander's radical aspirations, and within a few years convinced him that careful restraint was required to prevent popular revolution from once again disturbing the peace of Europe.

Yet liberal and revolutionary aspirations remained alive, particularly among educated men of the middle class. In 1830 and again in 1848–49, popular risings overthrew constituted authority in important parts of the continent. Yet the revolutionaries failed to create either a united Germany or a united Italy as they had hoped to do. France became a republic again (1848–52) until Napoleon III imitated his uncle the great Napoleon by converting his election as president into a personal empire, guaranteed by plebiscite. Great Britain escaped revolution, but launched upon a policy of piecemeal reform, expanding the franchise by degrees between 1832 (Reform Bill) and 1884, when almost complete manhood suffrage was introduced.

The failure of the revolutions of 1848 led many to despair of achieving really fundamental political change by reliance upon the will of the people. Yet Napoleon III in France (governed 1852–70) as well as a number of influential British statesmen felt that export of liberal and parliamentary government to other peoples of Europe was a good thing and ought to be encouraged. The Crimean War (1854–56) had the further effect of demonstrating unexpected weakness in the Russian autocracy, which had become the most energetic guardian of the political status quo in central Europe. Two daring political gamblers and diplomats, Count Camillo Cavour (d. 1861) in Italy and Count Otto von Bismarck (d. 1898) in Germany, seized upon the opportunities thus opened to them, and between 1859 and 1871 actually succeeded in uniting Italy around the kingdom of Sardinia and Germany around Prussia.

In Italy a constitutional monarchy prevailed, despite unrelenting opposition from the pope, who resented his loss of territorial sovereignty over central Italy. In Germany, however, Chancellor Bismarck established a constitution for the new imperial Germany (1871–1918) which preserved the prerogatives of the house of Hohenzollern intact. Unlike their Prussian rivals, the Hapsburg emperors of Austria found it impossible to come to terms with nationalism and the liberal demand for popular representative government. The numerous nationalities inhabiting their empire quarreled with one another so bitterly that no democratic consensus could emerge. Nevertheless, in 1914 some sort of parliamentary elective body existed in every important European country, even in Russia (from 1906); and every government tried to establish effective partnership between official policy and "public opinion" as expressed and generated through newspapers and political parties.

On the surface this constituted a tremendous victory for the ideals of popular government, ideals which in 1789 had seemed to most men of affairs to be no more than wild and impractical dreams. But in reality as they spread across Europe, liberal and democratic principles suffered drastic dilution by admixture with elements from the Old Regime. This was especially true in central and eastern Europe, where bureaucratic control from the top remained a far more vigorous reality than the parliamentary trappings of the Austrian, Russian, and German governments suggested. Even in the more truly liberal societies of western Europe, a wide variety of special interests — corporations, cartels, labor unions, political parties, churches, special occupational groupings like army officers, bureaucrats, lawyers, and others — had proliferated in such a way as to hedge round the theoretical sovereignty of the people as effectively as the theoretical sovereignty of the king of France had been hedged around on the eve of the Revolution itself by a similar proliferation of vested interests. As this occurred, of course, the revolutionary drive for liberal, democratic government which had inspired so many at the beginning of the nineteenth century wore itself out. The democratic ideal and the tarnishing realities of power had rubbed off on one another. Special privilege, far from fearing revolutionary unmasking by champions of the people, was more likely to have learned, like Bismarck, how to extend and entrench its power by manipulating the levers of democratic politics from behind the scenes.

Revolutionary ardor (or at least revolutionary rhetoric) passed therefore from liberal into socialist channels after the middle of the century. In 1848, Karl Marx (1818–83) and Friedrich Engels (1820–95) proclaimed in the *Communist Manifesto* their vision of how an international revolutionary proletariat might seize power and thereby inaugurate true liberty and equality. However attractive in itself, Marx's vision proved difficult to realize. Tumultuous quarrels accompanied the early stages of the international socialist movement, and it was not until after Marx's death that a somewhat more stable organization, the Second International Workingmen's Association (established 1889), came into existence. But the emergence of large and relatively well-disciplined socialist parties meant that these organizations, too, had begun to settle toward a *modus vivendi* with the parliamentary regime of the age. Hence in 1914 when war came to most of Europe, German and French socialists fought against one another cheerfully enough. Only a tiny fringe of extremists refused to violate the principles of international solidarity to which the whole socialist movement was officially committed.

Deliberate social change and popular government. Looking at this political evolution as a whole, it seems clear that the French revolutionaries and their liberal heirs accomplished two things.

First, the revolutionaries demonstrated beyond all reasonable doubt that governments were indeed man-made, and could be altered and manipulated more or less according to plan. The older idea that government was divinely instituted, and that some men were appointed by God to hold dominion over others, seemed less and less plausible in the face of the success that came to regimes professing to derive their powers from the people, not from God. The idea that social reform was an ongoing process grew out of the new political outlook. More and more men began to feel that if hardship or injustice existed, steps could and should be taken by deliberate action to remedy the situation. Society came to be looked upon as indefinitely pliable, to be altered bit by bit as changing standards of propriety and need came to be recognized.

All this was very different from older notions. Before 1789, most men had taken it for granted that they lived within a stable social structure whose institutions had been established by God's will and which, therefore, neither could nor should be altered. Hence, as the new liberal frame of mind spread, effective response to the social needs created by rapidly industrializing societies tended to come faster, and aroused less strenuous resistance than before.

Second, the political experience of the French revolution itself and of all European governments in succeeding decades showed that if political leaders were skillful enough to win the support of the majority of the population under their control, then government could achieve far greater practical power than any rulers of the Old Regime had been able to do. Universal military service was the most striking example of the way in which a government commanding the sympathy of the population as a whole could conscript manpower on a scale no monarch of the Old Regime would have dreamed of doing. A steadily mounting scale of taxation was an almost equally striking demonstration of the enlarged scope available to popular governments as against those which failed — as happened, for instance, in Austria — to establish an effective rapport with their subjects.

Enhanced flexibility and expanded power were thus the upshot of Western civilization's democratic revolution. It therefore constituted a true twin of the industrial revolution, which in its own sphere also enhanced flexibility and vastly enlarged the power available to Westerners. Taken together, the result was to raise the power and wealth of the Western style of life so far above those familiar to other civilizations as to make resistance to Western encroachment no longer possible.

Intellectual and cultural revolutions. The secret of Western preponderance over the rest of the world was not solely a matter of material superiority and political organization — important though these were. In addition, during the nineteenth and early twentieth centuries the intellectual achievement of Western science together with the artistic expression of Westerners' aspiration after truth and beauty attained a depth, power and sophistication unmatched elsewhere.

The scale and variety of cultural activity in the Western world between 1789 and 1917 make a brief summary unusually difficult. This is particularly true of art and literature, where among the romantics of the early part of the nineteenth century personal self-expression and originality came to be prized for its own sake. Interest in the unique historic past of each nation and region of Europe fed and was fed by the nationalistic movements of the age; and a rising valuation of national separateness tended to divide literature into distinct national schools.

Science, on the other hand, remained international and public, and perhaps for this reason it is easier to detect the main lines of its development. Two rival and basically imcompatible outlooks upon the word underwent extraordinary elaboration during our period, but shortly before the outbreak of World War I a series of conundrums and paradoxes began to make men aware of the defects and limitations of each of the two rival world-views.

The first of these was basically Newtonian. Four fundamental terms — matter, energy, space, and time — were put to work to explain all the phenomena of physical nature. The effort met with startling success. Indestructible matter, composed of molecules, atoms, and (after 1897) sub-atomic particles, was paired with an equally indestructible energy: and it seemed as though all chemical and physical changes could be explained as the result of combinations and recombinations of these two indestructibles within a uniform, infinite matrix of time and space.

Many phenomena that had previously seemed unrelated to one another fell into place as part of this grand scheme. In particular, the processes of chemical change came to be understood in terms of interactions among molecules, atoms, and electrons, absorbing or giving off energy with each change. As we have seen, this sort of understanding often allowed chemists to control and alter natural processes, thereby creating new industries and improving old products at an unprecedented rate. Similarly, such seemingly diverse phenomena as visible light, infrared, and ultraviolet rays, radio waves, X rays, and still higher energy radiation came to be viewed as parts of a continuous electromagnetic spectrum whose control and manipulation also began to extend human powers in dramatic ways just before the outbreak of World War I.

Yet just about the close of the nineteenth century, unsuspected weaknesses began to undermine the elegant clarity of this vision of the universe. Matter lost its solidity as first molecules and then atoms dissolved into tiny particles vibrating in comparatively vast emptinesses. Energy, too, sometimes seemed to come in particles or quanta. But what was most surprising and distressing of all was the strange results of experiments intended to measure the speed of the earth through space. For Albert Michelson (d. 1931), using very delicate and sensitive instruments, discovered that light appeared to travel with uniform velocity in every direction, even when launched from the rapidly moving platform of the earth. This result, first attained in 1887, seemed entirely incompatible with Newtonian notions of absolute space and time, for light launched in the direction of the earth's motion ought, by all ordinary logic, to move faster than light sent in the opposite direction, since in one

case the speed of the earth should be added, and in the other sub-
tracted from the absolute speed of light.

In order to bring mathematical order to this surprising result, Albert Einstein (1879–1955) proposed in 1905 that space and time
should be collapsed into a single space-time continuum whose nature was such that changes in the relative motion of any two bodies
affected measurements of one taken from the other. Laymen and
not a few scientists found this wrenching from familiar intuitive
ideas of space and time hard to accept. Equally, the discovery of
sub-atomic particles and of energy quanta which began to occur
very rapidly during the first decades of the twentieth century
brought the elegant simplicity of earlier theory into disrepair.
What had seemed about 1890 to be a well-understood, absolute
system of scientific truth, tested by experiment, validated by
innumerable practical applications, and lacking the elucidation of
only a few small corners of reality to achieve complete adequacy,
crumpled suddenly before a confusing welter of inconceivably
tiny and unimaginably vast phenomena that failed to fit the
familiar Newtonian scheme.

The second world-view of nineteenth-century Europe emphasized the fundamental character of time and saw all reality
— natural, biological, social — as part of an unending, develop-
mental flux. Men who pursued this vision of reality did not look
for absolute, universal laws such as those proposed by physicists
and chemists, but sought to comprehend patterns of evolutionary
innovation in particular circumstances and under given conditions.
Such men believed that reality, in whichever of its manifestations
especially interested them, was capable of seizing upon unique
strategic moments when some new possibility had opened to create
what had never been created before — thereby, perchance, pre-
empting the ground and inhibiting, or at least obstructing, any
later efforts to do still better.

The German philosopher, Georg Wilhelm Friedrich Hegel (d.
1831) pioneered the effort to view all reality as a process of unending change. Subsequently, geologists, biologists, archaeologists and
historians combined to open before men's startled eyes a vista of
terrestrial history unimaginably vast by comparison with anything

previously dreamed of. Geologic eons, organic evolution (first clearly proposed by Charles Darwin in 1859), and human history all seemed to belong together. Even the unchanging stars were presently brought within the scope of this evolutionary view, and astronomers began to speculate upon the birth and death not merely of individual stars, but of galaxies and of super-galaxies as well.

Such an ever-receding vastness was just as difficult to reconcile with the ordinary human scale of experience as was the inconceivably tiny world of sub-atomic physics which simultaneously opened beneath men's feet. Human values tied to a particular place and time seemed dubious indeed in a world where everything changed, and where nothing — unless change itself — remained absolute and eternal.

Revolutions in the arts. Art did not fail to mirror the expanding range of uncertainty that characterized European thought on the eve of World War I. A handful of painters, living mainly in Paris, twisted and then entirely discarded the use of perspective as an organizing principle for their art. Instead, Pablo Picasso (born 1881), Georges Braque (1881–1963), and others employed disjointed elements of optical experience, together with shapes only vaguely if at all reminiscent of observable reality, to create a pattern and suggest a mood. They repudiated, above all else, the idea of using painting as a vehicle to portray something outside or beyond the work of art itself.

Literature, being tied to language, was less international than painting and less radical in rejecting traditional forms. In Russia, however, the tension between the old Russian, Orthodox cultural traditions and new-fangled Western styles of thought and sensibility drove sensitive writers like Feodor Dostoyevsky (d. 1881), Ivan Turgenev (d. 1883), Leo Tolstoy (d. 1910), and Anton Chekov (d. 1904) to create a new moral universe, each for himself. This characteristic of nineteenth-century Russian literature lends its best productions a special resonance for many readers of the twentieth century who face a similar problem themselves. Outside of Russia, however, the literatures of Western nations continued to flourish within familiar and well-tried modes of thought and sensibility, along lines that had been fundamentally laid down in the age of the Renaissance.

Despite the comparatively conservative character of Western literatures, the changes that came to science, thought, and art, together with the drastic upheavals in routine resulting from the industrial revolution, and the changes in political and social structure ratified by the progress of the democratic revolution were so deep-going and massive that some men argue that Western civilization was in fact on the verge of breakdown in 1914 — when Europeans proceeded, of course, to complete the job by plunging into an unprecedentedly strenuous war. Yet one may just as well take a more optimistic view and believe that such discrepancies are no more than the signs of growth toward some new and as yet unachieved resolution of the diverse tendencies of our time. Future events may perhaps decide between the two interpretations.

In the meantime it is already clear that the difficulties into which Western civilization plunged at the beginning of the twentieth century entirely failed to hamper the spread of Western influence to other parts of the world, at least in the short run. Instead, vast new springs of power made the West overwhelming to others everywhere. A survey of how the major stems of mankind reacted to such an unprecedented confrontation will therefore be the theme of the next chapter.

XXVII

The Non-Western World Since 1850

TWO world historic processes have come close to completion since 1850. One of them is as old as civilization itself. Ever since civilized societies first came into existence, the wealth, power, and general attractiveness of civilized ways have tended to entangle simpler peoples in the venture of civilization. From about the mid-nineteenth century, the age-old retreat of barbarian and savage societies acquired a new velocity with the development of mechanical means of transport and communication. As a result, within scarcely more than a single century almost all the regions of the earth which in 1850 were still occupied by such simple societies have been either pre-empted by civilized settlers or else brought under civilized types of administration.

The second world transformation dates only from about 1500 when the European Far West began to outstrip the other major civilizations of the world. The upshot of Europe's three and a half centuries of energetic self-transformation was to endow Western soldiers, merchants, and missionaries with such formidable skills that even the best efforts of Moslems, Hindus, Chinese, and Japanese to stave them off proved woefully inadequate. Within a single decade, 1850–60, each of the four great Asian civilizations suffered irreparable invasion, with the result that the leaders of all the non-Western civilized peoples found themselves in almost the same situation as their barbarian and savage contemporaries who also had somehow to cope with the intrusive, mighty, and deeply foreign Western style of life.

Both processes thus reduce to one: the establishment for the first time in world history of a genuinely global cosmopolitan civilization, centered upon the West but embracing all the other varieties and cultural traditions of mankind as well, save for a few tiny and remote communities in such places as the mountainous interior of New Guinea or the upper Amazon, which retain an insulated autonomy to this day.

Impact upon Africa and Oceania. It is worth reminding ourselves how very recent the completion of this process really is. In 1850, for example, the interior of sub-Saharan Africa had not yet been explored by Europeans. The most famous African explorer, David Livingstone (d. 1873), made his first venture into the interior in 1849, and European eyes first looked across Lake Rudolf, one of the African Great Lakes, as recently as 1888. In the mid-nineteenth century, political conditions in most of Africa were very disturbed. Slave raiders, ivory hunters, and warrior tribes like the Zulus spread violence far and wide. Trade relations with Moslem and European agents, who had clustered in coastal towns from the sixteenth century and before, had already broken down the local self-sufficiency of most African societies. A few regions and peoples (e.g. the Pygmies of the Congo rain forest, the Dinka of the upper Nile, and the Bushmen of the Kalahari desert in southwest Africa) remained true to age-old hunting and gathering styles of life, and changed their ways little or not at all despite the trading and slave raiding which harrowed the Bantu and other agricultural peoples of Africa.

When European administration followed European explorers into the interior of Africa, local violence did not at first diminish much, since, despite the superiority of their arms, the number of European soldiers and administrators who undertook to rule vast territories was very small. Nevertheless, the European advance was rapid, spurred by national rivalries among British, French, and Germans. By 1914 only Ethiopia and Liberia remained officially independent.

EUROPEAN
PENETRATION OF AFRICA
to 1914

British
French
Italian
Portuguese
Spanish
German
Belgian

Principal Explorations
1800-1900
British
German
French

Scale of Miles
0   1000

The policies of European colonial administrations differed considerably as far as their immediate impact on pre-existing African societies was concerned. The British, for example, building upon the pattern of their rule in India, often preserved local tribal or territorial regimes, and relied upon advisers and inspectors to control local kings or chiefs. The French and Belgians more often tried to establish a Western type of bureaucratic administration, sometimes partly staffed by Africans who were educated in European-style schools. In either case, exposure to Western civilization and to at least some of its techniques and ideas penetrated African societies at a very rapid pace. The most striking testimony to this fact is that in less than three generations from the time European administration first began to reach inland nearly all of Africa again became politically independent (1951–65), but nevertheless preserved the administrative and economic frame European rulers had imposed upon that continent. Older tribal and religious orderings of African society appear to have become too weak to assert themselves against the new-fangled European styles of bureaucratic administration.

Other geographically extensive parts of the world also came within the circle of civilization only after mechanical transport made continental interiors more accessible. The continent of Australia, for example, saw the first European settlement in 1788, when the British government established a convict colony at Sydney. Free settlers soon followed, but penetration of the interior, and the destruction of native society which accompanied the spread of white settlement, did not get seriously under way until the discovery of gold in 1851 touched off a rush up-country to the gold fields. Similarly, the occupation of the western half of the United States and Canada barely began before 1850, and prospered only when railroads brought the fields and grasslands of the North American interior into effective commercial contact with world markets for grain and meat. Argentina and the southerly parts of Brazil had almost the same rhythm of development. In both North and South America, wherever white settlers advanced the Amerindian populations retreated, surviving, if at all, only in special reservations located normally in land the white men found unattractive.

Even in Asia, the period since 1850 has seen a very substantial advance of agricultural settlement and civilized society. The principal victims of this advance were nomads of the steppe, whose forebears had played such a prominent part in world history before the invention of gunpowder blasted their bows. Russians and Chinese divided the gains. The Chinese, for example, began to flood into Manchuria when the collapse of the Manchu dynasty in 1911 first opened those fertile grasslands to settlers. The Russians,

EUROPEAN PENETRATION
of the PACIFIC
1740-1914

420

similarly, launched a large-scale campaign in the 1950's to develop
the grasslands of Kazakstan for grain farming. Whether skillful application of modern techniques of water management will permit a
similar development of agriculture in Mongolia — long the center
and citadel of nomadic life — remains to be seen. The same is true
of Tibet, and of numerous sites in Chinese Turkestan, where oasis
settlements once flourished and, in all probability, can be made to
flourish again with only a moderate application of modern technology.

Simultaneously, uncounted thousands of peasants steadily
hacked away at the jungle in those parts of southeast Asia where
new land awaited the spade and plow, so that the remaining forest
dwellers of Assam, Burma, Siam, Laos, and the islands of the Indonesian archipelago, like their fellows of the Congo and Amazon rain
forests, are more and more restricted to shrinking pockets of jungle
wilderness.

Some primitive peoples entirely disappeared as a result of this
massive advance of agriculture and civilization. Others have made
the adjustment to living in a more constrained and complicated
world, and in several instances have begun to multiply their numbers very rapidly. This is true of such diverse peoples as the Maoris
of New Zealand, the Amerindians of both North and South America, and of most, but not all, African tribes. Each of these peoples
struck its own compromises between traditional patterns of life and
the social discipline required by ordinary citizenship in the great
world. However ingenious or locally successful such compromises
may be, it is hard to believe that the contribution of these peoples
to the cosmopolitan civilization of our time will be of great importance, since backwardnesses from their past continue to handicap
their present and cloud their future.

The Asian civilizations. The four great civilizations of Asia seem
destined to play a far more significant role. Interaction between the
heirs of Islamic, Hindu, Chinese, and Japanese civilizations on the
one hand and the spate of Western innovation on the other has
been and in the foreseeable future promises to remain, a central
axis, and perhaps *the* central axis, of mankind's history.

During the three or four generations which have elapsed since traditional orderings of society in each of the great cultural regions of the Old World irremediably collapsed, Chinese, Japanese, Hindus, and Moslems have reacted very differently to the problems facing them. The Moslems have been the least successful, for they can neither abandon the Sacred Law of Islam nor live any longer within its constricting bonds. The Japanese stand at the other extreme, having been able to maintain political independence and traditional deference patterns within their society while building a formidable industrial and military strength by means of massive appropriation of Western science and technology. As of 1966, China and India seem to occupy intermediary positions. They have clearer goals and greater ideological agreement as to how to achieve their goals than the Moslems, but have made less tangible progress toward the realization of their hopes than the Japanese.

Before considering the recent evolution of each of these parts of the world separately it seems worth pausing to emphasize how very recent is the disruption of traditional social patterns among the majority of mankind. Victory in the Crimean War (1853–56), which proved more fatal to Ottoman sovereignty than earlier defeats had been, and the Indian Mutiny (1857–58), which led to the abolition both of the Mughal empire and the East India Company, paralyzed initiative among the political leaders of the Islamic world; but only by degrees — in many cases not until World War I — did the lives of the Moslem rank and file feel the effect of the new balance of forces between Islam and the West.

Similarly, the outbreak of the Taiping rebellion, which ravaged wide regions of China for fourteen years (1850–64), no doubt announced the disruption of the Manchu dynasty and of traditional Confucian society. But until after 1949 the peasant mass of China simply suffered all the ills normally associated with the transfer of power from one strong dynasty to another, and heard only from afar of innovations generated in Shanghai and other coastal cities where the educated minority wrestled with foreign ideas in a way that had never happened before in Chinese history.

In India, where the benevolent despotism of the Indian Civil Service and a school system modeled on the British brought aspects of Western civilization to the sub-continent with a rush after 1857, and in Japan, where the initiative of cliques of Japanese samurai discarded the integument of Tokugawa Japan more ruthlessly than any foreigner could have done, peasants and townsmen began to experience the novelties of Western techniques and ideas a generation or more before the Islamic and Chinese heartlands felt any comparable wrench away from familiar routines. Yet even here, the horizon of effective Westernization extends no further than two or three generations. Such a length of time is very brief in the life of a human society numbering millions. It would be foolish to suppose that stable relationships or patterns likely to endure for very long have yet emerged from the past century's clash of cultures.

Islam's reactions to Western dominance. The dilemma confronting the heirs of Islamic civilization from about the middle of the nineteenth century was starkly simple: how to be Moslem without being a Moslem. That is to say, Islamic political and intellectual leaders had somehow to maintain a Moslem cultural identity vis-à-vis the West without remaining bound by the archaic prescriptions and intolerable rigidities of the Islamic Sacred Law which, for so many centuries, has constituted the controlling uniformity of Moslem civilization.

The only response that has so far won much support was to borrow the Western notion of linguistic nationality as a basis for creating modern, secularized nation-states. But this has the unfortunate effect of splitting Islam into a number of comparatively small nations, no one of which is likely to be great enough to regain the proud position Islam so recently occupied in the world. Nationalism has the further disadvantage of being incompatible with Islam's universalism. Any modern, secular-minded government ruling over a Moslem community cannot, therefore, command the wholehearted support of its people, since the teachers and preachers of Islam must of necessity deplore the degeneracy of a government that no longer even tries to conform to God's will as revealed through Mohammed. Hence nationalism has remained an ill-fitting garment, almost as awkward to wear as the Sacred Law itself, whose incompatibility with modern government and habits of mind lies at the root of Islam's crippling difficulty in coping successfully with the Western disruption of its traditional world.

The political fortunes of Islam reached their low point at the close of World War I when the Ottoman empire was partitioned among the victors. Before this final catastrophe, the western provinces of the Islamic world in Africa and the Balkans had all been sheared away, either by the rise of new independent Christian states in the Balkans or by the establishment of European colonial regimes in Africa. The same fate had also befallen Islam's eastern marches, as Americans in the southern Philippines, Dutch in Indonesia, British in India, and the Chinese and Russians in central Asia all closed in on Moslem states and peoples and forced them to accept a humiliating subjection. Hence, by 1914 only a slender band of states lying athwart the historical heartland of Islam retained even a tattered claim to independence: Afghanistan, Iran, and the Ottoman empire itself.

Yet the disaster of World War I (1914–18) presaged a partial political recovery. Outraged Turkish feeling stubbornly refused to accede to the decision of the victorious powers. Under the leadership of Mustapha Kemal (1880–1938), a resolute general and charismatic political leader, the Turks succeeded in defeating the would-be partitioners of their Anatolian homeland, and by 1923 had won the assent of the European powers to the repossession of Constantinople itself. The new, revolutionary regime that Mustapha Kemal fashioned in the heat of battle was secularist, nationalist, and completely indifferent to the West's liberal scruples against an indefinite expansion of governmental authority at the expense of private property and individual rights. Drastic internal reform, including the disestablishment of Islam, shift of the capital from the incurably cosmopolitan city of Constantinople to Ankara, and compulsory changes of manners — e.g. the unveiling of women and the wearing of hats with brims — shook traditional life to the core. Such enactments were accompanied by strenuous and organized propaganda, which attempted to plant a fierce pride in Turkishness and a sympathy for the regime among all ranks of society.

REALM OF ISLAM
SINCE 1850

Predominantly Moslem
Boundaries 1966
Political subjection
Moslem missionary advance

Boundary of the
Ottoman Empire
before WW1

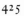
425

From 1925, when a usurping shah came to the throne, a similar though less drastic and less well-organized secularist revolution from the top came to Iran. Afghanistan, too, regained a more effective independence than it had enjoyed before the war.

Among the Arabs, however, a different reaction to the upheaval of World War I came to the fore. The peace settlement of 1919 assigned the richer and more settled portions of the Arab world to French and British colonial administrations. The peoples of Iraq, Syria, and Palestine baulked a little, but soon submitted. In Arabia itself, however, the puritanical Wahhabi reform movement came to power through the victories of Abdul-Aziz ibn-Saud (1880–1953), whose family had been the principal political and military protectors of the Wahhabi movement from its inception in the eighteenth century. By 1925 ibn-Saud had conquered most of the Arabian peninsula and in particular had gained control of the two holy cities of Mecca and Medina.

Yet by a supreme irony, ibn-Saud used his new-won power not to press forward with the effort to create a society and government truly pleasing to Allah, but to introduce such instruments of centralization as roads, airplanes, and telegraphic communication among the cities under his rule. Then, within less than a decade after the establishment of ibn-Saud's power, Western businessmen discovered enormous reserves of oil in Arabia, and by paying royalties on oil taken from the ground, began to shower the ruling dynasty with fantastic riches. Under these conditions the moral energy of the Wahhabi movement rapidly dissipated itself, betrayed by the new wealth that flowed from oil.

Secularism made rapid gains also in Egypt, Syria, and Iraq. Above all else, this spirit took the form of agitation for political independence from the French and British who had divided the Middle East between them after World War I. Iraq won independence — at least on paper — in 1932; but a far more genuine independence came to all the Arab nations after World War II, when European military bases and other trammels upon complete sovereignty were everywhere withdrawn. Yet even after these successes the Arabs suffered continuing political frustration. Their new states were not great and powerful, nor were they particularly resolute and skillful in creating the industrial and technical base upon which future national power might be erected. This was dramatically underlined in 1948 by the establishment of a Jewish state in Israel, whose existence constituted an affront to Arab pride, since it was carved out of land which had previously been occupied by Arabs, and which nearly all Arabs feel should belong to them again. But efforts to concert military measures against Israel persistently failed because of internal frictions among the Arab states themselves. These frictions were fed by the fact that the separate sovereignties into which the Middle East happened to be divided by the European imperial administrators after World War I had no very deep historical or geographical roots. Political multiplicity, indeed, confronts the more nearly Islamic ideal of a great pan-Arab empire. The resulting uncertainty as to political loyalties is further exacerbated by the fundamental Islam-secularist dilemma which Arabs feel with special sharpness since the faith of Mohammed is so peculiarly their own. For these difficulties no solution seems in sight.

The most embarrassing confrontation between Islam and modernity occurred in Pakistan. This new state was carved out of British India in 1947 to give the Moslems of the sub-continent a country of their own where they would be safe from oppression by the Hindu majority. The whole *raison d'état* therefore rested on religion. Yet efforts to create a constitution that would accord with Moslem precepts have uniformly failed. The country has in fact been ruled by army officers and bureaucrats who were trained, for the most part, under the British regime and who usually take their religion lightly enough in private, yet dare not question the religious basis upon which the state of Pakistan originally arose.

Despite these handicaps and frustrations, Moslem rulers have in practice regained political sovereignty all the way from Indonesia in the east to Morocco in the west. Only in Russian and Chinese central Asia do substantial communities of Moslems now remain under religiously alien rule. Perhaps in time the importation of Western technology and the development of industry will transform the social structure of Islamic societies in some decisive fashion and open fresh possibilities that now do not appear. To an outsider, educational, legal, and moral reform all seem prerequisite for really successful economic development; yet these imply inevitably a surrender of many distinctively Moslem traditions. And that is a course of conduct that cannot easily appeal to proud and sensitive peoples, whose faith in Allah has been so sorely tried by their recent defeats at the hands of Western upstarts, infidels, and apostates.

The Balkan Christians. Among the seventh of mankind that recognizes Mohammed as Prophet of God, neither the industrial nor the democratic revolutions of modern times can yet (1966) be said to have made much progress. In contrast, the two principal communities once subject to Moslem rule — the Christians of the Balkan peninsula and the Hindus of India — have each been able to respond far more successfully to the challenges inherent in the West's New Regime.

Balkan Christians won independence from Ottoman rule through a series of revolts and diplomatic crises, extending from 1803, when the Serbs rebelled against Turkish authority, until 1912–13, when the Turks were driven from all but a small bridgehead in Europe through the combined efforts of Bulgars, Serbs, and Greeks. Virulent and conflicting nationalisms, appealing to peasants as well as to townspeople, made the Balkans a political cockpit throughout the nineteenth century. Unlike the Moslems, the Balkan Christians felt no serious incompatibility between their traditional religion and the dictates of modernization along Western lines. Accordingly, economic and social development was fitfully but deliberately pursued by nationalistic governments in the nineteenth and early twentieth centuries, for it did not take much wisdom to realize that, as a minimum, national strength and security demanded local arms factories and a communications net that would allow rapid movement toward any threatened frontier. It was, however, only after World War II that efforts of this nature attained solid success. This was the case both in those areas which became Communist and in Greece, where a freer, more liberal society and a democratic parliamentary government prevailed. The result has been to weld Balkan society to the West, perhaps more securely than ever before, since even in Roman times the cultural gap between the Greek- and Latin-speaking halves of the empire always remained enormous.

The Hindus. The relation of the Hindu population of India to Western civilization was very different from the Balkan Christians'. After the shock of the Mutiny, which for a brief period in 1857 seemed to endanger British power in India, a benevolent but fundamentally autocratic civil service, whose members were recruited almost entirely from British universities, imposed a long series of reforms upon India. Their own liberal principles inhibited these civil servants from using governmental powers for any sort of forced-draft economic development; yet they did build a coherent railroad network that tied the entire sub-continent together as never before. In addition, British authorities organized an educational system which taught almost the same subjects as were taught in British schools and universities and used the English language for all higher instruction. The vast majority of Indians had no access to such schools. Yet the schools and universities did create a numerically small but very influential group of Anglicized Indians, most of whom found positions in government offices where they first assisted and in time took over responsibility from British officials.

Within this framework, India's reaction to Western civilization proceeded peacefully and comparatively quickly. Economic innovation rested very largely with outsiders: Parsis, Greeks, Britishers and others. Few Hindus were ready to risk private capital in new industrial or commercial ventures, preferring to use any surplus funds they might accumulate for old-fashioned village usury or for the purchase of land. During World Wars I and II, however, partial disruption of supply lines from Great Britain presented the administrators of India with a sudden need to find alternative sources of supply for thousands of needed items. Efforts to start new industries or expand existing ones therefore became urgent. Lines between private and state enterprise blurred or even disappeared under these wartime conditions. As a result, when independence came to India in 1947, a semi-socialistic economic regime was easily developed by building upon wartime emergency measures.

India's ability to meet the economic challenge presented by its rapidly multiplying peasant population, among whom customary routines and patterns of land holding often obstruct the introduction of more efficient agricultural techniques, remains one of the key questions of our time. Official planning and governmental initiative have not so far been able to prevent sporadic famine, a circumstance to which the Indian peasantry is, however, more accustomed than most.

In the sphere of politics, Indian response to the British presence was striking and unique. As we saw above, early in the nineteenth century, Ram Mohan Roy (d. 1833) used British ideas and rhetoric to agitate for a number of legal reforms in India. By 1885 enough Indians had been educated in British-style schools and universities to provide a sounding board and effective support for the Indian National Congress, which was organized in that year with the aim of pressing for eventual Indian self-government. After World War I, leadership of the Congress passed into the hands of Mohandas Karamchand Gandhi (d. 1948), nicknamed "Mahatma," i.e. "Great Soul," by his followers and admirers. Gandhi had been trained in the intricacies of English law, and as a political leader he combined the shrewdness of a lawyer with a direct appeal to India's religious traditions. In particular, he used the principle of nonviolence to organize massive civil disobedience campaigns, in which India's urban millions and even some of the villagers took part. British authorities were unable to suppress Gandhi's movement without violating their own ideas of the proper restraints upon the arbitrary use of power. Hence in 1947 the British government yielded and agreed to grant India's independence — a prospect which so frightened Indian Moslems that they withdrew to form their own state of Pakistan.

The achievement of independence confronted the government with the question of whether or not India would become a Hindu state to match Pakistan's official espousal of Islam. But when Gandhi was assassinated in 1948 by a fanatical adherent of a Hindu extremist group, massive reaction damped this issue as nothing else could conceivably have done. The result, therefore, was that a secular-minded administration under the leadership of Jawaharlal Nehru (d. 1964) guided India's first years of independence.

Whether the remarkable fusion between Indian traditional religious attitudes and the democratic ideals of the West which Gandhi fashioned will remain viable, or whether some other basis for Indian political life will assert itself, remains, like the question of India's economic future, one of the major issues of our time. Divisive nationalisms based on the linguistic multiplicity of Hindu India are already in the field. So is a vociferous Marxist party. But neither of these movements has so far won more than trifling local successes against the wider appeal of Gandhi and his successors in the Congress party.

China's response to Western dominance. The massive continuity and prolonged success of their civilization across so many centuries made it peculiarly difficult for Chinese literati to believe that uncouth foreigners could have anything really important to teach them. Hence, even after the imperial government found it necessary to hire foreign military experts to help suppress the Taiping rebellion, only a few mandarins dared or cared to take the lesson of China's weakness to heart. Their efforts to create the basis for a more efficient army and navy soon petered out, partly because of conservative opposition but also because the reformers themselves were half-hearted, and recoiled from any action that infringed upon traditional Chinese social patterns. But to create technically up-to-date military force would have required massive technological, educational, and administrative changes which the Chinese reformers of the nineteenth century were not themselves prepared to undertake. The inevitable result was further military humiliation, first at the hands of Europeans (1856–60) and then at the hands of the Japanese (1894–95).

Realization that Japan had been able within a single generation to equip its army and navy so as to outclass the Chinese armed forces come as a severe shock even to the most conservative mandarins. Yet efforts to cope with the problem of China's weakness remained ineffective, partly because agents of the rival European powers and of Japan began to swarm in upon Chinese officials, seeking special concessions and other advantages. To many Chinese, the government's concessions to foreigners looked like a cynical betrayal of the national interest. Hence, secret societies

aimed either at the expulsion of Europeans or at the overthrow of
the Manchu dynasty and the establishment of an authentically Chinese and presumably more patriotic government began to pro-
liferate widely, especially among students and other youth groups.
The so-called Boxer uprising (1900) showed how hopeless it was
to try to drive foreigners from China's shores without modern
arms. At the same time, the fact that the imperial court had lent at
least a backhanded support to the Boxers helped to discredit the
Manchu regime.

A great variety of reform measures were in fact undertaken. But
both before and after the abdication of the last Manchu emperor in
1912, tinkering with forms of government did not at first effect
basic changes. A rising level of violence and disorder in the provinces largely nullified official initiatives. Rising violence also had the
effect of checking Western economic penetration. Railroads that
did not run because of rebellion somewhere along the line, and
modern mines that operated only sporadically for similar reasons,
obviously were far less efficacious instruments of Westernization
than the same physical plant might have been in time of internal
peace. Moreover, by discouraging foreign investment outside the
limits of the zones actually administered by foreigners in Shanghai
and other port cities, civil violence tended to preserve a thoroughly
traditional social and economic order throughout China's interior.

Peasant discontent, based on land shortages, debt and heavy
rents, and taxes, fed civil disorder. Earlier Chinese dynasties had
repeatedly passed from the scene amid just such disasters. The
eventual consolidation of China under the Communists after 1949
also seems, at least superficially, to conform closely to ancient precedent. The relation of the Communist party and doctrine to the
new state resembles the traditional relationship of Confucian
schools and learning to the imperial government of China. And the
policy of the Chinese Communist government, which used its
power to expel foreigners and to reassert Chinese influence in the
disputed borderlands, exactly duplicated the policies earlier imperial governments had followed in such regions as Tibet, Annam,
Korea, and central Asia.

Nevertheless, it would be a serious mistake to conclude that

China has simply experienced one more traditional change of dynasty. Since 1905, when the ancient imperial examinations were abolished as the avenue of recruitment into the imperial bureaucracy, China's intellectual and political leaders have almost unanimously turned their backs upon Confucianism. This has had very important political consequences. Students, who in earlier times would have mastered the classics, swarmed instead into Western schools. Many enrolled in Japanese educational institutions and others traveled to the United States or Europe. Missionary schools in China itself expanded rapidly and new secular institutions were also set up. Hence a comparatively large number of young men and women encountered and enthusiastically embraced Western learning without always fully understanding it.

Sun Yat-sen's (d. 1925) naïve mixture of moral exhortation, social utopianism, and nationalism faithfully reflected the utter confusion prevalent among the first generation of Chinese students who sought to digest the intellectual culture of the West at a single gulp. Yet despite his intellectual confusions and extremism Sun Yat-sen became the founder of the Kuomintang party. Between 1911 and 1949, this party struggled for the control of China against local war lords, Japanese puppets, and Communist rivals. Then, after the prolonged strain of World War II, the more tightly disciplined and more intellectually coherent Communist movement took power in all of mainland China.

The appeal of Communism to Chinese minds is not difficult to understand. Marxism provided a clear explanation for all of China's recent humiliations by attributing them to the greed of wicked imperialists. It had the further advantage of giving "scientific" validity to the Chinese peasantry's hatred of foreigners and landlords, whom Marxists identified as class oppressors. At the same time, the completeness and philosophical sophistication of Marxism attracted educated and sensitive persons who, having repudiated all the pieties of their childhood, felt an acute need for articulate answers to all problems, both practical and theoretical.

Men caught in the midst of the harsh and painful disruption of traditional patternings of life probably need objects against which to direct pent-up frustration and hate. Under the same conditions we should expect intellectually inclined persons to seek systematic ideologies that will both explain what is happening and provide specific rules of conduct to give their lives structure and meaning. Communism, as developed in Russia and more recently in China, performs these functions very exactly — a fact which goes far to account for its widespread recent success among peasant societies just beginning to emerge from agrarianism.

Insofar as the enormous peasant mass of China is concerned, the confrontation with Western ideas and techniques began on a really massive scale only during and after World War I. Many of the leaders of Communist China personally bridge the gap between a thoroughly conservative Confucian world and their own new regime. Mao Tse-tung (1893–   ) himself, the principal Chinese Communist leader, started life as a student of Confucius and first met and accepted Marxism when in his twenties. This sort of experience, running through the lives of millions, assures a heavy carryover from traditional China. But how interaction between Chinese and Western cultures will proceed, and how the mixture of old and new, autochthonous and foreign, elements will proceed cannot be forecast. It has just begun.

Japan's Westernization. Defying Japanese law, Commodore Matthew Perry of the United States Navy sailed with a squadron of warships into Tokyo Bay in the summer of 1853. Perry then demanded an interview with the emperor of Japan and pressed for the opening of Japanese ports to American trade. Japan's reaction to this event was strikingly at variance with China's belated, troubled response to the West's challenge. In Japan traditional lines of social deference remained unbroken — at least until the end of World War II. But the traditional masters of Japanese society, the samurai (or more accurately, a faction drawn from that class), used their authority to revolutionize Japanese life in a very thoroughgoing way. Their overriding initial aim was military strength, i.e. a modern army and navy. To equip and maintain such forces required modern industry; modern industry required knowledge; and knowledge required schools. Japan's leaders proceeded with extraordinary energy to pursue all these implications, imitating the

West without scruple in order to create whatever they judged to be needful.

Their practical success was remarkable. As we just saw, Japanese soldiers and sailors defeated the Chinese in 1894–95. A decade later the Russians met the same humiliating fate. First Korea (1910) and then Manchuria (1931–32) were brought under Japanese imperial rule, and developed to provide fresh sinews for Japan's industrial and military growth. Invasion of China proper (1937) met with extensive initial successes too; but when the Japanese also attacked American, Dutch, and British forces in the Pacific (1941) the war merged into World War II. It ended (1945) with Japan's complete defeat and the loss of her former imperial possessions. Nevertheless, Japan's industrial recovery was rapid. Many Japanese products command a world market today, ranking with the best that any industrialized nation can produce.

The government played a very active part in initiating Japanese industrialization. Many new ventures were first begun by officials and only later sold to private entrepreneurs, whose relationship to the political cliques controlling the government remained very close. In addition, pre-existing artisan shops and small family enterprises were ingeniously mobilized for the production of new goods by a "putting out" system. This meant that a big firm might provide blueprints and perhaps raw materials, power tools, and credit to an artisan family, and in addition would undertake to purchase the product at a price that would allow the family to live modestly. Traditional reciprocal obligation between high- and low-ranking individuals and families assured the smooth functioning of this system. Similar ties mollified labor-management relationships in newly built mills and factories.

Industrial, technological, and scientific advances which brought Japan fully abreast of Western countries by the middle of the twentieth century were therefore not necessarily connected with liberal, democratic ideas or parliamentary government. In the initial stages, indeed, the policy of opening the country to foreign contact and changing familiar ways was generally unpopular. A democratic regime could not possibly have carried such a policy through. Indeed, it was only by appealing to traditional loyalty to the emperor, whose rights were restored by a *coup d'état* in 1868 (the Meiji restoration), and by emphasizing the nationalistic appeal of Shinto — a religious cult that treated the emperor as a god — that the Japanese revolution from above was able to surmount the troublesome first stage when the rank and file of Japanese society could not yet glimpse eventual success, and saw around them only a wanton destruction and disregard of traditional ways.

The fact that Japan acquired a constitution in 1889, cut mainly on the German model, did not of itself change the realities of Japanese politics. Informal groups of elder statesmen and trusted intimates still controlled affairs, despite noisy debates in the new Diet. A greater challenge to the power of oligarchic cliques arose from the ranks of the army. The introduction of universal military service in 1872 made the army into a very influential school of patriotism, where ordinary peasant boys could rise, by pursuing appropriate training, to officer rank. Junior officers in the 1930's therefore represented a new political element in the arcanum of Japanese government. More than once they resorted to assassination as a means of expressing their discontent with the policies of cabinet members and politicians. Such emphatic intervention in the political process was not without effect. Indeed, Japan's forward policy in Manchuria and China was largely the work of young hot-heads in the army who pushed their elders toward action.

After 1945, however, sharp reaction set in. American occupation forces attempted to democratize Japan by fiat from above, while the practical, irreverent example set by thousands of American soldiers worked from the bottom to reinforce social policy. Land reform eased peasant hardships, which before World War II had inflamed the ardor of young officers drawn from that class. Simultaneously, the erosion of the older clan and class lines as a result of changing manners and styles of living helped to give the new democratic forms of Japanese government greater reality than before. Yet the very structure of the Japanese language, which requires variant forms of address to indicate rank and status relationships between the speakers, seems to inculcate and sustain patterns of social deference that have no analogue in democratic societies of the West. Under such circumstances, it is surely too soon to be sure that Japan's industrial revolution will induce a plausible facsimile of the democratic revolution experienced by Western nations.

Such a survey as this ought to bring home the uncertainty and open-endedness of cultural interactions between Western and non-Western mankind. The mere numerical weight of those who are not directly heirs of Western civilization is enough to assure that the direction of mankind's future evolution will not be simple westernization. Instead there will surely be blending and intermingling of cultures, as there has always been in the past when men of divergent styles of life met and mingled. Yet in any foreseeable future the Western component of the mixture seems certain to be dominant, since power, wealth, and truth itself beckon men everywhere to pursue industrialization, democratization, and science — all of them stemming directly from the Western past.

XXVIII

The Western World Since 1917

THERE is a sense in which events since 1917 have magnified the West's advantage with respect to other peoples and cultures. Thus, for example, the development of tanks and airplanes during the First World War and of atomic weapons, electronic control systems, and rocketry, together with civilian uses for these and related devices during and since the Second World War, widened the gap between the technologically most advanced nations and the rest of the world. Moreover, as long as the richest and strongest among existing nations devote large sums of money and a large proportion of their trained manpower to systematic development of new technologies, it seems almost certain that the technological gap between the most advanced and more backward parts of the earth will continue to widen. Transfer of funds, whether as gifts or as loans, from developed to underdeveloped nations does not seem at all likely to close such a gap, though of course it can and sometimes does facilitate agricultural and industrial changes which may be of great importance locally.

From another point of view, however, the difference between Western and non-Western societies has radically decreased since 1917. As we have just seen, from about the middle of the nineteenth century, the leaders of Moslem, Indian, Chinese, and Japanese civilizations began to feel that their inherited societies required drastic and deliberate renovation. Old guidelines to behavior and traditional intellectual and moral certainties no longer seemed adequate; new ones were hard to find. Very similar sentiments have spread widely through Western nations since 1914–18, when many of the landmarks and illogical compromises of Europe's aging New Regime tottered or crumbled under the shock of war.

The Communist challenge. The most direct challenge to Western social and political practices came from Russia, where the revolutions of 1917 brought first a liberal and then a socialist and finally a Communist regime to power. Vladimir Ilyich Lenin (1870–1924) and his Bolshevik followers hoped and expected to see World War I provoke proletarian revolution in the highly industrialized countries of Europe, as predicted by Karl Marx. As long as Lenin lived the idea of using Russia as a launching pad from which to ignite revolution in Germany and elsewhere remained vivid. Many Russian Communists felt that they were merely conducting a holding operation on the flank of the capitalist world until such time as the dialectical forces of history would compel the industrialized peoples to enter the Communist camp. To make ready for that day, energetic propaganda and co-ordination of the efforts of Communist parties in all parts of the world seemed far more important than building a Communist society at home, or even establishing normal diplomatic relations with capitalist powers.

A full decade elapsed before it became reasonably clear to all concerned that Communist revolution was not imminent in western Europe or the United States. This confronted the Russians with quite a new challenge: how to overcome Russia's industrial backwardness, in order to be able someday to realize the dream summed up in Marx's phrase, "From each according to his ability, to each according to his need." The answer was found, under Josef Stalin's (d. 1953) tyrannously heavy hand, in a series of five-year plans, which projected rapid investment in factories, power plants, mines, communications, educational institutions, and all the other prerequisites for industrial expansion. Resources to support these efforts were gathered from the Russian populace by heavy taxation, and by direct appropriation of grain from the peasantry.

Collective farms, formed in the early 1930's, allowed the government to control agricultural operations more closely than before. Acute peasant discontent — manifested, for example, by the wholesale slaughter of farm animals at the time of collectivization — failed to achieve politically effective expression, partly because the most energetic and ambitious found it easy to leave the countryside in order to make a career in industry or industrial construction. To many — perhaps to most — Russians, hardships and brutality appeared justified by the urgent need to get on with the tasks at hand, in order to be able eventually to overtake and surpass the capitalist world.

Muddled liberalism. Meanwhile, the other nations of Europe and the United States were forlornly hoping for the world to return to normal. The three principal victors of World War I, France, Britain, and the United States, did return to normal in the sense that demobilized soldiers fitted again into civilian life without provoking any radical changes in the social or political order. In central and eastern Europe, however, the war left much deeper scars. In 1917–18, the Russian, Austrian, and German empires all collapsed, and a belt of new states extending from Finland in the north to Yugoslavia in the south emerged. In most of these new countries nationalist movements before and during the war had been partly movements of social revolution, directed against local ruling classes whose language happened to differ from that of the majority. But the new regimes established by the peace settlements of Versailles (1919–20) were quite unable to satisfy their supporters' revolutionary hopes. Resultant discontent very often drifted into Communist channels. Defeated Germany, too, developed a large and powerful Communist party, thus giving substance to Russian hopes for the spread of revolution westward.

Economic boom, based in part upon loans from the United States, seemed about to stabilize central and eastern Europe in the mid-1920's. But when in the 1930's crippling depression followed, the vague hope that liberal institutions and the free market would somehow muddle through seemed more and more absurd. This remained, nevertheless, the only foreign policy that French, British, and American statesmen could think of. Things were so bad at home that they quickly became obsessed by the task of relieving the symptoms of the depression within their own backyards. Communist hopes rose anew, for the depression seemed to conform to the predictions Marx had made about the increasing instability of capitalist economies. But it was not Communist but National Socialist (commonly abbreviated to Nazi) revolution that came to power in Germany (1933), and soon began to echo throughout Europe.

The Nazi-Fascist movement. Nazi doctrine and practice owed something to the example of Benito Mussolini's (d. 1945) Fascist regime in Italy, which dated from 1922. But the model offered by national mobilization as improvised during World War I was far more important. Adolf Hitler (1884–1945), the leader of the Nazi party, built his movement around veterans of the war who found no satisfactory niche in civilian life. Mussolini had done the same. Memories of the desperate comradeship of the trenches, where shared pains, joys, and dangers bound men powerfully together, haunted old soldiers whose civilian life lacked all value and meaning. Nazis and Fascists sought to create a similar comradeship in peacetime by demanding total subordination of individual and group self-interest to the service of the nation, as defined by themselves. Hitler also invented an enemy — the Jews — upon whom to focus hate and blame for all of Germany's difficulties and failures.

In practice Nazi rule meant energetic militarization of society, massive rearmament, road construction, and foreign trade controlled as much by political as by economic calculations. These enterprises, enthusiastically pursued, quickly absorbed Germany's unemployed, just as Communist Russia's planned industrialization also kept the work force busy — if not always well fed. A noisy propaganda aimed at restoring Germany's "rights" and claiming to safeguard civilization from the Communist danger accompanied the Nazi revolution.

Liberal and democratic governments were ill prepared to confront the simultaneous challenges of depression at home and Nazi, Fascist, and Communist totalitarianism abroad. Only the United States generated a partially effective response to the depression, when President Franklin D. Roosevelt (d. 1945) launched the

New Deal (1933). Like the Nazis and Communists, the New Deal drew upon wartime precedents for solving — or trying to solve — the economic depression. Meanwhile France and Britain dithered. The fact that small but influential groups in each country were attracted to fascist or communist ideas seriously hampered action. None of the Western governments — certainly not the United States — found any effective way of countering Hitler's growing power. Belatedly, when his plan for domination of Europe and his readiness to act on it became unmistakable, Britain and France declared war in September 1939.

World War II. The war of 1939–45 marked a great advance in the scale and precision of war mobilization. During World War I only Germany achieved something approximating rational coordination of civil and military demands upon resources — but only toward the end of the struggle. During World War II, on the contrary, all the major belligerents bent their economies out of shape by remarkably successful social engineering. Millions of men and women were taught new skills and moved to and fro to aid in the war effort. Calculations of supply flows and of industrial capacities governed military strategy. Bottlenecks occurred with disconcerting frequency at first, but as time passed, war planners increased the accuracy and skill with which they foresaw and forestalled such difficulties. Many of the devices — fixed prices, rationing, allocation of scarce raw materials, conscription of labor, etc. — used in the United States and Great Britain to give maximal force to the national war effort, resembled controls the Russians and Nazis had imposed in peacetime. The possibility of deliberately shifting human and material resources from their customary and traditional peacetime uses was strikingly demonstrated on every side. Just as the French Revolution had proven that governments were capable of being made and remade by men's deliberate choice, so it now appeared that the social and economic texture of society, which liberal thought had assumed to be natural and beyond deliberate human control, was in fact woven by human wills and could be rewoven to create new patterns so long as the rank and file were willing to submit to an energetic and purposive central direction.

Two other aspects of the wartime experience deserve emphasis.

First, both sides rapidly outgrew any merely national framework. The Germans overran and organized almost all of continental Europe to make it support a single war machine. The Japanese were less successful in east Asia, but within the limits of their narrower resources they did the same. The allied states, and particularly Britain and the United States, created a globe-girdling administrative war machine. Raw materials were gathered from the far corners of the earth and allocated in accordance with strategic plans agreed to from time to time at a series of summit conferences. Manpower and industrial capacity were similarly assigned war work according to reasonably precise plans that defined how much of what end products the armed forces of the allied nations would require. Finally, the allied armies campaigned almost as though they constituted a single trans-national force. The obsolescence of the sovereign national state — at least on the geographical scale of western Europe — was thereby made plain, for a political unit which cannot defend itself alone is not, in the traditional meaning of the term, sovereign, whatever legal forms or polite fictions may assert to the contrary.

Second, the major belligerents found it possible to plan invention and create new weapons on the basis of technologies which at the beginning of the war had not yet been discovered. Instead of waiting until a given device had been invented and then adjusting tactics and strategy accordingly, men set out to invent new weapons to fit specifications of performance based on tactical or strategic requirements. Among the awesome results of this venture were atomic bombs, jet planes, and long-distance rockets. Faint glimmerings of this sort of planned technological discovery had cropped up during World War I, when, for example, the second generation of tanks was built according to military planners' specifications; but wide-ranging resort to planned invention came only with World War II.

Postwar conflicts and co-operation. The significance of the wartime experience was much enhanced by the fact that there was no complete and general demobilization at the close of hostilities. Though the war ended with the utter defeat of Italy, Germany, and Japan, the victors quarreled almost immediately, so that by

1949, an American-led "free world" opposed a Russian-led "Communist world" which embraced not only eastern Europe, where Russian armies had brought revolution in their train, but the great bulk of China as well. The requirements of the aptly named "Cold war" compelled each side to maintain partial mobilization. This meant retention or reactivation of many of the instruments of economic and social control which had been first introduced or greatly expanded during wartime.

A striking aspect of the post World War II decades was a definite tendency toward the convergence of Russian and American social institutions. Growing complexity of industrial production in Russia compelled the Communists to rely more and more on market regulators to control the assortment of end products their factories produced. Simultaneously, elaborate controls and plans for future growth — some governmental and some developed by private corporations — have become a prominent part of the American economy. The contrast between Communist central planning and control and capitalist private initiative and competition is therefore no longer as sharp as it appeared to be in the 1920's.

Even more striking was the fact that both nations seemed able to plan technological invention in peacetime as well as in war. Estimates of the "lead time" required before a given technological breakthrough can be achieved have become part of national defense and industrial planning. In a limited sense, therefore, men have begun both in the United States of America and in the Soviet Union to plan not simply new applications of existing technologies but the future evolution of technology itself. Within surprisingly broad limits, it seems to be true that by directing enough trained minds to the solution of a particular problem, desired results can be achieved within a comparatively short period of time.

Though it is certainly too soon to be sure, the history of the relation of the Russian Revolution to other nations of the Western world seems about to recapitulate the history of the French Revolution in relation to Europe's Old Regime. The French revolutionaries began by challenging the Old Regime root and branch; but Napoleon was finally defeated by kings and aristocrats who had done a good deal to imitate the revolutionaries by bringing the people into closer partnership than ever before. During the rest of the nineteenth century, innumerable compromises between liberal, democratic principle and stubborn social realities were made. Such antagonists as secular, rationalistic liberals and the Roman Catholic church could and did learn to co-exist, limiting their warfare to occasional snide remarks. It seems possible that in the second half of the twentieth century a similar co-existence will develop between the Communists and their antagonists.

The free world has already adapted for its own use many of the devices of social engineering which were once monopolized by Communists. This has been so successful that Marxist doctrine now appeals mainly to the world's peasantries. Simultaneously, inside Russia and other Communist countries of eastern Europe the pluralism and intellectual open-endedness which has characterized Western civilization since the seventeenth century may be coming into the open. Certainly, it is getting more and more difficult to argue plausibly that the doctrines of Karl Marx as glossed by Lenin adequately describe the social and economic realities of the second half of the twentieth century. Since amendment of the sacred scriptures of Marxist-Leninism is impossible, Communists continue to pay lip service to traditional phrases, while thinking and acting according to variant and essentially independent professional standards. Western Europe passed through almost the same intellectual transformation in the late seventeenth century, when religious persecution and rigorous enforcement of orthodoxy ceased to prevail.

It appears to be possible, as we are all very much aware, for modern atomic warheads to end the human adventure on earth in a matter of a few days or perhaps hours. Life has always been precarious for individuals, and if it has now become more precarious than before for the species as a whole, this does not in itself expose us as private persons to dangers greater than those to which most of our ancestors were regularly accustomed. Our forefathers never knew from day to day when mortal disease or violence might strike them dead. Moreover, there is some reason to believe that the extreme power of atomic destruction may effectually inhibit future wars. At any rate, it is worth reminding ourselves that in spite of the numerous guerrillas which have raged in backward peasant lands since 1945, the world as a whole has experienced more of peace since World War II than it knew in the years after World War I. Wisdom and luck may yet operate upon the spectrum of human emotions in such a way as to permit survival of humanity for generations and centuries to come.

Our perils may indeed dwarf those of the past. So do our opportunities.

After the great European discoveries, inter-relations among the far parts of the globe became closer than before, and a number of histories reflect this fact by taking up inter-regional and trans-civilizational themes. Among those of special interest are: John H. Parry, *Europe and a Wider World, 1415–1715* (New York, 1949); John H. Parry, *The Age of Reconnaissance: Discovery, Exploration and Settlement, 1450–1650* (New York, 1963); P. M. Ashburn, *The Ranks of Death: A Medical History of the Conquest of America* (New York, 1947); Donald F. Lach, *Asia in the Making of Europe*, I: *The Century of Discovery* (Chicago, 1965); A. Grenfell Price, *The Western Invasions of the Pacific and Its Continents: A Study of Moving Frontiers and Changing Landscapes, 1513–1958* (Oxford, 1963); Walker D. Wyman and Clifton B. Kroeber, eds., *The Frontier in Perspective* (Madison, Wis., 1957); Robert R. Palmer, *The Age of the Democratic Revolution: A Political History of Europe and America, 1760–1800*, 2 vols. (Princeton, 1959, 1964); Hans Kohn, *The Age of Nationalism: The First Era of Global History* (New York, 1962); and W. S. and E. S. Woytinsky, *World Population and Production: Trends and Outlook* (New York, 1953).

EUROPE AND THE WEST. The plethora of books makes for confusion. A very popular and well-written general text is Robert R. Palmer and Joel Colton, *A History of the Modern World*, 2nd ed. (New York, 1956). The great European empires are treated by: Charles R. Boxer, *Four Centuries of Portugese Expansion, 1415–1825* (Chester Springs, Pa., 1961); C. H. Haring, *The Spanish Empire in America* (New York, 1947); W. B. Willcox, *Star of Empire: A Study of Britain as a World Power, 1485–1945* (New York, 1950). No comparable essay about the fourth great European empire, the French, is known to me. The following throw some special light on Europe's internal political evolution: Crane Brinton, *Anatomy of Revolution*, rev. ed. (New York, 1952); Laurence Lafore, *The Long Fuse: An Interpretation of the Origins of World War I* (Philadelphia, 1965); Hajo Holborn, *The Political Collapse of Europe* (New York, 1951); John Maynard Keynes, *The Economic Consequences of the Peace* (London and New York, 1920); H. Stuart Hughes, *Consciousness and Society: The Reorientation of European Social Thought, 1890–1930* (New York, 1958); Hannah Arendt, *The Origins of Totalitarianism*, 2nd ed. (London, 1961); Donald M. Wallace, *Russia* (London, 1877); Edward H. Carr, *The Bolshevik Revolution, 1917–1923*, 3 vols. (New York, 1951–52); Isaac Deutscher, *Stalin: A Political Biography*

447

(New York, 1949); Hugh S. Thomas, *The Spanish Civil War*, rev. ed. (London, 1965); Alan Bullock, *Hitler, a Study in Tyranny*, rev. ed. (New York, 1964).

Books treating of European science, technology, and economy of more than routine interest include: Alfred Rupert Hall, *The Scientific Revolution, 1500–1800* (Boston, 1954); Herbert Butterfield, *The Origins of Modern Science, 1300–1800* (London and New York, 1957); Abraham Wolf, et al., *A History of Science, Technology, and Philosophy in the Sixteenth and Seventeenth Centuries,* 2nd ed. (New York, 1951); Sir Eric Ashby, *Technology and the Academics: An Essay on Universities and the Scientific Revolution* (London, 1958); John U. Nef, *Industry and Government in France and England, 1540–1640* (Philadelphia, 1940); W. W. Rostow, *British Economy of the Nineteenth Century* (Oxford, 1948); Herbert Feis, *Europe, the World's Banker, 1870–1914* (New Haven, 1930).

It seems futile to suggest readings from the store of modern European and American authors: all the classics of our modern languages fall within such a scope. Similarly, no large-scale histories of the cultural development of modern times illumine the subject so well that they should be preferred to a direct plunge into the original texts.

Russian history perhaps should have special attention, since most readers of this book will probably know less of the Russian past than of that of other parts of the Western world. Michael T. Florinsky, *Russia: A History and Interpretation*, 2 vols. (New York, 1953, 1954), is a good text. Jane Harrison and Hope Mirrlees, trs., *The Life of the Archpriest Avvakum by Himself* (London, 1924), offers a precious and concise insight into the consciousness of an Old Believer. Other volumes of unusual interest are: Raymond H. Fisher, *The Russian Fur Trade, 1550–1700* (Berkeley, 1943); W. E. D. Allen, *The Ukraine: A History* (Cambridge, 1940); Richard E. Pipes, *The Formation of the Soviet Union: Communism and Nationalism, 1917–1923*, rev. ed. (Cambridge, Mass., 1964); John Maynard, *Russia in Flux*, ed. S. Haden Guest (New York, 1948). Two very interesting works trace the relations between Russia and China from their beginning: John F. Baddeley, *Russia, Mongolia and China*, 2 vols. (London, 1919), and Michael N. Pavlovsky, *Chinese-Russian Relations* (New York, 1949).

AFRICA. Aside from general histories of Africa mentioned in the bibliography to Part II, two books treat vividly of the European slave trade: H. A. Wyndham, *The Atlantic and Slavery: A Report* (London, 1935), and Eric Williams, *Capitalism and Slavery* (Chapel Hill, 1944). Leopold Marquard, *The Story of South Africa* (London, 1955), is a simple, well-written account.

THE REALM OF ISLAM. Modern historiography of the Islamic world remains in a quite unsatisfactory state of development. The following general essays are helpful: H. A. R. Gibb and Harold Bowen, *Islamic Society and the West*, I: *Islamic Society in the Eighteenth Century*, 2 parts (London, 1950, 1957); Gustave E. von Grunebaum, *Modern Islam: The Search for Cultural*

Identity (Berkeley, 1962); H. A. R. Gibb, *Modern Trends in Islam* (Chicago, 1947); Gustave E. von Grunebaum, ed., *Unity and Variety in Muslim Civilization* (Chicago, 1955). For the separate areas of Islam, consult: George Antonius, *The Arab Awakening* (London, 1938); Bernard Lewis, *The Emergence of Modern Turkey* (New York, 1961); Wilfred Cantwell Smith, *Modern Islam in India: A Social Analysis*, rev. ed. (London, 1947); Percy Sykes, *A History of Persia*, 2 vols., 3rd ed. (London, 1952).

INDIA. Percival Spear, *India: A Modern History* (Ann Arbor, 1961), and his revision of Vincent A. Smith, *The Oxford History of India*, 3rd ed. (Oxford, 1958), offer good general guides. K. M. Panikkar, *A Survey of Indian History*, 3rd ed. (Bombay, 1956), gives an Indian point of view. A better approach to the recent Indian climate of opinion and texture of experience may perhaps be had through two autobiographies: Mohandas K. Gandhi, *An Autobiography: The Story of My Experiments with Truth* (republished, Boston, 1957), and *Toward Freedom: The Autobiography of Jawaharlal Nehru* (New York, 1941). Percy Brown, *Indian Painting under the Mughals, A.D. 1550 to A.D. 1750* (Oxford, 1924), offers another kind of insight into Indian culture in the days of the Mughal empire's greatness. I know of no good history of that empire but its founder's memoirs, Annette S. Beveridge, tr., *Babur's Memoirs*, 4 vols. (London, 1912–21); and two books by W. H. Moreland, *India at the Death of Akbar: An Economic Study* (London, 1920), and *From Akbar to Aurangzeb: A Study in Indian Economic History* (London, 1923), are helpful.

CHINA AND JAPAN. E. O. Reischauer, J. K. Fairbank, and A. M. Craig, *A History of East Asian Civilization*, II: *East Asia: A Modern Transformation* (Boston, 1965), and George M. Beckmann, *The Modernization of China and Japan* (New York, 1962), offer general surveys of the modern history of the Far East. Charles R. Boxer, *Fidalgos in the Far East, 1550–1770* (The Hague, 1948), treats the Portuguese role skillfully. For Christian missions, see Kenneth Scott Latourette, *A History of Christian Missions in China* (New York, 1929), and Arnold H. Rowbotham, *Missionary and Mandarin: The Jesuits at the Court of China* (Berkeley, 1942). On politics, two books deserve special mention: Franz Michael, *The Origin of Manchu Rule in China* (Baltimore, 1942), and Ssu-yu Teng, John K. Fairbank, et al., *China's Response to the West: A Documentary Survey, 1839–1923* (Cambridge, Mass., 1954). Ping-ti Ho, *Studies on the Population of China, 1368–1953* (Cambridge, Mass., 1959), and the same author's *The Ladder of Success in Imperial China: Aspects of Social Mobility, 1368–1911* (New York, 1962); Chung-li Chang, *The Chinese Gentry: Studies in Their Role in Nineteenth-Century Chinese Society* (Seattle, 1955); and Hsiao-t'ung Fei, *Peasant Life in China: A Field Study of Country Life in the Yangtze Valley* (New York, 1946), all cast light on aspects of China's social order and disorder in recent centuries. For the break away from traditional Confucianism, consult Chow Tse-tsung, *The May Fourth Movement: Intellectual Revolution in Modern*

China (Cambridge, Mass., 1960), and, for the other side of the coin, Mary Clabaugh Wright, *The Last Stand of Chinese Conservatism: The T'ung-chih Restoration, 1862–1874* (Stanford, 1957). Osvald Sirén, *A History of Later Chinese Painting*, 2 vols. (London, 1938), offers the best available photographic sampling of modern Chinese art. Ts'ao Chan, *Dream of the Red Chamber*, tr. Wang Chi-chen (New York, 1958), offers a fragmentary translation of one of the classics of modern Chinese literature.

For study of Japan's recent history, see: George B. Sansom, *The Western World and Japan* (New York, 1950); Donald Keene, *The Japanese Discovery of Europe* (New York, 1954); Charles R. Boxer, *The Christian Century in Japan, 1549–1650* (Berkeley, 1951); and Hugh Borton, *Japan's Modern Century* (New York, 1955). Three distinguished treatments of diverse aspects of Japan's culture are: James C. Abegglen, *The Japanese Factory: Aspects of Its Social Organization* (Glencoe, Ill., 1958); Robert N. Bellah, *Tokugawa Religion* (Glencoe, Ill., 1957); and Peter C. Swann, *An Introduction to the Arts of Japan* (Oxford, 1958).

Reflection upon our place in world history is very much in order. A useful stimulant to this exercise of intelligence is Kenneth E. Boulding, *The Meaning of the Twentieth Century: The Great Transition* (New York, 1964).

World Maps

ARCTIC OCEAN

Greenla
Ice C

TUNDRA

TUNDRA

TUNDRA

TUNDRA

Alaska
20300

Bering Straits

Aleutian Islands

NORTH

PACIFIC

OCEAN

ROCKY MOUNTAINS

NORTHERN PRAIRIES

NORTH CONIFEROUS FORESTS

NORTH AMERICA

14495

Tropic of Cancer

NORTH

ATLANTIC

OCEAN

Equator

SOUTH

PACIFIC

OCEAN

Tropic of Capricorn

AMAZON

TROPICAL RAIN

FOREST

SOUTH AMERICA

Amazon

ANDES

6000

23293

SOUTHERN   OCEAN

Modified Gall Projection. Equatorial Scale 1 inch to 2050 miles (1:130m.) approx.

Dense northern forests

Natural grasslands

Permanent pack ice

Dense tropical &
sub-tropical forests

Deserts

Average minimum extent of
pack ice (autumn)

FIELD&FOR
LD&FOREST
FIELD&FOR
Field & forest-
mainly cultivated

Areas with
Mediterranean climate

Average maximum extent of
pack ice (spring)

ARCTIC OCEAN

0° 90° E

Arctic Circle

TUNDRA

NORTHERN CONIFEROUS FORESTS

Siberia

NORTHERN CONIFEROUS FORESTS

Siberia

URAL MTS.

Ob

BALTIC SEA

FOREST FIELD & FOREST FIELD & FOREST FIELD & FOREST
FOREST FIELD & FOREST FIELD & FOREST FIELD & FOREST
FOREST FIELD & FOREST FIELD & FOREST FIELD & FORE
FIELD & FOREST FIELD & FOREST FIELD & FOREST FIELD

E U R O P E

A S I A

Volga

EURASIAN STEPPE

L. Balkhash

Ukraine

Don

L. Baikal

13504

EURASIAN STEPPE

Manchuria

15526

Danube

Desert

ALTAI MTS.

TIEN SHAN 24406

BLACK SEA 18480

CASPIAN SEA

Oxus

Jaxartes

Turkestan

6000

Hwang

GOBI DESERT

FAR EAST

ADRIATIC

M E D I T E R R A N E A N

MIDDLE EAST

Plateau of Tibet

HIMALAYAS 29028

FOREST FIELD & FOREST
FOREST & FOREST FI
FOREST FIELD & FOREST
FOREST & FOREST FI

Indus

Ganges

ARABIAN DESERT

SAHARA DESERT

Nile

RED SEA

PERSIAN GULF

Bengal

ARABIAN SEA

BAY OF BENGAL

SOUTH CHINA SEA

Philippines

A F R I C A

C. Guardafui

CONGO TROPICAL RAIN FOREST

Congo

19340

Borneo

Sumatra

New 16503

Guinea

Java

Bali

INDIAN

SOUTH

Zambezi

Madagascar

OCEAN

ATLANTIC

OCEAN

AUSTRALIA

C. of Good Hope

SOUTHERN OCEAN

Antarctic Circle

6000

ANTARCTICA

Major ocean currents

• 13504'   6000 ft. contour and heights in feet above sea level

The Physical Environment

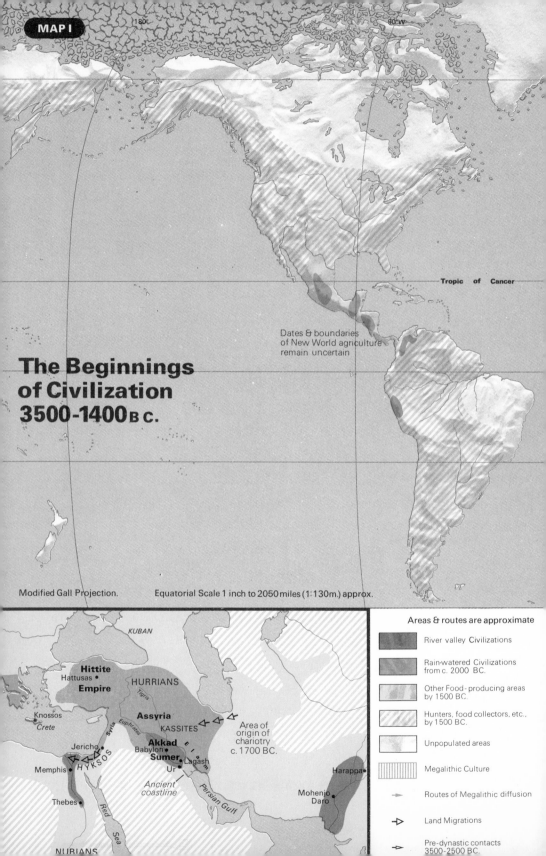

MAP I

The Beginnings of Civilization 3500-1400 B.C.

180° 90°W

Tropic of Cancer

Dates & boundaries of New World agriculture remain uncertain

Modified Gall Projection.   Equatorial Scale 1 inch to 2050 miles (1:130m.) approx.

KUBAN

Hittite
Hattusas •
Empire

HURRIANS

Tigris

Assyria

KASSITES

Area of origin of chariotry c. 1700 BC.

Knossos •
Crete

Syria
Euphrates

Akkad
Babylon •   E U L A M
Sumer •
Jericho •   Ur • Lagash

Memphis •   H Y K S O S

Ancient coastline

Persian Gulf

Harappa •

Thebes •

Red Sea

Mohenjo Daro •

NUBIANS

Areas & routes are approximate

River valley Civilizations

Rain-watered Civilizations from c. 2000 BC.

Other Food-producing areas by 1500 BC.

Hunters, food collectors, etc., by 1500 BC.

Unpopulated areas

Megalithic Culture

Routes of Megalithic diffusion

Land Migrations

Pre-dynastic contacts 3500-2500 BC.

Arctic Circle

INDO-EUROPEANS →

HITTITES

Achaeans

Malta

Minoans

LIBYANS

Mesopo-
tamia

Egypt

SEMITES

ARYANS

Indus

Indus
Valley

Shang
China

Nile

Equator

Tropic of Capricorn

Area of origin for
Middle Eastern seed
grain cultivation
c. 8000 B.C.

Area of origin for
South East Asian
root agriculture

Area of origin
of African
agriculture

Origin & Spread of Agriculture

▨ Areas of origin		▥ Extent by 3000 B.C.
⇢ ⇢ Routes of diffusion		▨ Extent by 1500 B.C.

© Oxford University Press

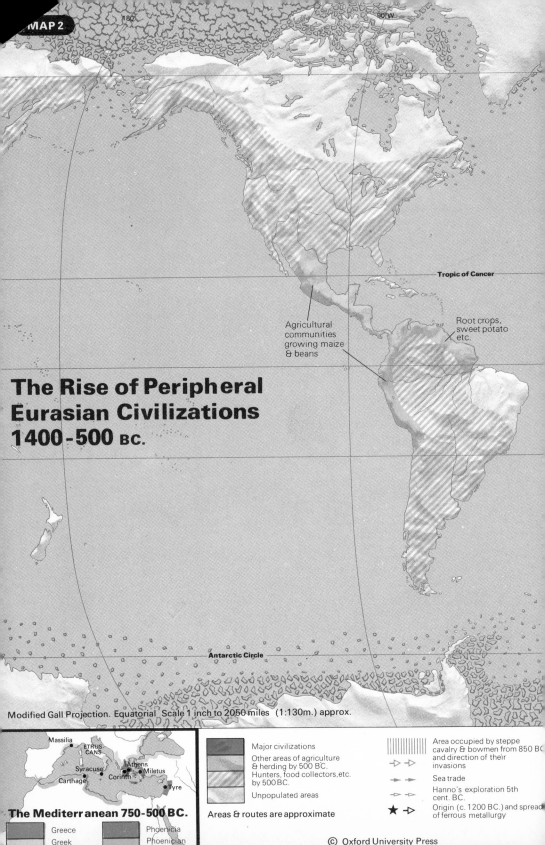

MAP 2

180° 90°W

Tropic of Cancer

Root crops,
sweet potato
etc.

Agricultural
communities
growing maize
& beans

The Rise of Peripheral
Eurasian Civilizations
1400-500 BC.

Antarctic Circle

Modified Gall Projection. Equatorial Scale 1 inch to 2050 miles (1:130m.) approx.

The Mediterranean 750-500 BC.

Massilia
ETRUS
CANS
Syracuse
Carthage
Athens
Corinth
Miletus
Tyre

Greece	Phoenicia
Greek	Phoenician

Major civilizations

Other areas of agriculture
& herding by 500 BC.

Hunters, food collectors, etc.
by 500 BC.

Unpopulated areas

Areas & routes are approximate

Area occupied by steppe
cavalry & bowmen from 850 BC
and direction of their
invasions

Sea trade

Hanno's exploration 5th
cent. BC.

★ ⟶ Origin (c. 1200 BC.) and spread
of ferrous metallurgy

© Oxford University Press

MAP 2

0°

90° E

Arctic Circle

Greece

Mesopotamia

Egypt

Hindu Kush

Indus

India

Yangtse

China

Nile

Philippines

Borneo

Equator

Madagascar

Tropic of Capricorn

Chariot & Cavalry Revolutions on the Steppe

SLAVS

GERMANS

C E L T S

SCYTHIANS

Early Scyth migration

TURKS

MONGOLS

Rome

Troy

Mycenae

Nineveh

Susa

Persepolis

Thebes

LIBYANS

ARABS

Loyang

DONGSON

Sack of Loyang
771 BC. may be
the work of
steppe cavalry

Sack of Nineveh
& overthrow of
Assyrian Empire
612 BC. by Scyths

Cavalry & bowmen
as on main map

Origin & spread of
chariotry

Migrations

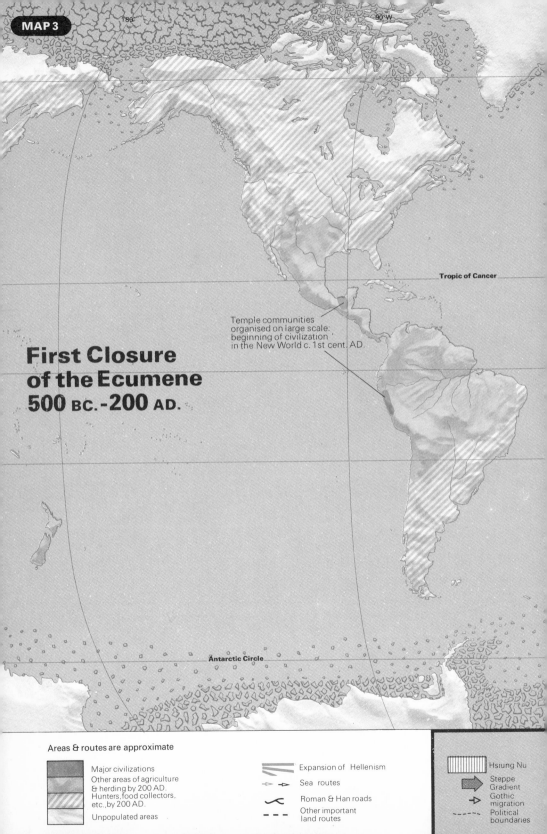

MAP 3

**First Closure
of the Ecumene
500 BC.-200 AD.**

Temple communities
organised on large scale:
beginning of civilization
in the New World c. 1st cent. AD.

Tropic of Cancer

Antarctic Circle

Areas & routes are approximate

Major civilizations	
Other areas of agriculture & herding by 200 AD.	
Hunters, food collectors, etc., by 200 AD.	
Unpopulated areas	

Expansion of Hellenism

Sea routes

Roman & Han roads

Other important
land routes

Hsiung Nu

Steppe
Gradient

Gothic
migration

Political
boundaries

Modified Gall Projection.   Equatorial Scale 1 inch to 2050 miles (1:130m.) approx.

MAP 3

Arctic Circle

0° 90°E

Rhine

Danube

Aral
Sea

Jaxartes

Urumchi Silk Road

Rome

Samarkand

Bactra

Athens

Merv

Silk Road

Indus

Loyang

Carthage

Seleucia

Alexandria

Ganges

Ujjain

Large
village
communities

Greek

traders

Kra

Equator

Beginning
of Bantu
expansion

Indonesian trade & migration

Tropic of Capricorn

Roman Empire

Light
in-
heavy

horsemen
conflict
armoured cavalry

with

E m p i r e   o f

Parthian
Empire

Kushan

H a n

C h i n a

Empire

Various
Indian
States

© Oxford University Press

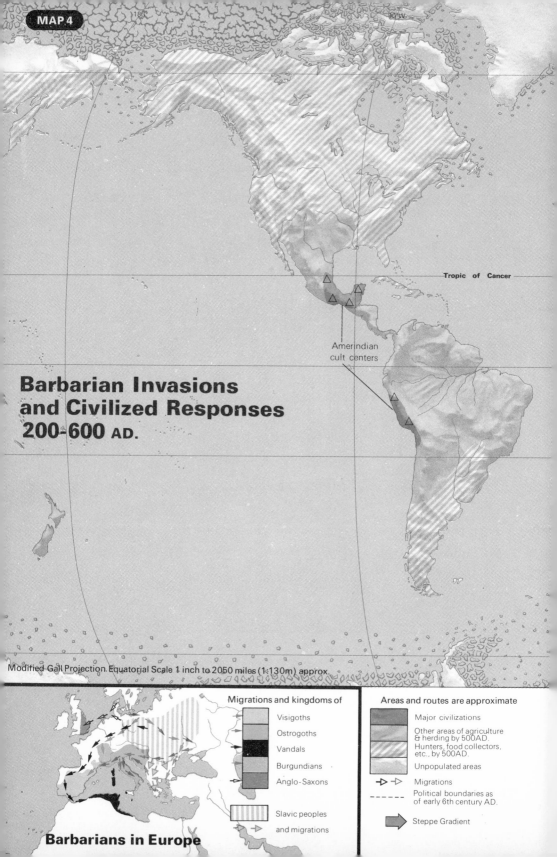

MAP 4

Tropic of Cancer

Amerindian
cult centers

Barbarian Invasions
and Civilized Responses
200-600 AD.

Modified Gall Projection. Equatorial Scale 1 inch to 2050 miles (1:130m) approx.

Migrations and kingdoms of

Visigoths

Ostrogoths

Vandals

Burgundians

Anglo-Saxons

Slavic peoples

and migrations

Areas and routes are approximate

Major civilizations

Other areas of agriculture
& herding by 500AD.

Hunters, food collectors,
etc., by 500AD.

Unpopulated areas

Migrations

Political boundaries as
of early 6th century AD.

Steppe Gradient

Barbarians in Europe

MAP 4

Arctic Circle

Britain

Huns

HUNS

Barbarian

Rome

Constantinople

Danube

L. Balkhash

TURKISH
PEOPLES

JUAN   JUAN

Manchuria

Kingdoms

Athens

East
Roman
Empire

Huns

Sui China

Yellow R.

Korea

Japan

Sassanian
Empire

WHITE
HUNS

Gupta
Empire

Tibet

Ganges

Yangtse

ARABS

Pataliputra

Ghana

NUBIANS

Ethiopia

Hadramaut

Arabian
Sea

Various
Indian
States

Bay of
Bengal

South
China
Sea

BANTU

Bantu
expansion
continues

Equator

Tropic of Capricorn

Major Religions by 600 A.D.

Judaism and Manicheism flourished as minority religions
along the Eurasian trade route

Monte Cassino

Nicaea

Jerusalem

Syria

Zoroastrianism

Alexandria

Buddhism
reaches Tibet
in 7th cent.

Kapilavastu

Ceylon

Malaya

Sumatra

Java

Extent of Hinduism

Areas of Indian influence

★ Origin and extent of Buddhism

★ Origin and extent of Christianity

★ Origin and extent of Confucianism

Spread of Graeco-Buddhist art

Other Arrows indicate spread of religions

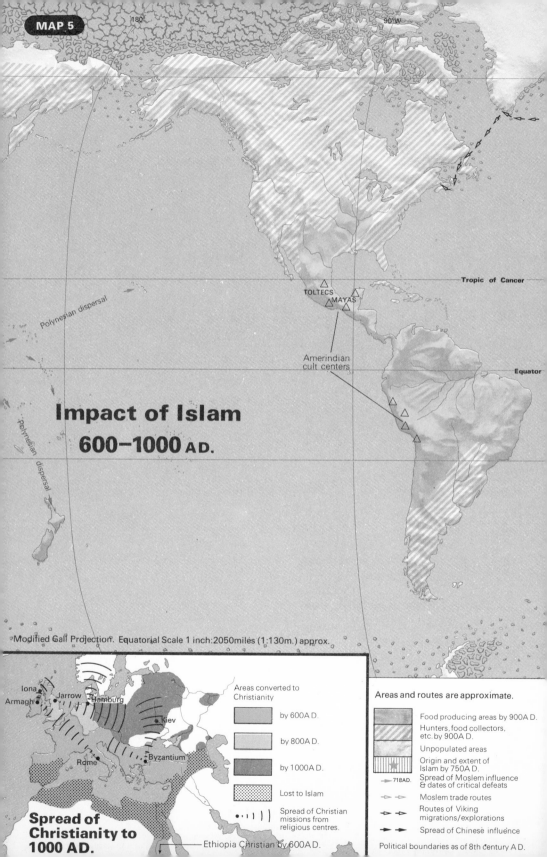

MAP 5

180°   90°W

Tropic of Cancer

△ TOLTECS
△ MAYAS

Amerindian
cult centers

Equator

Polynesian dispersal

Polynesian dispersal

Impact of Islam
600–1000 AD.

Modified Gall Projection. Equatorial Scale 1 inch:2050miles (1:130m.) approx.

Iona
Armagh   Jarrow   Hamburg
Kiev
Rome   Byzantium

Spread of
Christianity to
1000 AD.

Areas converted to
Christianity

	by 600 A.D.
	by 800 A.D.
	by 1000 A.D.
	Lost to Islam

•··ı ı ı   Spread of Christian
missions from
religious centres.

Ethiopia Christian by 600 A.D.

Areas and routes are approximate.

Food producing areas by 900 A.D.
Hunters, food collectors,
etc. by 900 A.D.
Unpopulated areas
Origin and extent of
Islam by 750 A.D.
→718AD. Spread of Moslem influence
& dates of critical defeats
⇢ ⇢ Moslem trade routes
⇨ ⇨ Routes of Viking
migrations/explorations
➤ ➤ Spread of Chinese influence

Political boundaries as of 8th century A.D.

MAP 5

Arctic Circle

Norway
VIKINGS
Sweden

Ireland

733AD.

Carolingian Empire

744AD.

718AD.
Byzantium

Byzantine Empire

Kingdom of Uighurs

T'ang China

751AD.

Ab·basid Caliphate

Tibet

T'ang China

Nanking

Japan

718AD.

Medina
Arabia
Mecca

Ghana

W African States
influenced by
Moslem traders

Ethiopia

BANTU

India

Polynesian

dispersal

**Empire
of
Srivijaya**

Tropic of Capricorn

Influence of the Steppe Gradient

CELTS

FRANKS

MAGYARS

AVARS
BULGARS

KHAZARS

SELJUKS

UIGHURS

	Slavic peoples		Turkish peoples
	Germanic peoples		Steppe Gradient

© Oxford University Press

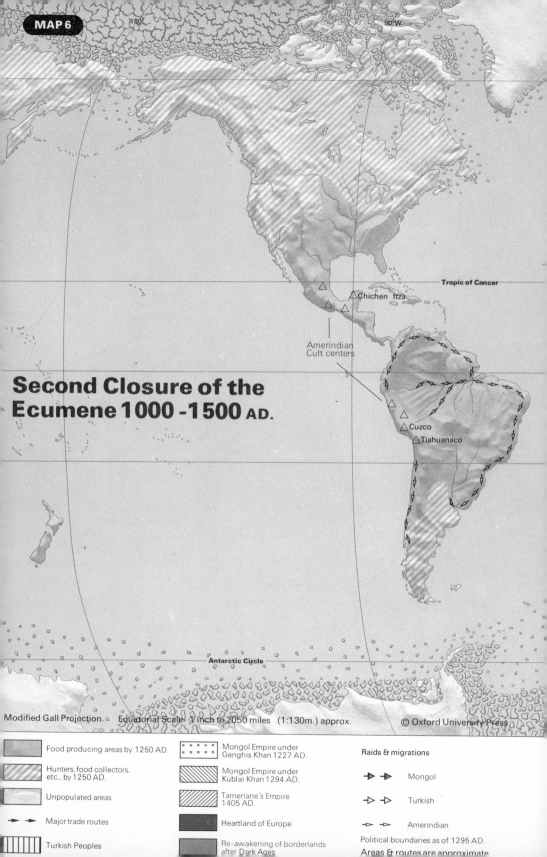

MAP 6

**Second Closure of the
Ecumene 1000 -1500 AD.**

180°   90°W

Tropic of Cancer

△Chichen Itza

Amerindian
Cult centers

△
△Cuzco
△Tiahuanaco

Antarctic Circle

Modified Gall Projection.   Equatorial Scale 1 inch to 2050 miles (1:130m.) approx.   © Oxford University Press

▨ Food producing areas by 1250 AD.	⬚ Mongol Empire under Genghis Khan 1227 AD.	Raids & migrations
▨ Hunters, food collectors, etc., by 1250 AD.	▨ Mongol Empire under Kublai Khan 1294 AD.	➡ ➡ Mongol
▨ Unpopulated areas	▨ Tamerlane's Empire 1405 AD.	➪ ➪ Turkish
➝ Major trade routes	▨ Heartland of Europe	➘ ➘ Amerindian
⦀ Turkish Peoples	▨ Re-awakening of borderlands after Dark Ages	Political boundaries as of 1295 AD. Areas & routes are approximate

MAP 6

0°   90°E

Arctic Circle

Elements of Chinese Culture
brought to W. Eurasia - paper,
printing, gunpowder

Scandinavia

Russia
Scotland   • Moscow

Lithu-
ania

England   Poland
Holy
Roman   Hungary   **Mongolia**
Paris   Empire   • Karakorum
France   East   GOLDEN HORDE
Roman
Empire   • Peking
Spain   Kdom
of
Sicily   Korea   **Japan**

Baghdad   Tibet   Fukien

Ming drove out
Mamluk   Mongols 1368 AD.
Emp.

Arabia

India   Annam

Ghana
Mali   • Hormuz

Calicut   Mindanao

Equator   Ceylon

Malacca
Sumatra   Borneo

Bantu migrations   Java

Farmers   Herdsmen

• Zimbabwe

Tropic of Capricorn

Major Religions in Eurasia in 13th century

Avignon
Rome   Byzantium
Acre
Jerusalem

▥ Moslem	▤ Orthodox Christian
▦ Hindu	▤ Other Christian
◪ Buddhist	➔ 1st Crusade
▨ Confucianist	⇨ 3rd Crusade
▧ Tibetan Lamaist	

MAP 7

180°   90°W

Hue

Cartier 1534-3

Quebec

Mass
La Salle 1681-82   Cabot 1498
New York
Va

Coronado
1640-42   de Soto
1539-42

Columbus 1492-9

Tropic of Cancer

AZTECS   M A Y A S   Cortez
1519-21

Equator

Pizarro
1531-33
INCAS

Rio de
Janiero

Tropic of Capricorn

Magellan 1519-22

The Great European
Discoveries 1450–1700AD.

Buenos
Aires

Tordesillas line
dividing New
World between
Spain and
Portugal

Cape Horn

Antarctic Circle

Modified Gall Projection. Equatorial Scale 1 inch to 2080 miles (1:130m) approx.

Areas and routes are approximate

Manchu home and conquests	Origins of Great Explorations	Areas of origin of slaves
Manchu expansion	Voyages of Discovery	Areas of slavery
Russian advance to Siberia	Areas of Amerindian high culture	Routes of slave trade
Mughal Empire	Political Boundaries as of 1550 AD	Bantu

© Oxford University Press

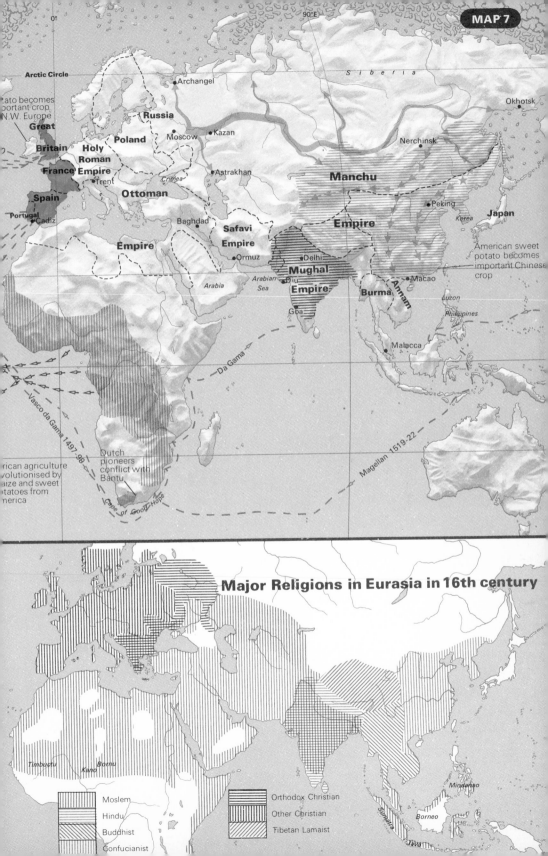

MAP 7

0°   90°E

S i b e r i a

Arctic Circle   •Archangel

...ato becomes
...ortant crop
N.W. Europe

Great   •Moscow   Kazan•   •Nerchinsk

Britain   **Holy**   **Poland**
              Roman   Crimea   **Manchu**
France   **Empire**
              •Trent   •Astrakhan

Spain   **Empire**   **Japan**

Portugal•   *Korea*
      •Cadiz   •Peking

                              •Baghdad   **Safavi**
Empire   **Empire**   American sweet
                                          •Ormuz   potato becomes
                                                        •Delhi   •Macao   important Chinese
                              Arabian   **Mughal**   crop
              Arabia   *Sea* •Diu
                                          Empire   **Burma** **Annam**
                                     •Goa   *Luzon*

                                                                            Philippines

                                                              •Malacca

                    Da Gama

Vasco da Gama 1497-98

African agriculture
revolutionised by
maize and sweet
potatoes from
America

                    Dutch
                    pioneers   Magellan 1519-22
                    conflict with
                    Bantu

Cape of Good Hope

Major Religions in Eurasia in 16th century

Timbuctu   *Bornu*
        Kano

                                                                            Mindanao

                                                              Sumatra   *Borneo*

                                                                            Java

	Moslem		Orthodox Christian
	Hindu		Other Christian
	Buddhist		Tibetan Lamaist
	Confucianist		

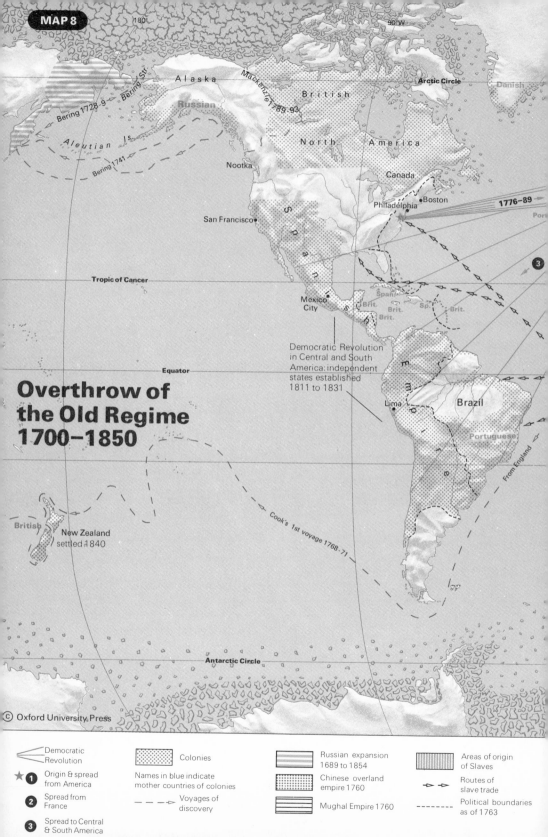

Overthrow of the Old Regime 1700–1850

MAP 8

180° 90°W

Bering 1728-9
Bering Str.
Alaska
Mackenzie 1789-93
British
Arctic Circle
Danish
Russian
Aleutian Is.
Bering 1741
North   America
Nootka
Canada
Boston
San Francisco
Philadelphia
1776-89
Port
3

Tropic of Cancer

Mexico
City
Spani
Brit.
Sp.
Brit.
Brit.
Brit.

Democratic Revolution
in Central and South
America: independent
states established
1811 to 1831

Lima
Brazil
Portuguese

Equator

British
New Zealand
settled 1840

Cook's 1st voyage 1768-71

From England

Antarctic Circle

© Oxford University Press

Democratic
Revolution

★ 1 Origin & spread
     from America

2 Spread from
   France

3 Spread to Central
   & South America

Colonies

Names in blue indicate
mother countries of colonies

- - - → Voyages of
         discovery

Russian expansion
1689 to 1854

Chinese overland
empire 1760

Mughal Empire 1760

Areas of origin
of Slaves

⊢→ ←⊣ Routes of
         slave trade

- - - - - - - Political boundaries
               as of 1763

Modified Gall Projection. Equatorial scale 1 inch to 2050 miles (1:130m) approx.

MAP 8

S i b e r i a

I m p e r i a l   R u s s i a

mocratic Revolution
Britain follows
eparate development
C17th - C19th

• St. Petersburg

Nerchinsk •

• Kiakhta

Manchuria

London
1789
1870

2

• France

Ukraine

KALMUKS

Volga

M o n g o l i a

I m p e r i a l

Peking •

Korea

Japan

Balkans

Constantinople

Kabul •

T u r k e s t a n

C h i n a

Nanking •

Nagasaki •

Kyushu

O t t o m a n

AFGHANS

SIKHS

British

E m p i r e

A r a b i a

Egypt

MARATHAS

British

Canton •

Taiwan

Hong Kong

Spanish

Mecca •

Bombay •

Calcutta •

Madras •

Danish

Spanish

Spanish

Pagan

Brit.

Brit.

African

Dutch

Tribal

French

Batavia •

Dutch

States

Port.

Cook's 1st voyage 1768-71

Tropic of Capricorn

A u s t r a l i a

British

French

South
Africa

Sydney •
settled 1789

Brit.

C. of Good Hope

Areas are approximate.

Areas predominantly Hindu (blue) and Moslem (red) by 1800

Hindu subjects of Muslim rulers

MAP 9

C a n a d a
(became a Dominion in 1867)

United

States

Heartland

Western

Tropic of Cancer

**The New
Regime
1850–1914**

Amazon

B r a z i l

New
Zealand

Argentina

Antarctic Circle

© Oxford University Press

Areas industrialised
by 1914

Areas in transformation
stage by 1914

Colonies

Breakdown of non-
Western civilizations

Expansion of Western Civilization

by sea   by land

Political boundaries
as of 1914 Other areas
& routes approximate

Modified Gall Projection. Equatorial Scale 1 inch to 2050 miles (1:130m.) approx.

MAP 9

Arctic Circle

S i b e r i a

gin of
ustrial
olution

R u s s i a

of
ivilization

Kazakstan

M o n g o l i a

Manchuria

Crimean
War
1853-6

Constantinople
Ankara

Turkestan

C h i n a

Japanese
penetration
1910

Tokyo

Baghdad

Tibet

Taiping
Rebellion
1850-64

Shanghai

Japan

Suez Canal
opened
1869

S a h a r a

A r a b i a

Indian
Mutiny
1857-8

Assam

Mecca

Congo

Ethiopia

Lake Rudolf

Siam

Philippines

Equator

New Guinea

Tropic of Capricorn

Kalahari
desert

A u s t r a l i a

Sydney

Areas predominantly Hindu (blue) and Moslem (red) by 1914

0°

90° E

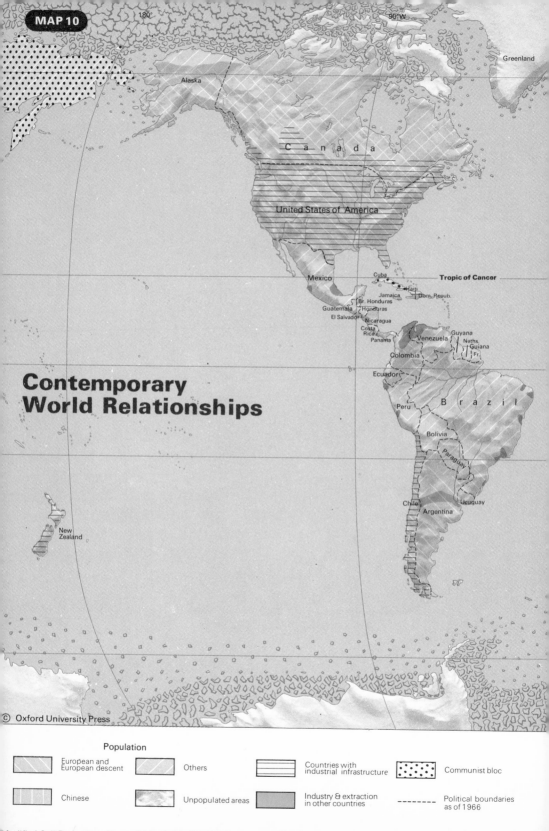

MAP 10

180°

90°W

Greenland

Alaska

C a n a d a

United States of America

Mexico

Cuba

Tropic of Cancer

Haiti

Jamaica — Dom. Repub.

Br. Honduras

Guatemala — Honduras

El Salvador — Nicaragua

Costa Rica

Panama

Venezuela — Guyana

Neths. Guiana

Colombia — Fr.

Ecuador

Peru

B r a z i l

Bolivia

Paraguay

Chile

Argentina

Uruguay

New Zealand

Contemporary
World Relationships

© Oxford University Press

Population

| | European and European descent | | Others |
| Chinese | | Unpopulated areas | |

Countries with industrial infrastructure

Communist bloc

Industry & extraction in other countries

Political boundaries as of 1966

Modified Gall Projection.   Equatorial Scale 1 inch to 2050 miles (1:130m.) approx.

MAP 10

Arctic Circle

Iceland

Norway
Finland
Sweden

Union of Soviet Socialist Republics

Mongolia

Chinese People's Republic

N
Korea
S

Japan

Morocco
Tunisia

Algeria
Libya
U.A.R.

Iraq
Iran
Afghanistan
Kashmir

Sp.
Sahara
Mauritania

Sa'udi
Arabia
W. Pakistan

Nepal

Mali
Niger
Chad
Sudan
Yemen
S. Arabia

Senegal
Guinea
U. Volta
Nigeria
Cameroon
Cent. Afr.
Rep.
Ethiopia
Somalia

India

Pak.
Burma
Laos
N
S
Viet
Nam

Sierra
Leone
Ivory
Coast
Liberia
Togo
Dahomey
Equat.
Guinea
Gabon

Thailand
Cambodia

Philippines

Ceylon

Malaysia

Equator

Congo
Repub.
Uganda
Kenya

Congo Rep.
(Brazz.)
Tanzania

Indonesia

New Guinea

Angola
Zambia
Mozambique

Rhodesia
S. W.
Africa
Botswana

Malagasy R.

Tropic of Capricorn

Australia

Repub.
of
S. Africa

Antarctic Circle

United
Kingdom

Denmark

Rep. of
Ireland

Neths.
W.   E.
Germany

Poland

Union of Soviet

Socialist Republics

Belgium
Lux.
Czechoslovakia

France
Switz.
Austria
Hungary
Romania

Italy
Yugoslavia
Bulgaria

Portugal
Spain

Albania

Greece

Turkey

Malta

Cyprus

Tunisia
Lebanon
Syria
Iran

Morocco
Israel
Iraq
Jordan

Algeria
Libya
U.A.R.
(Egypt)
Kuwait